Wagner is often held to have exerted a greater impact on modern culture than any other artist, yet the history of the reception of his works in Russia has until now remained largely unexplored. This book, which draws extensively on unpublished archival materials and other contemporary sources, aims to show that in certain important respects, Wagner's music and ideas found more fertile ground in Russia than anywhere else in Europe. Beginning with the first mention of Wagner's name in the Russian press in 1841, and ending almost 150 years later when the composer was finally rehabilitated during the years of *glasnost*, this study provides the first detailed account of Wagner's visit to Russia in 1863, and a history of the productions of his works in Russia both before and after the Revolution (including radical stagings by Meyerhold and Eisenstein). The book pays special attention to Wagner's important influence on the Russian modernist movement, focussing particularly on his impact on the leading Symbolist writers, Vyacheslav Ivanov, Andrey Bely and Aleksandr Blok.

CAMBRIDGE STUDIES IN RUSSIAN LITERATURE

WAGNER AND RUSSIA

Recent titles in this series include:

Petrushka – the Russian carnival puppet theatre
CATRIONA KELLY

Turgenev
FRANK FRIEDEBERG SEELEY

From the idyll to the novel
GITTA HAMMARBERG

The Brothers Karamazov and the poetics of memory
DIANE OENNING THOMPSON

Andrei Platonov
THOMAS SEIFRID

Nabokov's early fiction
JULIAN W. CONNOLLY

Iurii Trifonov
DAVID GILLESPIE

Mikhail Zoshchenko
LINDA HART SCATTON

Andrei Bitov
ELLEN CHANCES

Nikolai Zabolotsky
DARRA GOLDSTEIN

Nietzsche and Soviet culture
edited by BERNICE GLATZER ROSENTHAL

Russian literature and empire
SUSAN LAYTON

'Wagner Gallops into the Future'. Caricature published in *Iskra* (1863).

WAGNER AND RUSSIA

ROSAMUND BARTLETT

*Assistant Professor, Department of Slavic Languages
and Literatures, University of Michigan*

CAMBRIDGE
UNIVERSITY PRESS

Published by the Press Syndicate of the University of Cambridge
The Pitt Building, Trumpington Street, Cambridge CB2 1RP
40 West 20th Street, New York, NY 10011–4211, USA
10 Stamford Road, Oakleigh, Melbourne 3166, Australia

First published 1995

Printed in Great Britain at the University Press, Cambridge

A catalogue record for this book is available from the British Library

Library of Congress cataloguing in publication data
Bartlett, Rosamund.
Wagner and Russia/Rosamund Bartlett.
p.   cm. – (Cambridge studies in Russian literature)
Includes bibliographical references and index.
ISBN 0 521 44071 8
1. Wagner, Richard, 1813–1883 – Criticism and interpretation.
2. Wagner, Richard, 1813–1883 – Influence.
I. Title.   II. Series.
ML410.W13B195   1995
782.1'092–dc20   94–7607   CIP MN

ISBN 0 521 44071 8 hardback

In memory of A. B. B.

Contents

Illustrations

Acknowledgements for illustrations

Colour
1, courtesy of the Odessa Museum of Art; 2–5, courtesy of the Bakhrushin State Central Theatrical Museum; 6, courtesy of Oleg Khmelnitsky; 7–10, courtesy of Dmitry Gorbachev.

Black and white
1, 2, 4–8, 12, 21–3, 25–6, courtesy of the St Petersburg State Museum of Theatre and Music; 3, 9, courtesy of the Glinka State Museum of Musical Culture; 11, reproduced in N. Punin, *Pamyatnik tret'ego internatsionala* (Petrograd, 1920); 10, 13–14, courtesy of the Bakhrushin State Central Theatrical Museum; 15–18, 24, 27–32, courtesy of the Bolshoi Theatre Museum; 19–20, courtesy of Oleg Khmelnitsky.

Acknowledgements

The late Gerald Abraham was not exaggerating in saying that I had a 'big meal' in front of me when I consulted him at the beginning of my research, and I should like to thank the numerous institutions and individuals who have made the preparation of this gargantuan and variegated repast possible. First of all I would like to express my gratitude to the Warden and Fellows of St Antony's College, Oxford University for appointing me as the Max Hayward Fellow for 1993 and thus providing me with the ideal conditions in which to turn my doctoral thesis into a book. I am also extremely grateful to my colleagues at the Department of Slavic Languages and Literatures at the University of Michigan for allowing me to take a year of leave at such an early stage of my employment. Receiving a British Council Post-Graduate Scholarship in 1987 enabled me to spend a valuable year working in Soviet archives and libraries, while a generous grant from the Deutscher Akademischer Austauschdienst made it possible for me to make a research trip to the Richard Wagner Gedenkstätte in Bayreuth. I was also able to enjoy the unique resources of the library of the Warburg Institute, University of London, during my tenure there as a short-term Frances Yates Fellow in 1990. I am grateful to the Office of the Vice-President of Research at the University of Michigan for awarding me a publication subvention which has allowed the inclusion of colour plates in this volume, and to the Horace H. Rackham School of Graduate Studies in providing support for a visit to St Petersburg in May 1993, when I took part in the first conference on Wagner ever to be held in Russia.

xvii

I should also like to thank the many people who have given me assistance of various kinds over the last few years. Among the many Russian colleagues and friends who have been a source of invaluable practical assistance and helpful advice, I am particularly grateful to Anna Porfirieva, who was a model of scholarly generosity; without her help my access to many archival materials in Moscow would have been limited. I should also like to thank Inna Barsova, Marina Godlevskaya, Abram Gozenpud, Boris Kats, Oleg Khmelnitsky, Nikolay Kotrelyov, Lyudmila Kovnatskaya, Grigory Kruzhkov, Dina Magomedova, Irina Medvedeva, Lyudmila Rybakova, Dmitry Sarabyanov and the staff of the libraries and archives in which I worked in Moscow and St Petersburg. I am also grateful to the numerous people in England, Germany and the United States who have provided me with essential information and expert advice, especially Marina Baag, T. J. Binyon, Victor Borovsky, Patrick Carnegy, John Deathridge, Manfred Eger and Günter Fischer of the Wagner archive in Bayreuth, David Howells and the staff of the Taylorian Institution Slavonic Annexe, Carol Menzies of the Bodleian Library Slavonic Reading Room, Bernice Glatzer Rosenthal and John Warrack. For their encouragement and support, I am extremely grateful to my parents Paul and Hilary Bartlett, but most of all, I would like to thank three people from whose wisdom and expertise I have benefited greatly, and in whose debt I shall always remain: Gerard McBurney, who was a staunch and inspiring friend, Avril Pyman, without whom I would not have continued my studies at graduate level, and, above all, my advisor Gerry Smith, whose excellent guidance and fine judgement I shall continue to value in the years to come.

Notes on the text

The British system has been used for the transliteration of Russian words, with diacritics omitted. In proper names, *y* has been used for final ий and ый, *yo* has replaced ё, *ie* has replaced ье, and the apostrophe for ь has been omitted. Exceptions to these rules have been made in cases where there is a more commonly accepted spelling ('Tchaikovsky' has been used rather than 'Chaikovsky', for example), and also in those cases where authors use the romanised as well as the Russian versions of their names ('Medtner' and 'Laroche', for example, instead of 'Metner' and 'Larosh').

All Russian dates before 1 February 1918 are given according to the Old Style (Julian) calendar. All other dates are given according to the New Style (Gregorian) calendar.

Abbreviations

The following abbreviations have been used in the text and notes.

ed. khr.	*edinitsa khraneniya*
GATOB	Gosudarstvennyi akademicheskii teatr opery i baleta
Glavrepertkom	*Glavnaya repertuarnaya kommissiya*
GTsMMK	Gosudarstvennyi tsentral'nyi muzei muzykal'noi kul'tury im. Glinki, Moscow
GUS	Gosudarstvennaya uchenaya kommissiya
k.	*karton*
LN	*Literaturnoe nasledstvo*
op.	*opis'*
Narkompros	*Narodnyi kommissariat prosveshcheniya*
NEP	New Economic Policy
Persimfans	*Pervyi simfonicheskii ansambl'*
Proletkul't	*Proletarskaya kul'tura*
RGALI	Rossiiskii gosudarstvennyi arkhiv literatury i iskusstva, Moscow
RGB	Rossiiskaya gosudarstvennaya biblioteka, Otdel rukopisei, Moscow
RMG	*Russkaya muzykal'naya gazeta*
RMS	Russian Musical Society
Vkhutemas	*Vysshie gosudarstvennye khudozhestvenno-tekhnicheskie masterskie*

Introduction

No composer's works have had quite the same extraordinary after-life that Richard Wagner's music dramas and theoretical writings have done. After causing controversy all over Europe by denouncing contemporary theatre as corrupt and demanding social and artistic revolution in a series of inflammatory essays written after his participation in the 1849 Dresden Uprising, Wagner went on to change the face of opera with the composition of his seven 'music dramas'. It is of little significance that Wagner's political aspirations fell by the wayside, for there was revolution enough in the *Ring* to generate a public outcry, no more so than in Russia, where the most conservative critics at first saw the composer as nothing less than a musical Antichrist. Despite the success of his concerts in St Petersburg and Moscow in 1863, when Wagner became the first musician in Russia to conduct facing the orchestra, the Imperial Theatres tried to resist the production of his music dramas for as long as possible. Such was the clamour for tickets to the performances of the *Ring* in 1889 given by a German touring company, however, that in 1900 the Mariinsky Theatre finally succumbed to the inevitable, and began staging the first Russian production of the work. The Russian opera-going public now abandoned their favourites in the French and Italian repertoire as their enthusiasm for Wagner deepened; during the 1909–10 season seven works by Wagner were performed at the Mariinsky Theatre, and by 1914, performances of his works took up a quarter of the total number of performances in the preceding season. All further performances of his works were banned when Russia entered World

I

War I, however, thus bringing pre-revolutionary Russian Wagnerism to an abrupt end. During that time, however, Wagner had caught the imaginations of the Symbolist writers and their fellow musicians and artists, and exerted a profound influence on their creative works. Astonishingly, Wagner continued to exercise a hold over Russian minds during the first decade of Soviet power, when he was promoted as a paragon revolutionary artist by Anatoly Lunacharsky, the first Communist director of culture. During the early 1920s, when Moscow became the centre for artistic innovation, Wagner's works (particularly *Rienzi*) were enthusiastically staged once more, often in newly politicised versions, and designed by leading artists of Russia's avant-garde. The cultural revolution, however, dictated a shift in the official attitude to Wagner, whose other Janus face (the one looking towards mysticism, pessimism and reaction) could no longer be ignored. The new 'critical' outlook on Wagner meant that productions of his works now had to be justified ideologically, and could show only Wagner's hatred of capitalism, his optimism for the socialist future of mankind, and his identification with the rebellious masses. Hitler's rise to power in the thirties only accelerated Wagner's disappearance from opera repertoires and concert programmes. Yet the Nazi–Soviet Pact was to bring a late but rich bloom to Soviet Wagnerism: Eisenstein's production of *Die Walküre* at the Bolshoi Theatre in 1940, which was beyond doubt the most radical and innovative staging of the work to take place anywhere in Europe before World War II. The experience of producing Wagner's opera made a profound impression on Eisenstein, and he later acknowledged that it had been of prime importance to his experiments with colour film.

The story of Russia's long involvement with Wagner's music and ideas thus not only adds a small, but interesting and previously unexplored chapter to the composer's biography, but (particularly in the case of Meyerhold and Eisenstein) contributes very significantly to the history of Wagner stagings, and even that of opera production as a whole. Wagner's ideas also exerted a lasting influence on leading practitioners of

Russian Symbolism and many other artists and musicians during Russia's 'Silver Age'. What is particularly noteworthy about Wagner's influence on Russian culture is perhaps not the fact that it was so pronounced, but that – incredibly – it persisted until the end of the 1930s, where it had its final flowering in Eisenstein's production of *Die Walküre*. It is extraordinary that the ideas of a Romantic nineteenth-century composer should still be bearing fruit well into the twentieth century, by which time the heyday of the modernist movement had already long passed.

With the exception of Serov, most nineteenth-century Russian composers endeavoured, but mostly failed, to remain impervious to Wagner's imposing presence. The Balakirev circle, for example, both sensed and feared his colossal talent, but their intense desire to remain true to the precepts of Russian realist art which Stasov had instilled in them, coupled with an awareness of the relatively undeveloped state of Russian music, led to insecurities which often manifested themselves in the form of violent invectives directed against Wagner and his reforms. Cui, as the weakest of the group, was the most insecure: accordingly, his diatribes against Wagner were the most highly charged. Musorgsky, on the other hand, the greatest of the five, and also the most sure, had little need to expunge the fear of Wagnerian influence from his mind by means of vituperative attacks, for he was making discoveries of his own about opera and drama. That the hostile stance of the Balakirev circle was little more than a mask which hid quite different feelings is revealed by the cataclysmic effect that hearing the *Ring* had on Rimsky-Korsakov in 1889. Borodin too clearly harboured a furtive affection for Wagner's works. Tchaikovsky's feelings about Wagner, on the other hand, were complex. There was much he did not at first understand in Wagner's music (as his articles about the *Ring* demonstrate), but his almost obsessive desire to hear the composer's works, and discuss them in his writings – a habit maintained until his death – together with his late enthusiasm for *Parsifal*, combine to show that one should not be at all categorical about characterising his antipathy to Wagner. As often, it is a case of reading between the lines. At the end of the nineteenth century, when it was no longer possible to pretend that Wagner was really a second-rate composer with nothing to say, Russian composers all succumbed to his influence for a time: Glazunov, Prokofiev, Rakhmaninov, Skryabin and even Stravinsky, who took the scale of the Wagnerian orchestra to its limits in *The Rite of Spring* before reacting violently against it. Skryabin was the most deeply affected by Wagner, but given his links with the Symbolist movement, this was only to be expected. The influence that Wagner exerted on Blok, Bely and Ivanov, however, proves that the Symbolist Wagner had very little to do with the nineteenth-century composer Wagner that the Russian public flocked in droves to hear. All three writers were primarily attracted to the composer by his creative methods based on myth and symbol, which they believed were intimately connected to their own attempts to reveal the deeper realities behind the world of appearances. Each writer essentially responded to different aspects in Wagner's work, however. For Bely, it was the purely rhythmic element of Wagner's music which most excited him, and which he linked with the idea of Eternal Recurrence. Even a cursory glance over Bely's own writings will reveal how important the concept of rhythm was to him. In Wagner Bely prophetically divined the element in music which would increasingly come to the fore in the twentieth century. The structure of the Wagnerian music drama also strongly affected his own creative methods as he grappled with ways to achieve the emotional profundities of Wagner's musical leitmotifs by similar means in his prose fiction. Like Ivanov, Bely also believed that Wagner's symbolism made him the true founder of the Symbolist movement, but he did not share Ivanov's misguided belief that Wagner's music dramas also forecast the future development of Symbolism into universal mythmaking. Ivanov shared Blok and Bely's reverence for the *Ring*, but was transported most by *Tristan und Isolde*, in whose themes of love and death, joy and suffering he found echoes of the Dionysian myth which formed the core of his work. He also found evidence of Dionysian inspiration in the musical language of this work, whose chro-

maticism and apparent formlessness seemed to him to symbolise primordial chaos. Like Bely, Ivanov intuitively divined the
future of musical development; it was precisely the premonition of the disintegration of musical form which can first be
discerned in *Tristan und Isolde*, Wagner's most innovative work
musically speaking, which most attracted him in Wagner's
music. On the other hand, Ivanov fell prey to all the aspects of
Wagner's dramatic theories most vulnerable to criticism in
believing that the creation of a synthetic, music and myth-
based drama that would unite artist and spectator in the act of
holy creation was both realistic and feasible. In fact he went
one step further than Wagner in his call for the revival of
ancient tragedy in the form of the Dionysian rite, for Wagner
was always careful to stress that a return to Greek drama was
not a part of his programme for the 'art-work of the future'. All
three Symbolists at some point in their careers engrossed themselves in theorising on 'what was to come', visualising an ideal
future in which both society and art would be an organic
whole, as a reaction to the collapse of society, religion and
aesthetic values which they saw taking place around them.
Their receptivity to Wagner's theories shows that these writers
were as much Romantics as they were Symbolists. Like the
French Symbolists, they were drawing on the same German
sources of inspiration, but it is vital to recognise that they did so
not indirectly through their earlier French counterparts, but
directly, and principally from artists such as Wagner, Schopenhauer and Nietzsche, replacing European 'decadence', as they
did so, with their own brand of Solovyovian mysticism. As for
Blok, he had always been much more interested in the human
aspects of Wagner's *Ring*. He did not waste his time prophesying the Dionysian future of culture, nor did he share Ivanov's
conviction of the hierophantic role of the poet. But even he
towards the end of his life began to abandon the hard-won
realism of his later style in favour of hopelessly idealistic visions
of future synthesis. It is in fact an extraordinary phenomenon
that not only Blok, but also Bely and Ivanov, Skryabin, Meyerhold and Eisenstein – the Russian artists on whom Wagner's
ideas had the greatest impact – all at some point in their lives

began to preach the idea of synthesis: an organic art which would bring people together in a condition of all-embracing unity, as Wagner had dreamed. The question must be asked: what is it about Russian culture that makes its artists so receptive to, and uncritical of, all-embracing models? Perhaps it is not too far-fetched to suggest that there is a link between the enthusiasm of Russian artists for Wagner and the enthusiasm of Russian political activists of the same period for his compatriot Karl Marx, who, shortly before the composer sat down to pen his aesthetic tracts, was formulating an equally all-embracing solution to the problems of society, which ultimately hailed from the same source of German Idealism.

This study shows that Russia was peculiarly sympathetic and susceptible to Wagnerian ideas; certainly no other culture seems to have taken the composer's writings on art to heart as they did in Russia. Whilst France has been traditionally the country which is supposed to have taken Wagner for its own, that perception may now have to be substantially revised. The opinion was expressed on more than one occasion that Russia was bound to find in Wagner a kindred spirit. Several critics thought that Russia was far more likely to understand and appreciate Wagner than any other nation, whether as a result of its 'thirst for religious art', as Sergey Durylin believed, or the tendency it shared with Germany towards 'pessimistic idealism' and 'depth of feeling', as Viktor Kolomiitsov contended. Lev Kobylinsky-Ellis, meanwhile, placed not only the salvation of Russian Symbolism in Wagner's hands; he became convinced that Wagner's works were also capable of redeeming the entire Russian nation. It is peculiarly pertinent, in this light, to discover that singers such as Ershov had a way of 'Russifying' Wagner's heroes, because they found features in them common with the decidedly Slavic world of Dostoevsky's heroes (Tannhäuser as 'the sinner', Siegmund as 'the sufferer' etc.). Although Abram Gozenpud has rejected the idea that there was anything more than a superficial similarity between the themes of Dostoevsky and Wagner, in his biography of Ershov he nevertheless found it apposite to quote from Marietta Shaginyan's salient description of the quite natural transformation of Wagner's heroes from the *Ring* into holy fools, with whom Russian audiences could immediately identify. All this suggests that, as Emil Medtner so strongly believed, the affinities between German and Russian culture run much deeper than might previously have been supposed.

Wagner and nineteenth-century Russia

PART I

Eighteenth and nineteenth-century Europe

CHAPTER I

Reception and performance history, 1841–1863

RUSSIA ENCOUNTERS THE 'MUSIC OF THE FUTURE'

Wagner's name first appeared in the Russian press in June 1841, when the journal *Repertuar russkogo teatra* published a translation of his important early essay 'Über die Ouvertüre'.[1] This article had originally appeared only six months earlier in the *Revue et gazette Musicale* in Paris (where Wagner was based at the time), and its translation into Russian is something of a mystery, for nothing seems to have been known about this obscure 28-year-old composer in Russia at this time.[2] Indeed several decades were to go by before further Russian translations of writings by Wagner were issued. Wagner started properly coming into the public eye in Russia in 1842, when newspapers started to report on the première of *Rienzi* in Dresden,[3] but most Russians remained completely unaware of who he was until the early 1850s, when news of his notorious aesthetic theories began to spread abroad.

It was at concerts, rather than in the opera house that Wagner's music was first heard in Russia, and for very specific reasons. Opera in St Petersburg and Moscow under tsarist rule was government controlled, and repertoires were dictated by the extremely conservative tastes of the nobility, who were at that time in the grip of 'Italomania'.[4] The Russian public thus flocked in their thousands to hear the fashionable and prestigious Italian Opera in Petersburg, to whose further glory the Imperial Theatres Directorate devoted vast sums of money, while patronising the Russian Opera, on the other hand, was thought rather *infra dignitatem*, a situation which persisted until the 1880s. Years of neglect and under-funding by the Government had led to a distinctly moribund state of affairs; singers were paid a pittance (unlike their Italian counterparts) and productions were lack-lustre. It was therefore quite unthinkable that the Russian Opera should tackle radical and demanding new works by comparatively unknown composers such as Wagner, when it could barely cope with the existing repertoire.[5] It was even more unlikely, however, that Wagner's serious teutonic dramas should ever find a home amongst the often frivolous works on offer at the Italian Opera. Any chances of the Imperial Theatres Directorate even contemplating the production of a work by Wagner must have receded still further when Wagner took part in the 1849 Dresden Uprising, and went on to pen several lengthy and controversial treatises, calling, amongst other things, for social revolution and the abolition of all class-ridden artistic institutions, of which the Italian Opera was a glaring example.

Wagner's suggestions that the Royal Court Theatre in Dresden (where he had been kapellmeister since 1843) be nationalised and run democratically had not endeared him to his employers. Coming to the conclusion that the theatre was a 'mirror of a reactionary society that had first to be changed if he was to realise his artistic aims',[6] Wagner had increasingly become involved with left-wing politics, writing articles and speeches in which he openly called for revolution. And it was at some point in 1848 or early 1849 that he made the acquaintance of the great anarchist Mikhail Bakunin, one of the few Russians ever to make any real impression on him. Wagner found Bakunin's demand for the total destruction of all civilisation rather alarming, but he was nonetheless mesmerised by his titanic energy.[7] When rioting began in Dresden in May 1849, Wagner became directly involved in the famous Uprising, but (unlike Bakunin) he managed to escape arrest by fleeing to Zurich, where he began nine years of exile. It was here that he began to formulate his ideas for transforming opera into music drama; for the next few years, he stopped composing music in order to write several lengthy treatises, the most important of which are *Art and Revolution* (*Die Kunst und die*

Revolution) and *The Art-work of the Future* (*Das Kunstwerk der Zukunft*), both published in 1849, and *Opera and Drama* (*Oper und Drama*), published in 1851. Aleksandr Herzen, another Russian in exile who became acquainted with Wagner at this time, was an early admirer of these writings. In a letter he wrote to Wagner on 8 July 1852, he informed him that he had read his 'marvellous essay on the work of art of the future' and complimented him on an 'excellent understanding of the inter-relations of the arts, which ought to be joined in harmonious, concrete creation'.[8] It is doubtful that anyone in Russia had read Wagner's writings with such apparent care at this time, and with such inflammatory titles like *Art and Revolution*, there was little chance of them ever passing the censor for publi-cation in Russian translation. They certainly won Wagner wide notoriety in Russia, however, as they had done throughout Europe, and eventually there was sufficient curio-sity for people to want to hear his music. The first public performance of music by Wagner finally took place on 15 March 1856, when the overture to *Tannhäuser* was heard at a concert organised by the St Petersburg Philharmonic Society.[9] In subsequent years, the Society also tackled the *Faust-Ouvertüre*, excerpts from *Der fliegende Holländer* and the prelude to *Lohengrin*, but performances were infrequent.[10]

The situation regarding public concerts in Russia in the middle of the nineteenth century was not exactly a healthy one, for it was not as if the metropolitan concert societies would have been able to take up the cause of promoting Wagner's works in the absence of full-scale productions, even had that been their objective. Public concerts had only begun to be given in Russia on a more or less regular basis from 1770 onwards,[11] and, until the relaxation of the draconian restric-tions imposed by the Imperial Theatres (who wished to main-tain their monopoly), could only be held during Lent, when the opera season was over. When only a handful of organi-sations existed which arranged orchestral concerts, there was little hope of Wagner ever attaining any lasting popularity during the five-week concert season each year. When the Russian Musical Society (RMS) was founded in 1859 (the first organisation in Russia to hold concerts throughout the winter season), the situation was barely altered, since its director Anton Rubinstein was no admirer of Wagner.[12] Music by Wagner was performed at only eleven concerts (out of an approximate total of seventy) held during the seven-year period of his jurisdiction.[13] Wagner fared rather better at the hands of Nikolay Rubinstein, director of the Moscow branch of the RMS. Between 1860 (the year of its foundation) and 1866, music by Wagner was performed at almost twice the number of concerts.[14] Once music by Wagner began to be performed at concerts in Russia, however, the number of articles on the composer in the Russian press began to increase considerably. Russian critics, mistakenly applying the label 'Zukunftsmusik' to any music they heard by Wagner, now felt qualified to pass judgement on the composer himself, and it was at this point that the bitter polemics surrounding Wagner's name in the Russian press (which were to rage for the next sixty years) began to divide musical opinion into opposing factions.[15] With each successive year, Wagner and his theories attracted more and more attention, to the extent that over 225 articles and reports were written about the composer in the Russian press during the 1860s, compared with the paltry few written each year during the previous decade.[16]

Many of the early opinions expressed about Wagner in Russia were of a dilettante nature, for there simply was no professional music criticism in Russia until the second half of the nineteenth century,[17] and not until 1862, indeed, was there a critic in Moscow who even maintained a regular column on musical matters.[18] Somewhat predictably, most of the enthusiastic amateurs who made up the small community of Russian music journalists took immediate exception to Wagner and his newfangled theories about opera. Chief amongst Wagner's Russian opponents was the venerable Aleksandr Ulybyshev, who refused to recognise any music written after Mozart and regarded Wagner as a musical apostate.[19] Ulybyshev's conservative views were shared by other leading critics of the day such as Nikolay Melgunov, Feofil Tolstoy, Yury Arnold and Sergey Rachinsky. The German-born critic Berthold Damcke also vilified Wagner and his music whilst acting as foreign correspondent for the Russian press between 1857 and 1860.[20] For these critics, rejection of the traditional operatic form was nothing short of heresy. But whilst they were swift to ridicule Wagner's iconoclastic theories of the 'art of the future', which they found deeply shocking, it is unlikely that any of these critics had ever heard more than a couple of overtures by Wagner or read his writings. Possibly they had seen full scores of the early operas, but it is probable they had only ever set eyes on the four-hand piano versions of their overtures which the journal *Nuvellist* began issuing from 1856 onwards.[21] Hence much opinion was inevitably based on rumour rather than hard evidence.[22] It is ironic that it should have been a writer who was the first in Russia to perceive Wagner's greatness. In 1858, the poet and essayist Pyotr Vyazemsky remarked prophetically in his diary that Wagner's music was 'not only the music of the future, but the music of eternity'.[23]

The few Wagnerians in Russia at this time were heavily outnumbered. Before Wagner's visit to Russia, only two critics ventured on to the pages of the Russian press to defend the composer against the increasingly scurrilous attacks: the composer Aleksandr Serov and the critic Konstantin Zvantsov. The latter, who completed the first Russian translations of *Tannhäuser* (1862) and *Lohengrin* (1868), entered the arena with an article in *Syn otechestva* in 1857, in which he poured scorn on Ulybyshev's primitive ideas about Wagner,[24] but the level of his journalism was really no better than that of his foe. In Serov, however, Wagner found a gifted ally, for his animated and well-informed articles raised the quality of music criticism in Russia to unprecedented levels of professionalism. At the same time, his caustic sarcasm won him many enemies and ensured that the arguments about Wagner were always highly charged.

Serov became acquainted with Wagner's writings before he heard any of his music, first reading *Opera and Drama* in 1852 (a year after its publication), and treating it with a healthy scepticism. By the time he discovered *The Art-work of the Future* two years later, however, those feelings had been replaced by an unbounded admiration.[25] A similar change of heart took place with regard to Wagner's music. When Serov first heard the overture to *Tannhäuser* at the Philharmonic Society concert in 1856,[26] he found it 'absorbing, and even striking, but certainly not beautiful, and incapable of bringing any pleasure from a musical point of view'.[27] During his first trip abroad in 1858, however, he heard six performances of *Tannhäuser* in a row,[28] and by the time he returned to Russia, his conversion to Wagnerism was complete.[29] During his next visit to Germany the following year, he met and became friends with Wagner himself.[30] Serov now dedicated himself to the propagation of Wagner's ideas and music in Russia. As well as writing numerous articles, and giving a poorly attended lecture series, he managed to persuade the Imperial Theatres Directorate to include music by Wagner at one of its Lent concerts.[31]

It seemed the efforts of Wagner's tireless Russian 'apostle' were finally rewarded when the Imperial Theatres began seriously to entertain Serov's proposal that they should stage *Tannhäuser* under his general direction. In May 1860, the director of the Imperial Theatres visited Wagner in Paris to invite him to spend the following winter in St Petersburg. During that time, it was suggested, he could supervise the production of *Tannhäuser* and give some concerts. Since rehearsals were shortly to begin for the Paris première of *Tannhäuser*, however, Wagner was in no position to accept this attractive offer, but no alternative dates could apparently be entertained by the Imperial Theatres emissary.[32] In 1862, Zvantsov (whom Serov was later to call 'more ardent a Wagnerian than Wagner himself')[33] made another attempt to arrange for the production of *Tannhäuser*. This new project enjoyed the active support of several Russian singers who wanted to know from Wagner personally how *Tannhäuser* should be staged, and Zvantsov travelled to Germany for the purpose with letters of introduction to Wagner. Hopes were dashed again, however, by the Imperial Theatres' lack of commitment.[34]

Serov's cult of Wagner did not endear him to the rest of the composing fraternity in St Petersburg. Aleksandr Dargomyzhsky, by this time the doyen of Russian music, shared the same year of birth with Wagner and an interest in the dramatic possibilities of opera, but had very little else in common with him. He first became acquainted with Wagner's music in 1856, when Serov lent him the piano arrangement of *Tannhäuser*, and his verdict was that there was 'much poetry' in the libretto, but that Wagner's vocal writing was unnatural.[35] He found Wagner's aesthetic theories as unpalatable as his music and subjected both to a relentless stream of mockery in the satirical journal *Iskra*. Dargomyzhsky's hostility to Wagner, however, is most probably attributable to insecurity, and it is interesting to note that parallels were subsequently drawn on more than one occasion between his and Wagner's compositional methods.[36] Dargomyzhsky found Wagner's music threatening, and feared that his theory of the 'art of the future' would 'interfere with the development' of the young Russian school, and 'halt its momentum'.[37] None of the five composers in the Balakirev circle who made up this 'young Russian school' (which formed between 1856 and 1862) would ever admit to feeling threatened by Wagner, but the eloquent silence with which most of the group greeted the first performances of his music in Russia and his arrival in Petersburg speaks volumes. Neither Musorgsky or Balakirev expressed any real opinions about Wagner in their writings, although the latter's hatred of Wagner was apparently 'intense',[38] and was equalled in ferocity only by that of César Cui, who from 1864 acted as the group's spokesman in the press.[39] Rimsky-Korsakov was moved to write a great deal about Wagner in later life, but for the present was under the spell of Balakirev. Borodin was the sole member of the group to have actually heard operas by Wagner performed (he had heard *Der fliegende Holländer*, *Tannhäuser* and *Lohengrin* in 1861 in Mannheim).[40] Whatever nascent feelings of respect he might have begun to nurture towards the composer, however,[41] had to be suppressed when he joined ranks with the Balakirev circle in 1862. Pyotr Boborykin, a close associate of the group who never remembers them talking about 'the creator of the "music of the future"', confirms that 'they had no enthusiasm for Wagner whatsoever'.[42] Vladimir Stasov, the group's chief ideologue, also played an important role in fostering anti-Wagner sentiment. As a promoter of Russian nationalism and realism, it was perhaps inevitable that he should be repelled by Wagner. His antipathy became more pronounced, moreover, when Serov began to bring Wagner into the *Ruslan i Lyudmila* controversy which arose at the end of the 1850s,[43] thus bringing a once close friendship to an abrupt end. Although he never engaged in full-time journalism, Stasov led a virulent and prolonged campaign in the name of Russian music against Serov and the pernicious doctrine of Wagnerism.[44]

WAGNER'S VISIT TO RUSSIA

By the 1860s, Wagner had become something of a musical celebrity, and in November 1862, he received an invitation from the St Petersburg Philharmonic Society to conduct two concerts of his own music the following year for a fee of 2,000 silver roubles. At the time, Wagner was living in Vienna, struggling to get *Tristan und Isolde* performed at the Court Opera. But after seventy-seven rehearsals, the opera was still not ready for its première, and Wagner therefore decided to accept the invitation to go to Russia, hoping the trip might be financially advantageous for him. Accordingly, he despatched a letter of acceptance to the Philharmonic Society, in which he also imprudently suggested that the august charitable body might also act as an agent to secure some concerts for his own benefit.[45] A second letter that he sent to this effect in January 1863 finally provoked a nettled reply from the Society, reminding Wagner of its philanthropic purpose. The invitation was not withdrawn, however, and Wagner telegraphed back shortly afterwards to accept the Society's invitation on their terms.[46] Shortly afterwards, he set out on his journey to St Petersburg, elated by the success of the concert he had just conducted in Prague and by new hopes for the production of *Tristan*.

Wagner was filled with unease as he crossed the border into Russia, having last crossed it illegally in 1839 when leaving Riga,[47] and his apprehensions increased when the train he was

travelling on came to an abrupt halt and was closely searched
by the police. Although it transpired that they were looking for
participants in the latest Polish uprising, the composer could
not quell his fears entirely. 'Not far from the capital', he wrote
in his autobiography, 'the empty seats were suddenly filled
with people whose large Russian fur hats made me all the more
suspicious, inasmuch as the wearers fixed me with an incessant
stare. But suddenly the face of one of them lit up in transfiguration, and he hailed me enthusiastically as the man whom he
and several other members of the Imperial Orchestra had
come out to greet.'[48] Ironically, Wagner did in fact have
good reason to be suspicious, for unbeknown to him, the
notorious 'Third Department' had branded him as a 'suspicious and politically suspect person'.[49] Despite the fact that
Wagner had been granted a full amnesty in 1862, the Third
Department resolved to keep him under strict surveillance
throughout his stay. The secret police's file on Wagner was
opened by Prince V. A. Dolgorukov (responsible for the surveillance of all foreigners in St Petersburg), and consists of five
reports compiled by a secret agent. Cognisant of Wagner's past
as a revolutionary and his acquaintance with Bakunin,
Dolgorukov evidently considered that Wagner's presence in
the capital posed a political threat. Inciting the Russian people
to overthrow their government was really very far from
Wagner's mind by this stage, however. Under the tutelage of
Schopenhauer's life-renouncing and pessimistic philosophy, to
which he had succumbed in 1854, he had become convinced of
the futility of revolution, and the only exhortations he was
planning to make in St Petersburg were motivated by financial
rather than political considerations. The following statement
by the Third Department agent in fact tactfully suggests that
Dolgorukov might have unduly magnified the political danger
represented by Wagner: 'Although he took part in the disturb-
ances in Germany in 1848 [*sic*], these days Wagner seems to
have settled down: last summer he lived very modestly in
Biebrich on the Rhine.'[50] Not satisfied by Wagner's apparent
pacifism, Prince Dolgorukov none the less ordered that the
composer be kept under close observation throughout his stay.

—Публика для музыки «будущаго»—
Вагнера.

1. Caricature of the audience at Wagner's Russian concerts published in
the satirical magazine *Iskra* (St Petersburg, 1863).

Upon arrival in Petersburg on 12 February, Wagner settled into a German pension on the Nevsky Prospekt and was soon inundated with visitors. The constant throng of people around the composer thus made the secret agent's task a difficult one. One of Wagner's first visitors was Serov, who proved to be an invaluable source of assistance throughout his stay. As well as assiduously translating the composer's programme notes and vocal texts for the forthcoming concerts, Wagner's Russian acolyte also strove to secure the best singers for the concerts (there being, of course, no impresarios at that time to fulfil that function).[51] Wagner wrote the first of many letters from Russia to his friend Josef Standhartner three days after his arrival, in which he complained of his 'horrifying journey' and the cold Russian weather ('It's winter here, sleighs and ice!').[52] From this letter we also learn that Wagner had held his first rehearsal on 14 February and that it had been most successful. 'The orchestra is very good, very strong (24 first violins), intelligent and competent', he wrote, 'and they are thrilled to play at last under a decent conductor.'[53]

Wagner gave his first concert on 19 February[54] in the Hall of the Nobility (the *Blagorodnoe sobranie*), with 130 musicians at his disposal selected from the Imperial Orchestra. His Russian audiences were entertained to excerpts from all his most recent works. In fact they even heard many excerpts from works Wagner was still writing (namely the *Ring* and *Die Meistersinger*). Thus the Russian public were amongst the first ever to hear the famous *Ritt der Walküren*, and the *Feuerzauber* music from *Die Walküre*, for example, the forging songs from *Siegfried*, and the overture to *Die Meistersinger*, as well as such well-tried favourites as the overture to *Lohengrin*. All these pieces had only ever been performed a handful of times before at concerts held elsewhere in Europe before Wagner's Russian tour. Quite by chance, Wagner's first concert was held exactly two years after the emancipation of the serfs, a day on which the anniversary of Alexander II's coronation was also being celebrated, and Wagner was therefore asked to conduct the orchestra in a performance of the national anthem. It was apparently given a rather chilly reception by certain members of the audience.

The secret agent appointed to monitor Wagner's movements took particular notice of this fact and noted that 'some people got up and walked out as soon as they heard the first notes; they were all young people with beards'.[55] Wagner, who remained blissfully unaware of the Third Department's machinations, had evidently disappointed the young radicals in the audience, and it would no doubt have been to their great chagrin had they learnt how pleased he actually was to perform the anthem. 'How tragic this tsar seems to be', he wrote to his friend Marie Kalergis-Mukhanova after his first concert, 'the things I have learned about him make me view him as God's emissary to Russia. Yes, precisely him, this noble, deeply well-meaning emperor. But what bitter experiences await him, I wonder?'[56] The day after his first concert, he wrote to Mathilde Maier in exalted (and exaggerated) tones: 'The concert is over. It was quite frightful; I've never had such a warm reception as I've had here in Russia!!! The audience – three to four thousand people[57] – almost devoured me!!! ... When I had to repeat the *Lohengrin* prelude, my nerves began to give way and it was if the whole orchestra – 130 people – were transformed into angels and were greeting my arrival in heaven with particularly ecstatic music. It was a sublime, moving moment! ...'[58]

Wagner's second concert, held on 26 February, was remarkable for the fact that his subsequently familiar practice of combining the prelude (*Liebestod*) and the conclusion (*Verklär-ung*) from act three of *Tristan und Isolde* was here employed for the first time.[59] His third concert, held on 6 March at the Imperial Opera House (home to the Italian Opera during the season), was a benefit for himself. The previous two concerts had been extremely successful and the third was evidently no exception, if we are to take Wagner at his word:

The concert itself succeeded beyond expectation, and I do not ever recall being received more enthusiastically by an audience than was the case here, for even the initial applause was so stormy and lasted so long that it overwhelmed me, something which was otherwise not easy to achieve. The fiery devotion of the orchestra itself seems to have contributed greatly to the enthusiasm of the public. For it was my one hundred and twenty musicians themselves who repeatedly instigated the tempestuous outbursts of applause, an event that appeared unprecedented in St Petersburg. From some of them I heard such exclamations as 'Let us admit we didn't know until now what music is!'[60]

Wagner's concerts inevitably aroused much interest in the St Petersburg music world. The 20-year old Tchaikovsky long retained his memories of Wagner's conducting, as is clear from his letter to Nadezhda von Meck of 1879, where he comments on a concert conducted by Edouard Colonne:

[Colonne] is not first-rate, but still a very sound conductor ... However, in all my life I have only ever seen one such conductor ([Colonne] commanded none of the authority or power that transforms the orchestra until all the players become as if one soul, one great instrument) and that was Wagner when he came to give concerts in Petersburg in 1863 and conducted some Beethoven symphonies. Whoever did not hear those symphonies performed with Wagner conducting cannot fully evaluate them or comprehend their unattainable greatness.[61]

There is no evidence that Musorgsky or Borodin attended any of Wagner's concerts, but in a letter of 18 February 1863, we find Cui inviting Balakirev to 'go and see Wagner' the following evening.[62] A letter to Rimsky-Korsakov (who was abroad on naval duty) from Balakirev contained the improbable verdict that the concert had contained 'nothing new or interesting'.[63] Wagner had the chance to observe Balakirev's conducting during his stay in St Petersburg, and on 5 April he attended the second concert of the Free Music School, the occasion of Balakirev's second public appearance as a conductor.[64] In his autobiography, Wagner does not mention Balakirev by name, but records his attendance at a concert held at the Chamber of Commerce and recollects being 'received there on the steps by an extremely drunken Russian, who introduced himself ... as the conductor'.[65] One wonders, if this was not Balakirev,[66] who that 'drunken Russian' might have been.

During his stay in St Petersburg Wagner wasted no time in gaining admittance to court. That financial rather than artistic

2. 'Music for the Unborn (Wagner's Zu Kumft Musik)' by N. Stepanov, cartoon depicting Wagner and Serov published in the satirical magazine *Iskra* (1863). Caption: <u>Composer</u>: 'It's strange – the French didn't appreciate my music of the *future*, but the Russians do. Why is that?' <u>Answer</u> 'Because Russians now live in the *future*'.

concerns were uppermost in Wagner's mind during his Russian visit is confirmed by his letter to Standhartner of 15 February, in which he bemoaned his failure to gain an introduction, despite the fact that he had only been in the capital three days.[67] Through the connections of his patron Marie Kalergis, however, Wagner eventually succeeded in receiving an invitation to the salon of Grand Duchess Elena Pavlovna's lady-in-waiting, Editha von Rhaden. And on 27 February, he wrote to Mathilde Maier, telling her he had already spent one evening 'in society' with the 'spirited and informed' Grand Duchess, who had expressed a desire to be acquainted with the text of *Die Meistersinger*.[68] Wagner subsequently spent at least five evenings (the first of which took place on 25 March)[69] reading both the *Ring* and *Die Meistersinger* to her.[70] Whilst at court Wagner also met Count Matvey Vielgorsky, an important figure in Russian musical life at that time, and the composer Count Boris Fitingof-Shel, who invited Wagner to lunch. Recollecting his guest later, he wrote that Wagner 'spoke loudly and distinctly; when he considered his point proved, a rather imperious tone appeared in his voice as if to forbid objection'.[71] The Count later visited Wagner in Florence in 1876 and was dismayed that the composer was on this occasion not nearly as genial or as sociable as he had been during his visit to Russia, and lamented that 'During that time he had changed from the Wagner who had come to us thirteen years ago into the demi-god from the Bayreuth Olympus.'[72]

After the Petersburg concerts, Wagner spent twenty hours travelling to Moscow to give some concerts there at the invitation of the Imperial Theatres Directorate, which hoped to profit by the proceedings. The cold indifference that Wagner encountered in his relations with Russian officialdom in Moscow was in marked contrast to the official pomp of Verdi's visit a few months earlier.[73] Leonid Lvov, head of the Bolshoi Theatre (whom Wagner dismissed as 'paltry'[74]) recognised only Italian opera and wanted to have nothing to do with the visit.[75] Moscow seemed to make more of an impact on Wagner than Petersburg had done. Beyond writing on 15 February to Josef Standhartner that Petersburg was not making an 'unfavourable impression' on him,[76] and on 19 February to Mathilde Maier that he liked the city 'very much',[77] his only other observation on life in the Russian capital was that the climate was vile.[78] In Moscow, however, Wagner felt as if he was in a quite different country. 'So now I'm in Asia, really in Asia, my child!', he wrote to Mathilde Maier on 9 March, shortly after his arrival: 'The Kremlin is a conglomeration of wonderful buildings from *A Thousand and One Nights*; from it you have a view of this city of 400,000 inhabitants and 800 churches, some of which have five domes; everything is colourful, bright, gilded, domed – so weird and wonderful that I had to burst out laughing in amazement.'[79]

Rehearsals for Wagner's Moscow concerts were begun immediately after his arrival with 100 musicians selected from the Imperial Orchestra. As far as musical standards were concerned, Moscow was very much a backwater compared to Petersburg and Wagner was slightly disappointed by the lower calibre of the orchestra, who were usually fed an unrelenting diet of Italian opera and ballet music. Wagner's arrival was a great event for the few Wagnerians in Moscow, however, and his rehearsals were attended by Nikolay Rubinstein, the noted writer Vladimir Odoevsky, the 'cellist Karl Albrekht and the critic Nikolay Kashkin, whose colourful memoirs are a source of much interest and amusement. During the first rehearsal, according to Kashkin, Beethoven's 5th Symphony was played straight through without a correction, 'for the orchestra was electrified by the presence of a European celebrity'.[80] Wagner encountered problems with the singers, however. The tenor Mikhail Vladislavlev insisted on singing the *Schmiederlieder* from *Siegfried* in the Italian manner to which he was accustomed, and the German text eventually had to be translated into Russian for him to be able to sing it at all.[81]

Wagner had arrived in Moscow in spring when the snow was beginning to melt and his contraction of influenza due to the inclement weather forced him to postpone his first concert (which had been scheduled for 10 March). The three concerts held at the Bolshoi Theatre finally took place on 13, 15 and 17 March. Rubinstein was embarrassed by the Imperial Theatre's haughty disdain of Wagner after the dazzling reception that they had given Verdi, and he decided to hold a dinner for Wagner to which musicians, rather than high-placed officials and aristocratic opera lovers would be invited. The forty guests included Odoevsky, Prince Nikolay Trubetskoy (a director of the Moscow branch of the RMS), the writer Konstantin Tarnovsky,[82] the Austrian pianist Anton Door, the publisher Pyotr Jurgenson and Nikolay Kashkin. The dinner was a modest affair since the orchestral players received a meagre salary, but it was evidently a very convivial occasion, with numerous toasts in the Russian fashion. Ultimately it also became rather riotous, to judge from Kashkin's account, with Wagner becoming so exuberant that he decided to 'show off his gymnastic prowess by jumping over a card table'. Naturally, all this was helped along by the consumption of excessive quantities of wine, and Wagner became eventually so drunk that he had to be carried off to Kashkin's apartment to be sobered up with soda water.[83] Wagner made relatively few social calls whilst he was in Moscow, but at the urging of Marie Kalergis, he paid a visit to Vladimir Odoevsky on 14 March. Odoevsky did not immediately offer to become his patron, however, so Wagner did not judge the visit to be a success.[84] Odoevsky, however, who first heard music by Wagner in 1857, when he heard a performance of *Tannhäuser* in Berlin, seems to have remained oblivious of Wagner's rather mercenary designs, as his jubilant diary entries and articles testify.[85]

Wagner returned to St Petersburg on 19 March to give three more concerts and to further his cause with the Grand Duchess. He was by now enjoying himself immensely. 'I am the "lion" here', he wrote to Standhartner on 27 March, 'and have to say that I have made an unexpectedly thrilling impression on the Russian public.'[86] Wagner's final concert in Russia took place on 5 April and was held in aid of the families of inmates at the St Petersburg debtors' prison. This charitable occasion was held under the highest auspices and was attended by the cream of society (including, we may presume, Elena Pavlovna herself, whose idea it had been that Wagner should participate). Prince Suvorov, governor-general of Petersburg, presented Wagner with a silver drinking horn on behalf of the beneficiaries, and in a letter to Mathilde Maier the following day, Wagner wrote that the tsarevich had also presented him with an enormous diamond ring.[87]

Wagner had originally come to Russia with the intention of giving two concerts and leaving the country by the end of February. Because of the financial gains to be made from giving more concerts, however, and, more importantly, the prospect of acquiring patronage from the Russian aristocracy, his stay in Russia had been considerably prolonged. As far as he was concerned, the evenings he had spent at court reading his works to Elena Pavlovna represented a good investment, for he was convinced 'something good' would come out of his relations to this 'important lady'.[88] Initially it seemed that Wagner's supposition was correct, for Elena Pavlovna made Wagner a gift of 1,000 roubles (since his last concert was a charity event), intimating that she might renew the amount yearly until his position improved.[89] Wagner's Russian venture had indeed been very lucrative and at the time of his departure (he had now been in Russia for almost two months) he was already nurturing plans to return the following year. He wrote to Minna Wagner on 8 April: 'I will only come again if the Directorate engages me for a concert series with a significant fixed honorarium. That could well happen and then I would always be able to earn enough for the whole year in Petersburg.'[90] Further patronage from Elena Pavlovna might have been forthcoming, but Wagner made his financial appeals too swiftly, and the Duchess (no doubt offended by his lack of grace and unmoved by his gift of a luxury edition of the *Ring*)[91] just as swiftly withdrew her support. Over the course of the next year, Wagner wrote numerous increasingly desperate and sycophantic letters to Editha von Rhaden, in which he complained of feeling 'abandoned', asserted that his Petersburg experiences were his only 'happy moments for many years' and requested her help in arranging 'six big concerts' for him to conduct in Petersburg.[92] Next he proposed that the Imperial Theatres Directorate engage him on a five-year contract to spend several months each year in Petersburg, so that he could make the orchestra 'the best in the world' and raise musical standards.[93] Wagner was still intent on making another trip to Russia the following year, but did nothing to further his cause by asking why the 1,000 roubles promised for 1 January by Elena Pavlovna had failed to materialise: 'I am racking my brains as to whether I omitted to do something and thus incurred the delay. Surely no one doubts my gratitude?'[94] It took a long time for Wagner to realise that nothing would be forthcoming from Elena Pavlovna. On 14 March 1864, he wrote again to Editha von Rhaden: 'I wanted to go to Petersburg a week ago, to stay. I wanted to throw myself at the feet of the Duchess and ask her to take me on in any capacity, give me a quiet room, a servant, some pocket money – a couple of hundred roubles a year. The awful climate no longer frightened me . . .'[95] But in this same letter, he had the temerity to suggest that Elena Pavlovna should pay an annual pension to his wife Minna until her death. For various reasons, Wagner's second visit to Russia never took place. The Philharmonic Society tried to invite Wagner to Petersburg again in 1866, but by this time King Ludwig II had become the composer's patron. Wagner wrote in November of that year to decline the invitation, explaining that Ludwig II's support had provided him with the means to devote himself now wholly to composition (thus rendering fund-raising concert tours unecessary), but adding that he was glad he had left a good impression and that he nurtured fond memories of the excellent orchestra he had conducted.[96]

WAGNER'S CONCERTS IN THE RUSSIAN PRESS

If Wagner's visit had been preceded by polemics, the concerts he conducted in Russia only served to intensify the arguments surrounding his 'futuristic' theories. Feofil Tolstoy was supposedly one of Russia's more eminent critics, but his reviews of two of Wagner's Petersburg concerts show up his decidedly amateur skills as a journalist, not to mention his obscurantist musical views. The tone of these pieces (which do not really discuss the music performed at all) show that Wagner and his

music left this critic in a state of near apoplexy. Before
Wagner's visit, conductors in Russia had always stood facing
the audience, and Tolstoy thought Wagner's 'picturesque position' with both hands raised *facing* the orchestra highly
objectionable. Conducting a well-known piece by heart he
conceded, was 'perhaps alright, but we do not see why it is
necessary to look the artists in the face'.[97] Tolstoy also took
exception to Wagner's 'mysterious telegraphic signals', for to
conduct with such 'unusual devices', in his view, could only
'confuse the orchestra'; the concert conductor in his opinion
should be nothing but a 'living metronome' whose sacred duty
is solely to ensure that the orchestra keeps time.[98] The fact that
Wagner performed his own works along with Beethoven's
struck Tolstoy as the height of presumption, and it is evident
from his description of the apparently dumbfounded audience
at Wagner's second concert that he was really expressing his
own feelings:

And so the members of the audience were lost, at least partly, in the
waves of music intended for the pleasure of their descendants ... It
must be confessed that this submergence produced an unpleasant
sensation for the majority, judging by the fact that more than half the
audience left after Master Pogner's speech without waiting for the
praised overture to *Die Meistersinger* ... Our audience was, as it were,
perplexed to hear this outlandish music, in which previous forms
have been replaced by some sort of ill-defined wavering and comprehensible melodies by audacious and sometimes wild fantasy.
Many were bewildered and really did not know whether to laugh or
cry.[99]

Tolstoy was even more strongly affected by listening to *Tristan
und Isolde*, likening it to the sort of nightmare produced by
taking substantial quantities of hashish: 'Your head spins, your
thoughts become more and more muddled, certain phrases
repeat themselves stubbornly and importunately a multitude
of times, becoming more and more like huge apparitions;
others quickly change like an incomprehensible assortment of
words, like the following: ocean, pineapple, divinity, money,
gloom, light, etc.'[100] The anonymous critic from *Golos* was as
sceptical about Wagner's music as Tolstoy, although he was at

least prepared to acknowledge the huge success of his concerts. The critic's final judgement on the composer, however, was that 'Wagner's source of creativity – whatever his fanatical followers may say – is not inspiration, and not his soul, but his intellect ... Wagner wants to compose by reason. It is obvious he is mixing art with science.'[101]

Written in quite another vein are the three reviews by Mavriky Rappaport in *Syn otechestva* and Serov's in *Yakor'* and *Sankt-Peterburgskie vedomosti*. 'I cannot remember there being such general excitement for a long time', wrote Rappaport after Wagner's first concert: 'Everyone was noticeably enjoying themselves, the huge hall was full and the silence which reigned during the performance was unprecedented ... The wizard who achieved such a transformation with a wave of his baton was R. Wagner. Never has Beethoven's 'Eroica' Symphony ... made such an impression.'[102] The rather breathless tone continued in Rappaport's second article, published two days later, where he asserted that the public's excitement had reached its zenith at Wagner's first concert when he had called for the national anthem to be sung (which certainly does not concur with the Third Department's version of events). Rappaport demonstrated a knowledge of Wagner's ideas superior to that of his fellow critic Tolstoy by including in his third review a brief exposé of Wagner's reformist ideas about opera and a discussion of his reasons for supporting them.[103]

After the feuilletons of Tolstoy and Rappaport, Serov's articles cannot but strike one with their clarity, insight and sheer professionalism. Serov wrote three articles discussing Wagner's Petersburg concerts; two for *Sankt-Peterburgskie vedomosti*,[104] and one for *Yakor'*.[105] In the first, Serov outlined Wagner's career to date and dismissed the composer's many detractors, declaring that Wagner's visit was the greatest musical event in Russia since Berlioz's tour in 1847.[106] Serov's second article was written after Wagner had already given his first two concerts. Unable to restrain his withering contempt for Tolstoy's quaint notion that conductors should be nothing more than metronomes, he proclaimed (with characteristic belligerence) that it would be a profanation even to polemicise with someone who called *Lohengrin* 'ballet music' and *Tristan und Isolde* a 'nightmare'.[107] Before moving on to an appraisal of the concerts themselves, Serov discussed Wagner's work in general terms, taking every opportunity to demonstrate the informed knowledge of Wagner's works he had acquired through his friendship with the composer. Wagner scored his greatest success, according to Serov in his article for *Yakor'*, at his last concert before leaving for Moscow. In the closing paragraphs of this article, Serov's exaltation knew no bounds:

For a musical critic who has been preaching in Russia the importance of Wagner to the general evolution of music, the strong and profound impression made on the Petersburg public by Wagner both as conductor and composer was a most joyous occasion, a real *triumph* ... Music plays a fairly prominent role in our public life, but, as is well known, there is still very little real understanding of music here. One thing however is certain, and the welcome given to Richard Wagner by Petersburg has reinforced that certainty: our public, with its integrity and freshness, brushing aside all prejudice, with its candour, its warm and direct appreciation of everything that is genuinely good, is the greatest and best public in the world ... There was not one empty seat. There was a multitude of people even on the stage, among the musicians of the orchestra, in the wings. The very novelty of Wagner's music, its unusual and unprecedented, unimaginable boldness in orchestration in the excerpts from the opera *Die Walküre* carried the entire audience away to the most extreme limits of its ardent appreciation.[108]

Wagner's Moscow concerts were not given the same coverage as those he had given in the Russian capital, although Vladimir Odoevsky tried to compensate by writing three lengthy articles under different pseudonyms. Odoevsky, one of Russia's finest nineteenth-century prose writers and a man with a profound knowledge of music, was one of the few people in Russia at that time who perceived the true importance of Wagner's visit: 'How can one describe in a newspaper article the deep impression which was produced by this concert! For this concert was *an epoch for us!* Everything was new here: the deeply thoughtful music, the melody, the harmonic links, the orchestration, and the performance with the most delicate nuances ...'[109] As well as providing his readers with an enthusiastic account of Wagner's life and artistic views, Odoevsky also subtly exploited the occasion to put forward some fairly partisan views. Using Wagner's concerts as a weapon with which to batter Italian opera (with Verdi emerging as the chief villain), Odoevsky compared the music in Verdi's 'so-called operas' to an exhibition consisting of pictures of bonnets and crinolines, and expressed amazement that people should be still questioned on their preference for 'Verdi or Wagner, *Rigoletto* or *Tannhäuser*'. For Odoevsky, Wagner's concerts in Moscow were clear signs of a new artistic epoch in which French and German opera would finally eclipse Italian music:

The theatre was absolutely full, the enthusiasm of the audience quite unprecedented, and the orchestra itself, carried away by the surge of excitement and amazement before this brilliant artist, more than once took part in the general applause. All this proves that we are entering a new artistic era and that our musical demands have risen. Is there a hope that instead of the strings of Verdi's polkas we will now be able to listen to real operas by such people as Gluck, Mozart, Méhul, Weber, Beethoven and Wagner?[110]

The intelligence and conviction which marks Odoevsky's writing is notably absent in the two reviews by Nikolay Melgunov, who approached Wagner's music and ideas in an extremely detached manner. In his view, Wagner was obviously a 'product of Germany', and a composer who was first and foremost an 'aesthetic theoretician', since his point of departure was a 'system'.[111] Wagner's theory of the *Gesamtkunstwerk*, moreover, he dismissed as 'simply aesthetic communism' that could allow nothing 'individual'. He was also sceptical that Wagner's 'operatic pantheon' could be truly 'all-embracing', since an opera written by a single person, he argued, could not possibly be superior to one written by two. Wagner's 'Icarus-like' theories, he concluded, were 'obviously pure utopia'.[112]

A different note sounds in the closing stages of Melgunov's second review, however. As with Odoevsky, reviewing Wagner's concerts also presented Melgunov with the opportunity to air his views on a subject of deep concern to him. Whereas Odoevsky put forward a general appeal for Russia's musical horizons to be enlarged, Melgunov's overriding concern was the promotion of native music. It is not a reproach that Wagner happens to be German, he wrote, 'on the contrary, we Russians should relate more freely to foreign theories and developments. Why should Russia fawn on Italians and Germans? If we were free from prejudices against one school or another we should then be able to use their instructive example to develop our own music all the more effectively and all the more swiftly find our own representative and authentic music.'[113] Melgunov recommended that Wagner should return to Russia for the staging of one of his operas, so that the Russian public could judge the composer's great talent properly:

We Russians, as a northern people, are more able than the French (not to mention the Italians) to understand the innovator who has broken all links with routine and boldly thought of re-creating dramatic music on new foundations. Everyone would benefit: both our public and our orchestra and our composers, if they could get taken up by the extremes of the new direction; eventually our social life would benefit, for a production of one of the operas of the radical reformer would inject an active current into our sleepy aesthetic pond and would awaken in us the desire to insist that the mediocre Italian troupe be replaced by a company equally mediocre but at least Russian . . .[114]

This was first of many subsequent occasions when the idea was put forward that Russians were more likely to appreciate the genius of Wagner than other nations. It was also the first of many subsequent occasions that Wagner's name was identified with artistic reform in Russia. The history of Wagner's visit to Russia would not be complete without mentioning the delightful barbs directed at Wagner's 'Zukunftsmusik' in 1863 by the satirists of *Iskra*. N. Stepanov produced the following skit, for example:

Man at ticket office:

MAN: Could I have a ticket to Wagner's concert please?

REPLY: What sort of ticket do you want? One with or without understanding of the music?

MAN: Well, one with understanding of course.

REPLY: Then I'm afraid you will have to wait a bit: tickets only
come on sale in fifty years' time.[115]

Another cartoon appeared showing Wagner conducting to
an audience of babies: 'the public for Wagner's music of the
future',[116] while the following issue showed a large picture of
Wagner with the caption: 'Wagner is galloping into the future
while Wagner's Russian admirer, as courier, gets the horses
ready at the way-stations. The action for Wagner's opera takes
place before the earth's creation, the music is for waking the
dead on the Day of Judgement.'[117] Wagner and his theories
still had a long way to go before they were either accepted or
understood in Russia.

CHAPTER 2

Reception and performance history, 1863–1890

'Oh Moscow! Oh Bayreuth!!!'[1]

THE FIRST RUSSIAN WAGNER PRODUCTIONS

Although it was *Tannhäuser* that Serov and Zvantsov had so vigorously campaigned to bring to the notice of the Imperial Theatres Directorate, in the end *Lohengrin* was the first opera by Wagner to be staged in Russia. Konstantin Lyadov, chief conductor at the Mariinsky Theatre, chanced to hear the work in Berlin in 1865,[2] and decided that it ought to be performed in St Petersburg. The theatre's prospective repertoire had first to be sanctioned by the tsar and his government, however, who in June 1866 decided to reject the *Lohengrin* proposal under the pretext of insufficient resources and doubts about its possible success.[3] Political apprehension may have been the real reason for the refusal, for although Wagner could now boast Ludwig II as his patron, he may have still been seen as a dangerous figure in the eyes of the Russian government. However unlikely it may seem, it was perhaps felt that approving *Lohengrin* for performance would be tantamount to condoning Wagner's past as a revolutionary. The government's decision came as a shock to the cast, who had already begun rehearsals, however, and the director of the production even wrote to appeal, claiming that the Russian public was now 'sufficiently prepared to listen to serious music' and that the 'artists themselves' wanted to perform the work.[4] Permission to stage *Lohengrin* was finally given two years later, and the opera's first Russian performance took place on 4 October 1868, eighteen years

after its German première and several years after its performance in other major European cities.[5] The disputes over the
nature and legitimacy of Wagner's artistic reforms had continued unabated in St Petersburg since his visit, and the
production of *Lohengrin* inevitably aroused much interest in the
capital. The critic for *Sovremennaya letopis'* described the excitement at the first night:

In the intervals there was animated conversation throughout the
theatre: in the foyer, in the bar, in the auditorium, in the corridors.
The arguments about the relative merits of Italian and Wagnerian
opera reached such a pitch that in the upper circle it almost went as
far as 'divine judgement' for two youths, that is to say a duel, as if to
correspond to the 'divine judgement' which ends the first act in the
opera itself . . .[6]

Opinions about Wagner were already sharply divided, and the
production of *Lohengrin* served only to intensify the animosity
felt on both sides of the dispute. Musorgsky, Cui, Rimsky-
Korsakov, Balakirev and Dargomyzhsky (who, like their
mentor Stasov, perceived Wagner and his music as a serious
threat to the integrity of Russian music), treated *Lohengrin* with
'complete contempt' when they attended the première, 'while
from Dargomyzhsky there came an endless stream of ridicule,
mockery and venomous criticism'.[7] Balakirev, meanwhile,
informed Nikolay Rubinstein that he had been to see *Lohengrin*
'for the first and last time'.[8] It was César Cui who poured most
scorn on the production, however. Although he professed a
certain admiration for Wagner's theories, Cui abhorred
Wagner's music, and the composer became a frequent victim of
his malicious jibes in *Sankt-Peterburgskie vedomosti*, to which he
had been contributing regularly since 1864. In one of his very
first reviews, Cui had formed the following opinion of the
Lohengrin prelude: 'I cannot understand why the public should
like this prelude. There are no musical ideas in it, the endless
unhealthy screeching of the violins is unbearable and is made
all the more unpleasant by the fact that we are just hearing one
sound the whole time, devoid of any content or musical idea,
and it is all so incredibly long . . .'[9] Seeing the opera on stage
did not impel Cui to modify his views. While Wagner was a

composer deeply devoted to opera, in his opinion, who had studied and thought carefully about all its aspects, he was at the same time 'a completely untalented artist, with no creative ability'. Cui's considered opinion was that he had never heard a 'more colourless and boring opera'.[10] Antagonism between Serov and the Balakirev circle was now at fever pitch and Serov seized every opportunity to pour withering scorn on his foes. His first review of *Lohengrin* took the form of an open letter to Wagner, in which he apologised for the 'obscure pen-pusher' (Cui), who had declared himself Wagner's 'bitterest enemy, recognising only Schumann, Berlioz, Glinka and . . . a handful of unknown Russian musicians'.[11] He also apologised for the Russian production's excessive realism, finding it incompatible with the opera's mythical and mystical content. Vladimir Stasov was incensed:

Just listen to this: our singers are supposed to get carried away by German sentimental hysterics . . . and reject the striving for truth and realism which constitutes the main task of our time! . . . Let him not think that Wagner's music is capable of putting down roots in our country . . . What are Wagner's dreams and utopias to us . . .? What do we need his models of tastelessness, talentlessness and crudeness for, other than to see more clearly what is no good for us and what we should certainly not follow . . .[12]

Serov remained undeterred, however. In his second review of *Lohengrin* (this time for *Novoe vremya*), he defiantly maintained that the Petersburg production was a unanimous success due to the 'curiosity and great respect' shown by the Russian audience: 'Whilst "in the capital of the civilised world" [Paris] people are still set against Wagner, here [in Russia] he immediately scored a complete victory and met no opposition at all. This is a remarkable event in the chronicles of Slavonic art and has great significance for the fate of musical drama in Russia.'[13] Serov, as we have already seen, was often prone to hyperbole, but he was not the only critic to write favourably about *Lohengrin*. Mavriky Rappaport, cautiously optimistic that Wagner's music would signal the end of the hegemony of Italian opera in Russia, also responded with enthusiasm:

The public has followed the opera with the utmost attention and while still under the influence of *La Traviata* and all kinds of Leonoras, is instinctively conscious of the wide gulf which separates Wagner from composers of other operas and greatly respects his work. This is a great step forward. But the time will come when the majority will become convinced that the tender caressing of the ears with empty sounds is not opera . . .[14]

The correspondent for the Moscow-based *Sovremennaya letopis'* also proclaimed the production to be a success: 'The production of the opera has been extremely painstaking. The musical side has been excellently rehearsed . . . everything has been handled superbly and with a . . . verisimilitude moreover, so rare in our productions of *grands opéras*.'[15] The critic and music professor Aleksandr Famintsyn, who joined ranks with Serov and Zvantsov as another early supporter of Wagner in Russia, wrote the most voluminously about *Lohengrin*, but the three laudatory (and derivative) articles he wrote for *Golos* did not attempt to evaluate the production in any way.[16] Despite the paeans of praise from one section of the press, it cannot truly be said that the first Russian production of *Lohengrin* was an unqualified success. The critic Mikhail Stanislavsky was probably correct in identifying a lack of unity as its chief shortcoming for, whatever effect the production was attempting to achieve, he believed, was destroyed by the differing styles of performance amongst the cast, some of whom sang in the time-honoured Italian manner to which they were accustomed, and others in the more realistic 'Russian style'.[17] It seemed, then, that Wagner posed no immediate threat to the various factions in the Russian music world: 'The Italomanes stopped worrying about the future of the various *Ernani*s, *Sonnambuli*, *Lucia*s, *La Favorita*s, *Lucrezia*s and other operas from the transalpine repertoire. Our innovator-populists also secretly rejoiced. Wagner had proved to be too *aristocratic*. His music did not throb with the life of the common people. The subject alone with its kings, dukes and counts and "slavishly" devoted warriors had sickened the radical circles of contemporary Russian society.'[18]

In 1873, *Lohengrin* was re-rehearsed and performed with a much greater success, which was undoubtedly largely due to the talents of Eduard Napravnik, who replaced Lyadov in 1869. Yet when the Russian Opera decided to risk staging *Tannhäuser*, Napravnik was initially doubtful of it being either adequately performed or well received.[19] The first Russian performance of *Tannhäuser*, however, which took place on 13 December 1874 (twenty-nine years after its Dresden première),[20] unexpectedly scored a 'spectacular success'.[21] 'The set was highly elegant; it was an utter triumph',[22] recollected the critic Aleksandr Volf subsequently. Without Serov to whip up the indignation of the Balakirev circle (he had died in 1871), there was far less antagonism and controversy surrounding the production of *Tannhäuser* than there had been six years earlier when *Lohengrin* was performed; responses in the press were generally muted.[23] The production of *Tannhäuser* (which was Napravnik's first major success) did much to raise the prestige of the Russian Opera. Even the nobility – who otherwise only recognised Italian opera – now apparently began to 'drop by' the Mariinsky theatre, which was still not quite seen as a respectable place of entertainment: '"We came to hear the overture to *Tannhäuser*", was the excuse given by representatives of Petersburg "high life" if unexpected meetings occurred in the corridors of the theatre.'[24]

BAYREUTH AND ITS RUSSIAN CRITICS

The first Bayreuth *Festspiele* began to attract attention in the Russian press in May 1876, and over ninety-six articles about the festival and a serialised biography of Wagner were to be published in Russian newspapers and journals before the year was out.[25] Two Russian composers, Tchaikovsky and Cui, were sent as correspondents to cover the first performances of the *Ring*, accompanied by the critics Herman Laroche, Aleksandr Famintsyn, and Mikhail Ivanov. Other Russian visitors included Konstantin Zvantsov, Nikolay Rubinstein, Karl Albrekht, Serov's widow and son Valentin, the future painter.[26] Tchaikovsky's thoughts on Wagner had begun to crystallise after 1868, when he became a music critic for *Russkie vedomosti*. Although Laroche maintains that Tchaikovsky had hurled 'direct abuse' at the *Lohengrin* prelude in 1864,[27] the composer's attitude had changed by the time his first public pronouncement on Wagner appeared in 1871. Reviewing a Moscow RMS concert, he wrote that the 'superb' prelude to *Lohengrin* was perhaps Wagner's 'most successful and inspired composition',[28] a view which remained largely unchanged over the course of his lifetime. Like the Balakirev circle, Tchaikovsky was extremely critical of Wagner, but also like his Russian contemporaries, he was never indifferent to either his music or his theories, as can be deduced from the numerous reviews in which he felt compelled to present his views about the composer and his theories. By the time he arrived in Bayreuth, Tchaikovsky had formed the conviction that the composer was 'principally a symphonist' whose 'false aesthetic theories' had led him astray into the world of opera.[29] This was also a opinion that never underwent any substantial revision.

Tchaikovsky clearly found his visit to Bayreuth an overwhelming experience. The music to *Das Rheingold* he found 'an impossible chaos through which extremely beautiful and extraordinary details shimmer', but his reaction to *Götterdämmerung* was that he had never heard anything 'so boring or protracted'.[30] These were opinions he expressed privately, however. In the articles Tchaikovsky produced for *Russkie vedomosti*, he was far more equivocal. Only in the last of his five articles on the Bayreuth Festival did Tchaikovsky actually concern himself with the performances of the *Ring*, and even then, he was reluctant to pass judgement: 'Even if the *Ring* does seem boring at times, even if much of it is confusing and incomprehensible at first, even if Wagner's harmony suffers from over-complexity and over-subtlety, even if Wagner's theories are false, even if most of them are pointless quixotry ... the *Ring* still constitutes one of the most significant events in the history of art ...'[31] This reluctance was due in part to his fear of Karl Klindworth, his 'faithful but despotic' friend, before whom he trembled, according to Laroche, 'like an aspen leaf'.[32] Klindworth, the gifted German pianist who became

Tchaikovsky's colleague at the Moscow Conservatoire in 1868, was a close associate of Wagner and a most ardent propagandist of his music. Wagner entrusted him alone with the completion of the piano arrangements of the *Ring*.

Despite Tchaikovsky's generally negative feelings about Wagner, he continued to take an active interest in the composer after his visit to Bayreuth, and seized every opportunity to attend performances of his works during his frequent trips abroad. He also continued to expound at length upon their shortcomings to his correspondents.[33] Yet he was also the first to admit that he had been influenced by Wagner's music,[34] and from 1884 (when he began to study *Parsifal*) a growing respect for the composer can be clearly discerned in his pronouncements,[35] suggesting that his aversion to Wagner may well have been unduly exaggerated by certain critics.[36] If one attempts to set Tchaikovsky's attitude to Wagner in context, one has to conclude that, with the exception of Serov and Laroche, it was remarkably more sophisticated than that of his contemporaries. Tchaikovsky must be commended for the comparative consistency of his views and the unfailing honesty with which he confronted his frequent inability to understand or appreciate Wagner's masterpieces. One cannot but be impressed by the maturity and comparative objectivity of his writing, moreover, when one compares his music reviews with those of Cui. The reviews Cui sent back from Bayreuth, in which he did not neglect to stress that the Russian method of opera writing was superior in every way to Wagner's, were as usual not distinguished by any particular originality, depth of insight or journalistic flair, although it must be said that they were not quite as cantankerous as many of his previous attacks on Wagner.[37] Laroche, who, like most serious critics, regarded Cui's writing with a mixture of amusement and contempt, was surprised to discover that Cui had even attended a reception at Wahnfried and found this apparent volte-face highly hypocritical.[38] Laroche wrote four articles about the Bayreuth Festival for the Russian press.[39] For all their clarity, they are not as incisive or as detailed in their criticisms as his previous reviews of Wagner's early works, and in later years he came to realise

the folly of travelling to Bayreuth in 1876 with so little preparation.[40] Laroche had written his first review of Wagner's music
for *Moskovskie vedomosti* in 1869. When he maintained in that
review that the Russian public was much more interested in
Wagner's music than in his theories,[41] he was really talking
about his own feelings, for he himself had no sympathy with
any of Wagner's reformist ideas (and thus held almost dia-
metrically opposed views to Cui, who did have a certain
respect for Wagner's theories). Due to his staunch defence of
classical ideals in music, and his sharply critical attitude to
Wagner's mature works, Laroche was usually firmly placed in
the 'anti-Wagner' camp by Soviet musicologists. Neither his
description of *Lohengrin* as a 'revelation' in 1878 (like Tchaikovsky, he held *Lohengrin* to be Wagner's greatest work),[42] nor
his membership of the Richard-Wagner-Verein's Moscow
branch, seem to tally with this conclusion, however. The
Moscow branch of the Richard-Wagner-Verein was set up in
1878 by Karl Klindworth.[43] Besides Laroche, the members
listed by *Bayreuther Blätter* for 1886 included the musicians Karl
Albrekht, the young Anton Arensky (future teacher of Skryabin and Rakhmaninov), Pavel Pabst and the pianist and
conductor Vassily Safonov. Wagner evidently enjoyed some
popularity amongst female music lovers in Moscow, since
twenty-three out of the fifty-nine members listed are women.[44]
In January 1886, a certain Vladimir Iznoskov claimed in the
French Symbolist journal *La Revue Wagnérienne* that a Wagner
association existed in St Petersburg which gave popular concerts.[45] If this was an official branch of the Wagner-Verein,
however, no details of its membership were ever filed to *Bayreuther Blätter*, which incorporated regular information about
the various branches of the Verein in the early years of its
publication.

Despite the success of *Tannhäuser* in 1874 and the wide
publicity attracted by the Bayreuth Festival in 1876, resistance
to Wagner in Russia was still proving hard to break down. On
22 October 1879, *Rienzi* was performed in Russia for the first
time at the Mariinsky Theatre, thirty-seven years after its
German première. But despite the lavish amounts invested in

the production, the result was a fiasco and the opera was removed from the repertoire in 1880 after only six performances.[46] Performances of Wagner were sparse in St Petersburg, but music lovers in Moscow had to wait until 1889 for a Wagner opera to be staged in Russian. Ironically enough, Wagner was first performed in Moscow in Italian by the resident Italian opera company, and the success of its production of *Tannhäuser* in 1877 encouraged its sister company in St Petersburg to 'succumb to the spirit of the times',[47] by performing *Tannhäuser* during the 1878–9 season, and *Lohengrin* in October 1880.[48] An Italian production of *Lohengrin* followed at the Bolshoi Theatre in 1881, and in 1887, the work was even performed by Savva Mamontov's private opera company in Moscow, conducted by Enrico Bevignani.[49] Russian productions of *Lohengrin* and *Tannhäuser* only took place at the Bolshoi Theatre in 1889 and 1898 respectively. These operas now began to enjoy a certain degree of popularity, and were no longer thought too avant-garde and difficult to perform. In no way could it be said, however, that Wagner had really conquered the public imagination. Performances of these two operas continued to be infrequent, because the Director of the Imperial Theatres, Ivan Vsevelozhsky (who held the post from 1881 until 1899) loathed Wagner.[50] The vigorous promotion of Russian music, moreover, which began after 1881 (when Alexander III became tsar and abolished the Italian Opera),[51] also ensured that Wagner's works were never given a prominent place in the repertoire. Wagner was not only unpopular because the Russian Opera felt it should stage only works by fellow countrymen. As the critic Mikhail Stanislavsky commented, Wagner was also discriminated against because of 'the fierce Germanophobia gripping us during the eighties and nineties'.[52] Alexander III may have had a 'passionate love of music', but his 'aversion to Bismarck and to the pan-Germanic policies of his late father' were also apparently well known.[53] According to Karl Klindworth, these 'famous anti-German feelings', to which he attributed a cool reception of an excellent performance of Wagner's 'Kaisermarsch' in 1871, had been present even in the previous decade.[54] Yet Wagner was not completely without support in Russia. In 1882, a critic wrote in exasperation about the absence of Wagner's works in the repertoire:

> We put forward the hope, that at some point, if not in the near future, the Egyptian pyramids of the Petersburg Russian Opera, covered at the moment in the mould and moss of indifference to musical progress, will clean themselves up and cease to present themselves as immobile objects for historical research by astounded contemporaries – then, perhaps, the time will come for the Russian public to be acquainted with the works of Wagner . . .[55]

The time was to come seven years later, when a company from Germany toured Russia to perform the *Ring*. Only seventeen years later, however, did the Russian Opera feel sufficiently emboldened to tackle the production of one of Wagner's music dramas. The second Bayreuth Festival, which was held in 1882, again attracted Russian visitors, with Famintsyn, Karl Albrekht and Zvantsov returning for the second time. Other Russians included the critics Nikolay Kashkin and Vsevolod Cheshikhin, Count Fitingof-Shel, the artist Pavel Zhukovsky and Josef Rubinstein, a gifted pianist from Kharkov.[56] Both Rubinstein and Zhukovsky (the half-German son of the famous poet) were intimates of Wagner's circle during the last years of his life. Zhukovsky, who completed the initial designs for the first production of *Parsifal*, had introduced himself to Wagner in 1880 and had remained on close terms with the composer and his family thereafter.[57] Rubinstein's relationship with Wagner was altogether more problematic, however. He had met Wagner in 1872, having been introduced to his works by Serov (whom he had known in Petersburg, when he worked as *Kammerpianist* for the Grand Duchess Elena Pavlovna between 1869 and 1871). Rubinstein was ready to forego his potentially brilliant career as a concert pianist in order to devote himself to the *Meister* and was accepted as a close friend and colleague. Due to his serious psychiatric problems, however, and also because of Wagner's notorious anti-Semitism, this was a friendship fraught with difficulties, although Rubinstein was filled with such despair and loneliness after Wagner's death that he eventually took his own life.[58] Shortly before the tragic event in

1884, he attended his last performances at Bayreuth, where he met the composer Aleksandr Glazunov, who recalled how utterly transformed Rubinstein became when he spoke about Wagner.[59]

THE FIRST PERFORMANCES OF THE *RING* IN RUSSIA

In February 1889, Russia at last gained its first chance to see some of Wagner's music dramas performed when Angelo Neumann, director of the German opera in Prague, brought his touring opera company to Russia. This was the last major tour for the 'Richard Wagner-Theater', after visits to many other major European cities,[60] and between 28 February and 22 March, they performed four cycles of the *Ring* (conducted by Karl Muck), as well as two concerts of Wagner's works.[61] Since none of the constituent parts of the *Ring* had yet been performed in Russia, this was a great event, and according to the daily paper *Teatr i zhizn'* (which followed events closely and included daily synopses), no less than the 'whole of Petersburg' gathered to attend the first performance of *Das Rheingold*. Despite Zvantsov's misgivings about the enterprise,[62] the four cycles sold out completely and Neumann judged the Russian tour to be a great success. Not only did the Russian orchestra compare favourably with that in Bayreuth in his view, but he also considered that the male chorus in *Götterdämmerung* was the best he had ever heard.[63] Mikhail Stanislavsky confirmed that the orchestra indeed acquitted themselves extremely well and recalled that the first cycle was performed with 'outstanding success'.[64] In his opinion, this was largely due to the presence of the German prima donna Therese Malten, for he found almost all the other singers in the cast mediocre. Malten had only been booked for the first cycle, but Neumann was forced to persuade her to stay, after a vociferous display of indignation from the audience at the beginning of the second cycle necessitated police intervention.[65]

These performances of the *Ring* made a great impression on Aleksandr Benois and Nikolay Strakhov, to name but two of the writers and artists who attended them, whilst Rimsky-

Korsakov and Glazunov went as far as attending every single rehearsal.[66] From 1889 onwards, Rimsky-Korsakov's attitude to Wagner changed radically in favour of his works.[67] Interestingly, Vladimir Stasov's views on Wagner also underwent some revision. Although Stasov remained firmly convinced of Dargomyzhsky's superiority as a reformer of opera, he confessed a great admiration for *Die Meistersinger* (which was both realistic in its treatment and nationalistic in its subject material, the two prime criteria in art, in his view) and came to respect much of Wagner's symphonic writing.[68] Borodin, who had earlier criticised Wagner perhaps out of a desire to maintain solidarity with his colleagues, also seems to have nurtured a growing respect for Wagner towards the end of his life; in 1881 he travelled specially to Leipzig to hear the *Ring*.[69] Musorgsky, who died in 1881, found Wagner an alien figure in all respects, but nevertheless recognised the composer's strength as an artist, and respected him for his determination to grapple with new forms (which was, after all, the task he had set himself).[70] Cui and Balakirev, however, maintained their position of unwavering hostility (born of a mixture of fear and insecurity) for the rest of their lives.[71]

Many members of the Russian court attended performances of the *Ring* in 1889, including Alexander III himself, and the tsarina, who rarely visited the theatre during Lent.[72] According to Cosima Wagner's friend Countess Marie Wolkenstein, wife of the Austrian ambassador to St Petersburg, the audience had grown 'warmer with each performance until *Götterdämmerung* was greeted with fiery enthusiasm'.[73] The *Ring* was such a success, in fact, that not only was a request made by the Imperial Theatres Directorate for another cycle to be performed (which Neumann turned down), but the tsar himself requested that the troupe perform the *Ring* in Moscow.[74] Despite the dismissal of artistic life in Moscow by a Petersburg official from the Imperial Theatres, the tetralogy was also received well in Moscow, even if box office returns were not quite as high as they had been in St Petersburg. The Imperial Theatres were keen for Neumann and his troupe to return the following year, but all efforts to arrange a second tour, both in

1890 and in 1891, had to be abandoned.[75] The signing of the Franco-Russian Alliance was partly responsible for rendering conditions 'less favourable' to Wagner in the 1890s, according to Mikhail Stanislavsky: 'It was impossible even to mention German, German people and German art ... Our young people were gripped by Franco-Russian enthusiasm and tried to show their patriotic feelings by an assault on the Germans sitting peacefully with a mug of beer in the Zoological Gardens. In those conditions it would have been utter quixotry even to dream of repeating the experience of 1889 and give another series of Wagner performances.'[76] Yet Wagner was now steadily gaining supporters in Russia. As Stanislavsky points out, the thousands of Russians who visited Paris each year could not have failed to have noticed Wagner's name on theatre posters there and wondered at the reason for Wagner's 'strict ostracism' in their own country.[77] Russian Wagnerians had either to content themselves with sporadic performances of *Lohengrin* and *Tannhäuser*, which usually took place when there were visiting soloists from abroad (such as Dame Nellie Melba and the de Reszke brothers who came to St Petersburg in 1890),[78] or go abroad themselves. In 1889, *Russkoe bogatstvo* published an account of a visit to Bayreuth by a certain 'S. K-verina', who had opted for the latter course, and attended performances of *Parsifal* with her sister, also a 'passionate' Wagnerian.[79] As a resident of southern Russia, the author had evidently had very little opportunity to hear any music by Wagner: 'Wagner is not popular here in the south, in fact no one has even heard of him. Anyone who has read something about him in reviews or has heard the *Tannhäuser* overture ... considers it his duty to remark with aplomb: "Oh, Wagner is just a lot of noise ... and screeching." '[80] After the Bolshoi Theatre's valiant but dismal attempt to stage *Siegfried* in 1894,[81] no doubt many more such voices were heard. After the première on 27 January 1894 (for which there had apparently been forty-six rehearsals), there were only two further performances that year. The production was revived for two performances in 1896 (one of which was attended by Lev Tolstoy), after which it was deleted from the repertoire. The reaction of the audience after a concert conducted by Gustav Mahler in March 1897 which included the 'Siegfried Idyll' and the overture to *Rienzi* indicates that, thirty-four years on from Wagner's visit, the Russian public were really no nearer understanding or appreciating his music. 'The Russian public appears to have been as uneducated as it was impolite', writes Mahler's biographer Henry-Louis de la Grange, 'its main interest was in the soloists.'[82]

WAGNER AND NINETEENTH-CENTURY RUSSIAN LITERATURE

Wagner was not a figure of supreme importance to writers in nineteenth-century Russia as he was to the Symbolists in the early years of the twentieth century; indeed few nineteenth-century Russian writers expressed any enthusiasm for either his music or his theories. Yet serious comparisons have on occasion been made between Wagner's works and the writings of the three great Russian novelists of the late nineteenth century (Turgenev, Dostoevsky and Tolstoy), which demand that the links between Wagner and nineteenth-century Russian writers should not be entirely overlooked.

As noted earlier, Herzen, Vyazemsky and Odoevsky were amongst the first Russian writers to react positively to Wagner's music, but the poet and critic Apollon Grigoriev was probably the first Russian writer to call himself openly a 'Wagnerite'. In an article on Russian theatre published in the opening issue of *Epokha*, the journal of the Russian *pochvenniki*,[83] founded by Dostoevsky's brother Mikhail in 1864, he declared that as a democrat, it followed that he was 'a Wagnerite, for the principle which determines that opera is drama – a principle which currently Wagner represents in its highest and purest form – is a thoroughly democratic one that gives pleasure to the masses rather than dilettantes'.[84] That Grigoriev became interested in Wagner was undoubtedly due to the influence of Serov, with whom he became acquainted in 1854.[85] There were certain distinct similarities between Wagner's artistic views and the populist aims of the *pochvenniki*, however, as Richard Taruskin has pointed out: Grigoriev's 'principles of "organic criticism", emphasizing such things as transcendence, inclusiveness, richness of allusion, ties to the soil and to ancient heritages, placed him – and the *pochvenniki* generally – among the few in Russia hospitable to Wagner and "Wagnerianism" '.[86] Grigoriev helped to further the Wagnerian cause in Russia by publishing Serov's articles on the composer, first in *Teatral'nyi i muzykal'nyi vestnik*, which he edited in 1860, and subsequently in *Yakor'*, which was set up as an interim measure when *Vremya*, the first organ of the *pochvenniki*, was banned by the censor. Although Grigoriev maintained that 'Wagnerism' was the inevitable outcome of musical evolution and was keen to praise Wagner as a creator of tragic drama 'par excellence', he was anxious to emphasise that he was no adherent of the policies of 'extreme' Wagnerism, which he characterised as the 'strange ideal of merging all forms of dramatic art into one' to create opera, as if to deny prose drama an independent existence of its own.[87] After Grigoriev, the poet, playwright and novelist A. K. Tolstoy, who spent much time in Germany, was probably the next Russian writer to take a passionate interest in Wagner.[88] The same cannot be said of Nikolay Chernyshevsky, however, who, like many of his contemporaries, passed judgement on Wagner without ever hearing a note of his music. In a letter of 1881, he wrote with great arrogance (and no less ignorance): 'As far as Wagner and his "music of the future" is concerned, I maintain (and I do not think I am wrong) that he is a half talent (with excessive vanity) and a half idiot, while his music is a lengthily stewed *kasha* composed of good bits by other people (Beethoven, for example) and his own stupid ideas. This is to judge from what I have read about Wagner. I have not heard any of his music.'[89]

Two other founder members of Russian *pochvennichestvo*, Fyodor Dostoevsky and Nikolay Strakhov, were divided in their opinions about Wagner. In 1873, Dostoevsky had claimed (perhaps under the influence of Serov, with whom he had also been on close terms) that Wagner's music, which was 'full of noble aims', showed that German art was 'still alive and still inspired by the highest aspirations'.[90] Six years later, however, he was of the opinion that Wagner's music was 'the most utterly boring German rubbish'.[91] He might understandably therefore have been shocked if he had known that in 1913, the critic Arkady Gornfeld would write a substantial article comparing him to Wagner.[92] As Gornfeld points out, Wagner was Dostoevsky's senior by eight years and outlived him by two, but their creative careers very largely coincided (*Rienzi*, Wagner's first success, was premiered in 1842, while Dostoevsky's *Poor Folk* was published in 1846; *The Brothers Karamazov* was finished in 1880, *Parsifal* in 1882). The external similarities do not stop there, for apart from the fact that Wagner and Dostoevsky combined publicistic and creative careers, both writer and musician also became embroiled in left-wing politics early on in their lives, with dire consequences. Dostoevsky was arrested and exiled in 1849 for his involvement with the Petrashevsky circle, while Wagner fled Germany that same year after the Dresden Uprising to avoid arrest. The shock of these events caused a lengthy hiatus in the creative work of both artists, who also both eventually eschewed political radicalism in favour of decidedly reactionary views, although Gornfeld perhaps oversteps the mark as far as Wagner is concerned, when he maintains that both preached the ideas of 'traditional religiosity and official nationalism' during their last years,[93] for Wagner, unlike Dostoevsky, was never a practising Christian. As well as these external similarities, there are also a number of interesting internal similarities between the works of Dostoevsky and Wagner which should not be totally ignored.[94]

Despite the apparent lack of common ground between Wagner's mythological world of gods and medieval knights and the seemingly concrete nineteenth-century world of Dostoevsky's characters, both are linked by the fact that their creators (both of whom interestingly enough have been named as precursors of Freud) are far more interested in the psychology of their characters, and in the ideas they represent, than in their surroundings. It could therefore be successfully argued that the inner world of Dostoevsky's and Wagner's characters (be the emphasis on irrational or on unconscious behaviour) is deliberately far more convincing than the external world that these characters inhabit, more convincing even than their existence itself. Not for nothing did Dostoevsky choose to situate *Crime and Punishment* in St Petersburg, that most phantasmagoric of cities, for 'it had a basic unreality which made it seem likely to evaporate altogether as the mists rose'.[95] A similar analogy occurred to Theodor Adorno when analysing the 'detachment from time' of Wagner's characters. The only reason they can function as 'universal symbols', he writes, 'is that they dissolve in the phantasmagoria like mist'.[96] The character of Sonya Marmeladova in *Crime and Punishment* could be described as just such a character or symbol. While it seems at first that she is a living being, when one looks deeper one realises she is in fact an 'apparition', a symbolic, even mythical creature.[97] Despite their very different artistic concerns, Dostoevsky and Wagner are also fundamentally linked by the idea of redemption which runs through their work, and also by the theme of compassion, which in Wagner surfaces most strongly in *Parsifal*. The interesting links between the eponymous hero of that work (*Durch Mitleid wissend/Der reine Tor*)[98] and Alyosha Karamazov or Prince Myshkin (often described as a 'Holy Fool')[99] have, interestingly, been alluded to by Thomas Mann: 'When it says, in the preliminary draft [of *Parsifal*] that Klingsor is the daemon of secret sin, the wild ragings of impotence in the face of sin, we feel ourselves transported into a world of Christian insight into remote and hellish psychological states – the world of Dostoevsky.'[100]

Strangely enough, Dostoevsky's fellow *pochvennik* Nikolay Strakhov was one of Wagner's most fervent supporters in Russia. Strakhov was also a close friend of Lev Tolstoy, who in the fifth chapter of the seventh part of *Anna Karenina*, completed in 1877, describes an argument Levin has with his friend Pestsov about the 'merits and shortcomings' of Wagnerian art.[101] No doubt this conversation was a mirror of the arguments Tolstoy had with Strakhov, for the composer was a particular *bête noire* of his. Strakhov visited Bayreuth in 1884, where he heard three performances of *Parsifal*,[102] and he followed the Russian performances of the *Ring* avidly in 1889.

Afterwards he attempted to explain the work to Tolstoy, who commented baldly in his diary: 'It is terrible to see the level of utter madness to which people have descended. I must write about art.'[103] In the summer of 1895 Tolstoy was to be found at Yasnaya Polyana studying the text of the *Ring* in preparation for this projected 'article on art',[104] and one evening was entertained to excerpts from the work played on the piano by the composer Sergey Taneev. Afterwards, according to Taneev, Tolstoy 'attacked Wagner's subjects, saying that he, a nineteenth-century Christian, did not want to know what Scandinavian gods got up to and was amazed that Nikolay Nikolaevich [Strakhov] actually liked these childish fairy-tales'.[105] On 18 April 1896, Taneev shared a box with the Tolstoys at the fourth performance of *Siegfried* at the Bolshoi Theatre. In a letter to his brother the following day, Tolstoy was unable to speak calmly about it. 'It is a stupid puppet show not even good enough for children', he wrote, 'with pretension and pretence, complete falsity and absolutely no music.'[106] Taneev found Tolstoy's wholesale dismissal of Wagner so unreasonable that he even found himself defending a composer with whom he himself had very little sympathy. Tolstoy viewed Wagner's works as worthless, noted Taneev in his diary, because they were not immediately comprehensible and accessible to everyone; any desire to make art complex, as far as he was concerned, concealed decadence and a lack of content.[107] In January 1897, Tolstoy finally began work on *What is Art?* and in its thirteenth chapter, he gave vent to these feelings,[108] making no allowance for the fact that the primitive performance of *Siegfried* he had seen did no justice to the work and bore almost no resemblance to more representative German productions.[109]

It is ironic, then, that Tolstoy himself was actually compared to Wagner even during his lifetime. The interest in Schopenhauer that both shared is well known, and in 1893 Strakhov discussed a recently published study of the philosopher in a letter to Tolstoy, in which that 'strange fact' was remarked upon.[110] In 1901, the music critic Aleksandr Khavsky also noted some similarities between Wagner and Tolstoy. Khavsky believed Tolstoy had erred about Wagner in *What is Art?*, for in his opinion their artistic views led ultimately to the same conclusions: 'Both proceed from a firm belief in the high purpose of art for the common good, both see this as impossible in the conditions of our cultural life at present, both reject contemporary art as the child of this culture and both are drawn towards the people in a democratic rejection of our capitalist class-structure.'[111] Laroche and Turgenev also found affinities between Tolstoy and Wagner,[112] but it was Thomas Mann who most clearly defined what those affinities were. It was not just that Tolstoy and Wagner both employed the leitmotif as a structural device in their works (Tolstoy most notably in *Anna Karenina*); they also exemplified, Mann believed, the nineteenth-century tendency towards creation on a large scale: 'Tolstoy too has the same vast naturalistic range, the same democratic immensity ... He has often been criticized for ... his endless repetitions and underlinings ... while of Wagner Nietzsche writes that at all events he is the most *impolite* of geniuses ... repeating a thing so many times until it drives you mad ...'[113] The *Ring* and *War and Peace* may indeed be considered to be the most ambitious nineteenth-century creations in their respective fields. Mann found an even greater affinity in 'the social-ethical ambience' shared by both artists: 'It signifies little that Wagner saw art as a kind of sacred mystery ... while Tolstoy dismissed it towards the end of his life as a frivolous luxury. For in so far as it *was* a luxury Wagner dismissed it too. He thought to apply its cleansing and sanctifying powers to the cleansing and sanctifying of a corrupt society ... he was closely akin to the Russian novelist in his social ethos.'[114]

While Dostoevsky and Tolstoy rejected Wagner outright, Turgenev's position was more complicated. Due to his involvement with Pauline Garcia-Viardot, who had known Wagner since 1860, he could hardly avoid coming into contact with Wagner's music. Indeed, as he spent most of his time abroad after 1862 (a Wagner concert in Petersburg in 1859 appears to be the only occasion on which he heard music by Wagner performed in Russia),[115] Turgenev was one of the first Russians to hear some of Wagner's works performed on stage. He was present at the Paris première of *Tannhäuser* in 1861, and in 1869 attended the first performance of *Die Meistersinger* in Karlsruhe and the dress rehearsal for *Das Rheingold* in Munich.[116] In 1863, Turgenev accompanied Garcia-Viardot to a concert of excerpts from *Die Walküre* in Karlsruhe, conducted by Wagner, whom he met shortly afterwards.[117] Like Dostoevsky, Turgenev was almost Wagner's exact contemporary; Turgenev was born five years later than Wagner, but both died in 1883. Irene Masing-Delic has maintained that Turgenev 'intensely disliked' Wagner's music,[118] but it is perhaps more accurate to define his position as one of extreme ambivalence. Marie Kalergis reported after the concert in 1863, for example, that Turgenev 'was mad about "The Ride of the Valkyries", but revolted by "Wotan's Farewell"'.[119] After hearing *Das Rheingold* in 1869, Turgenev complained that both the music and text were 'unbearable', and later that Wagner's 'eternal dissonances' produced 'a most unpleasant impression' on him.[120] In 1871, however, he was 'forced to admit' that the prelude to the third act of *Die Meistersinger* was 'powerful music'.[121] Turgenev's position with regard to Wagner was in some ways very close to that of Tchaikovsky, who could only sympathise with characters who experienced feelings that he also felt and understood. Turgenev too found it difficult to identify with such unreal characters as Lohengrin and Brünnhilde; Wagner's music, he wrote, 'expresses inhuman feelings, and his characters are not [ordinary] people; I cannot identify with them'.[122] Since it transpires from the above that the negative feelings Turgenev had about Wagner's music seemed to outweigh the positive ones, it comes as a surprise to learn that his third novel, *On the Eve*, written between 1860 and 1861, might have been written under the influence of *Tristan und Isolde*,[123] whose libretto was first published in 1859. There is in fact no hard evidence to suggest that Turgenev was acquainted with the text to *Tristan* (which was not performed on stage until 1865), or even that he knew its 'general plan'.[124] Therefore Irene Masing-Delic's hypothesis, which rests upon the supposition that Pauline Viardot might have talked about the work with Turgenev in July 1859, is, as she herself admits, highly tenuous.[125] Furthermore, it makes no allowance for the fact that Turgenev might have become acquainted with the *Tristan* legend through sources other than Wagner's opera. The parallels Masing-Delic draws between Turgenev's hero Insarov and Tristan are indeed striking, and should in no way be dismissed out of hand, but given the wide gulf separating Wagner's and Turgenev's artistic preoccupations, it is unlikely that they are anything more than fortuitous.

Dmitry Tsertelev's 'In Memory of Wagner' was the first piece of Russian lyric poetry to be directly inspired by Wagner, and was composed shortly after a visit to Wagner's grave in Bayreuth in 1887. With its atmospheric evocation of images from Wagner's operas, Tsertelev's poem is a triumphant affirmation of their enduring resonance, despite the death of the 'magician' who had created them.[126] Tsertelev had a keen interest in German culture and mythology, and that, coupled with his devotion to the philosophy of Schopenhauer, made Wagner an obviously attractive figure to him.[127]

PART 2

Wagner and Russian modernism

CHAPTER 3

Reception and performance history, 1890–1917

THE ROLE OF *RUSSKAYA MUZYKAL'NAYA GAZETA*

Although performances of Wagner's works remained infrequent in the 1890s, the stream of articles on Wagner's music and aesthetic ideas in the Russian press was gradually increasing each year. Not only had the first Russian monograph on Wagner appeared,[1] but journals such as the weekly *Artist* were now publishing regular articles on Wagner-related subjects. It was *Russkaya muzykal'naya gazeta* (*RMG*), however, which played the greatest role in the dissemination and popularisation of Wagner's music and ideas in Russia. Founded in Petersburg in 1894 under the editorship of Nikolay Findeizen, a prolific musicologist who was to write over 300 articles in his lifetime, *RMG* was Russia's first serious music journal. Despite some initial scepticism with regard to its survival (most music publications had hitherto been short-lived), regular issues were published, first monthly, then weekly after 1899, until 1918. Despite the seriousness of its purpose, *RMG* was a highly partisan paper. A constant battle was waged to raise musical standards in the capital, particularly in the Imperial Opera theatres, whose artistic policies *RMG* considered conservative and unimaginative. In its first issue it also became clear that the promotion of Wagner was another major cause, for both Findeizen and his chief colleague Evgeny Petrovsky were avid Wagnerians, and it is to be assumed that they were the authors of the unsigned musical chronicles that appeared in *RMG* every week, deploring the absence of works by Wagner in the repertoire and chastising the Imperial Theatres Directorate.

In its first issue, *RMG* reported the Imperial Theatres Director-ate's announcement that another proposed tour by Angelo Neumann's troupe had been cancelled.[2] Unlike Mikhail Stanislavsky, *RMG* blamed the cancellation of the tour on those Russian music critics opposed to Wagner: 'One has only to remember the shameful howling which was raised during the first performances of Wagner's tetralogy, and that there were sufficient ... attacks and insinuations from a certain group of Petersburg hacks that the second proposed visit from the "Wagner" company a few years later did not take place.'[3] *RMG* was not unaware of the difficulties it faced in its propa-ganda of Wagner. In acknowledging that the composer still enjoyed comparatively little popularity in Russia, however, the paper attributed this to the fact that the public had had little chance to acquaint themselves with his works, and laid the blame squarely with the Imperial Theatres Directorate, which, it claimed, deliberately 'suppressed' Wagner.[4] In April 1896, *RMG* pointed out, for example, that there had been forty performances of French operas at the Mariinsky Theatre that season and thirty performances of Italian operas, compared to only six performances of a single opera by Wagner.[5] An example of the kind of resistance to Wagner that *RMG* was trying to break down can be found in an article in *Teatral'nye izvestiya* in September 1896, where Wagnerism is described as a 'disaster' brought from the West.[6]

Besides its campaign against the conservative forces in the Russian musical world, *RMG* also promoted Wagner by reg-ularly publishing articles about his music and translations of his writings. In 1897, for example, it began the gargantuan task of publishing Wagner's major treatises, beginning with a trans-lation by the critic Aleksandr Koptyaev of *The Art-work of the Future* which was serialised in twenty parts. Koptyaev prefaced his translation by stressing that the prejudice against Wagner in Russia was based on sheer ignorance: 'We know the word Wagnerism better than Wagner himself. We put on *Tannhäuser* and *Lohengrin*, but fear the other operas like the plague. There is very little on Wagner in our music criticism and our literature on him must be almost the poorest in Europe.'[7]

In September 1897, rumours were rife in the Petersburg press that Theodor Löwe, director of the Breslau Opera Theatre, had signed a contract to tour Russia with a troupe of German singers the following Lent for the performance of works by Wagner. Fears that this tour would also be cancelled proved to be unfounded, and between 22 February and 27 March 1898, Löwe, as well as the famed interpreter of Wagner's works, Hans Richter (conductor of the first perform-ance of the *Ring*), Julius Prüwer and Bernhard Stavenhagen conducted a total of thirty-one performances of works by Wagner, including *Der fliegende Holländer*, *Die Meistersinger*, *Tristan und Isolde*, *Lohengrin*, *Die Walküre* and *Siegfried*. Amongst the many well-known singers who took part in the tour were Therese Malten, Theodor Reichmann, Ernest van Dyck, Jean and Edouard de Reszke and the Russian-born Felia Litvinne. *RMG* provided its readers with introductions to each of the works not yet performed in Russia,[8] as did Koptyaev,[9] yet appreciated that the battle to familiarise the Russian public with Wagner's works would be a long one. The journal was quite correct to identify fear as one of the chief obstacles that needed to be surmounted before Wagner could gain popularity in Russia: 'It is nowhere as difficult to fight with prejudice as it is here in Russia. Musicians and critics ... stagnate in their stubborn rejection of the German composer. Perhaps they are just frightened of Wagner, perhaps they fear that his colossal genius will crush their own musical composition. Only rarely does one meet a Russian musican with an authoritative name who would be prepared to confess his ignorance before Wagner ...'[10]

Judging from the coverage of the tour in *RMG*, the 1898 Wagner performances were not a complete triumph, although one German paper wrote enthusiastically about the success of the first performance of *Der fliegende Holländer*, observing that it must have been 'acutely depressing' for the Directorate, whose 'short-sightedness and resentment' had held the work back from the St Petersburg public for decades.[11] Hans Richter reported to Cosima Wagner that *Die Meistersinger* had made a great impression, but that only the orchestra deserved any real

3. The set for *Tannhäuser* (Bolshoi Theatre, 1898).

praise.[12] Both *Siegfried* and *Die Meistersinger* suffered numerous cuts, whilst the production of *Lohengrin* combined Hans Richter, Felia Litvinne and Therese Malten with a Russian chorus, half of whom sang in their native language and half in Italian, resulting in what Mikhail Stanislavsky called 'a sort of babel in terms of the mixed styles and languages'.[13] Only *Tristan und Isolde*, which played to packed houses for its three performances, scored any real success, but Cui (cast by *RMG* as the Russian Salieri)[14] inevitably found it 'intolerable'. Feeling bound to warn his fellow-countrymen of the dangers of the 'decadent infection' of Wagnerism before it reached Russia, he defined Wagnerites as people either naturally prone to decadence or blind to reason,[15] and proposed the following experiment to simulate the experience of listening to *Tristan und Isolde*:

Find in your flat a door handle which will creak particularly expressively, make it creak for three and a half hours – that is to say the length of *Tristan und Isolde*, listen to this screeching with reverence, convince yourself that this is a leitmotif composed by Wagner and I am convinced that after such a seance there will result an impression and a shock to the nerves that is equal to that gained from Wagner's opera ... The desire to see something profound when there is nothing there at all may have pernicious consequences and may even lead to insanity – I'm saying this quite seriously, there have been cases ...[16]

Unfortunately for Cui, the following season marked a turning-point in the history of Russian productions of works by Wagner. Not only did the Mariinsky Theatre stage its fourth Wagner opera (the first in twenty years), but it now also felt sufficiently emboldened to tackle for the first time the production of *Tristan und Isolde*, one of Wagner's music dramas. The decision was taken with extreme reluctance, for the innate conservatism which governed the tastes of the Imperial Theatres Directorate had hitherto determined that only *Tannhäuser* and *Lohengrin* could be accommodated into the canon of what it deemed was opera. As mentioned earlier, Ivan Vsevolozhsky, Director of the Imperial Theatres from 1881 to 1899, could not bear Wagner, and according to Ivan Ershov, the tenor who was to transform Russian attitudes to Wagner almost single-handedly, he was not alone: 'The whole organisation was hostile to Wagner. Wagner's music met with suspicious opposition. They just about tolerated *Lohengrin* and *Tannhäuser* on the stage, but turned these romantic operas into trite performances in the Italian style. Rumours went around that "Wagner ruined singers' voices" and deafened audiences with orchestral thunder.'[17]

After the relative success of the first Russian performances of *Tristan und Isolde* the previous year, Felia Litvinne had entreated Vsevolozhsky on several occasions to produce the work ('Mais, pensez donc, M. le Directeur, cette mort magnifique!'), but had always been met with a flat refusal ('Oui, mais quelle vie ennuyeuse!').[18] Having signed a contract with the Mariinsky, however, she was adamant that the work be included in its repertoire, and eventually her determination was rewarded. After the tours by Neumann's and Löwe's companies, it had now become traditional to perform Wagner during the Lent Season, and the first Russian production of *Tristan und Isolde* was premièred on 5 April 1899. Although the cast included Litvinne in the role of Isolde, who was 'one of the greatest singers that has ever existed' in the eyes of Sergey Volkonsky,[19] the production was not judged to be a success. Owing to his dislike of Wagner's late operas, Napravnik had handed over the conducting to Feliks Blumenfeld. Despite Blumenfeld's passion for Wagner, this was a difficult work for the young conductor to make his debut with. The performance was further marred, according to *RMG*, by the fact that the title roles were sung in French, while the supporting roles were sung in Russian. The discrepancy in height between the imposing (and rather corpulent) figure of Litvinne and the French tenor who was her partner also cannot have enhanced the general impression.[20] *RMG* nevertheless considered the production a minor triumph, and expressed the hope that it would 'remain a *permanent* and *vital* part of the repertoire'.[21] Only then, it suggested in its seasonal retrospective, would the work 'cease to frighten or arouse the doubts and aversion of listeners brought up on *Faust* or *Roméo et Juliette*'.[22] G. P. Kondratiev, one of the directors at the Imperial Theatres, evidently thought otherwise. Although *Tristan und Isolde* had been considerably shortened, he found that it was 'boring and ridiculously long', and that 'the beginning of the love duet was like dogs barking accompanied by a fidgeting orchestra'.[23] It was undoubtedly due to the influence of figures such as Kondratiev that there resulted such a 'banal' repertoire at the Mariinsky Theatre, where, according to *RMG*, an atmosphere reigned that was 'barbarian' and 'inimical to art'.[24] Yet change was nigh. In July 1899, Sergey Volkonsky took over from his uncle as Director of the Imperial Theatres. Not only was he favourably disposed to Wagner, but he also realised that a Russian production of the *Ring* was long overdue. His first priority was to revive *Tristan und Isolde*, however. Four performances were given in his first season as Director, in which the entire cast now sang in Russian. Another major step forward was the casting of Ivan Ershov as Tristan. Ershov's performance elicited an enthusiastic response from *RMG* and marked the beginning of an historic career, founded on his unique interpretations of Wagner's heroes.[25] *RMG* found these performances far more 'painstaking and serious' than those the previous season.[26] *Tristan und Isolde* was still not popular with the public, however. Some greeted it with catcalls, while others decided to leave before the end, so that Tristan's last monologue was accompanied by 'the sound of footsteps and the slamming of doors in the stalls'.[27] At the beginning of the 1899–1900 season, a new production of *Tannhäuser* was also presented at the Mariinsky Theatre after a two-year absence from the repertoire. It was welcomed by *RMG*, which appreciated not only the new scenery, but the 'clear signs of careful attention' that had been paid to the artistic side of the performance. For once, it seemed that the singers did not seem to be exclusively concerned with their own performance, and *RMG* noted that there was 'a noticeable attempt to cultivate ... a feeling of ensemble, a feeling for which is generally poorly developed amongst first-class Russian singers'.[28]

WAGNER AND THE 'SILVER AGE' OF RUSSIAN CULTURE

It was not just on a whim that Volkonsky decided to encourage the production of Wagner's music dramas at the Mariinsky, for his interest in Wagner was a reflection of the new currents in art which were beginning to make themselves felt at the turn of the century in Russia. In particular, Volkonsky had strong sympathies with the 'World of Art' (*Mir iskusstva*), a group of Petersburg artists and aesthetes who were united by their distaste for the preaching of moral ideas that had become so characteristic of painting and literature in Russia at the end of the nineteenth century. Indeed, in their determined anti-realist stance, in their interest in individual and inner experience, and in their refusal to sub-divide the 'world of art' into its constituent parts, they embodied much that was characteristic of the artistic aspirations of late nineteenth- and early twentieth-century European culture. There was also an undeniable air of *fin-de-siècle* decadence in the intense aestheticism of the 'World of Art' group, personified in the colourful figure of their leader, Sergey Diaghilev, and all these factors combined made it somewhat inevitable that Wagner would prove to be an attractive figure to them, as he had been in preceding decades to the French Decadents, with whom the phenomenon of 'Wagnerism' had properly begun.[29] It comes therefore as no surprise to learn that Wagner was indeed a figure of towering importance to both Diaghilev and Aleksandr Benois, leading figures in the 'World of Art' group. Benois had been won over to the Wagnerian cause in 1889, when he attended the performances of the *Ring* in Petersburg, which 'completely transformed' his musical tastes: 'The very first chords of *Das Rheingold* made me feel that here was a new elemental force, and this feeling persisted during all the four days that the tetralogy lasted. For a considerable time afterwards, I remained under the spell of the music; I was in a state of exaltation, not unlike what one experiences on mountain heights or on the shore of the ocean.'[30] Benois was particularly moved by Wagner's musical evocations of nature, which were linked, in his eyes, to his concurrent enthusiasm for Böcklin, whose paintings had also revealed to him the 'very essence of nature'.[31] But he was dismayed by the clichéd scenery in Neumann's *Ring* production. When he came to design *Götterdämmerung* in 1902, he made a concerted attempt to render more faithfully what was suggested to him in Wagner's music. Diaghilev had become a Wagnerian in 1890, and had visited Bayreuth to attend the *Festspiele* in 1896.[32] He had initially harboured hopes of becoming a practising musician, and it is telling that he chose to perform Amfortas' monologue from *Parsifal* and the prelude to *Lohengrin* at a private concert in 1893.[33] Wagner's music, as Richard Buckle says, 'filled him with a sense of glory',[34] while the blatant eroticism of works such as *Tristan und Isolde* appealed to his more sensual side. In December 1899, he wrote an article about the first Russian production of *Tristan und Isolde* for *Mir iskusstva*, the journal of the 'World of Art' group,[35] and it was *Tristan* which he heard shortly before his death in Munich. Diaghilev had visited Bayreuth for a second time with Stravinsky in 1911, but had then rebelled against his former god in favour of contemporary music. When he came back to Wagner at the end of his life, however, he shed 'bitter tears'.[36]

In 1899, *Mir iskusstva*, the modernist journal that Diaghilev had founded with Benois and their friends in 1898, published translated extracts from Henri Lichtenberger's influential literary and philosophical study of Wagner's music and ideas.[37] This was the first time in Russia that an article about Wagner appeared in a non-musical journal as part of a particular artistic credo, and *Mir iskusstva* continued to publish other materials concerning Wagner until its closure in 1904.[38] With the emergence of the 'World of Art' movement, then, it can be said that Russian Wagnerism (traditionally the province of non-musicians) had truly begun.[39] It is no coincidence that several of the artists who had links with 'The World of Art' also took an intense interest in Wagner. Mikhail Vrubel, for example, was a particular admirer of *Tristan und Isolde* and the *Ring*,[40] and in 1899, he painted a portrait of the art patroness Princess Tenisheva as a Valkyrie.[41] Vrubel's passion for Wagner may have been kindled by his friend and fellow-artist Valentin Serov, who had inherited his late father's veneration for the composer.[42] Serov visited Bayreuth several times, and went often to the theatre with Benois to hear Wagner.[43] Their colleague Nikolay Rerikh had become a Wagnerian at the age of fifteen, when, like Benois, he heard the *Ring* performed by Neumann's troupe in 1889. The experience affected him deeply and he later came to feel a strong affinity between Wagner's music and his own creative aspirations.[44] He particularly loved *Die Walküre* and made several sketches in 1907, hoping that he would one day receive a commission to design a production of the work.[45] Rerikh's innovation was to use colour to convey the emotional content of the music. 'I feel a particular bond with music', he later wrote, 'and just like a composer writing an overture, who chooses a certain tonality, I pick a particular scale – a scale of colours, or rather a leitmotif of colours, on which I base my whole system. When I designed *Die Walküre*, for example, I felt the first act in black and yellow tones . . .'[46] In 1912, Rerikh was appointed designer of a production of *Tristan und Isolde* at the Zimin Theatre in Moscow, and made over twenty costume designs before World War I brought the production to a halt. In the first act, the predominant colours were to be red (symbolising both love and destruction) and yellow (symbolising happiness and treachery), whilst in the second act, lilacs and blues were intended to convey alarm and fear.[47] Viktor Borisov-Musatov was another contemporary artist associated with the Symbolist movement who equated colours with musical tones. He was particularly inspired by Wagner's 'endless melody', which he considered was present in painting. He attempted to achieve music's syncretism of structure and image[48] by seeking to convey 'rhythm and equilibrium' and a 'melodic fluidity' in his pictures.[49] Vassily Kandinsky, one of the founders of abstract painting (and an artist with close links to modernist writers such as Andrey Bely), claimed that hearing Wagner's *Lohengrin* at the Bolshoi Theatre was, together with seeing one of Monet's 'Haystacks', an event that stamped his whole life and shook him to the depths of his being:

I saw all my colours in my mind; they stood before my eyes. Wild, almost crazy lines were sketched in front of me. I did not dare use the expression that Wagner had painted 'my hour' musically. It became, however, quite clear to me that art in general was far more powerful than I thought, and on the other hand, that painting could develop just such powers as music possesses.[50]

Wagner's works also had an earth-shattering effect on Kuzma Petrov-Vodkin. After hearing *Siegfried* in 1911, he marvelled at Wagner's ability to 'turn the soul inside out'. 'The bird's song is still ringing in my ears', he wrote in a letter afterwards; 'his music stimulates in me a desire to work, and listening to it, I dream about my picture; it is the purest art, nothing in it jarred.'[51]

It was on modernist writers, however, that Wagner was to have his greatest influence in Russia. The Imperial Theatres managed to resist the production of Wagner's music dramas until the beginning of the twentieth century, but the Russian opera-going public then quickly succumbed to the inevitable fashion of Wagnerism, which succeeded in gripping first St Petersburg and then Moscow with an intensity that more than made up for its tardiness. At the same time, Wagner began to enjoy a great popularity with a certain section of Russia's literary élite, who were drawn by the sheer elemental power of Wagner's music, by the mythological subjects that he had chosen to construct his music dramas around, by the inherent symbolism of these subjects and by the ritualistic element which belongs to all myth-based art. These writers were transported by the extreme sensuality of Wagner's writing, by the universality of his themes, and, since the perception of metaphysical realities was an overriding concern for them, by the composer's persistent interest in the unconscious stirrings of his protagonists. They were also thrilled by Wagner's *unendliche melodie*, the apparent formlessness of his works that suggested a vast stream of consciousness, and by his approach to art as religion. Wagner had brought tragic drama to the operatic stage and combined it with symphonic music, the result of which was an emotional expressiveness that had an explosive effect on receptive listeners. He had created a fairy-tale world of myth which these writers could both escape into, and identify with, as allegorical of the world in which they themselves lived. These writers were Aleksandr Blok, Vyacheslav Ivanov and Andrey Bely, the second-generation Russian Symbolists, for whom art was the 'key to the world of absolutes', and music above all a 'redemptive revelation'.[52] If French Symbolism was 'arguably the "second flood of the same tide as Romanticism" and of German Romanticism (especially *Frühromantik*) in particular, with Wagner as the priestly intermediary', as Edmund Wilson and Raymond Furness have argued, then second-generation Russian Symbolism was undoubtedly the third and final flood of that same tide.

Mir iskusstva had become the first platform for the Russian Symbolists, and when it folded in 1904, the literary journal *Vesy* (*The Scales*) arose to take its place as Russia's most progressive artistic periodical, and devoted its attention exclusively to what it called in its opening editorial 'decadence', 'symbolism' and 'the new art'.[53] As will be seen in the following chapter, Vyacheslav Ivanov, a leading representative of the second generation group of Symbolists (who were united by their interest in the mystical philosophy of Vladimir Solovyov as well as by their links to the German Romantic tradition), perceived in Wagner's music certain ideas that he considered seminal to the development of Symbolist art, and encouraged their discussion in the journal. Valery Bryusov, the editor of *Vesy*, and a 'first generation' Symbolist more concerned with decadence than mysticism, showed no particular interest in Wagner himself but complied initially with Ivanov's wishes.[54] Accordingly, an article appeared late in 1904 which discussed Wagner as a 'symbolist', and was replied to by Ivanov, followed by reviews of several recent German Wagner publications. *Zolotoe runo* (*The Golden Fleece*), another modernist journal sympathetic to the Symbolist cause, which was founded in 1906, devoted more attention to music than *Vesy*, and Emil Medtner, who became its chief music critic, contributed lengthy articles in 1907 and 1908 about the annual Wagner performances in Munich.[55]

Although Wagner exerted his greatest influence in Russia on the three main second generation Symbolists Aleksandr Blok, Andrey Bely and Vyacheslav Ivanov, other poets linked with the movement were also occasionally inspired by his works. Ivan Konevskoy was the first Russian modernist writer whose writings were directly influenced by Wagner. In 1897 (three years before his untimely death), the twenty-year old Konevskoy visited Bayreuth during his first trip abroad to hear

Parsifal. Hearing the work inspired two short verses entitled 'Bayreuth', the first of which explores the power Wagner's music exerts on the listener, while the second muses on the significance of the last sounds in *Parsifal*.[56] Six years later, Innokenty Annensky also wrote a poem invoking *Parsifal*,[57] which had received its first full concert performance in Petersburg a few months earlier.[58] Another contemporary writer who appears to have been inspired by Wagner is Venedikt Livshits, who included a poem entitled 'The Valkyrie' (*Valkiriya*) in his first collection of poetry which was published in 1911.[59]

Although the fashion for Wagner amongst the opera-going public continued right up until the beginning of World War I (and would have certainly continued beyond 1914 if the ban forbidding the performance of his works not been enforced), the closure of *Vesy* in 1909, and the founding of a new journal, *Apollon*, reflected the crisis the Symbolist movement was undergoing, and signalled a change in artistic climate which was less hospitable to Wagnerian idealism. Although Blok, Bely and Ivanov continued to revere Wagner, by 1913 Symbolism had been eclipsed by Acmeism, a movement which constituted a revolt against the mystical transcendentalism and myth-creation of the Symbolists, a renewed emphasis on the 'word' (rather than 'music') and a move away from Germanic high seriousness in preference of Romanic irony. In Wagnerian terms, this change in climate is best exemplified by a poem written by Osip Mandelstam in 1914 entitled 'The Valkyries fly, the bows sing' (*Letayut val'kirii, poyut smychki*), a matter-of-fact evocation of a performance of *Die Walküre*, composed in the neo-realist style of the times.[60] It is clear from this eight-line poem, in which Wagner's opera is described as 'cumbersome', that Mandelstam was no Wagnerian. No longer are the Valkyries linked with emanations of the 'Eternal Feminine', neither are they symbols of Russia. Far from identifying Wagner's music with other worlds, Mandelstam instead fixes his attention (in typical Acmeist fashion) on the concrete, external details of this world: the footmen waiting on the marble steps of the theatre ready with the heavy fur coats of their employers and the cabmen huddled outside round bonfires. It is perhaps surprising, in this context, to detect signs of obvious Wagnerian influence in *Gondla*, the fourth play of Nikolay Gumilyov, another leading theorist of Acmeism, which was published in 1917.[61] Traces of *Tristan und Isolde* and the *Ring* are nevertheless evident in its ninth-century Icelandic setting, for example, in the fact that key events take place while its hero is being taken to Iceland by sea and in the act of redemptive self-immolation which ends the play. But perhaps this is not all that surprising given that Gumilyov drew from the same sources that Wagner used in composing the *Ring* (the Old Norse Eddic poems) for his play. Interestingly, Gumilyov's pupil, Georgy Adamovich, wrote several poems before the Revolution under the direct influence of Wagner. A poem entitled 'Siegfried', (*Zigfrid*), for example, was included in his first collection, *Clouds* (*Oblaka*), which appeared in 1916, and evokes the hero of *Götterdämmerung* remembering the blue sea of flame, like an 'abandoned paradise', which once surrounded Brünnhilde.[62]

THE FIRST RUSSIAN *RING* AND THE RISE OF RUSSIAN WAGNERISM

The success of *Tristan* in 1900 gave Volkonsky the courage to broach the subject of the *Ring* with his colleagues,[63] who with reluctance must have agreed that the Mariinsky Theatre could no longer postpone the production of Wagner's most famous work. The conservative Laroche observed that 'it was not without some wise caution that the Directorate made the decision to introduce the *Ring* into the Mariinsky repertoire',[64] and at first it was proposed that *Die Meistersinger* be staged instead. Eventually the Directorate sanctioned the production of the *Ring*, but only on the condition that *Die Walküre* was staged first. The first performance took place on 24 November 1900, thirty years after its Munich première, and was conducted by Napravnik. To judge from the review in *RMG*, the tide of public opinion was slowly beginning to turn, for the cast (with Ershov as Siegmund, and Litvinne as Brünnhilde) received prolonged curtain calls; the production was pronounced 'an undoubted success'.[65] The praise from *RMG*'s exacting critic was certainly not unqualified, but it is evident from the review's tone that the production now gave cause for encouragement, rather than exasperation (which was the case previously). At least one of the *Die Walküre* performances was attended by Nicholas II, who was particularly impressed with the orchestra's performance, and summoned Napravnik afterwards to the Imperial Box to congratulate him.[66]

Theatres other than the Imperial opera houses were now beginning to venture warily into the Wagnerian repertoire. *Tannhäuser* was performed in Kharkov in 1899, and in Nizhny Novgorod in 1900.[67] In 1901, a production directed by Vassily Shkafer and designed by Vrubel was performed by Savva Mamontov's private opera company in Moscow,[68] and both *Tannhäuser* and *Lohengrin* had now become part of the operatic repertoire in Kazan, Perm and Tiflis. This was not sufficient for some, however. 'Wagner will only be represented in this season by *Tannhäuser* and *Lohengrin* of course', complained the Tiflis correspondent for *RMG*, Vladimir Derzhanovsky (one of whose pseudonyms was 'Wotan'); 'to dream of a production of *Tristan und Isolde*, the tetralogy and other works would be simply foolish: in Tiflis that will only happen in the twenty-first century – not earlier'.[69] The public seemed more favourably disposed towards Wagner now, but the conservative tastes of the Petersburg Russian Musical Society meant that Wagner was still discriminated against in their concert repertoires, which *RMG* found aggravating: 'The Eighth Symphonic Concert showed (a) that boring tastes and a lack of any artistic sense still persist in the programme compilations, and (b) that the definite anti-Wagner tendency manifested by the St Petersburg RMS management does not prevent the public from liking Wagner and enjoying his music; if the public demands an encore of the brilliant Prelude to Wagner's *Parsifal* there is nothing they can do about it!'[70]

When the Mariinsky Theatre staged *Siegfried* in 1902, Volkonsky had already been replaced by Vladimir Telyakovsky. Volkonsky may have been a man 'with a genuine artistic and poetic nature' who had the 'best intentions to serve art', as

4. Felia Litvinne as Brünnhilde (Mariinsky Theatre, 1900).

Napravnik thought,[71] but he had met with much opposition within the Mariinsky and was forced to resign as Director at the close of the 1900–1 season. Telyakovsky, an erudite and energetic administrator (who had long experience in the army), did not possess his predecessor's appetite for radical innovation to such a degree, but was also concerned to raise the standards at the Imperial Theatres. The first performance of *Siegfried* took place on 4 February 1902, with Ivan Ershov in the title role.[72] It was particularly in this part of the tetralogy that Ershov excelled. As Siegfried, writes his biographer Abram Gozenpud, Ershov 'had no rivals, either in Russia or in the West'.[73] Ershov excepted, *RMG* found the production of *Siegfried* 'grey, mediocre and unremarkable',[74] but by March, the production had evidently rapidly improved, since the journal now declared that it had scored a 'definite success with the public'.[75]

It was approximately at this time that the Bolshoi Theatre also started to take an interest in Wagner. Moscow had always been considered a backwater compared to the more cosmopolitan, northern capital, and the Bolshoi Theatre was (despite the good intentions of its disastrous staging of *Siegfried* in 1894) an even more reactionary institution than its sister theatre in St Petersburg. Like the Mariinsky, the Bolshoi was also beset by the problems of bureaucracy and conservatism which the Imperial Theatres Directorate brought to bear on artistic life, as the soprano Nadezhda Salina so well describes: 'When I first came to the Bolshoi Theatre (1 January 1888), it was really more like a government department than a temple of free art. Almost the whole first decade of my service (for it was 'service' rather than work) passed under the flag of conventionalism [*kazenshchina*] and bureaucratic arbitrariness ... The artists were not a collective, a friendly family, linked by the common interest of great work ...'[76] Salina was not the only person to find fault with artistic standards at the Bolshoi Theatre. In 1898, Nikolay Kashkin (pseudonymously) published a damning critique of not only the repertoire, but also the productions, the directors, the conductors and the bureaucrats at the Bolshoi, who, in his eyes, were simply 'not interested' in what they were supposed to be doing. There was 'no style' at the Bolshoi Theatre, he complained; every composer (whatever his nationality) was measured by the same 'lifeless musical-bureaucratic formalism, which tries to rid itself of

5.   Ivan Ershov as Siegfried (Mariinsky Theatre, 1902).

artistic work like office papers'.[77] In Kashkin's opinion, the repertoire featured insufficient operas by Russian composers, and insufficient works by Wagner; instead there was a surfeit of Verdi (who was really 'not so popular at the present time') and Meyerbeer (which showed the influence of 'provincial tastes').[78] A quick glance at the repertoires from 1891 to 1897, the period falling within Kashkin's scope (which show an even greater percentage of French and Italian opera than in Petersburg), reveals his accusations to be palpably true. Kashkin also upbraided the theatre for wasting time and resources:

Wagner's *Tannhäuser* was nominated for production. The parts were naturally distributed beforehand. From highly competent sources we have discovered that the scenery, props and costumes were all ready but as the opera has not yet been performed, all the outlays have been in vain so far. Those near to the highest theatrical spheres have said that the production of a one-act ballet called *The Cricket* prevented *Tannhäuser* from being performed ... If the obstacle in the form of *The Cricket* is just a *façon de parler*, and they simply were not up to learning *Tannhäuser*, then one should not even be thinking of increasing the troupe's activities but rather bringing it into order so that it would be possible to accomplish the proposed plan of action.[79]

Ironically, just as Kashkin's study was published, the mood at the Bolshoi Theatre began to change. When at the beginning of the 1890s, Grand Duke Sergey Vladimirovich became Governor of Moscow, a small court formed, and 'the theatrical bureaucrats began to stir'.[80] Reform only began in earnest, however, when the theatrical administration received word from St Petersburg that Sergey Vladimirovich's German-born wife Elizaveta Fyodorovna (sister to the tsarina Alexandra) was fond of Wagner, and then, recalls Salina 'they began enthusiastically staging his operas':

The Bolshoi theatre began to move like a bear in his lair after a long hibernation. It was as if some fresh air had roused the indifferent sleepiness of the artists, lulled by the monotony of the repertoire and the boredom of the inactive life inside the theatre. The production of operas such as *Lohengrin*, *Tannhäuser* and *Die Walküre* with their large choruses, complex ensembles and many characters even aroused Altani's artistic feelings and he showed once more how talented a musician he was. His interpretations of the overture to *Lohengrin* and the 'Ride of the Valkyries' could ably bear comparison with the performances of these pieces by the well-known foreign conductors ...[81]

If one examines the Bolshoi Theatre repertoire during this time, one can indeed note a sudden increase in the number of performances of Wagner operas. From 1894 to 1898 there had been a total of three performances of works by Wagner at the Bolshoi, and then ten performances were suddenly included in the 1898–9 season. The 1899–1900 season opened with the afore-mentioned production of *Tannhäuser*, which had never been in the Bolshoi repertoire, and was followed by productions of *Die Walküre*, conducted by Ippolit Altani, which was first performed on 24 February 1902, and *Der fliegende Holländer*, first performed on 19 November 1902, which preceded the first Petersburg production by nine years. Even *Siegfried* was revived for one performance in 1900. At the end of January, the critic Ivan Lipaev reported from Moscow on the state of Wagnerism in Russia's second capital for *RMG*:

Wagner ... is gaining a firm foothold in Moscow. He has acquired firm and staunch admirers. They have promoted him fairly successfully, especially when Kes came. Hans Richter also strengthened support ... not to mention the constant performance of his works at concerts and Jurgenson's publication of his operas ... In a word, *Wagnerovshchina* has put down fairly strong roots here and the German reformer's music can be heard every week.[82]

As Lipaev suggests, the concerts given by foreign conductors on tour did a great deal to advance the Wagnerian cause in Russia, as their programmes invariably included excerpts from one or other of the music dramas. Arthur Nikisch, a renowned interpreter and propagandist of Wagner's works, had been regularly visiting Russia to conduct concerts since 1895,[83] while other eminent visitor conductors included Felix Weingartner who toured in 1898,[84] Hans Richter and Willem Kes who came in 1899,[85] and Max Fiedler who came in 1902.[86] Siegfried Wagner was invited to conduct *Die Walküre* in Moscow in 1902,[87] but declined the invitation in favour of his brother-in-law Franz Beidler, who travelled from Bayreuth to conduct *Die Walküre* and, later in the year, the première of *Der*

fliegende Holländer.[88] The number of Russian visitors to Bayreuth was also steadily increasing each year, although the
prohibitive costs of tickets meant that the festival enjoyed its
greatest popularity with the titled nobility.[89] Ivan Lipaev was
able to attend the *Festspiele* in 1902 as a correspondent for
RMG,[90] however, and other Russian visitors that year included
Sergey Rakhmaninov, Konstantin Stanislavsky and Valentin
Serov.[91]

The 1902–3 Russian opera season included thirty performances of operas by Wagner; an increase on previous years but
still a paltry figure when set against the 1,204 performances in
Germany, for example, the 139 performances in Austria and
the 76 performances in France.[92] Even thirty performances was
extravagant for the conservative section of the Russian press,
however. Mikhail Ivanov, for example, was a prominent critic
who held extremely conservative musical views, and he led a
vigorous campaign against the performance of Wagner's works
in the pages of the reactionary newspaper *Novoe vremya*. A
review he wrote in September 1902, for example, is a case in
point: 'It seems to me that the Directorate has been wasting its
energies in bothering about Wagner so much recently. Of
course the repertoire must be as varied as possible, but do we
have to be saturated with Wagner and nothing else but
Wagner? With the exception of *Parsifal*, the Petersburg public
is already well acquainted with all of his works ...'[93] Needless
to say, *RMG* found Ivanov's attempts to prove that Wagner
was 'unnecessary and harmful' extremely tiresome, and subjected his diatribes against Wagner to endless ridicule.[94]

The highlight of the 1902–3 season was the première of
Götterdämmerung at the Mariinsky Theatre, with sets designed
by Benois, and painted by Konstantin Korovin. Benois was one
of the first real artists that Imperial Theatres commissioned to
design an opera production at the Mariinsky (a practice that
Mamontov had first introduced in his private opera company),
and the scenery therefore attracted as much criticism from the
press as the performers. When Benois had first heard the *Ring*
in 1889, he had been unimpressed by the sets, which were
based on the traditional pseudo-romantic Bayreuth model, and

was glad of the chance to create a production that he felt would be true to life. The first performance (which took place on 20 January 1903) did not meet with universal approval, however. The singers, for example, had grown accustomed to the traditional painted flats (which followed the standard European set design for Wagner's works) and they did not like the change. Benois argued in his defence that the style of traditional productions was 'old-fashioned' and 'tasteless', and that he was trying to make a break from the old designs which he found artificial and cloying.[95] He had aimed to imbue the set with a feeling of genuine nature rather than its stylised representation, but his gentle, small-scale response, 'in subdued tones of grey, blue and brown', it was felt, did not suit Wagner's grandiose and epic images.[96] *RMG* recognised the 'attempt to introduce something new into the sphere of decorative art', but although it found the designs 'pleasing and interesting', there was nevertheless much, in its opinion, that was unsuccessful, aroused 'confusion', and broke the scenic illusion.[97] Diaghilev was equally critical, but not just because he resented his friend working for the Imperial Theatres, with whom he had recently parted on unfriendly terms. While praising certain elements, he condemned the designs as 'delightful water-colours', maintaining that their realism had nothing to do with the spirit and character of Wagner: 'We see a beautiful spot of northern countryside with a pile of stones ... arranged like pieces of furniture ... It is this little spot, transported, it seems, from the province of Perm, which is to depict that terror-stricken rock on which Wotan sends his winged daughter to sleep. It is here that great feats are to be accomplished, and gods and heroes are to interract ...'[98] The problem was partly to do with the fact that Benois was not given full control over the production, partly that his designs were executed by another artist, and partly that he lacked experience in the theatre.[99] Benois accepted much of the criticism, but remained satisfied (as indeed Diaghilev did) with his design for the concluding scenes of *Götterdämmerung*, where he had been able to exercise more influence.[100] Whatever Mikhail Ivanov's artistic sensibilities were, his response to the production of yet

another Wagner opera was predictable: 'I consider the production of *Götterdämmerung* <u>absolutely</u> superfluous, just as all
the other Wagner productions have been recently', he fulmi-
nated; 'what is the point of all these Wagner operas, and who
are they put on for?'[101] Ivanov renewed his attacks on Wagner
at the beginning of the 1903–4 season, somewhat incredibly
blaming the 'over-abundance' of operas by Wagner in the
Mariinsky Theatre repertoire on the theatre administration's
bias towards the composer.[102]

The year 1903 marked the twentieth anniversary of
Wagner's death and the ninetieth anniversary of his birth.
Glazunov, Rimsky-Korsakov and Taneev went to Berlin to
attend the unveiling of a statue of Wagner,[103] and *RMG*
celebrated the occasion with book reviews and articles, including Nikolay Findeizen's account of Wagner's visit to Russia,[104]
which was the first article to explore Wagner's Russian connections. Ivan Lipaev, meanwhile, published the first Russian
guidebook for visitors attending the Bayreuth festival, which
included information on the journey from Moscow, for
example, a summary of Russian opinion on Wagner, and a
bibliography of the books and articles about the composer that
had so far appeared in Russian. This was a very timely publication according to *RMG*, 'since the number of Wagnerians in
Russia is growing all the time and there are many enthusiasts
who visit the Bayreuth Festival almost every year'.[105] In
Moscow, Wagner's popularity was also now increasing
steadily. In March 1904, for example, Willem Kes conducted
concerts of excerpts from *Tristan und Isolde* and *Die Meistersinger
von Nürnberg* (neither of which had yet been performed there),
and the Moscow correspondent for *RMG* was astonished by the
response from the audience: 'All I will say is that the audience
here listened not only with careful attention; they were obviously won over by the beauty and lightness of Wagner's
work.'[106] There was a hiatus in the Mariinsky Theatre's *Ring*
production during the 1903–4 and 1904–5 seasons. Of its constituent parts, all but *Das Rheingold* had now been performed,
but despite the fulsome praise of *RMG*, which described the
annual *Ring* performances as the 'main artistic event of the

season',[107] its pleas to complete the work were met with deafening silence on the part of the Imperial Theatres Directorate. Provincial opera theatres, meanwhile, continued to stage productions of the two stalwarts from the early Wagnerian repertoire. At the end of 1904, for example, *Lohengrin* was performed in Irkutsk, Kiev, Odessa and Saratov, and *Tannhäuser* was given one performance in Zhitomir.[108]

There was still very little serious critical literature about Wagner in Russia besides the regular articles that appeared in *RMG*, but the situation was somewhat rectified in 1905 by the publication of a Russian translation of Lichtenberger's *Wagner: poète et penseur* (1898),[109] which suggested that there was now an audience for such a work. Vsevolod Cheshikhin's *History of Russian Opera from 1674 to 1903* (*Istoriya russkoi opery s 1674 po 1903 godu*), published in 1905, confirmed that Wagner's supporters did indeed now outnumber his detractors. In Cheshikhin's analysis, Wagner's popularity was part of the overall vogue for foreign music in Russia which had begun with the 'Italomania' in the eighteenth and nineteenth centuries:

Foreign mania is one of the worst ailments in Russian cultural life. In opera it is expressed by a decrease in interest in the national Russian element and an increase in interest in everything fashionable and foreign ... At the end of the nineteenth, and at the beginning of the twentieth centuries, the same habit of 'singing in a foreign tongue' manifests itself in Russian 'Wagnerism': his operas dominate the Imperial Theatres' repertoire and do not leave any room for Russian operas; imitation of Wagner is obviously a 'vogue', which all Russian contemporary composers have to reckon with, and only the best of them moreover (Rimsky-Korsakov, for example in *Kashchei*) are able to succeed in more or less reconciling 'their own' national Russianness with the foreign element.[110]

RMG (which no doubt would have only been satisfied if works by Wagner took up 100 per cent of the repertoire) would not have agreed with this evaluation. At the end of 1905, it produced a list of the number of performances of operas performed in Russia during the 1904–5 season, the aim of which was to point out that none of Wagner's operas had been performed more than 17 times during the season (the number of *Tann-*

häuser performances), whereas *Eugene Onegin*, for example, had been given 194 performances, *Carmen* 163 and *Faust* 161.[111]

The Mariinsky Theatre's production of *Das Rheingold*, conducted by Napravnik (who had visited Bayreuth the previous summer along with Blumenfeld),[112] and designed by Aleksandr Golovin, was finally given its first performance on 27 December 1905, with Ershov as Loge. It was not received well by the press, however, not least because the work's unity was destroyed by the insertion of an interval halfway through. *RMG* in fact refrained from reviewing it at all until the end of the season, since it held that most first performances of Wagner operas in Russia resembled rehearsals.[113] The critic Aleksandr Ossovsky appreciated the amount of work that had been invested in the production but maintained there was 'little feeling and even less enthusiasm'. His main criticism was the lack of a style 'of any kind' in the production; poetic beauty, he held, had been replaced by 'plain prose', and Golovin's designs, in his view, had turned Wotan into a king from a children's fairy tale.[114]

Although at the end of the 1905–6 season *Tannhäuser* and *Lohengrin* were respectively still only the 39th and 46th most frequently performed operas during the season,[115] the resistance to Wagner in Russia was now largely overcome. In 1906, Russian musicians had actually taken part in the *Festspiele* for the first time, when Viktor Valter, leader of the Mariinsky Theatre orchestra (and author of many books and articles about Wagner) and his 'cellist colleague Arkady Sasonov spent nine weeks in Bayreuth during the summer playing in the orchestra. Valter had been writing as a music critic since 1897 and his reports on the festival were published in *RMG* later that year.[116] It was in 1906 that Russian studies of Wagner's operas and translations of his writings began to appear, including *Art and Revolution* (which must have earlier encountered severe problems with the censor due to its inflammatory title)[117] and *Opera and Drama*.[118] Viktor Kolomiitsov considered the publication of Vyacheslav Ignatovich's analysis of the *Ring* in 1906 'most timely';[119] 'in view of the interest the public is showing towards Wagner's operas, in view of most of

6.   Ivan Ershov as Lohengrin (Mariinsky Theatre, 1905).

the public's lack of comprehension not only of his ideas, but even the contents of his works, and also in view of the almost complete absence of explanatory brochures on this topic'.[120] Kolomiitsov, one of Russia's most committed Wagnerians, and author of countless translations, books and articles about the composer,[121] pointed out that the Russian translation of Henri Lichtenberger's study was too costly for many people to acquire and that the ideas in the recently published translation of Max Nordau's notorious *Degeneration* (1892) were too 'superficial', 'comical and vulgar' to be of any value. The Wagner 'cult' was a rather predictable target in Nordau's bilious attack on the degeneracy of *fin-de-siècle* culture. Amongst other things, Nordau detected manifestations of persecution mania, megalomania, mysticism and anarchism in Wagner's writings, and regarded the 'erotic madness' he found in the texts of his music dramas as 'a form of Sadism'.[122]

It was no coincidence that an article had appeared in *RMG* at the end of 1905 which was expressly devoted to analysing the performances of Ivan Ershov,[123] for it was Ershov who was largely responsible for popularising Wagner's works in Russia. Without his contribution, in fact, it is doubtful whether Wagner would have attracted such a following in Russia, and had he accepted Cosima Wagner's invitation in 1901 to go and sing at Bayreuth,[124] he would probably have achieved world renown. Moscow could boast no other tenor of his calibre, which is perhaps why the performances of his operas at the Bolshoi Theatre always remained fewer in number than those in Petersburg. The reason why Ershov played such a crucial role in the popularisation of Wagner's operas in Russia was due not only to his vocal powers, but also to his supreme dramatic talent; where others just sang the Wagnerian roles with pathos, Ershov gave enthralling performances with his vivid and convincing interpretations. His life had begun prosaically enough in the kitchens of the provincial house belonging to the family for whom his mother worked, and at the age of sixteen, he was employed as a locomotive driver. Four years later, however, friends raised the money to send him to the Petersburg Conservatoire, and since his debut in 1893, he had acquired a repertoire of forty-seven roles. According to Eduard Stark (whose pseudonym was 'Zigfrid'), however, everything paled 'before the characters created by him in the Wagnerian repertoire. He could claim immortality just for his interpretations of Tannhäuser, Tristan, Loge, Siegmund and Siegfried.'[125] Ershov's first Wagnerian role was Tannhäuser, which he sang in 1895. This was not only the beginning of Ershov's fame, but also the beginning of Russian Wagnerism, according to Eduard Stark: 'for the first time, the whole character of the German legend became visible; *Tannhäuser* was not only sung but acted'.[126] Ershov's passion and directness made a decisive break with tradition, for Nikolay Figner, the previous Tannhäuser, had sung in the 'European style' with stylised gestures.[127] So much energy and feeling did Ershov invest in his roles in fact, that his contemporary B. Mazing recalled that he would actually blanch when stabbed by Hagen each time and involuntarily blush upon discovering Brünnhilde to be a woman.[128] On 3 December 1905, Russia's other great singer, Fyodor Chaliapin, sang 'Wotan's Farewell' (from *Die Walküre*) at a Ziloti concert in Petersburg, and it was one of the rare occasions when Chaliapin consented to sing Wagner; the Dutchman was the only role he sang in full-scale productions.[129] Chaliapin had developed his own particular style of singing that was well suited to the Russian realist tradition and he evidently did not find it as easy to identify with Wagner's mythical figures as Ershov did.[130] *RMG* commented that Chaliapin 'did not possess the strength or beauty of voice for Wotan', finding his distinctive manner of 'dramatising' his performance also 'not quite appropriate'.[131] The concert series that the pianist and conductor Aleksandr Ziloti had founded in 1903 was considerably enriching concert life in St Petersburg and was also helping to further the Wagnerian cause. The RMS concerts had been highly innovatory when they first began, but by the beginning of the twentieth century, they had started to become increasingly 'academic', with programmes leaning ever more heavily on the classical repertoire. Ziloti wanted to educate the 'empty' public who went to concerts only to hear famous names like Chaliapin. If 'serious music' was performed, he reasoned, the public could not fail to leave his concerts better informed.[132] Ziloti was intent on promoting new music through his concerts, and their programmes often featured music by Rakhmaninov, Sibelius, Franck or Glazunov, but he was also keen on Liszt and Wagner, and had gone to Bayreuth in 1893. Concerts whose programmes consisted entirely of music by Liszt and Wagner regularly featured on the schedule.

Whilst Ershov's role cannot be overestimated, two other parties also played seminal roles in reversing Russian attitudes to Wagner: the conductor Eduard Napravnik and the Mariinsky Theatre troupe. Napravnik was never an enthusiast for Wagner in the way that some of his contemporaries were, but under his tutelage, the Mariinsky Theatre orchestra proved more than equal to the task of performing Wagner's difficult scores.[133] Napravnik transformed an orchestra accustomed to accompanying Italian arias into a first-rate ensemble, and when Vassily Shkafer began directing at the Mariinsky in 1906, the reigning 'Richard Wagner cult' he found there was largely due, in his opinion, to Napravnik's efforts:

An honoured place in the repertoire was given over to Wagner as the whole Lent season was taken up with the *Ring* subscriptions. The performances, conducted by E. F. Napravnik, were distinguished by such a high musical level that the well-known German conductors invited by the orchestra and chorus for special benefit performances (Muck, Mottl, Hans Richter and Nikisch) would express their admiration of the Wagner performances to Eduard Frantsevich when visiting him ...[134]

As well as the exceptional talents of Ershov and Litvinne, the most renowned interpreters of Wagner in Russia, Shkafer also recalls the 'huge enthusiasm' for the *Ring* shown by the singers, who were gripped in an elemental way by Wagner's music.[135] These singers must have been amongst the younger members of the troupe, for *RMG* had little good to say of their elder colleagues. The paper had fought a vigorous campaign for the tetralogy to be performed in full, and had succeeded. Nevertheless it was still very critical of artistic standards overall in the Mariinsky Theatre, as was manifest in its review of the 1908 season, for example:

> The main season has finished and no great impressions have remained with us. In fact, compared with last year, the lack of colour, sluggishness and dwindling of artistic feeling not to mention all other feeling has significantly increased ... During Lent the 'Wagner season' will begin (it threatens to become a tradition). Once again we will have to make do with a home-spun production. Once again the trusting subscribers will enjoy a provincial imitation of the huge tetralogy, sung and performed in the 'Faust-Carmen-Onegin' – or in other words – specific Mariinsky spirit and style' ...[136]

Part of the problem lay with the singers, according to *RMG*, who were mostly 'invalids'. Young singers who saw their hopes come to nothing soon became 'past their best and dried up in the stifling and stale routine of the opera department'.[137]

An example of the growing fashion of Wagnerism in Russia was the first full performance of the score of *Parsifal* in Russia, arranged by Count Aleksandr Sheremetiev in 1906. To circumvent the thirty-year copyright regulation, the opera was performed in Vsevolod Cheshikhin's translation at three separate concerts on Sunday afternoons, beginning on 19 February. Musical standards were not apparently very high. Each member of the orchestra played 'smoothly and evenly', according to *RMG*, but without any regard to the other players, and the conducting was 'primitive'. The use of an electric light for the Holy Grail, moreover, was condemned as utter bad taste.[138]

During the 1906–7 season, *RMG* continued the important task of publishing the legacy of Wagner's prose writings. By far the most important event for Wagner followers in Russia that season, however, was the first complete performance of the *Ring* at the Mariinsky. The sixteen-year-old Sergey Prokofiev (on whom the *Ring* 'made a great impression'), managed to get a subscription to one of the three cycles, 'but not without some effort, since a huge queue of people wanting to hear Wagner had formed at the box office'.[139] According to Telyakovsky, the production attracted not only the attention of the musical world in Russia, but the whole of Europe: 'The audience, having only recently acquainted themselves with Wagner, now filled the theatre with such excitement that tickets were only obtainable with great difficulty.'[140] 'Any art imbued with the spirit of the new is condemned to overcome the huge force of public moral inertia before gaining recognition', commented Aleksandr Ossovsky, who remarked that the public looked unusually serious and attentive for the performances of the *Ring*. This proved that the previous resistance to Wagner had now largely disappeared, according to Ossovsky, as 'what was incomprehensible to Tchaikovsky, Laroche, Stasov and Cui' was now 'accessible to the masses'.[141] Mikhail Ivanov predictably led 'the artillery attack on Wagner' afterwards,[142] although his tirades were now becoming ever more ludicrous and anachronistic in the light of public opinion, which was now changing so dramatically in favour of Wagner. To coincide with the performances of the *Ring*, he contributed a lengthy article on Nietzsche and Wagner to *Novoe vremya*. Although it purported to discuss Nietzsche's attitude to Wagner, the article was in actuality merely a vehicle for Ivanov to lambast Wagner once again, this time for his 'self-satisfied egoism',[143] 'arrogance and self-deception'.[144] In another tendentious review he wrote that year, he wrote that Mariinsky Theatre had been turned into nothing less than a 'heathen temple', to which sacrifices had been brought to the 'idol' Richard Wagner. Yet even this most curmudgeonly of Wagner's Russian critics was forced to acknowledge the composer's popularity amongst St Petersburg's opera-going public: 'Many – women included – sit with the score in their hands, ruining their eyes in the darkness in the attempt to understand what is going on on stage.'[145] It is telling that Ivanov also mentions Wagner's popularity amongst the nobility in this review. As the section of society brought up almost exclusively on Italian opera and light-hearted melodrama, it might at first appear odd that the upper classes should have suddenly discovered a passion for Wagner, one of the most intellectually demanding of all operatic composers. Whether the Russian nobility really enjoyed and understood his works will remain a matter for conjecture, but there were in fact certain specific reasons why a vogue for Wagner's operas developed amongst the Russian upper classes. It was not unknown for the personal tastes of the Imperial family to influence the operatic repertoires, and as the German-born tsarina Alexandra was supposed to have liked Wagner's operas, Nicholas II therefore probably encouraged their inclusion in the repertoire. This also may partly explain why Wagner was performed in St Petersburg far more frequently than in Moscow, and why he enjoyed a greater popularity there. For if the tsarina enjoyed listening to Wagner, then it followed that the rest of the Court would enjoy listening to Wagner as a matter of course. Telyakovsky maintains that 'they went to listen to Wagner because his operas were fashionable, but they found them very boring',[146] and N. V. Tumanina has corroborated this view, asserting that the Russian nobility in general had little understanding of music, and preferred ballet to opera: 'Wagner's operas were even more difficult for upper-class society to understand than those by the *kuchkisty*, but they diligently attended the performances, copying the court.'[147]

With the first complete performance of the *Ring*, Russian Wagnerism had begun in earnest, as Viktor Valter's assesssment indicates: 'In Russia, the country next to Wagner's motherland, which is honoured to have contributed a few prominent pages to his biography, the name of Wagner is becoming ever dearer and closer to us; people are learning to grasp and understand him more deeply and more clearly.'[148] Three cycles of the *Ring* were given at the Mariinsky Theatre in 1908, but according to Eduard Stark, there were enough people wanting tickets for three more cycles. 'The evolution in tastes over ten years surpassed all expectations', he wrote later, for it was now as difficult to obtain tickets for *Die Walküre* and *Siegfried* as it had apparently been for *Aida*, when the tenor Nikolay Figner was at the height of his powers.[149] Stark rejected the idea that Wagner's popularity was just a passing fashion, for he thought it hardly possible that people blindly following a fashion would really want to sit through the six hours that the Russian performance of *Götterdämmerung* lasted.

In his opinion, the Russian public had finally come to understand exactly what music drama was in comparison to ordinary opera, and could now listen to Wagner's 'endless melody' as dramatic dialogue, without worrying about its resolution; 'the absence of rounded numbers with effectively placed final notes had ceased to shock'.[150]

The year 1908 marked the twenty-fifth anniversary of Wagner's death, which provoked a stream of articles and commemorative lectures.[151] In April 1908, a series of talks was given in memory of Wagner at the Tenishev School in St Petersburg. Lecturers included Yosif Ashkinazi, a critic from Odessa, who (like Eduard Stark) signed his articles as 'Zigfrid', Evgeny Braudo, who was to contribute much to Russian 'Wagneriana' over the course of his lifetime, and Sergey Bulich, a professor of Sanskrit at Petersburg University, who had visited Bayreuth in 1888.[152] Another lecture was given by A. P. Koptyaev, and was accompanied by Ershov, who sang excerpts from *Tannhäuser*.[153] Several concerts were also given in 1908 to commemorate the anniversary of Wagner's death. Sheremetiev compiled a programme of excerpts from Wagner's works to show the composer at different stages of his career (accompanying the third act of *Parsifal* with pictures shown on a screen), and Arthur Nikisch conducted a concert given by the Imperial Court Orchestra which consisted exclusively of works by Wagner.[154] As Russian interest in Wagner rose steadily, so too did the demand for literature on the composer. Two guides to the *Ring* were published in 1908,[155] and *RMG* noted that Sofya Sviridenko's book had proved so popular it had to be reprinted, which was 'a very rare occurrence'.[156]

Sviridenko is an interesting figure in Russian musical history, for not only was she (as far as can be ascertained) almost the sole woman to write about Wagner in Russia at the beginning of the century, but she was also one of the very first (if not actually the first) female Russian music critics. In 1911, she was awarded the M. A. Shakmatov prize by the Academy of Sciences for the completion of the first full translation of the Edda legends. She was also an avid Wagnerian, and at the age of twenty-six, she became a regular contributor to *RMG*,

writing exclusively on Wagner and Russian Wagner productions. She was an exacting critic and apart from Ershov's
performance, she found very little to commend the Petersburg
production of *Ring*. The crudely designed scenery and 'colourless performances' given by most of the cast combined with
Napravnik's sometimes 'flawless' conducting and Ershov's
masterful interpretations of the Wagnerian roles to create an
overriding impression of 'extreme unevenness', in her opinion.
In *Siegfried*, she wrote, the 'drab scenery and pathetic lighting
effects' contrived to conjure up an 'October day in the narrow
courtyard of a government building' rather than the intended
'blinding summer day'. Another major defect was the
Mariinsky's habit of casting different singers for the same part
for each of the four operas, pointing out that as many as three
different Brünnhildes had sung in one of the subscriptions in
1908. Yet another shortcoming were the gaps of anything up to
seventeen days between each performance, when the tetralogy
was ideally supposed to be performed on consecutive days.
'Probably no one would be surprised if they thought of performing just one act each evening, starting with the third',
Sviridenko fumed ('everything is possible in our country'). In
her view, the bureaucracy was chiefly at fault: 'Everything that
comes from the state "producers" is practically an outright
failure, it is crude, suffused with complete ignorance of artistic
matters and an utter contempt for Wagner ... who only
recently was "hounded and cursed" by the same musical
administrators who have now taken him up on the wishes of the
management.'[157]

Apart from her guide to the *Ring*, Sviridenko published
another, more substantial work on the subject in 1908 in
which, after a detailed discussion of each of the characters in
the tetralogy, she gave full vent to her feelings of indignation
about the Petersburg production.[158] As well as pointing out the
numerous faults in the Russian translations of the librettos, she
railed against the 'excessive' number of cuts in the Russian
production, which led, she believed, to many non-sequiturs in
the text.[159] None of the tetralogy's constituent parts was in fact
performed without cuts except *Das Rheingold*. More than sixty

cuts were made in each of the other parts, leaving only the first act of *Die Walküre* intact: 'It is not the trilogy [*sic*] of *Der Ring des Nibelungen* which has been performed on the Mariinsky stage, but eighty-two excerpts from this trilogy, which somehow belong to each other.'[160]

The Mariinsky Theatre had now staged all but two of Wagner's music dramas, but the atmosphere was very different in Moscow. After seven seasons in which Wagner's operas had constantly been included in the repertoire, three seasons had now passed without a single one of his works being performed.[161] In December 1908, however, *Lohengrin* was revived with new singers in the main parts: Leonid Sobinov and Antonina Nezhdanova. Reporting from Moscow for *RMG*, Yury Engel described the production as an 'important event': 'After several years of determinedly suppressing Wagner, our Imperial Opera has somehow got around to remembering this "really pretty decent" composer. How can we not envy you in St Petersburg being able to listen to *Tristan und Isolde* and *Das Rheingold*? Whatever one's attitude to Wagner, the most important thing is first to know him. And here in Moscow, his music is really very little known.'[162]

The significance of this production of *Lohengrin* lay in Sobinov's innovative interpretation of Lohengrin. Having extensively studied the literary sources for the opera, he had come to the conclusion that the traditional portrayal of the opera's eponymous hero was based on false premises. Instead of presenting Lohengrin as a fearless German warrior, Sobinov decided to portray him as a young Celtic knight, full of knowledge but lacking in faith.[163] Lohengrin became one of Sobinov's most famous roles, and one which he sang until his retirement in 1933.[164] Despite the apparent success of the new *Lohengrin* production, some critics still claimed to perceive a certain resistance to Wagner. 'Let us not close our eyes to the truth', wrote a correspondent for *Novosti sezona*: 'In our country people do not like Wagner very much. Here at the Bolshoi Theatre people listen to Wagner's operas either because they have a subscription [including other operas] or because of some unusual circumstance. People find Wagner boring. I do not mean the select band of cognoscenti and music lovers, but the crowds on whom the box office depends.'[165]

A significant event in the history of Russian productions of Wagner's operas was the first performance of *Die Walküre* in Kiev in February 1909, which was the first Russian-language staging of one of Wagner's music dramas outside Petersburg and Moscow. Lengthy preparations were undertaken for the production, which entailed the theatre's manager, director Nikolay Bogolyubov and conductor travelling to see the work in Munich the preceding year.[166] According to *RMG*'s correspondent, 'all Kiev' came to the first night (including 'people indifferent to art'), and 'it was immediately noticeable that people had come to see an exceptionally interesting performance, not just something run-of-the-mill'. The production had its detractors, with one member of the audience calling the Valkyries' war cry 'jackdaw squawking', for example, but such 'archaeological specimens' were fortunately few in number, and the performance was judged 'remarkably good' on the whole.[167]

MEYERHOLD'S PRODUCTION OF *TRISTAN UND ISOLDE*

The 1909–10 season was memorable for two Wagner productions: the first Russian production of *Die Meistersinger*, staged by Sergey Zimin's private opera company in Moscow,[168] and a new production of *Tristan und Isolde* at the Mariinsky Theatre, directed by Vsevolod Meyerhold, who had been appointed as a director for the Imperial Theatres in 1908. *Tristan* was given its first performance on 30 October 1909, and like *Die Meistersinger*, was sung in a new translation by Viktor Kolomiitsov.[169] Meyerhold's production of *Tristan* not only ranks as one of the most intereseting Russian Wagner productions (it was certainly the most radical pre-revolutionary production), but also as one of the most interesting of all Wagner stagings. It was the first time that an avant-garde director was given free rein in the Imperial Opera (in fact the first time a director was given any rein there at all), and it was also Meyerhold's first operatic production. Telyakovsky, indeed, could have appointed no more radical a director to enliven the staid, traditionalist atmosphere of the Imperial Theatres, for Meyerhold's seemingly unquenchable zest for experimentation and his mercurial nature had already won him notoriety.

Meyerhold's first production for the Imperial Theatres – Hamsun's *At the Gates of the Kingdom* – was first performed on 30 September 1908, which gave him a whole year to prepare for *Tristan*, his next project. It should be pointed out straightaway that Meyerhold did not come to this production unprepared, and this was not only because he had already staged two extracts from the work in Finland in July 1907.[170] As L. Arnshtam has pointed out, music was Meyerhold's 'element, his passion'.[171] This love of music had begun in childhood, and Wagner became a serious interest for Meyerhold when he was eighteen.[172] He was an enthusiastic violinist, and even toyed with taking music up as a career at one point,[173] but instead made music an indispensable part of his theatrical productions. Boris Pokrovsky has attested that 'theatre and music existed for him indivisibly, whether he was staging Tchaikovsky, Verhaeren or Ostrovsky. The musicality of his direction was astonishing ... He did not subsitute music for theatre, he turned theatre into music.'[174] Music became for Meyerhold an important instrument with which to tackle the problem of Symbolist theatre, and introduce the abstractionist approach demanded by the new mystical dramas by writers such as Maeterlinck. In 1904, he had told Chekhov that his play *The Cherry Orchard* was 'abstract, like a Tchaikovsky symphony'. Instead of the overblown naturalism favoured by his erstwhile teacher Stanislavsky, Meyerhold envisaged, as Edward Braun has noted, 'a production in which music and movement would be used not simply as components of a life-like scene, but as the means of pointing theatrically what is truly significant in the action, the sub-text, the unspoken dialogue of emotions'.[175] It is when Braun mentions Meyerhold's interest in conveying the 'unspoken dialogue of emotions' that we can immediately see why Wagner came to play such a prominent role in the development of his theatrical technique. Even before he came to work on *Tristan und Isolde*, Meyerhold was already trying to apply Wagner's methods of transmitting 'inner dialogue' through the orchestral score to the dramatic stage, by using the actor's physical movements. In an important essay in the collection *Theatre. A Book About the New Theatre* (*Teatr. Kniga o novom teatre*) published in 1908, Meyerhold explained that the new means of expressing the 'ineffable, of revealing that which is concealed' had been required for his first 'stylised' production (Maeterlinck's *Death of Tintagiles*) at the Theatre Studio in 1905:

Like the singer's phrase in the 'Musikdrama', the actor's word in the drama is an insufficiently powerful means of conveying inner dialogue ... Just as Wagner employs the orchestra to convey spiritual emotions, I employ *plastic* movement ... The difference between the old theatre and the new is that in the new theatre speech and plasticity are each subordinated to their own separate rhythms and the two do not necessarily coincide.[176]

It is not surprising that Meyerhold's article was published alongside those by Symbolist writers such as Sologub, Chulkov, Bryusov and Bely who had no direct involvement in the theatre. All the Russian Symbolists became intensely preoccupied with the problem of the 'crisis' in Russian theatre in one form or another from approximately 1905 onwards, and Meyerhold's desire to 'penetrate behind the mask', inspired by the abstractions of the 'new' dramas, brought him naturally into contact with their ideas. The Symbolists intuitively perceived the watershed that drama had come to, and started theorising endlessly on the dimensions of an ideal theatre of the future which would also be socially cohesive.[177] Wagner was naturally a prominent figure, both as one of the first artists to attempt to convey ideas through consciously symbolical means and also as a promoter of a people's theatre which would unite actor and public. Meyerhold was on particularly close terms with Vyacheslav Ivanov, who had since 1904 been preaching the idea (inspired by Wagner and Nietzsche's *The Birth of Tragedy*) that music should become the 'Dionysian' substratum of theatre (from which the 'Apollonian' dream could arise). Meyerhold's debt to Ivanov becomes apparent in the fifth part of his article ('Stylized Theatre'), where he writes, for example: 'But thanks to such dramatists as Ibsen, Maeterlinck, Verhaeren and Wagner, the theatre is moving back towards its dynamic origins. We are discovering the precepts of antiquity. Just as the sacred ritual of Greek tragedy was a form of Dionysian catharsis, so today we demand of the artist that he heal and purify us.'[178] It is not unreasonable to suggest that it was Ivanov who initially inspired Meyerhold to take the form of the Wagnerian music drama as his dramatic model for stylised theatre, as Meyerhold certainly came to consult with Ivanov on his *Tristan* production in 1909, as will be discussed in the following chapter. Meyerhold, then, approached *Tristan und Isolde* with the utmost seriousness. After immersing himself in Wagner's essays and correspondence, Gottfried von Strassburg's version of the legend, critical and biographical works on Wagner (by Glasenapp, Mendes, Lichtenberger and Chamberlain, for example), works on *Tristan und Isolde* (by Koptyaev, Golther, Müller, Fritz Koegel, von Wolzogen, M. Kufferath, Heinrich Porges and Karl Grunsky), and the writings of Schopenhauer, Nietzsche, Nordau, Rolland, Schiller, Schlegel, Lessing, Craig, Adolphe Appia (*Die Musik und die Inszenierung*) and Georg Fuchs (*Revolution des Theaters*), to name just some of the authors he consulted,[179] he produced a substantial article outlining his approach to *Tristan*,[180] although as A. L. Porfirieva wrily remarks, 'the impression forms that he was planning to write an epoch-making aesthetic study of Wagner's work at the very least'.[181] Meyerhold made seventy-one (largely unpublished) pages of notes on Wagner's theories alone.[182]

Meyerhold's article in essence represents a logical continuation of the ideas expressed in his article for *A Book About the New Theatre*, now applied to the operatic medium.[183] Inspired by the writings of Appia, Fuchs, the Symbolists, and by Japanese theatrical technique,[184] but mostly by Wagner himself (it should also be stressed that Appia, Fuchs and the Symbolists were themselves, to a greater or lesser extent, influenced by Wagner), Meyerhold advocated that the production of *Tristan und Isolde* should be determined by its musical score. As Anna

7. Ivan Ershov as Tristan (Mariinsky Theatre, 1909).

Porfirieva has shown, Wagner's discussion of the function of music in his music dramas had a decisive influence here, for Meyerhold returns to this question again and again in his notes: 'Music really was the foundation from which "arise the images, the action and the drama". Thus Wagner's concept unexpectedly received its realisation in the new Russian theatre, the first phase of which was Meyerhold's production of *Tristan*.'[185] A naturalistic production would not be appropriate, he argued, because the actors have to *sing*. Although his goal was realism (Wagner, Chaliapin, Borodin and Musorgsky represented 'realism without veering into naturalism' in his eyes),[186] Meyerhold believed that only a stylised production could remedy the absurdity of actors singing. His idea was that the actors should reveal the 'world of the soul' depicted in the score by specific physical movements and gestures dictated by the principle of rhythm. The foundation of these movements Meyerhold sought in mime and dance (for its rhythmic 'flexibility of expression'). By dance, Meyerhold followed Appia's interpretation: 'I do not mean those light parlour entertainments of what passes for dance in the opera, but the *rhythmic* life of the human body in its whole scope. Dance is to the body what pure music is to our feelings: an imaginative, non-rational form.'[187] But, as his own notes and also the notes he made from Wagner's writings reveal,[188] he was also following Wagner himself, who wrote, for example, in *The Art-work of the Future*: 'By means of Rhythm does Dance become an art ... Rhythm is the natural, unbreakable bond of union between the arts of Dance and Tone ... If Rhythm ... is the very Mind of Dance ... so is it, on the other hand, the moving, self-progressive Skeleton of Tone.'[189] That Meyerhold was directly inspired by Wagner is made clear by his statement that Wagner was right to claim that 'the plastic movement of the body, represented by musical rhythm, serves as the basis of all true art'.[190] In his notes, Meyerhold writes that 'dance enables the spectator to grasp the rhythm of the performance in the broad sense of the word. Of course, not in the dance class, where one learns the pas-de-quatre, but in *pantomime*.'[191] Meyerhold takes issue with Wagner's criticism of pantomime in his notes, claiming that only pantomime can make the actor 'comprehend the strength of rhythm'.[192]

What finally resulted in the production were almost statuesque poses and sculpted groupings (each of which was designed to convey a whole musical phrase)[193] that Meyerhold drew from Wagner's conception of the stage as a 'pedestal for sculpture'.[194] He achieved this by rather mechanical means, according to Lidiya Ivanova's recollections:

> He complained about the singers' usual gestures and did an imitation of them which was killingly funny. He boasted of his idea. He ordered sets to be made that were so complicated, unwieldy and dangerous for the slightest move that the unfortunate singers had to stand motionless like pedestals for fear of breaking a leg. The actors were very angry about this, but the producer rubbed his hands with delight, for he had achieved the production he wanted.[195]

Meyerhold's synthetic conception also extended to the scenic realisation of his production of *Tristan und Isolde*. Despite arguing against the setting of Wagner's music dramas in particular historical periods, Meyerhold nevertheless set *Tristan und Isolde* in the medieval France of Gottfried von Strassburg, which he claimed corresponded to the 'medieval colouring' in Wagner's music. Aleksandr Shervashidze's costume designs were based on a stylised adaptation of the miniatures of Strassburg's contemporaries. Also because of the highly illustrative nature of Wagner's music, Meyerhold felt it unecessary to adhere to Wagner's stage remarks. In the first act, the stage was dominated by a vast red and white checkered sail, which was part of Meyerhold's attempt to achieve stylisation through the economy of gesture (it was left to the powers of the audience's imagination to evoke the rest of the ship). Similarly, in the second act, there was nothing but a stone wall and gate, silhouettes of leafless trees and a few boulders, and it was left to the powers of the orchestra to summon up the garden and bank of flowers demanded in the libretto, as 'the mere contemplation of foliage on the stage would be as flagrantly tasteless as illustrating Edgar Allen Poe. In the second act, our designer depicts a huge towering castle wall, and in front of it . . . there burns the mystical torch which plays such an important part in the drama.'[196] Meyerhold was also trying to implement Fuchs' ideas for a relief stage to overcome the limitations of the Renaissance stage, by placing the actors at the front of the stage amongst 'practicable reliefs' against a painted backdrop. In his attempt to make theatre three-dimensional, he was also concerned to break up the flat surface of the stage (which can be seen most visibly in the scenery for the third act of the production).

Meyerhold's production of *Tristan und Isolde* was predictably highly controversial, for what direction there had been in Russian operatic productions prior to Meyerhold's debut had concentrated on the vocal interpretation of roles – the purely formal side of performance had hitherto been ignored. As Porfirieva has noted, there were three main complaints from critics: firstly, that Meyerhold had ignored Wagner's remarks; secondly, that his choice of historical setting was arbitrary and thirdly, that the static acting did not correspond to the passion of the music.[197] *RMG*, for example, which had hitherto criticised Wagner productions at the Mariinsky for being obsolescent and staid, now found everything too avant-garde. In its view, Meyerhold and Shervashidze had committed an act of gross irreverence before Wagner and had turned *Tristan und Isolde* into a 'strange and ridiculous spectacle' where 'artificiality' and 'affectation' had replaced the simplicity Wagner had supposedly desired.[198] The renowned Bayreuth conductor Felix Mottl came to conduct *Tristan und Isolde* in January 1910, which gave *RMG* the excuse to direct another torrent of abuse against 'the scenic outrage' and 'desecration' of Meyerhold's production,[199] yet Mottl apparently found it the most impressive he had yet seen.[200] Meyerhold took all the criticism he received in a serious vein, particularly that of Benois,[201] whom he took the trouble to reply to, setting out his reasons for his artistic decisions in great detail.[202]

The production of *Tristan und Isolde* was a very significant one for Meyerhold, as it furnished some of the essential principles of the theatrical method that he would continue to develop and refine for the rest of his career. Wagner had revealed the vital importance of rhythm, and as Edward Braun

8. Aleksandr Shervashidze, costume design for Meyerhold's production of
    Tristan und Isolde (Mariinsky Theatre, 1909).

has said, 'there was no production by Meyerhold which did not reaffirm his conception of rhythm as the basis of all dramatic expression'.[203] Wagner's specific use of music as the 'language of the soul' also had a lasting influence. In his famous production of *The Government Inspector* in 1926, Meyerhold again used music as a means of achieving his constant goal of theatrical synthesis – in which all elements of performance (from the actor down to the scenery) were subordinated to the director's single conception.[204] Paul Schmidt is correct to point to Wagner when describing Meyerhold's production of *Woe from Wit* in 1928, in which music was no longer 'an accompaniment, no longer simply mood music, melodramatic background' but an 'integral part of the drama' where 'emotion and action are both expressed by music',[205] for we can trace the roots of this 'innovation' to his experiments with *Tristan und Isolde* in 1909. Meyerhold himself confirmed Wagner's importance to him as a theorist at the very end of his life: 'I've read all of Wagner in German. People know him as a composer and as the author of librettos, but he also wrote ten volumes full of the most interesting articles. I've studied them all. If you go and find the pages I've covered with notes, you will immediately understand what has interested me.'[206]

FROM WAGNERISM TO *WAGNEROVSHCHINA*

The lack of interest in Wagner shown by the Bolshoi Theatre persisted while Meyerhold was shocking the Petersburg musical world, but excerpts from his works were frequently performed at concerts during the 1909–10 season. Wagner was now the Philharmonic Society's most frequently performed composer in fact, and eight excerpts from his operas were performed at the nine concerts in the season, one of which was wholly given over to Wagner. Together with Beethoven, Wagner was the most popular composer during the first season of the concert series founded by Sergey Kussevitsky in 1909, and another whole concert was devoted to Wagner during the 1909–10 'historical concerts' season organised by the composer Sergey Vasilenko, who was a passionate Wagnerian. The third

act of *Tristan und Isolde* was also performed for the first time in
Moscow at one of the ten RMS concerts held that season.[207]
Wagnerism was now a growing fashion which had inspired its
own literature in Russian, and the bibliography section in
RMG in February 1910 was devoted to the ever-expanding
Russian 'Wagneriana'. The books reviewed included guides to
Tristan und Isolde, which had been written to coincide with the
opera's recent revival,[208] Kolomiitsov's translation of the esoteric dramatist Edouard Schuré's study of *Tristan*,[209] and the
collected articles César Cui had written about the *Ring* in 1876.
The latter was appended as a humorous item, and *RMG*
observed that it had little of interest to offer on the tetralogy
and possessed value only 'as a historical document':

Despite all the attempts by our music critics to convince the public of
the dangers, harms and redundancy of Wagnerism, it is putting down
ever stronger roots here. Apart from Serov's apologia forty to fifty
years ago, almost all critics up until the end of the 1890s were
surprisingly unanimous in warning the public against being captivated by Wagnerism ... But in spite of all obstructions, the musical
infection of Wagnerism is affecting more and more of the public. So
none of the inoculations from our musical physicians ... have done
any good! Apart from *Parsifal*, Petersburg has seen all of Wagner's
operas. In Moscow *Tannhäuser* and *Lohengrin* have even been staged
by private opera companies ...[210]

Although the regular artistic chronicle and bibliography sections in *RMG* were always unsigned, it has been assumed that
they were written either by Nikolai Findeizen or his editorial
colleague Evgeny Petrovsky. The above-mentioned review
section was probably written by Findeizen since the passage
cited above bears a strong resemblance to a particular part of
his review of the Russian translation of Schuré's monograph of
Wagner in *Ezhegodnik imperatorskikh teatrov*,[211] which was
written at approximately the same time in 1910:

Twenty years ago at the first performance in St Petersburg of *Der Ring
des Nibelungen*, who could have thought that interest in Wagner would
soon bring forth here a whole literature on the Bayreuth master?
Have not all those tirades, attacks and gibes ... with which Russian
anti-Wagnerians frightened the public and musicians, actually

helped after the death of Serov, the first and most staunch supporter of Wagner's ideas in St Petersburg? The operas and music dramas of the Bayreuth master, staged one after the other at the Mariinsky Theatre, have brought about such a great interest in the life and works of the late Bayreuth reformer that his most difficult and complicated operas are being staged by private companies in Moscow and even by provincial theatres, together with which, the demand for literature about Wagner has begun to grow ever greater.[212]

The expanding Wagner literature did not escape the attention of Mikhail Ivanov. 'What is appearing at the moment on Wagner can hardly be called new literature', he protested with acrimony in *Novoe vremya*; 'What can one now say about him that was not said when he was alive or in the first years after his death? Who has not written and discussed him?'[213] Other studies on Wagner by Russian authors published in 1910 included Mikhail Stanislavsky's book-length investigation of the reception of Wagner's works in Russia.[214]

An unprecedented seven Wagner operas were performed during the 1909–10 season, which made up 25 per cent of the overall repertoire. The *Ring* cycle was performed three times as usual during the Lent season, but now with a different conductor for each of the four operas. The 27-year old Nikolay Malko conducted *Das Rheingold*, Napravnik conducted *Die Walküre*, Albert Coates conducted *Siegfried* and Eduard Krushevsky conducted *Götterdämmerung*.[215] Napravnik's conducting, according to Nikolay Bogolyubov, was always orderly and precise, which reflected his character. The volcanic nature of Albert Coates,[216] however (who had to change his shirt at each interval), contrasted sharply with Napravnik's composure: 'if under Napravnik, Wagner's music radiated the light of an altar to some unknown god, then this same music under Coates, taken at double speed, definitely had something in common with a Bacchic orgy'.[217]

Wagner had indeed become fashionable. *Tannhäuser* was chosen for a gala charity performance on 6 April 1910 at the Mariinsky Theatre which was conducted by Nikisch and featured Vaslav Nijinsky dancing to Mikhail Fokine's choreography.[218] In summing up the 1909–10 season for the *Ezhegodnik imperatorskikh teatrov*, Vyacheslav Karatygin, who wrote a great deal about Wagner during his long career as a critic, concluded that the performances of Wagner really deserved 'their own section':

Wagner in Russia is really a special chapter in the history of Russian musical culture. How many obstacles were raised to stop Wagner's operas becoming established in Russia by our 'kuchkisty': Tchaikovsky [*sic*], Cui, Stasov, Borodin, not to mention minor composers and critics – all were set against Wagner, all cursed his music with foul language, all thought his work confusion and charlatanism … how great must be the energy and pathos of these brilliant works if for a good third of the century their rays had to penetrate Russia from Germany through huge and seemingly insuperable clouds of aesthetic prejudice and antipathy before illumining us at last with their full and joyous light …[219]

The first issue of *RMG* in 1911 opened with a review of musical life in Russia during the past year, in which it claimed to have discerned a change in the public's attitude to music, marked by a 'transition from unconscious musical enjoyment and entertainment to a conscious attitude to art'.[220] This transition was probably not entirely unconnected to the fact that works such as Wagner's music dramas had now largely replaced the most frivolous of French and Italian operas which had hitherto dominated the Russian operatic repertoires. In the fifty-odd years that had passed since the inception of the Russian Musical Society, concert life had considerably expanded, both in Petersburg and Moscow. Many new concert series had sprung up, and new music journals were also beginning to appear. The most important of these was the progressive Moscow weekly *Muzyka*, which began publication in November 1910. Under the editorship of Vladimir Derzhanovsky (who, as we have seen earlier, was a keen Wagnerian) the journal was inevitably favourably disposed towards Wagner, and many articles about the composer were to appear on its pages over the following years. Despite Eduard Stark's optimistic reading of the situation, there was really no escaping the fact that the vogue for Wagner was not dictated by purely musical considerations. 'The audience at the Wagner sub-scriptions was quite special,' Nikolay Bogolyubov wrote: 'It was then considered a sign of *bon ton* (although many were bored) to be a Wagnerite and sit without an interval for an hour and forty minutes as it was with *Götterdämmerung*. Black tie, dinner jackets, ball gowns and the finest fragrance of Paris perfume – these were the external signs by which one could immediately tell without even hearing any music that one was at one of the Wagner performances. It was fashionable!'[221]

The *Ring* was performed as usual during Lent in 1911, and in her annual report on the performances in *RMG*, Sviridenko noted that because of the current 'Wagner fashion', they were now frequented by crowds from the 'musical non-intelligentsia' because *'così fan tutte'*. She also perceived that the Imperial Theatres Directorate was becoming increasingly indifferent to the artistic side of the performances because it was assured such high box office returns.[222] Meanwhile, Russian 'Wagneriana' was augmented in 1911 by the publication of the first two parts of an (ultimately unfinished) critical biography of Wagner by Nikolay Findeizen,[223] the first volume of a Russian translation of the composer's autobiography, edited by the important modernist literary critic Akim Volynsky,[224] a translation by Viktor Kolomiitsov of Wagner's 1870 essay *Beethoven*,[225] and Viktor Valter's substantial study of the composer.[226]

It was in 1911 that 'Wagnerism' finally reached Moscow. The Bolshoi Theatre's activity during the season proceeded largely 'under the sign of Wagner' wrote Yury Engel,[227] who later commented that this was 'particularly significant when one remembers that only three to four years ago Wagner was not performed *at all* during one season'.[228] Indeed, after six seasons in which at most two of Wagner's works were included in the repertoire, there were suddenly six in the 1911–12 season, including Moscow's first production of *Götterdämmerung*. The cancellation of the first performance due to the indispo-sition of two singers caused great commotion, as the journal *Studiya* reported: 'The event of the day, the subject of all conversation and quarrels in the wide musical world of Moscow is the cancellation of *Götterdämmerung*. All Moscow was looking forward to the first performance . . . and was extremely unpleasantly shocked by its being cancelled, just before the première.'[229] Emil Kuper had spent two years rehearsing the orchestra for the production,[230] and when it finally received its first performance, it was favourably reviewed by *RMG*[231] and *Muzyka*,[232] although Oskar Riesemann, writing for *Studiya*, thought the production was flawed by cliché and conventionality. In particular, he criticised Leonida Balanovskaya, who performed the role of Brünnhilde, for singing at the footlights (as if performing a coloratura solo) and for facing the public rather than Siegfried.[233] The sets (designed by Konstantin Korovin) were not popular with any critic. In D. Varapaev's view, they 'did not even justify modest expectations' and were 'limp and completely lacking in originality', and compared poorly with Vrubel's designs for Mamontov's company, for example.[234] The sets designed for productions by private opera companies, it should be noted, were by no means flawless either, however. The Zimin theatre, for example, staged *Tannhäuser* in 1911, and Riesemann claimed that the designs showed 'neither verisimilitude nor fantasy', and thought that the bacchanalia opening the first act resembled 'a family dance at a second-rate club'.[235]

Apart from the new production of *Götterdämmerung*, *Das Rheingold* was also given its first performance at the Bolshoi Theatre during the 1911–12 season. *Siegfried*, which had been removed from the repertoire in 1903, because 'the public were simply too frightened by it',[236] was also revived, but without any degree of success, it would seem.[237] Four cycles of the *Ring*, meanwhile, were performed during the 1911–12 season in Petersburg, one of which took place for the first time in the winter season. The performance was spread over a month, with one part performed on consecutive weeks. There were arguments for and against performing *Der Ring des Nibelungen* in the middle of the usual repertoire. By performing the tetralogy in Lent, in isolation from other operas, *RMG* maintained that at least a vague suggestion of the atmosphere of the Bayreuth Festival was preserved. Both artists and audience were usually tired at the end of the long operatic season, however, and there was 'definitely more life' in the winter performance of *Die Walküre*, according to *RMG*, which now placed the opera in a position of equal popularity with the wildly successful *Carmen*.[238] Another innovation during the 1911–12 season was the restoration of many cuts, which had the result of making *Die Walküre* a whole half-hour longer. 'The winning back of more than ten pages of beautiful music from "non-existence" – such is the great success of Wagnerism at the Mariinsky Theatre', commented Sviridenko drily.[239] Aleksandr Andreevsky, who devoted a long article to the journal *Studiya* about the *Ring* performances in 1912, was highly critical of the long gaps between performances, which, he claimed, totally contradicted the artistic idea of a work designed to be performed on four consecutive evenings. He also regretted that the work was performed so often, and argued that it would inevitably soon become debased. Andreevsky also found fault with Ilya Tyumenev's translations of the librettos, pointing out several examples in which the stress, through infelicitous translation, fell on the wrong word. The unity of the Russian production was also destroyed, he felt, since different artists had been commissioned to design each part of the tetralogy.[240]

A private opera company had staged the first Russian production of *Die Meistersinger* in Moscow in 1909 and it was a private opera company which staged the opera for the first time in St Petersburg. The 'Theatre of Musical Drama' (the Wagnerian overtone in its title was quite intentional) was founded in December 1912 by Sergey Lapitsky, and *Die Meistersinger* was one of its first productions. The Mariinsky Theatre was planning its own production, and had even acquired a copy of Kolomiitsov's translation. But 'as usual', wrote Kolomiitsov in 1912, 'the matter has dragged on and been postponed from year to year' since artistic life in Petersburg was governed by 'the arbitrariness of blind chance'.[241]

The major event of 1913 was the celebration of the centenary of Wagner's birth. A plethora of articles appeared in magazines and journals, the greatest concentration of which inevitably appeared in *RMG*, which produced a special commemorative issue. Numerous books were also published to

ПАМЯТИ

РИХАРДА ВАГНЕРА

ПО СЛУЧАЮ 100-ЛѢТІЯ ДНЯ РОЖДЕНІЯ И 30-ЛѢТІЯ ДНЯ
КОНЧИНЫ ВЕЛИКАГО ХУДОЖНИКА.

(СЪ 24 ИЛЛЮСТРАЦІЯМИ).

Цѣна этого № 30 коп.

Рихардъ Вагнеръ.—Гравюра Фел. Валлотонъ.

9. Cover of special commemorative issue of *Russkaya muzykal'naya gazeta*
celebrating the 100th anniversary of Wagner's birth (May 1913).

commemorate the event,[242] two of which were issued by Emil
Medtner's Symbolist publishing house Musaget,[243] whose
journal *Trudy i dni* (founded the previous year) included a
'Wagneriana' section contributed to by Medtner, Lev Kobylinsky-Ellis, Marietta Shaginyan and others. To celebrate the
centenary, Nikolay Findeizen also travelled round Russia,
lecturing on Wagner at branches of the RMS in Vilnius,
Ivanovo-Voznesensk,   Samara,   Saratov,   Ekaterinoslav,
Kherson, Poltava and Kharkov.[244] K. Eiges contributed an
article on Wagner's artistic reforms to *Russkaya mysl'*, in which
he commented on the latter's influence in Russia:

If, as far as Germany is concerned, one could say that Wagner is now
at the zenith of his popularity, and that at the moment he stands
almost above any criticism, then here in Russia over the last ten years
his authority has grown slowly but surely with each year that has
gone by. That Wagner's 'music dramas' have noticeably ousted
operas of the usual old-fashioned type in our main theatres and
decisively influenced the works of our operatic composers (Rimsky-
Korsakov and especially Rakhmaninov) is beyond any doubt, and in
most recent years a certain coolness towards Wagner is explained, at
least in Moscow, by another partly analogous enthusiasm in our
society, and that is enthusiasm for the work of Skryabin ... All
further musical development after Wagner will be made under his
influence; hardly any major composer of our time has escaped it.
Suffice it to name Grieg, Rimsky-Korsakov, Rakhmaninov,
Skryabin ...[245]

In his book *Wagner and Russia*, published by Musaget, Sergey
Durylin claimed that Wagner was bound to acquire greatest
popularity in Russia, due to its thirst for religious, myth-based
art.[246] In 1913, Viktor Kolomiitsov also published a study in
which he claimed that Russia was likely to understand and
appreciate Wagnerian art better than any other nation. Kolomiitsov's thesis was that despite Russia's isolation from the rest
of Europe, she had many 'spiritual features' in common with
Germany, namely a similar depth of feeling and 'a tendency
towards pessimistic idealism', which also meant that Tchaikovsky was 'best understood' in Germany.[247] Kolomiitsov's
ideal was the creation of indigenous Russian music dramas,
which would be performed to a darkened auditorium in a

'theatre-temple' built on the Bayreuth model. People would enter it with reverence, he hoped, and leave behind their daily lives to lose themselves in the mysteries of art, where there would be no room for thought of prima donnas and conductors: 'If we, Wagner's Russian adepts, propagandise his music, then it is mainly in the firm hope that Russian artists will one day produce genuine music drama, which we have only had in embryonic form here so far.'[248] Kolomiitsov justifiably saw the Moscow Arts Theatre (founded in 1898) as a definite, albeit indirect, by-product of Bayreuth. Like the *Festspieltheater*, it was austerely decorated, and latecomers were barred so that no attention should be detracted from the performance.

In 1913, the Mariinsky Theatre's sympathies 'for the brilliant Richard I' remained 'at their previous high level',[249] while the demand for the *Ring* subscriptions in Moscow, which was first performed as a complete work at the end of 1913, had now grown to such an extent that mounted policemen and officers had to be called in the following year to preserve order at the box office.[250] All that remained beyond Russia's grasp was *Parsifal*, but when its thirty-year copyright ran out on 31 December 1913 (19 December according to the Julian calendar), it was immediately performed by Aleksandr Sheremetiev's concert society,[251] and accompanied by the publication of no less than five guides and brochures.[252] The initiative for staging *Parsifal* came from the composer and conductor Aleksandr Khessin, who from 1910 had been the artistic director of Sheremetiev's society, and had heard the work during his visits to Bayreuth in 1894 and 1904.[253] While Sheremetiev's considerable financial resources ensured that the production could go ahead, enormous problems lay ahead for both the orchestra and the singers, who for the most part lacked the necessary professional skills and coped 'with difficulty'.[254] By far the greatest problem as far as Khessin was concerned, however, was the task of instilling in Sheremetiev (an 'incorrigible dilettante') the 'character and style for performing Wagner'.[255] Had Litvinne not fallen ill, the first Russian performance of *Parsifal* would have taken place on the day the copyright ran out,[256] but instead took place on 21 December in a private presentation at the Ermitazh theatre (attached to the Winter Palace) before the Imperial family, the diplomatic corps, representatives from the State Duma and senior government officials.[257] It was thus a grand occasion. On the first night, the arrival of the Imperial family was announced by an elderly master of ceremonies in full dress uniform and decorations: 'The endless procession filled the whole gallery. Finally the Imperial couple appeared with the entire Imperial family, then their retinue and invited guests in ceremonial dress, stars, ribbons, decorations, the women *décolletées* in their magnificent apparel.'[258] Two further performances of *Parsifal* were given at the Ermitazh theatre for Military Academy students before the production transferred to the Theatre of Musical Drama.

The last new Wagner production at the Mariinsky before the 1917 Revolution was *Die Meistersinger*, which was finally performed in March 1914, and which *Muzyka* regarded as the only 'interesting' production in the season.[259] In 1914, performances of Wagner's works still made up over a quarter of the Mariinsky Theatre repertoire, and there were naturally some who thought this was excessive, but as Yury Keldysh points out:

Although this criticism of a bias towards Wagner's operas was largely justified, the productions of Wagner's operas were amongst the greatest achievements of the Russian opera at the turn of the century. The outstanding success of many of them are witness to the significant development in operatic performance and to the higher level of the audience's aesthetic standards.[260]

Boris Asafiev, who was to become the Soviet Union's foremost critic and musicologist, claimed that the annual Wagner performances at the Mariinsky (where he worked from 1910) represented the theatre's highest levels of artistic attainment, and were of serious social and educational significance. In the intervals, he wrote, there were 'philosophical and musicological arguments, discussions about the score, criticism and enthusiasm for the performers, conversations between Italophiles and Wagnerites, intellectual fireworks from writers and historians, poets and artists, passion and eagerness from young girls, rejecting contemplation for the world of feelings.'[261]

In the 1914–15 season, the Bolshoi Theatre was planning productions of *Tristan und Isolde*, *Parsifal* and *Die Meistersinger*,[262] while the Zimin Theatre was planning to stage *Lohengrin*, *Parsifal* and *Tannhäuser*,[263] but when Russia entered World War I in August 1914, works by German composers were immediately removed from all repertoires, thus bringing pre-revolutionary Wagnerism in Russia to an abrupt end.

WAGNER AND RUSSIAN MUSIC IN THE PRE-REVOLUTIONARY PERIOD

None of the major Russian composers at the beginning of the twentieth century managed to escape Wagner's influence, even if it was a passing phase for most of them. Despite his claim in 1909 that he was 'much better' than Wagner,[264] for Aleksandr Skryabin, Wagner was 'the only genius for whom he felt not only respect, but who was able to affect him powerfully', according to the critic Leonid Sabaneev, himself a rabid Wagnerian:

Götterdämmerung made a great impression on him,[265] while the *Feuerzauber* [from *Die Walküre*], with its mighty play of light and colour shook him to the roots[266] and made him think even more intensively about his own 'colour symphony'. He greeted the very mystical idea of the Nibelung tetralogy, in which he saw occult meaning and symbolic significance, as one of the nearest approximations of the human spirit to his idea of the Mystery. Wagner limited himself, according to Skryabin; he could not rise above the theatrical plane and therefore his reforms had not essentially reformed anything . . .[267]

Wagner's influence on Skryabin has often been remarked upon;[268] and his outlandish and utopian vision of the 'Mysterium', a synaesthetic and synthetic work combining religion and philosophy, which would transport all participants into a state of ecstasy and transform the universe, indeed represents a logical continuation of some of Wagner's ideas. Wagner was also a common denominator in Skryabin's links with the Symbolists.[269] His theurgic aspirations, together with his interest in Eros and his desire that audiences should become active participants, in particular brought him very naturally into line with Vyacheslav Ivanov, with whom he came into close contact in 1913. Although it is not possible to establish when exactly Skryabin first heard music by Wagner, it may well have been at one of the Wagner sessions that Sergey Taneev held at his home from 1894 onwards. At the time, Taneev was markedly hostile towards Wagner, but after studying the score of *Götterdämmerung* with the Sabaneev brothers, he inadvertently turned Leonid Sabaneev into a Wagnerian, and even surprised himself by finding the work actually rather interesting.[270] Several other Wagner evenings were held subsequently, the first of which was attended by Rakhmaninov, Goldenveizer, Georgy Katuar and Skryabin. The composer Katuar was a *rara avis* at that time: a musician in Moscow (which Sabaneev called an 'amusing province' in terms of the standard of musical life there) who already was a Wagnerian.[271] Rakhmaninov, on the other hand, found it difficult to muster any real enthusiasm for Wagner at this stage. During Taneev's *Tristan und Isolde* soirée, he 'sat in a rocking chair in the corner with the score, from time to time issuing gloomy remarks: "Still another 1,500 pages to go"'.[272] In 1902, however, he visited Bayreuth after being given tickets as a wedding present, and the works he heard there apparently made a 'deep impression' on him. He later acknowledged Wagnerian influence, moreover, in his first piano concerto and in his opera *The Miserly Knight* (*Skupoi rytsar'*).[273] Taneev may have maintained his hostile stance towards Wagner to the end of his days,[274] yet the recent translation and publication of his diaries from 1895–1909, which were written entirely in Esperanto, reveal not only that the composer was a frequent topic of his conversations, but that he was still studying the scores of his music dramas in 1907.[275] In 1903, indeed, he was happy enough to go to Berlin to attend the unveiling of a statue to Wagner in Berlin, as mentioned earlier, and spent most of the week he stayed there trying to acquire tickets for the Wagner performances held at the same time (he even admitted enjoying *Die Meistersinger*).[276]

Several of Stravinsky's early works (his song cycle *The Faun and the Shepherdess* (1906), for example, and his 'Scherzo

Fantastique' (1907–8) reveal his youthful enthusiasm for Wagner,[277] but it had all but disappeared by the time he visited Bayreuth with Diaghilev in 1911.[278] Later he was to condemn Wagner in no uncertain terms: 'So, from music shamelessly considered as a purely sensual delight, we passed without transition to the murky inanities of the Art-Religion, with its heroic hardware, its arsenal of warrior-mysticism and its vocabulary seasoned with an unadulterated religiosity.'[279] Prokofiev admitted that Wagner had a 'huge influence' on him at the end of the first decade of the twentieth century,[280] and Nikolay Myaskovsky, who was to become a close friend, was also attracted to the composer during these years.[281] Other composers who succumbed to Wagnerian influence at the time include Anatoly Drozdov,[282] and Sergey Vasilenko, for whom Wagner was a 'god'.[283] Nikolay Nabokov, however, was infected with the 'scarlet fever of Richard Wagner's music' only in the early 1920s, when studying music in Stuttgart. He had seen one performance of *Die Walküre* in Petersburg in 1914, and surmised that he might have been infected somewhat earlier had the war not put a stop to any further performances, and perhaps also if that particular performance had possessed a little more atmosphere:

I remember only one incident of this armour-laden Teutonic drama; a forty-by-thirty foot cloud painted on a large sheet of metal slowly creaked across the stage. It was cluttered with incredibly fat and incredibly blonde females in winged copper helmets.[284]

CHAPTER 4

Wagner and the Russian Symbolists: Vyacheslav Ivanov

'The Spirit of music seemed to them to be embodied in the work of Wagner, whose direct, almost innate symbolism blossomed in myth, the highest manifestation of the symbol, for myth is symbol realised as action.'[1]

WAGNER IN IVANOV'S LIFE

It is no coincidence that Beethoven, Wagner and Skryabin are the composers whose names stand out most in Ivanov's writings, since Ivanov believed the three composers were 'joined to each other by their common aspirations and by the link of continuity'.[2] Any attempt to discuss Ivanov's interest in Wagner, however, must take account of the important role which music played in his life generally. Although ignorant of technique, Ivanov was 'musical to the highest degree', according to his daughter Lidiya, who believed that the stuff of which her father's soul had been woven 'contained many threads of Beethoven'. Beethoven was the composer Ivanov was 'linked with his whole life from his very youth',[3] and throughout the year following the death of his second wife Lidiya Zinovieva-Annibal, his friend Anna Mintslova would each evening play him a Beethoven sonata on the family piano. Music was in fact constantly heard in the Ivanov home. Not only was Lidiya Zinovieva-Annibal a fine singer, and their daughter a violinist (who later studied composition with Respighi in Rome), but several of Ivanov's close friends were practising musicians who would come and play to him on the piano for hours, or discuss their latest compositions with him. One of the friends who played on the family piano was Skryabin, with whom in 1913 Ivanov began an intense friendship which lasted until the composer's death two years later. Ivanov's interest in Wagner must also be understood in the context of the deep love of German literature, philosophy and music he developed from an early age under the 'completely formative' influence of his mother.[4] Although it is safe to assume that the concert halls and opera houses of Moscow were favourite haunts during his adolescent years,[5] it is unlikely that Ivanov heard much music by Wagner until he left Russia in 1886 to study in Berlin. Here he was free to immerse himself in the culture of the country he was to make his home for the next few years, however, and later commented that at this time he knew 'nothing on earth more pleasurable and richer in spiritual content than German classical music'.[6] Amongst other things, Berlin was a city with a major opera house, and in the years in which he was becoming acquainted with the philosophy of Schopenhauer and Nietzsche (whose *Birth of Tragedy* he read with particular interest in 1891), Ivanov was no doubt also attending performances of Wagner's music dramas for the first time. Although it is not possible to corroborate this supposition with any hard evidence, the references to Wagner in the literary and philosophical essays Ivanov began to publish from 1904 onwards make it clear that he was by that time acquainted with at least the *Ring*, *Die Meistersinger* and *Tristan und Isolde*, and had also perused some of Wagner's early theoretical writings (the first collected edition of which was published in 1887).[7]

When Ivanov eventually returned to Russia in 1905 with Lidiya Zinovieva-Annibal, they inaugurated weekly soirées at their new home in Petersburg, and the famous 'Wednesdays', as they came to be known, immediately became a focus of artistic life in the city. Besides Ivanov himself, many of those who attended his famous *jours-fixes* were Wagner enthusiasts and it therefore comes as no surprise to learn that Wagner was sometimes performed at them. In February 1906, for example, Pyotr Mosolov played piano transcriptions of Wagner's works to an audience which included Blok and his wife and mother (who were all fanatic Wagnerians), Sergey Gorodetsky (who would later translate *Die Meistersinger*), and Evgeny and Alek-sandr Ivanov, who were considered 'exceptional experts and connoisseurs of Wagner'.[8] Like Wagner and the German Romantics before him, Ivanov saw life as ideally indivisible from art, and his 'Wednesdays', with their mixing of artists and musicians, academics and theatre directors, writers and poli-tical theorists, became in their own way a kind of *Gesamtkunst-werk* on the Wagnerian model. In his writings, Wagner had dreamed of resurrecting the spirit of Greek tragedy by bringing together different kinds of people and art forms in an idealistic synthesis, and he thus must have been an appealing figure for a poet for whom a 'constant striving towards integration, towards synthesis' was 'probably the single most important feature' of his thought.[9] Not surprisingly, Wagner featured prominently in a lecture he gave in Baku in 1922 which was specifically devoted to the synthesis of the arts,[10] and it was this same interest in artistic synthesis which attracted him to Skry-abin, and which led him to study the Lithuanian painter-composer Čiurlonis, who had tried to fuse the worlds of art and music in his creative work.[11] Ivanov's interest in synthesis even carried over into life itself, as Nikolay Berdyaev noted: 'Ivanov never exacerbated disagreements, never led sharp quarrels, he always sought the rapprochement and union of different people and different tendencies, loved to work out common platforms ... Ivanov always wanted to transform people's meetings into Platonic symposia, he always referred to Eros. Collective spirituality [*sobornost'*] was his favourite slogan.'[12]

Wagner's music dramas were of course just coming into vogue in Petersburg when Ivanov returned to Russia in 1905, and it seems reasonable to assume that he may have sometimes attended performances of works by the composer whose name was appearing regularly in the essays he wrote at this time, although again there is no hard evidence to prove it. There seems no doubt, however, that Ivanov went to see Meyerhold's radical new production of *Tristan und Isolde*, which would always remain his favourite work by Wagner. Meyerhold spent the summer of 1909 preparing for his production, and on at least one occasion visited Ivanov to talk further about Wagner with his friend.[13] Ivanov retained his interest in Wagner even after the decline of the Symbolist movement in 1910 (despite the somewhat ambivalent feelings of rapture or laughter that his music seemed alternately to arouse in him).[14] After the Revolution, on 17 May 1919, he gave a lecture on Wagner to delegates at conference on extramural education before a performance of *Die Walküre* at the Bolshoi Theatre, shortly after the work was revived there the previous month, and he gave another lecture on the composer in conjunction with a new production of *Lohengrin* in Baku. The strength of Ivanov's affection for Wagner's music is perhaps best gauged from the fact that in August 1924, when he finally emigrated, Ivanov took his family almost straight from the station upon arrival in Berlin to the opera, as he had noticed that *Die Meistersinger* was to be performed that night.[15]

IVANOV'S CONCEPT OF MUSIC

The first reference to Wagner in Ivanov's writings occurs in 1904 in his first published article, 'The Hellenic Religion of the Suffering God' (*Ellinskaya religiya stradayushchego boga*),[16] in which he makes the bold assertion that music is responsible for bringing about a revival of the spirit of Greek tragedy: 'The other arts have not created anything in recent centuries so essentially new, so exclusively ours as music has. Gogol was right to glorify it as our art. But the dithyrambic soul of music is the soul of Dionysian purification. Under its charms we still shudder with the reverberations of ancient orgiastic rites. It prophesies the Dionysian future of our culture ... it is strong enough to return us to a religious comprehension of all things.'[17] Named as the chief harbinger of this new cultural era is Beethoven, whose 9th Symphony has 'finally implemented in spirit the Dionysian dithyramb after so many centuries of oblivion'. Beethoven, according to Ivanov, was not just a creator of sounds, but the founder of a 'new synthesis of life' and 'a new attitude to the world'.[18] Since he was Beethoven's successor in certain important respects (and certainly saw himself as such), it is not surprising that Wagner is also named by Ivanov as a herald of the new Dionysian age approaching: 'Not only did he try to revive ancient tragedy, in a certain harmony of music, poetry and acting, but he also dreamed of the organisation of a future synthetic art, an organisation that would recall the ancient actors' groups, the "craftsmen of Dionysus". He even speaks in his theoretical works about Dionysus and the Dionysian essence of tragedy and alludes to the musical nature of the Dionysian rite.'[19] References to Dionysus may indeed be found occasionally in Wagner's writings,[20] but it should be pointed out that Ivanov rather overplays their significance.

Whilst Ivanov initially talks of music in 'The Hellenic Religion' in relatively concrete terms (that is, by naming composers and specific compositions), it becomes increasingly apparent that he not only regards music as an art form but also as an abstract symbolic concept. In this dual approach to music, Ivanov's position was similar to that of his fellow Symbolists, Aleksandr Blok and Andrey Bely. Music for Bely, Blok and Ivanov had essentially very little to do with the ideal of euphonious verse, as it did for first generation Symbolists like Balmont, for example (who were inspired by Verlaine's dictum 'de la musique avant toute chose'), but everything to do with metaphysics.

Immanent within Ivanov's concept of music are a whole cluster of associations, the most obvious of which (given Ivanov's interest in tragedy, music, the Hellenic spirit and Dionysus) appear to be Nietzschean in origin, and, more specifically, emanate from the philosopher's early work, *The Birth of Tragedy out of the Spirit of Music* (1872). When Ivanov pins his hopes for cultural regeneration on music, for example, inspired by the art of Beethoven and Wagner, he is essentially echoing Nietzsche's claims of the Dionysian spirit being awakened in the music of Beethoven and Wagner in *The Birth of Tragedy*. And when he writes that Beethoven and Wagner are heralds to a new Dionysian age, Ivanov repeats Nietzsche's basic idea in part 19 of that work: 'Out of the Dionysiac recesses of the German soul has sprung a power ... I refer to German music, in its mighty course from Bach to Beethoven, and from Beethoven to Wagner ... Let us now recall how the new German philosophy was nourished from the same sources ... To what does this miraculous union between German philosophy and music point if not to a new mode of existence ...?'[21] It is important to remember, however, that what Nietzsche implied with his 'spirit' of music was hardly his own invention. His argument that tragedy arose out of the spirit of music was highly coloured by his contact with the ideas of Schopenhauer and Wagner, an issue which needs clarifying.

As with his preoccupation with Greece and ancient tragedy, it is important to recognise that Nietzsche's worship of music fitted into a tradition. Music assumes a central importance in *The Birth of Tragedy*,[22] but Nietzsche was not the first to exalt its powers. Music had gained ascendancy as the supreme art form for the early German Romantics. Wackenroder was probably the first to seek to penetrate its mysteries and praise it as 'the ultimate revelatory experience'.[23] The glorification of music was subsequently emulated by Hoffmann, Tieck, Novalis and others, but reached its apotheosis in Schopenhauer's theory that music possessed the best means of expressing the irrational essence of being. Within Schopenhauer's pessimistic philosophy, set forth in *The World as Will and Representation* (1819), art occupied a position of fundamental importance. Schopenhauer argued that art provided the sole means for redemption and transcendance (other than total renunciation to achieve a state of nirvana) from an existence of ceaseless striving dictated by the cosmic forces of being, which he called the 'will'. Music was supreme amongst the arts, according to Schopenhauer, because it was a direct reflection of this will, or noumenal reality. Music, he argued, was able to penetrate our consciousness without intermediary, referring 'to the most innermost being of the world and of our own self',[24] whereas the other arts were tied to images and reflected phenomena rather than their essence. By natural extension, therefore, music could be interpreted as a means by which to comprehend the world.

Schopenhauer's philosophy of music corroborated Nietzsche's definition of the Apollonian and Dionysian impulses present in all artistic creativity. Whereas Apollo according to Nietzsche represented harmony, stasis, reason, the principle of individuation and the plastic arts, Dionysus symbolised chaos, irrationality, dynamism, oneness, and above all music. The latter are all features closely related to Schopenhauer's 'will' and they are also, moreover, features commonly associated with the music of Wagner (especially his *Tristan und Isolde*), upon whom Schopenhauer's ideas exerted a lasting influence. Nietzsche certainly saw Wagner's music as Dionysian in the early years of their friendship, and he is at pains to point out in *The Birth of Tragedy* that its conception owed much to both Schopenhauer and Wagner:

Among the great thinkers there is only one who has fully realized the immense discrepancy between the plastic Apollonian art and the Dionysiac art of music. Independently of Greek religious symbols, Schopenhauer assigned to music a totally different character and origin from all the other arts, because it does not, like all the others, represent appearance, but the will directly ... Richard Wagner set his seal of approval on this key notion of all this esthetics when he wrote in his book on Beethoven that music obeys esthetic principles quite unlike those governing the visual arts and that the category of beauty is altogether inapplicable to it ... Once I had become aware of this antinomy I felt strongly moved to explore the nature of Greek tragedy, the profoundest manifestation of Hellenic genius.[25]

This statement has important implications for the discussion of Ivanov's concept of music. It has been common to downplay Wagner's role in *The Birth of Tragedy*, but his influence on the work and therefore on Ivanov's concept of music should not be underestimated. Ivanov avows that Beethoven's 9th Symphony has restored the 'Dionysian dithyramb' in spirit, yet Nietzsche barely mentions Beethoven in *The Birth of Tragedy*, still less the 9th Symphony.[26] What references there are to Beethoven undoubtedly occur as a result of the inspiration of Wagner, whose lengthy Schopenhauerian analysis of music under the guise of a panegyric to Beethoven was issued in 1870, before Nietzsche wrote *The Birth of Tragedy*. Because Beethoven had introduced song into the 9th Symphony at its culmination, Wagner regarded this work as the justification and cornerstone of his aesthetics, and Ivanov was perhaps drawing directly

from the ideas expressed in *The Art-work of the Future* (some of
which bear a striking resemblance to certain passages in 'The
Hellenic Religion'), where the composer first elaborates that
idea:

The last symphony of Beethoven is the redemption of Music from out
of her own peculiar element into the realm of *universal* art. It is the
human evangel [*sic*] of the art of the Future. Beyond it no forward
step is possible; for upon it the perfect Art-work of the Future alone
can follow, the *universal Drama* to which Beethoven has forged for us
the key. *Thus has Music of herself fulfilled what neither of the other severed
arts had skill to do.*[27]

It was actually Wagner too, and not Nietzsche, who first
formulated the idea that music was the 'matrix' of drama,[28]
when he wrote in his essay, 'The Name "Musikdrama"', that
music felt 'called to re-assume her ancient dignity, as the very
mother-womb of Drama'.[29] This is an idea which Ivanov
repeats in 'The Hellenic Religion', when he writes that
'perhaps once again genuine tragedy will arise from the matrix
of music; perhaps the resurrected dithyramb will 'prostrate
millions into the dust'[30] as is sung in the only dithyramb of the
new world – the 9th Symphony of Beethoven'.[31] One should
also not forget that if Nietzsche had never met Wagner or
heard his music, *The Birth of Tragedy* would never have been
written. M. S. Silk and J. P. Stern have shown not only that
The Birth of Tragedy 'had a Wagnerian stimulus behind it and
discernible "Wagnerian connection"', but that 'the decision to
write a whole book on the basis of that material was prompted
by Wagner's personal advocacy ... Received opinion, based
unduly on the word of his sister Elizabeth, has it that Nietzsche
began with the idea of a large book on Greek culture which,
under Wagner's influence and against its author's real incli-
nations, was gradually whittled down to a book on Greek
tragedy – and Wagner. Our conclusion, overall, is rather that a
large book on Greece was not a serious possibility for long, if at
all; that the actual book written was, in an important sense,
Wagnerian from the start.'[32] Ivanov would have agreed with
this judgement, for he himself acknowledges in 'The Hellenic

Religion' that *The Birth of Tragedy* flowed from Nietzsche's experiencing the 'complicated mixture' of Schopenhauer's philosophy and Wagner's music.[33] Since Ivanov's interest in Nietzsche focussed almost exclusively on *The Birth of Tragedy*, it would thus seem of some importance to bear in mind this 'complicated mixture', a point that has frequently not been made on the numerous occasions when the question of the philosopher's influence on Ivanov has been raised.[34] Of course one should also remember that both Schopenhauer's theory of music and Wagner's ideal of an all-embracing art form that harked back to Greek tragedy were themselves intimately connected with the ideas of the early nineteenth-century German Romantics. At the root of Ivanov's ideas on myth and music, then, lie basic precepts of German Romanticism, a fact Ivanov was not unaware of to judge from an entry he made in his diary in 1909.[35]

The nuances of Schopenhauer, Wagner and Nietzsche by no means exhaust the symbolic associations within Ivanov's concept of music (he also aligns music with the origins of language and religion and with artistic creativity). In Ivanov's writings after 'The Hellenic Religion', for example, his concept of music acquires another layer of meaning. In his 1904 essay 'Athena's Spear' (*Kop'e Afiny*), he claims that music is 'the only art of the new world about which one can say that the pathos of people's [*vsenarodnyi*] art is still alive amongst us',[36] for it is an art which he believes is communal by its very nature.[37] Music comes to be linked to the key Ivanov concept of *sobornost'*, conveying a sort of collectivism in a spiritual sense and organic unity. The word *sobornost'* has both Russian Orthodox and Slavophile connotations reminiscent of Khomyakov,[38] from whom Ivanov seems to have borrowed the term. Yet there is a connection with Wagner here too. The resemblance between Khomyakov's and Wagner's ideal of freedom in unity and their insistence of the moral superiority of the commune[39] are striking but hardly surprising. The common denominator is again German Romanticism of which both Khomyakov and Wagner were products. Thus even in his Slavophilism, Ivanov was drawing from the same source of German Romanticism.

WAGNER AND RUSSIAN SYMBOLISM

Like the French Symbolists some twenty years earlier, Ivanov's reverence for Wagner partly emanated from a conviction that the composer's use of symbol-like leitmotifs to enrich and deepen the psychological content of his music dramas had laid the foundations of the Symbolist movement. The clarification of Wagner's significance, moroever, he felt was central to the Symbolist debate, as it unfolded on the pages of *Vesy*, the first modernist journal in Russia specifically devoted to the Symbolist cause. Towards the end of 1904, the first year of *Vesy*'s publication, Ivanov wrote to Valery Bryusov, the editor of the journal, to complain that discussion of Wagner had not appeared frequently enough on its pages, arguing that 'the question about Wagner should have been discussed constantly in *Vesy* for it had not been resolved, and was of 'major significance not just to music, but to all art'.[40] And Ivanov had spoken in no uncertain terms about the lofty mission of *Vesy*. In a letter written that October to Bryusov, he had declared that it was time for the Symbolists to define themselves as a movement, maintaining that *Vesy* was 'not just a journal to be read, but an organ of a kind of collective self-affirmation, a kind of living process in Russian (or, if you like, European) consciousness'.[41] What discussion there had been of Wagner in 1904 in fact had been mostly introduced by Ivanov himself in his essays 'Nietzsche and Dionysus' ('*Nitsshe i Dionis*') and 'Athena's Spear'. Although it is an exaggeration to claim that these articles were the first to arouse interest in the theories of Wagner and Nietzsche in Russia,[42] Ivanov was nevertheless the first writer in Russia to tackle the question of Wagner's significance to contemporary art. We should not forget that the first serious literary and philosophical study devoted to analysing Wagner's music and ideas to appear in Russia (a translation of Henri Lichtenberger's monograph) was only published in 1905. Whilst Wagner never openly referred to his leitmotifs as symbols, he nevertheless described them as emanating from the mythic action performed on stage in a way which suggests that this was precisely how he regarded them.[43] In *Opera and Drama*, Wagner defined their chief functions as

instruments of remembrance and premonition,[44] and it was no
doubt the mnemonic qualities of the leitmotif which enhanced
Wagner's appeal for Ivanov. It is hardly necessary to point out
the importance for Ivanov of remembrance, which he defined
as the principle of being, and as 'collective energy'.[45] 'The gift
of memory infused in us' he wrote, 'awakes in us the remembrance of the soul of the world.'[46] For Ivanov, renunciation
and forgetfulness were identifiable with Non-Being, which led
ultimately to moral and spiritual death.[47] This is perhaps why
references to *Parsifal*, Wagner's last work, are hard to find in
Ivanov's work, for its spirit of resignation was utter anathema
to everything he stood for.

The question of Wagner's position with regard to Russian
Symbolism was intimately connected in Ivanov's eyes with the
question of his being a Dionysian artist, which he had first
broached in 'The Hellenic Religion'. In his essay 'Nietzsche
and Dionysus', published in *Vesy* in 1904, he reiterated this
view by arguing that Nietzsche's attraction to Wagner was
inevitable, since the composer was an artist 'dedicated to the
service of the Muses and Dionysus'.[48] In 'Letter from Bayreuth', a reply to that article, however, a certain Max Hochschüler[49] forced Ivanov to reconsider whether Wagner really
was as Dionysian as he made him out to be. The Dionysian
elements in Wagner's work unconsciously displayed 'clear
features of symbolism', in Hochschüler's view, which meant
that Wagner represented the 'transition from Romanticism to
Symbolism',[50] but it was his belief that there was nothing
'purely Dionysian' in Wagner.[51] Arguing that Wagner's aim
was to 'preach moral ideas' rather than to 'serve Dionysus with
musical orgies', Hochschüler declared that one of Wagner's
greatest mistakes in the *Ring* had been to confuse symbol with
allegory. The *Ring* was partly Dionysian, he conceded, but
Brünnhilde's dialogue with Wotan in the second act of *Die
Walküre* introduced the first 'Apollonian' element in the work.
Parsifal, on the other hand, was completely Apollonian, Hochschüler alleged, because symbols had now been replaced by
allegory, and 'the sharp, dark dissonances' by 'bright, pure
harmony'.[52]

Wagner's great achievement, Hochschüler believed, was to

have constructed his music dramas by using leitmotifs, many of which were genuine symbols.[53] Yet whilst the purpose of the leitmotif was to act as a symbol, Hochschüler argued, Wagner had not drawn a sufficiently sharp and clear line between textual illustration based on description, and dramatisation based on leitmotifs. Only leitmotifs, in his view, which were 'fathomlessly deep' and 'endless in meaning', could penetrate the essence of phenomena and thus become symbols.[54] During his moments of greatest inspiration, 'moments of Dionysian ecstasy and orgy', Hochschüler maintained, Wagner had created symbolic leitmotifs 'of genius', but his music vacillated between 'flashes of genuine Dionysianism' (when he tore the veil of appearances from a phenomenon and penetrated its essence) and 'refined, crystalline, calm Apollonian clarity' which had nothing to do with intoxication, and never delved beyond the appearance of things.[55] In the final part of his article, Hochschüler argued that both Wagner and Nietzsche had turned in the direction of Apollonianism. Nietzsche's tragedy did not lie, as Ivanov had maintained, in the fact that he 'understood the Dionysian principle aesthetically and life as an aesthetic phenomenon'.[56] Hochschüler claimed that Nietzsche had in fact yearned to 're-experience the Dionysian principle as a life principle and dreamed of achieving this in Bayreuth where he thought he would experience genuine mysteries'.[57] But instead of realising that Wagner's music dramas were not wholly Dionysian (which meant that they ultimately remained 'spectacles') Hochschüler argued, Nietzsche had concluded that it was not enough to be Dionysian and had consequently turned 'to the other god'. He concluded that it was Wagner, not Nietzsche, who had understood the Dionysian principle aesthetically.

Ivanov found Hochschüler's article very stimulating, and in a letter to Bryusov soon after it appeared, wrote to concede that Wagner was not a wholly Dionysian artist. He was not prepared to back down completely, however:

It is an extremely good article. He ascribes to me more than I said, so he is polemicising with points I am in agreement with. Of course

Wagner is not a pure Dionysian. But that his 'art was dedicated to serving the Muses and Dionysus' is quite true: his *merit* lies in the fact that he was the first artist to talk about Dionysus in theoretical articles. I'm glad that Shick [*sic*] has applied the method of my article on Nietzsche to Wagner. That means it is effective. The remark on the leitmotif being a symbol is important. My friend Ostroga, a professor at the conservatoire here[58] and a composer, wants to write more about Wagner's leitmotifs: it is necessary to differentiate between the symbols and non-symbols amongst them; apart from that, there is much which is taken for a leitmotif that is determined by purely thematic development . . .[59]

After Ostroga had written his article, Ivanov wrote to Bryusov again about the question of the split between Dionysos and Apollo in Wagner:

Ostroga, about whom I've written to you, has brought me the first part of his observations – *substantielles et approfondies* – on the subject of Hochschüler's 'Letter from Bayreuth' . . . and is writing the second part. He is contending in the first part the possibility of establishing the evolution from Dionysus to Apollo in Wagner, proving that in the *Ring* he is already non-Dionysian. In the second part comes his musical interpretation of the leitmotifs. It would seem that this polemic is significant to understanding Wagner's role. Ostroga writes in French. I don't think that this would be an obstacle to publishing his work. But if you want I will translate it here. Write straight away to tell me about this. The article concerned with Hochschüler's theses evidently should not lag behind the theses themselves . . .[60]

On 22 November 1904, Ivanov wrote to Bryusov once more on the Wagner question. This time it was to inform him that he too had decided to enter the discussion:

I wanted to write a small postscript to the article by Ostroga sent to you about leitmotifs . . . which is painstakingly written and able, in my opinion, to assist the explanation of the important questions raised by Shick [*sic*] by virtue of its polemics and technical corrections. But my piece, in view of its contents and form has turned out to be something for the main section of the journal. And the brevity of the article seems to be its advantage from the point of view of form . . . As you can see, *je plaide ma cause* as well in the capacity of author of choral tragedies, which only achieve their full effect, as I see it, when enveloped by musical symphony.[61]

Ostroga's article never appeared, but 'Wagner and the Diony-sian Rite' (*Vagner i Dionisovo deistvo*), Ivanov's supposed 'post-script', appeared in *Vesy* in February 1905. Originally the article was also to have the heading 'To the author of the "Letter from Bayreuth"' but Ivanov subsequently asked Bryusov to remove it as he felt his article was addressed equally to Andrey Bely, for example, his 'fellow supporter of the mystery'.[62]

IVANOV'S ART OF THE FUTURE

Wagner was not only important to Ivanov as a precursor of the Symbolists. As an artist who believed that myth was the 'highest power thinkable' for the poet,[63] he also pointed the way to the future, for Ivanov saw the symbol as the germ of myth, and likened their relationship to that between acorn and oak.[64] 'True symbolism must reconcile the Poet and the Crowd in a great people's art', Ivanov wrote in his 1904 essay 'The Poet and the Rabble' (*Poet i chern'*); 'the era of alienation is passing. We are proceeding along the path of the symbol to myth. Great art is mythopoeic art.'[65] And it was with Wagner's work, Ivanov believed, that 'the restoration of primordial myth as one of the determining factors of national conscious-ness' had begun.[66] Ivanov believed that in ancient times each myth had contained a certain truth which both poet and people had access to, since they were one, an opinion voiced by Wagner in *The Art-work of the Future* where he declared that the 'public art of the Greeks, which reached its zenith in their Tragedy, was the expression of the deepest and the noblest principles of the peoples' consciousness'.[67] When the poet and the people became alienated from each other, however, Ivanov believed that myth had been forgotten by the people, and only fragments of it remained as incomprehensible symbols in the poet's consciousness. He was convinced that these symbols, which he defined as 'metaphysical truths', would contribute to the new mythopoeia. Like Wagner, who sought in myth 'to reveal in images the most profound insights into the meaning of life and the riddle of being',[68] Ivanov wished to use myth to re-enact the Dionysian truths of death, resurrection and rebirth. Both placed great importance on the creation of new myths. Wagner created the *Ring*, which was his own re-working of the German legends, while Ivanov attempted literally to revive ancient tragedy by re-working Greek myths. Wagner's music dramas certainly must have been in Ivanov's mind as a model, however, for as Anna Porfirieva has shown, his first drama *Tantalus* (*Tantal*), completed in 1904, bears unmistakable traces of their influence. Not only does the play's central scene of sacrifice appear to shadow the ending of *Das Rheingold* by featuring a rainbow stretching up towards the gods (echoing the rainbow Wotan and Fricka mount to reach their newly built home in Valhalla), but Adrastiya's question-ing of her oracle calls to mind Wotan's scenes with Erda in the third act of *Siegfried*, and the scene where Tantalus dreams he has drunk from the cup of ambrosia is reminiscent of the final scene in *Tristan und Isolde*.[69] It was after completing *Tantalus* in 1904 that Ivanov began to set out his theory for an ideal communal art which was to provide the solution to the prob-lems of social alienation, and Wagner was his chief model, as his close friend Olga Deschartes has confirmed:

Immediately after finishing the tragedy (in 1904), V. I. asked himself whether and how it was possible to overcome individualism and 'cellularity' [*tsellyulyarnost'*] in art and life. With three articles (written respectively in 1904, 1905 and 1906[70] and appearing in the periodical press at that time) he answered: yes, it is possible; it is possible through 'restoring the chorus in all its ancient rights'.[71] And V.I. had already identified the 'founder' of this restoration and named him: Wagner ...[72]

Ivanov's conclusions in 'The Hellenic Religion' had been that tragedy had a religious and collective foundation and that intimate art should be transformed into an ideal synthetic art through mysticism. In his subsequent essays, he put forward a utopian, and very Wagnerian, vision of a drama that would be a distillation of myth and music and a synthesis of art forms, which would also unite the poet with the people.

It was in 'Wagner and the Dionysian Rite' that Ivanov first began to theorise on his ideal art of the future. While he never specifically refers to any of Wagner's writings on the theatre, his acknowledgement that Wagner had been the first to advocate a 'synthetic' work of art in his writings confirms that he was at least partially acquainted with them. Convinced still of Wagner's Dionysian inspiration, he writes: 'Wagner the theoretician could already perceive the Dionysian element of the Tragedy he was reviving and already called Dionysus by name. Artists' communes, sharers in one common "synthetic" work-Action, were in his mind, truly communes of "Dionysian craftsmen". The world-enveloping idea of his life and his great daring were indeed inspired by Dionysus.'[73] Perhaps Ivanov had in mind *The Art-work of the Future*, where Wagner does indeed discuss the idea of artistic communes:

Artistic man can only fully content himself by uniting every branch of Art into the *common* Art-work ... the purpose of each separate branch of art can only be fully attained by the reciprocal agreement ... of all the branches in their common message ... The Art-work of the Future is an associate work, and only an associate demand can call it forth. This demand ... is practically conceivable only in *the fellowship of every artist* ... The *free Artistic Fellowship* is therefore the foundation, and the first condition, of the Art-work itself.[74]

Both Ivanov and Wagner looked to ancient Greek tragedy as an ideal art form, and both emphasised the necessarily religious nature of true art.[75] Ivanov recognised Wagner's aspirations, but was not satisfied with the idea of the *Festspiele*, which took place in a purpose-built temple to art, such as Bayreuth. 'He was already gathering people to the festival and mystic rite', writes Ivanov, but they were still only 'festive holy spectacles, and not the mystical choral dance [the *khorovod*]'.[76] With the foundation of the mystical *khorovod*, he declared, the chorus would once again play a leading role, as it had done in ancient tragedy. In *Opera and Drama*, Wagner had explained that by bequeathing 'its emotional significance for the drama in the modern orchestra alone', the chorus of Greek tragedy would be able to evolve 'to an immeasurable wealth of utterance'.[77] Its 'individual human semblance', meanwhile, was to be 'lifted from the *orkhestra* and placed upon the stage, there to unfold the germ of human individuality indwelling in the Greek chorus to the topmost flower of self-dependence as the immediate doer or sufferer in the drama itself'.[78] For Ivanov, Wagner's orchestra was the Dionysian element of his music dramas – it was a sacred 'chorus' which enabled the 'assembled crowd' to 'mystically become one' with its elemental voice.[79] But it was not enough for him that the 'gathered crowd' assembled, in his view, to 'create' and not just to 'contemplate', for although the audience became 'ideal molecules of the orgiastic life of the orchestra', they were nevertheless still an audience, whose participation was latent and not active. Wagner's Dionysian chorus was only 'primordial chaos'.[80] For Ivanov's future 'Mystery', which would transform the crowds 'into genuine participants of the Rite, into the living Dionysian body',[81] the 'dithyrambic chorus' had to be 'freed and revived in all its ancient rights'.[82]

While Ivanov approved of Wagner building a special theatre for the performance of his music dramas, he remained critical of the fact that in the middle of the amphitheatre seating (deliberately constructed in the Greek style) Wagner had not left space for the *orkhestra*, the place in front of the stage where the chorus traditionally danced in Greek drama. It was not enough for him that Wagner had made his Bayreuth orchestra 'invisible' in an attempt to break down the barrier between the performers and the audience; the bridge had still not been 'thrown across the cavity of the invisible orchestra from the kingdom of Apollonian dreams into the realm of Dionysus: to the *orkhestra* which belongs to the collective community'.[83] In Ivanov's art of the future, the *orkhestra* would be physically joined to the stage, and there would be two choruses: one directly linked to the dramatic action and another larger chorus of participants, which he called in populist fashion the 'commune' [*obshchina*].[84] Although Ivanov stresses that the coming 'Mystery' would be 'deepened and enrichened by means of the Symphony', it is not surprising that, as a poet, he was adamant that speech should prevail over song. Ivanov wanted the protagonists of this Dionysian art form to speak

rather than sing, and visualised his 'tragic actor' speaking forth
from the 'womb of instrumental music'.[85] His conclusion in
'Wagner and the Dionysian Rite', then, was that 'the struggle
for the democratic ideal of the synthetic Rite' was 'the
struggle for the *orkhestra* and for the collective word'.[86]

In his essays following 'Wagner and the Dionysian Rite',
Ivanov continued to formulate his definition of the coming
'Mystery', most notably in 'Presentiments and Portents' (*'Predchustviya i predvestiya'*), published in 1906. Here Ivanov predicted that the 'critical' period he and his contemporaries lived
in would soon be replaced by an 'organic' one marked by the
'dynamic' art of music. The appearance of the Russian novelists, Nietzsche and Wagner gave him cause to believe that there
would be a general gravitation towards the 'reintegration of
cultural energies'. A new, people's art would supersede 'intimate' art.[87] Ivanov defines his ideal people's art as drama
combined with music, because, as he puts it, music alone 'does
not have the strength to solve the problem of synthetic theatre':
'the drama is in fact drawn to music, because only with music's
aid is it able to express its dynamic nature and Dionysian
character to the full'.[88] Although Wagner later abandoned his
earlier ideals in favour of the pre-eminence of music, in *Opera
and Drama* he had advocated an art based on the equal participation of music and drama:

I have made it the goal of this book to prove that by the collaboration
of precisely *our* Music with dramatic Poetry a heretofore undreamt
significance not only can, but *must* be given to Drama[89] ... If Poet
and Musician ... mutually go under in the offering that each brings
each the offering of his very highest potence, then the Drama in its
highest plenitude will be born ...[90]

Throughout *Opera and Drama* in fact, Wagner repeatedly
stresses the importance of poetry in its union with music to
create the ideal synthesis: 'But [Beethoven's] most decisive
message, at last given us by the master in his *magnum opus*, is the
necessity he felt as a *Musician* to throw himself into the arms of
the Poet, in order to compass the act of *begetting* the true, the
unfailingly real and redeeming Melody.'[91] Wagner gave too
much prominence to the individual singers in his music

dramas, according to Ivanov. He had neglected 'the spoken word and the dance, the mass vocalism and the symbolism of the multitude', and had therefore stopped in mid-course, leaving his final word unspoken.[92] He had tried through the creation of new myths to break through into 'mystical realism', but remained a symbolist.[93]

Although Ivanov was critical of the fact that 'those who gather at the *Festspiele*' were only envisioned as molecules of the 'orchestra's orgiastic being', he nonetheless regarded music drama as the only art form capable of putting an end to the current 'crisis' in the Russian theatre, which mirrored the contemporary problems of acute social alienation. Like his fellow Symbolists, Ivanov saw enormous potential in the theatre as a uniting force after the shock of the 1905 Revolution, which had revealed the enormity of the gulf between the intelligentsia and the rest of the population. In Ivanov's view, the yawning gulf separating the 'poet' from the 'crowd' was symbolised by the row of footlights in the theatre, dividing the 'players' from the 'community' in 'two alien worlds, one exclusively active, the other exclusively contemplative'. In his vision of the theatre of the future, Ivanov envisioned music retaining its supremacy in the 'symphony' but felt the chorus had the greatest role to play in healing the rift: 'We see no other means of fusing stage and auditorium other than by unleashing the hidden and suppressed Dionysian element in the orchestral symphony and in the independent, musical and rhythmic life of the chorus.'[94] Ivanov defines the orchestral symphony as a 'metaphysical chorus of universal Will' and the chorus as 'our collective [*sobornoe*] self'.[95] The two elements are thus very closely allied to his concept of myth as the 'postulate of collective self-determination' and the 'hypostasis of a certain essence or energy',[96] which would seem to be confirmed by Ivanov's statement that 'the problem of the chorus is indissolubly linked to the problem of myth and with the establishment of realistic symbolism'.[97] There is much in common here with Wagner's view of myth as 'the view-in-common of the essence of things',[98] and the expression of 'public conscience'.[99] Both Wagner (at least initially) and Ivanov saw artistic freedom as

synonymous with political freedom. Art, in their view, was not
only capable but responsible for bringing about social amelior-
ation. The masses [*narodnye massy*] have an instinctive feeling
for true art, writes Ivanov in 'Presentiments and Portents'; a
myth-based art, he claims, would be a people's art and the
concern of the 'community' [*obshchina*] by its very nature.
Political freedom, he continues, can only be achieved 'when
the choral voice of such communities is the genuine referendum
of the people's true will'.[100] Wagner had held similar beliefs.
'The Art-work of the Future must embrace the spirit of a free
mankind',[101] he writes in *Art and Revolution*; 'it is for art therefore, and art above all else, to teach this social impulse
[towards the free dignity of man] its noblest meaning.'[102]

Although Ivanov was not alone in formulating idealistic
theories of a future art-form, his vision was perhaps the most far
removed from reality. It was hardly surprising, therefore, that
it attracted some fierce criticism. Ivanov further fuelled cause
for attack by publicly supporting his friend Georgy Chulkov's
doctrine of 'mystical anarchism' in 1906.[103] Chulkov believed
that Wagnerian theatre was not only important 'as a remarkable phenomenon, but as a tragic attempt to found religious
theatre',[104] and it thus comes as no surprise that Wagner
figures prominently within the doctrine of mystical anarchism,
which was in essence an ill-conceived and chaotic re-working
of some of Ivanov's more exotic ideas.[105] Dmitry Filosofov was
amongst those who took a jaundiced view of Ivanov's ideas on
the theatre, and his 1906 article 'Mystical Anarchism' (*Misticheskii anarkhizm*), reveals to what extent people were aware at
the time of the derivative nature of some of those ideas:

It's finally time to give up these naive ravings about some kind of
joint orgiastic rites, leading to a condition of ecstasy. V. Ivanov's
dreams of some sort of theatre of the future are just as naive. A new
Bayreuth will not save anyone, and if it is possible to have a genuine,
cultured theatre that unites people, then it will not of course be the
cause but the result of people united already. Ivanov's theatre can
only be a product, a consequence of the people's religious life, but
it is not possible to create this religion by any kind of mystical
aestheticism ...[106]

Despite the 'shortcomings' of Wagner's music dramas, they were the only works of art which Ivanov could point to as a prototype for his own 'art-work of the future'. And since it cannot be mere coincidence that the ideas Ivanov puts forward bear a remarkable similarity to those expressed in Wagner's essays, it would seem that Ivanov drew much inspiration from them – more, perhaps, than he cared to admit. It was Wagner, after all, as Ivanov acknowledges, who had issued a call 'to merge artistic energies in a synthetic art which would absorb into its focus the spiritual self-determination of the people'.[107] It was Wagner who had first sought a synthetic art based on drama,[108] and it was Wagner who had preceded Ivanov's call for actors and spectators to merge into 'one orgiastic body':[109] 'In common ... shall we close the last link in the bond of holy Necessity; and the brother-kiss that seals this bond, will be the *mutual Art-work of the Future*. But in this, also, our great redeemer and well-doer ... the *Folk*, will no longer be a severed and peculiar class; for in this Art-work we shall all be *one*.'[110]

WAGNER IN IVANOV'S POETRY

Although comparatively little of Ivanov's poetry seems to have any specific connection with music, his early verse was perceived by several of his contemporaries as being Wagnerian in texture. The critic L. Galich, for example, noted this quality in a review of Ivanov's second collection in 1906, and it was a point which Lidiya Zinovieva-Annibal particularly remarked upon in a letter written a few days after his article appeared.[111] In his review, Galich expressed his frustration with the excessive musicality of *Pilot Stars* (*Kormchie zvezdy*), Ivanov's first collection, which was published in 1903: 'It angered me that the sumptuous verses of Ivanov ... did not become clear with the passing of time, did not become fluid and transparent but continued to hum dimly with heavy dissonances like the chorus in Wagner's operas ... I was compelled to speak out against Ivanov ... I could not fail to attack an art in which "la musique," as in Verlaine's poetic catechism, was "avant tout."'[112] Interestingly, the parallels between Wagner and

Ivanov were also not lost on Ivanov's close friend, the poet and composer Mikhail Kuzmin, who thought that Wagner's librettos would sound very much like Ivanov's verse if they were 'transposed' into Russian.[113]

The Wagnerian qualities of Ivanov's early verse detected by his contemporaries partly stem from his fondness for using bare roots and stressed one-syllable words, as well as accumulations of consonants at the beginning and ending of words,[114] tendencies to be found in the texts of Wagner's music dramas. One only has to cast a brief glance over the third part of *Opera and Drama*, in which Wagner discusses in detail the specific sort of poetry he plans to write for his music dramas, to realise that he and Ivanov seemed to share similar ideas about poetic language. Wagner devotes several pages in *Opera and Drama*, for example, to demonstrating that poetic expression could be enhanced by the placing of consonants at the beginnings of words, and he also explains how poetic speech could be brought closer to its 'purer original' by giving stress only to condensed 'significant root-syllables'.[115] Although desirous that everyday speech should provide the source for poetic expression (since contact with the 'people' was all-important), Wagner was nevertheless conscious that 'our sentences are diffuse and endlessly expanded', and therefore proposed the grasping of 'the sensuous substance of our *roots of speech*' so that 'the purely-human core shall alone remain'.[116] Wagner's insistence on the use of the 'old primal roots' of language, which had been preserved by the people 'beneath the frosty mantle of its civilisation',[117] proceeded from a hope that his new music dramas would once more bring the artist and the people together in the presentation of myth, as in the times of Greek tragedy. Ivanov's poetic language suggests that his aims were rather similar, a supposition that is borne out in his essay 'The Poet and the Rabble'. There is no way of telling whether Ivanov ever studied either *Opera and Drama* or the poetic texts that Wagner wrote for his music dramas with any care. The fact that more than one person found that Ivanov's poetry possessed a particularly Wagnerian sonority, however, suggests that he might have unconsciously absorbed some of Wagner's ideas about language as he listened to the music dramas performed on stage, even if he did not openly draw from them.

Only one poem by Ivanov is directly linked to Wagner. 'Tristan and Isolde', (*Tristan i Izolda*), a Wagner-inspired study of love and death, is the last of four 'Hymns to Eros' (*Gimny Erosu*) written in 1915, and the only one with a title. Ivanov's 'Hymns to Eros' were first published (together with poetry by Balmont, Pasternak, Khlebnikov and Shershenevich) in an Imagist anthology which appeared in 1920,[118] but subsequently also appeared (with slight variations and without either the 'Hymns to Eros' or 'Tristan' titles) in the second part of Ivanov's important cycle 'Man' (*Chelovek*), a work composed between 1915 and 1919, but only published as a complete work in 1939.[119] Their earlier publication has never been remarked upon in any edition of Ivanov's poetry. *Tristan und Isolde*, which Ivanov regarded as Wagner's most Dionysian opera, must have indeed held a powerful attraction for him, for its intoxicating mixture of love, loss of self, suffering and death, were themes central to his own work.[120] It was Wagner above all, Ivanov believed, the creator of *Tristan und Isolde*, who had looked directly into the eyes of chaos to seek, 'in metaphysical eroticism, union with the first principles of being'.[121] Its protagonists, he wrote, 'arise from the wave of dark chaos, of universal Meon [non-being], in convulsions of tragic passion, in order once more to sink and disappear into it, paying as individuals for the expiatory revenge of their birth, as old Anaximander said, with their deaths'.[122] Wagner was indeed an important figure for Ivanov: the first artist to have raised the 'veil of Isis' and expressed with his music the chaos that lay behind it.

CHAPTER 5

Wagner and the Russian Symbolists: Bely, Medtner and Ellis

MUSIC DRAMAS IN PROSE: BELY'S 'SYMPHONIES'

As with Vyacheslav Ivanov, there was something of an inevitability about Bely's attraction to Wagner in his student years, for he had developed a passion for German music and literature at an early age. His nanny had introduced her young charge to the entrancing world of German poetry and legend by reading him works by Uhland, Eichendorff and Goethe as well as the traditional Hans Christian Andersen tales,[1] and many years later Bely speculated that his unswerving devotion to German culture had perhaps begun with those bedside tales:

Maybe that is why there is within me to this day a love for old Germany (and for Germany generally), for German music (Beethoven, Schumann, Wagner), painting ... poetry (Goethe, the Romantics, Nietzsche), philosophy (Kant, Leibniz, Schelling, Schopenhauer, Rückert and Nietzsche again), science ... and mysticism (Eckhart, Böhme and Rudolf Steiner from our time). Everything that I love in the West is involuntarily tied for me somehow with Germany.[2]

Music was the art form that Bely was first drawn to. Not only does he claim to have 'worshipped' music from infancy,[3] but to have been able to recognise composers' names from the age of four, the first of which, interestingly, was that of Wagner.[4] It was also during 1884 that he experienced his first 'musical revelations', when his mother (who was a gifted pianist) whiled away the winter evenings by playing Chopin and Beethoven. Bely was profoundly affected by this magical nocturnal world of music that he instinctively felt was different to the diurnal world of 'professors', 'rational explanations' and 'Darwinian theories of evolution' that his mathematician father inhabited.[5] From the beginning, what excited him about music was the fact that it was not reducible to inflexible laws, and contained something unfathomable. He was also captivated by musical rhythm.

It is difficult to pinpoint when Bely first came into contact with Wagner's music, as references to specific concerts and operas in his writings are rare. Although according to one autobiographical source it was in 1897,[6] in another he claims that it was in 1898 that he first heard music by Wagner, when he began to attend the orchestral concerts for which his mother had taken a subscription: 'My great passion for Tchaikovsky began; I found the composer Rebikov's works very interesting . . . as well, both Mama and I began seriously to be absorbed by the music of Wagner; Wagner appeared in my field of vision.'[7] Bely's tastes, then, were nothing if not catholic at this time. Wagner was still at the centre of Bely's attention the following year, and his diary entries for February and April 1899 record his particular interest at the time in Grieg's songs and orchestral suites and Wagner's *Ring*.[8] The passion the nineteen-year-old Bely developed for Grieg concurrently with Wagner (inspired by his new-found enthusiasm for Ibsen, Hamsun and other 'northern' writers)[9] was intense, but relatively short-lived and had an impact only on his early writings. Bely's involvement with Wagner, on the other hand, was far more diffuse, and spread over a more extended period, affecting both his early and late work. That this 'mad passion'[10] for Wagner began in 1898 is significant, for that was precisely the year in which the tide of hostility towards Wagner in Russia began to turn. At the end of the 1897–8 season, there had been only three performances of works by Wagner in Moscow in as many years. In the 1898–9 season, however, the Bolshoi Theatre suddenly included ten performances of works by Wagner in its season. Admittedly these were performances of Wagner's early works *Tannhäuser* and *Lohengrin* (and therefore less likely to fire Bely's imagination),[11] but in that same season a whole host of eminent conductors (including Richter, Nikisch, Weingartner

and Kes) came to Moscow to conduct orchestral concerts, and
excerpts from Wagner's music dramas featured prominently in
their programmes.[12] It was undoubtedly at these concerts that
Bely underwent his initiation into Wagner's music.

Bely's father Nikolay Bugaev appears to have had some
indirect contact with Wagner, but did not encourage his son's
interest in the composer. Bely relates that his father had
written an opera libretto entitled 'Buddha', which apparently
elicited great interest from Wagner when Serov showed it to
him during one of their meetings, the last of which took place
in 1869.[13] It would be something of an exaggeration to claim
that this marked the beginning of the 'Wagner cult' in the
family, however,[14] for Professor Bugaev never accompanied his
wife and son to the concerts they went to; the 'new trends'
meant nothing to him, according to Bely, and in Grieg and
Wagner he heard only 'noise'.[15]

Bely had already begun to develop a serious interest in
writing by this time,[16] but until 1899, he was more interested in
pursuing music than literature as a career. The Bugaev family
were friendly with Sergey Taneev, who told Bely that he had
'the hands of a musician', while another acquaintance heard
his piano improvisations and declared that he was a composer
rather than a poet.[17] Yet in the end Bely was not content to be
just one or the other. Like Wagner, he dreamed of uniting the
two worlds of music and poetry, feeling within himself the
'conjunction' of poetry, prose, philosophy and music.[18] He
knew his creativity should combine all these spheres, but at
first he was unable to conceive of a means of doing so. One of
the people he discussed this question with was Taneev, who
noted a conversation he had with Bely in October 1900 in his
diary, where he writes that they talked about 'recurrence in
music and about uniting visual and aural impressions'.[19] In the
end, Bely's first serious experiments with prose writing were an
attempt to illustrate his musical compositions.[20] In 1899 (the
year in which he entered Moscow university to study natural
sciences) he produced a work he called the 'Presymphony', and
went on to write his first 'Symphony' in 1900, the second a year
later, while the third and fourth were begun in 1902.

The question of Wagner's influence on Bely's 'Symphonies' has been touched upon by many critics,[21] but never investigated in any detail. Bely's opinion that symphonic music was superior to operatic music[22] certainly does not rule out Wagner as a possible source of inspiration, since evidence seems to point to the fact that Bely found inspiration in the *nature* of symphonic music, rather than in the symphonies of specific composers or symphonic form *per se*, and Wagner is certainly included in the list of composers whose music he claimed provided the inspiration behind his 'Symphonies'.[23] And although Wagner was indeed an operatic composer, the music in his operas has little to do with operatic music in the traditional sense and everything to do with dramatic-symphonic music in the tradition of Beethoven, whom Wagner considered his direct predecessor. Bely's interest in writing a 'symphony', it seems, lay in the fact that 'in a symphony we contemplate the sum total of all possible images in a given connection, all possible combinations of events, which come together to form a vast and fathomless symbol'.[24] His use of the term may well imply the word's literal meaning of 'sounding together', just as much as use of the traditional sonata form of the first movement of the symphony, which some critics have tried to locate in his 'Symphonies'.[25] Emil Medtner was also probably close to the mark when he commented that the word 'symphony' should be understood here figuratively, like the terms 'picture' and 'portrait'.[26] With the exception of the references to the *Ring* in Bely's fourth 'Symphony', *The Goblet of Blizzards* (*Kubok metelei*), which were added when he began to re-write the work in 1905, Wagner had little influence on the actual content of the 'Symphonies'. Their mythological worlds, do, it is true, contain Wagnerian echoes, and the medieval knights, old kings, swans, giants, gnomes and dragons may perhaps have been inspired by works such as *Lohengrin* or the *Ring*. It is unlikely Bely had seen these works performed on stage at this point, however, and the influence of Grieg and Ibsen would seem to be far stronger here. It was in the area of technique that Wagner proved most influential. In a later autobiographical memoir, in fact, Bely quite baldly declared that his method of composition for *A Goblet of Blizzards* had been directly inspired by Wagner. With phrases as his material, he explained, he wished 'to proceed as Wagner had done with melody', using the themes as a 'strong line of rhythm' which would absorb subsidiary themes 'according to the rules of counterpoint'.[27] Elsewhere he declared equally explicitly that the subjects of his first four books had been drawn from 'musical leitmotifs'.[28] As Roger Keys has commented, what Bely was actually trying to do here was advance a 'new theory of semantic structure in literature'.[29] As a Symbolist, Bely found that conventional imagery was inadequate to the task of giving expression to the deeper realities underlying everyday life he was interested in exploring, and Wagner's intrinsically symbolic compositional methods presented him with an ideal model for deepening the psychological and emotional texture of his prose. It was not for nothing that Bely had talked to Taneev about recurrence in music, for this is exactly how the leitmotifs in Wagner's music dramas function: forever recurring, but endlessly developing – both harmonically and thematically – and interweaving with other motifs to create a complex, multi-layered and unified artistic structure. The potential for employing such methods in literature was obviously enormous. As Raymond Furness has pointed out, the powers of the leitmotif 'to enrich and enhance were found to be of unprecedented intensity', and affected the works of such major modernist writers as Proust, Mann and Woolf.[30] It is possible that Bely had learnt about leitmotifs by studying Wagner's *Opera and Drama*, as Ada Steinberg suggests.[31] The only reference to this work in Bely's writings, however, occurs in the commentary to his 1903 essay 'The Forms of Art' (*Formy iskusstva*), which gives no indication that he had paid it particularly close attention. It is perhaps more plausible that Bely was directly inspired by Wagner's music in his attempt to use verbal equivalents of leitmotifs in his work.[32] The extent of his success is another matter, since the ambitiousness of his philosophical ideas rather outstripped the technical possibilities of his material, as he was to discover, but his continued use of the leitmotif as a purely stylistic device in his novels was later to work to great effect.[33]

MEDTNER AND BELY: A WAGNERIAN FRIENDSHIP

As well as employing the device in his writings, Bely also had a habit of using the word leitmotif in his memoirs and correspondence, particularly when he wished to convey the tenor of a particular period in his life, the dominant characteristic of a particular person, or a theme in his work. That he did so was due almost entirely to the powerful influence of his friend Emil Medtner,[34] an inspirational and intellectually formidable lawyer-turned-musicologist who saw the world through the prism of Wagner's *Ring*. Five years Bely's senior, Medtner came from an old German family which had settled in Russia in the eighteenth century. The artistic tradition in the family was strong; Medtner's great-grandfather had been a leading actor at the German Court theatre in Petersburg (who had apparently corresponded with Goethe and Wagner),[35] and two of his brothers were professional musicians. Nikolay Medtner indeed, the most famous member of the family, became a composer and pianist of considerable renown.

In his memoirs, Bely describes being briefly introduced to Medtner in 1901 on the street,[36] his curiosity already aroused by having heard that he was a solitary figure, who had independently come by much of what he and his friends considered to be the 'pulse of the new culture'.[37] It was not until April of the following year, however, that Medtner and Bely became properly acquainted, when they met at a rehearsal for a concert conducted by Arthur Nikisch.[38] The Wagnerian note to their relationship was struck almost immediately, according to Bely, who claims in his memoirs (though probably with the benefit of hindsight) to have seen Medtner from their very first meeting as a 'Wälsung', the tragic race of human beings doomed to suffering in Wagner's *Ring*: 'He was dressed in a dark grey coat and gloves and held a cane in his hand; he was also holding a brimmed hat. I saw a thin nose ... a thick beard ending in a narrow wedge ... firmly pursed lips, ready to explode into sarcasm, a small forehead ... an irregularly shaped skull, lightly covered with dark brown curls: all this brought to mind a mixture of viking and wolf, and the leitmotif of the Wälsungs – the theme of the sun – arose for a moment.'[39]

Towards the end of the rehearsal, which Bely sat through entranced as he listened to Medtner's discourse, it seemed to him that it was no longer Nikisch conducting Schubert, but Medtner conducting Nikisch. Medtner had turned Nikisch's rehearsal into a 'lecture on European culture' by 'simply outlining the musical themes and their development in connection with philosophy',[40] and had then manoeuvred the discussion onto the subject of Nietzsche, claiming, like Novalis, that culture was 'music'.[41]

After the publication of Bely's *Second Symphony* that same month, Medtner recognised him as a true writer and during the long walk that he invited him to go on, the 'bonds of friendship' were securely tied.[42] Medtner proclaimed Bely's 'Symphony' as the 'music of the dawns',[43] and once again dazzled his younger friend, appearing to him as a Siegfried figure, ready to do heroic battle with the dragon of degeneration:

We sat on a bench; I listened to [Medtner's] brilliant examination of the card theme [from Tchaikovsky's *The Queen of Spades*] and its link with the heart-rending theme of the *Pathétique*; out of the dazzling analysis of this link between the themes arose the theme of fate, and naturally the leitmotif of Medtner's theme was revealed in it – at that moment he seemed to be a kind of Siegfried, raising his 'Nothung' (his cane whirling in the air) above Mime and Alberich, above the chimeras of the degeneration of culture.[44]

While he would always retain an intense love for Russian culture (in his early days, he had been a fervent Slavophile),[45] Medtner's first allegiance was to German culture, and to Beethoven, Kant, Wagner and Goethe above all. In his opinion, Wagner and Nietzsche had represented the last great developments in culture after whom had followed a relentless decline and regression that was most clearly manifest in contemporary French music (which he found particularly abhorrent). Fortunately Bely happened to be a particularly receptive subject for the 'militant Germanophilia' his friend felt it almost his moral duty to preach,[46] and he later confessed that he had Medtner to thank for his love of German culture.[47]

Bely's 'turbulent' meetings with Medtner continued through

May 1902, during which time he fell more and more under his friend's spell.[48] After a heated exchange of letters throughout the summer, he spent 'almost every evening in unending conversation' with Medtner until the latter's departure to Nizhny Novgorod at the end of October 1902 to take up a job as censor.[49] During that time, the Medtners' apartment became a 'musical academy' for Bely,[50] where he would come into contact with the most eminent personalities from Moscow musical life.[51] Medtner, 'refined and brilliant', would 'conduct' the conversation like an 'albatross circling the sky',[52] and invariably finding that music could best illustrate the points he wished to make, he would command his brother to play to Bely, but then stop him to 'heatedly read a dazzling lecture, comparing certain chords with similar progressions in Wagner and Schumann and linking up these chords with the problems of European culture'.[53] Music was Medtner's great passion, and the subject of most of his writings. Like no other, he was able to 'penetrate' music, according to Bely: 'he took our souls captive with it; with music he looked at the mystery inherent within us, grasping each person's leitmotif'.[54] Although Bely had acquired a certain amount of knowledge about Wagner on his own, he acknowledges in his memoirs that it was Medtner who first truly 'raised' the composer before him.[55] The Medtner brothers seemed to spend a good deal of time studying Wagner and their enthusiasm undoubtedly rubbed off on Bely. When Nikolay went to stay with Emil in 1905, for example, he took with him the score of *Das Rheingold* which he wanted to study with his brother 'from A to Z'.[56] Their analysis of the *Ring* was still underway in the winter of 1911, although by this time they must have been familiar with every note. 'First of all the libretto was read through', recalled V. K. Tarasova later; 'then Uncle Kolya played. The whole of the *Ring* was read through in this way. The performance was always stopped for discussion of what was being played.'[57] The Medtner brothers seized every opportunity to hear works by Wagner during their frequent trips abroad and finally managed to go to Bayreuth in 1912, an event of great importance to them. 'Our most important trip was to Bayreuth to

hear Wagner,' Nikolay wrote in a letter at that time; 'we had
the impression that it lasted a whole eternity rather than just a
week, and that we had not just been in Bayreuth, but travelled
over the whole globe, the whole universe.'[58] Emil Medtner was
no ordinary Wagnerian, for not only was his knowledge of
Wagner superior to that of most practising musicians, but he
was almost exclusively obsessed with the *Ring*, seeing it as
nothing less than a kind of paradigm of the world, in which
people could be categorised as either Wälsungs or Nibelungs
(mostly the latter). Because he regarded himself as a tragic
figure, he predictably enough identified with the Wälsungs,
seeing himself as both Siegmund (whose other name 'Wölfing'
he assumed as his pseudonym) and Siegfried. The Wälsung
leitmotif, Medtner considered, was 'his story about himself'.[59]
Bely, who was mesmerised by the mythological Wagnerian
world which materialised before him, would often explore the
theme of Siegfried's death in their conversations with Medtner,
who would comment to his friend that there was something
exquisitely sweet in the Wälsung theme that made his heart
miss a beat: 'It is a love of death ... You know, I once fell
ill ... before I became ill, the Wälsung theme arose involuntarily before me: tam-ta-ta-tam ... ta-tam-tam ...'[60] In
the published version of Bely's memoir *The Beginning of the
Century*, Medtner's confidence reads slightly differently (Bely
had an obsessive habit of revising everything he wrote): 'Day
and night before I fell ill, my blood rang with the themes of the
Wälsungs, interwoven with the theme of the 'Ruin of Valhalla'; it felt as if I had drunk up the sun; and the sun within
me became poison: the death of the sun within me is my theme,
my fate ... Be wary of my theme; it will threaten you.'[61]
Medtner thus brought the symbols of Wagner's *Ring* into Bely's
'everyday life', illustrating its events with scenes from the
'battle of Gunther and Siegmund' (sic), for example, the
'freeing of Brünnhilde' by Siegfried, or the famous sword
forging scene from *Siegfried*. 'In the raised dust of civilisation',
writes Bely, 'he saw the smoke from the blazing of Valhalla; his
motto was "cut off Fafner's head".'[62] Russia, according to
Medtner, was a sleeping Brünnhilde who would soon be

awakened by her German Siegfried,[63] for nothing less than the entire European political situation was mapped out on a plane seemingly lifted straight from Wagner's *The Wibelungs*:[64]

To those close to him, he would often talk about the Wölfings, Wolfs[65] and Welfs, or Guelfs; about the Hohenstaufens,[66] in whom the Ghibellines crossed with the Welfs;[67] about Friedrich Barbarossa, who would one day rise from his sleep;[68] the theme of fate crossed to Germany, beloved by Medtner; he followed this theme right up to Bismarck, whom he idolised.[69]

In his more pessimistic moments, which, it must be said, outweighed his optimistic ones (in general, Medtner was as pessimistic about the human race as Wagner, and did not really believe that 'Siegfried' could be victorious), he predicted a rather gloomier scenario. Conscious of the link between the Nibelung myths and the legends surrounding Attila, King of the Huns (in one version of the myths, Brünnhilde becomes Attila's, rather than Gunther's wife), his racist views led him to fear that the 'Aryan' world would soon have to struggle with the 'dark invasion' of the Huns.[70] Bely does not seem to have been too perturbed by his friend's more unsavoury characteristics. Inspired by Medtner's example, however, the word 'leitmotif' now began to appear in his writings in a way that made it clear that he saw it as interchangeable with the word 'symbol' (it was a habit he maintained to the end of his days), and he also began to view his life in terms of classic scenes from the *Ring*. Not only did he start to cast his contemporaries as characters from the tetralogy, he even took the analogy one step further, by likening situations to those in Wagner's life.

It was soon after meeting Medtner that Bely wrote his first major theoretical article, 'The Forms of Art' (*Formy iskusstva*),[71] in which he argued that the world of art had followed a path of evolution from architecture to symphonic music, which was the 'germ of the art of the future'.[72] Amongst the numerous items in Bely's bibliography for this article is Wagner's *Opera and Drama*,[73] whose ideas he may have discussed in his conversations earlier that year with Medtner (who possessed a first-edition copy of *The Art-work of the Future* which had belonged to his great-grandfather).[74] There is nothing to indicate that

Opera and Drama had a particularly strong impact on the composition of 'The Forms of Art', beyond Bely's general advocacy of the desirability of artistic synthesis, yet Wagner does indeed occupy a prominent position in this article, and it is one that is roughly analogous to that ascribed to the composer by Vyacheslav Ivanov (with whom Bely was as yet unacquainted) in his essay 'The Hellenic Religion', written at approximately the same time. Under the powerful influence of Schopenhauer's aesthetic philosophy and Nietzsche's *Birth of Tragedy* (which he first became acquainted with at approximately the same time as he first encountered Wagner), Bely, like Ivanov, had come to see music as the superior art form, and as a symbol for metaphysical reality: 'To formulate our thought in the language of Schopenhauer – all art leads us to the pure contemplation of the World-Will; or, to speak in the spirit of Nietzsche – every form of art is determined by the degree to which the spirit of music is revealed in it.'[75] Bely and Ivanov also concurred in seeing Wagner's music as the embodiment of metaphysical reality (as Nietzsche had done in *The Birth of Tragedy*), which for them was a confirmation that a new cultural era dominated by music was imminent. Bely felt that the human spirit was at a watershed, and 'the growth of music up to Beethoven and the broadening of its sphere of influence from Beethoven to Wagner' was for him (and for Ivanov) the supreme representation of an 'increased gravitation towards religious questions'.[76] Like Ivanov, Bely viewed drama as moving in the direction of music, a tendency realised to a significant degree with Wagner's music dramas: Wagner was 'the first musician who consciously reached out his hand to tragedy as though in an attempt to facilitate its evolution in the direction of music'.[77] Bely's conclusion was that the 'symbolism' and musical character of contemporary plays indicated that drama was destined to return to 'mystery', whence it evolved, and 'extend into life'.[78]

'The Forms of Art' made such a great impression on Aleksandr Blok that he felt an 'organic need' to enter into correspondence with Bely.[79] Whilst he found Bely's article 'brilliant and outspoken', he nevertheless had some criticisms to make, the chief of which was that its author had failed to distinguish between religion and art, and should certainly not have equated music with the Apocalypse. (Bely had maintained that music was 'not of this world', and had quoted from the Revelation of St John to argue that the 'apocalyptic music' of the Archangel's trumpet might 'awaken us to a final understanding of the phenomena of the world'.)[80] To 'avoid temptation' in Blok's opinion, it was necesssary

to shout and cry out about boundaries, about limits, that the apocalyptic trumpet is not 'the stuff of art' . . . You have not said the final word, and for that reason your last pages are horror and doubt . . . You hid your face precisely when it became necessary to say whether or not music was the ultimate. The main thing is, what sort of music is this anyway? Is it really a 'form' of art?[81]

Blok conceded that music could indeed be a kind of transfiguration in that all art offers the possibility of transcendence, but pointed out that it did not necessarily lead to salvation. To illustrate his point, he alighted on two scenes from the *Ring*, in which Wagner had written deliberately seductive music to depict what was, in his view, essentially demonic: the incestuous love of brother and sister, and the incitement of a person who knows no fear to further elevation of the will: 'Is there not after all in Wagner the horror of "holy flesh"?[82] Are not after all Siegmund and Sieglinde intoxicatingly holy, and also the voice of the bird "that starts to sing" to Siegfried, "luring", infernal?'[83]

In his reply to Blok, Bely acknowledged that it was a mistake to have failed to lift the 'veil' completely by referring to music both as an art form and as a symbol of the 'soul of the world'.[84] He also agreed that if music was the door to 'other worlds', then the other-worldly could indeed be both 'good' and 'evil' (just as the 'Apocalyptic trumpet signified both joy and horror'). It was Bely's conviction, furthermore, that the utterly different reactions that music aroused in people were dependent on whether the forces of good or evil were dominant in their personalities. Again using Wagner as an example, he explained that the overture to *Tannhäuser* terrified him, but moved others.[85] Bely was in general agreement with Blok's observations about the demonic side of Wagner's music, but felt that the interval changes in certain chords running through all of his works suggested that the composer had sometimes consciously suppressed the urge to turn all art into 'holy flesh'.[86]

While Blok had been correct to identify the struggle between 'Christ' and the 'Antichrist' as one dichotomy in music (represented in symphonies, for example, by 'the musical theme itself, deviation from it in numerous variations and return through the fire of dissonance'),[87] Bely argued that the struggle between the 'aesthetic' and the 'mystical' constituted a dichotomy on the 'perpendicular' level, which manifested itself in rhythm. It was not for nothing, he wrote that 'the greatest of musicians', Beethoven and Wagner, were 'rhythmical, recurrent to the utmost', for rhythm was linked to the idea of Eternal Recurrence, which was 'musical in its very essence'.[88]

'The Forms of Art' was published in December, 1903. Two months earlier, Bely and his fellow 'younger generation' Moscow Symbolists had formed a group called the 'Argonauts' in an attempt to distinguish themselves from the 'older generation' who proclaimed Symbolism as a literary school, with links to the traditions of the French poets. Unlike Bryusov, who had a passion for establishing everything in a 'clear, precise and certain way', teaching that 'Symbolism arose as a movement in such and such a year', the Argonauts understood the word 'Symbolism' in a wider, in a less defined way,[89] and were interested in 'the problem of the new culture and a new existence, in which art was the linchpin'.[90] There was something very Wagnerian in fact about the whole idealistic nature of the Argonauts' aspirations towards mythicisation of all human behaviour and artistic activity. It is hardly surprising, then, that Wagner was a pivotal figure for Bely at this time. The lack of a set outlook amongst the Argonauts meant that there was some disagreement over whom they revered as artistic mentors, but as far as Bely was concerned, Medtner had made him see the significance of German culture in contemporary art as 'indisputable', so that 'Nietzsche, Wagner, Grieg, Ibsen, Hamsun and the other Germans and Scandinavians always outweighed the Baudelaires, Verlaines and Maeter-lincks'.[91]

After Medtner left Moscow at the end of 1902, the two friends did not meet for a year and a half, but Wagner and Nietzsche were names that frequently arose in the regular correspondence that they maintained in the mean time. When Bely visited Medtner in Nizhny-Novgorod in March 1904, the conversation the friends had begun in 1902 now 'continued like a phrase halted by a comma',[92] and Medtner renewed his efforts to mould Bely into a latter-day German Romantic: 'And once again arose Wagner and Schumann and Nietzsche and the Goethe Society; suddenly, like a conductor, pulling back the curtain, [Medtner] portrayed me against a back-ground of Goethe, Novalis, the Schlegels, Tieck, Schelling ... Amongst various "Lucindes" and "Öfterdingens" he inserted my image, so that I saw myself as a Romantic.'[93] After returning to Moscow, Bely resumed his correspondence with Medtner, who continued to discuss Wagner frequently in the letters he sent to his friend.[94] Towards the end of 1903, Medtner had shared with Bely his desire to translate *The Art-work of the Future* into Russian for *Vesy*, which was about to begin publication the following month.[95] At the time, Bely had relayed back to his friend that Bryusov was keen for Medtner to collaborate, but reluctant to publish a translation of such length.[96] In September 1905, Medtner returned to the idea in a letter in which he stressed to Bely how timely it would be for a Russian translation of Wagner's ideas to appear, and reminded his friend how important those ideas had been for the young Nietzsche.[97] Early the next year, Medtner left his job as censor in order to devote himself to literary and musical pursuits, and became chief music critic of *Zolotoe runo* when it was founded in 1906. When he was looking for a pseudonym to write his articles under, Bely had declared that there was nothing to look for. He was 'Wölfing', since 'he had developed that theme already'.[98]

. For a writer so obviously preoccupied by music and musical themes, it is perhaps surprising how little these feature in the lyric poetry which Bely wrote at this time.[99] There is nevertheless a case to be made that a faint Wagnerian subtext lies beneath some of his early poetry, particularly the mythical poetic world of the third part of *Gold in Azure* (*Zoloto v lazuri*), Bely's first collection of poetry, published in 1904. The poem 'Serenade' (*Serenada*), for example, evokes a flock of seven white swans, whom Bely calls the 'swans of Lohengrin'.[100] The fact that Bely speaks of seven swans would seem to suggest that the poem has more to do with the thirteenth-century French epic *Le Chevalier au Cygne* (in which six out of seven children are turned into swans) than with Wagner's hero.[101] It is in the thirteenth-century German epic *Lohengrin* (the main source for Wagner's opera) that we find the knight of the Swan who goes under that name, but this version of the legend features only one swan. That notwithstanding, it is unlikely that Bely was unconscious of the Wagnerian allusion, since *Lohengrin* was the most frequently performed and best known of all Wagner's operas in Russia. Another early poem which has a Wagnerian subtext of a more obvious kind is 'The Duel' (*Poedinok*), where the intervention of a valkyrie in a battle between Thor, the god of thunder, and a fearless viking summons to mind Brünn-hilde's intrusion into the battle between Siegmund and Hunding in *Die Walküre*.[102] Elsewhere, a poetic description of a journey to a rocky crag with a 'crown of fire' also has unmistak-eable associations with the *Ring*,[103] as do the appearance of various giants, Mime-like gnomes and dragons in other poems.[104] The hypothesis that Bely's early poetry was indeed influenced by Wagner's *Ring* might appear to some to be far-fetched. Both *Die Walküre* and *Siegfried* had become part of the Bolshoi Theatre repertoire by 1904, however, and Bely himself actually suggests that the appearance of gnomes and giants in his verse owes something to Wagner in his memoir *The Beginning of the Century*, where he directly identifies the gnome figure in his poem 'The Oldest Friend' (*Starinnyi drug*) with Wagner's Mime. This five-part cycle, an archetypal example of a poem which Bely later re-worked several times, was dedi-cated to Emil Medtner and composed soon after the latter left Moscow at the end of 1902.[105] In *The Beginning of the Century*, Bely describes the poem as being about 'the return, in a dream, of an old forgotten friend calling out from the catacomb for sun, air and freedom':[106] 'My closeness to E. K., the intensity that always fired electric currents of ideas between us, made me think of a meeting of friends who had been parted for centuries and who had not been able to bring their only conversation to an end; they meet, and the interrupted conversation flows [once again] in a brilliant torrent.'[107] The 'old friend' fears that the 'gnome' from the grave ('Mime') will come back to part him from his friend again, and only removes his battle-worn helmet (Bely is perhaps seeing his 'old friend' in his beloved guise as a Wälsung) after reassurance that this will never happen. 'Mime' does reappear, however, to imprison the friends once more in their respective graves. 'The oldest friend is me' was Medtner's immediate response when Bely sent the poem to him in Nizhny Novgorod. 'Thirty years later I understood', Bely wrote subsequently: 'these "graves" were the ideologies which drove us apart and caused the break up of a wonderful friendship. After 1915 we did not meet; Medtner had become an "enemy".'[108] Fate had taken a hand in events, according to Bely, when Medtner's book *Reflections on Goethe* (*Razmyshleniya o Gete*) appeared, forcing Bely to write *Rudolf Steiner and Goethe* (*Rudolf Shteiner i Gete*) in answer to it: 'the perfidious Nibelungs triumphed, the poem came true'.[109]

THE SLAYING OF THE DRAGON: BELY AS SIEGFRIED

It should be pointed out that the habit of characterising people in terms of Wagner's *Ring* was not peculiar to Medtner. Bely's very first piece of theoretical writing (a letter he wrote to Dmitry Merezhkovsky, in which he took issue with some of the latter's 'neo-pagan' ideas about religion and the apocalypse) had led Olga Solovyova to see Bely as a Siegfried figure, who was fighting with the powers of darkness that she considered Merezhkovsky to represent. Solovyova had placed high hopes in Merezhkovsky after reading his book *Tolstoy and Dostoevsky*, which was serialised in *Mir iskusstva* during 1900 and 1901. At that time, Merezhkovsky's star was in the ascendant and for certain people, according to Bely, he was nothing less than a

Russian Luther, because of his mission to bring about a religious revival.[110] Solovyova was desperately disappointed by her
first meeting with Merezhkovsky, however, as she had
expected to encounter a figure with the same religious ideals as
her late brother-in-law, Vladimir Solovyov. Her growing sus-
picion of him, combined with an intense neuroticism, led her to
magnify the significance of Bely's first meeting with Merezhkovsky out of all proportions. In her unbalanced state, Bely
now assumed the features of a Siegfried, who was to do battle
'with the dreadful serpent' Merezhkovsky in the name of the
purity of Solovyov's religious ideal.[111] Yet this was not an
accurate scenario, at least in Bely's view, who felt he was going
along to see Merezhkovsky to 'discuss things, rather than to do
battle':[112] 'I did not feel myself to be a "Siegfried"; I did not
feel Merezhkovsky to be a "serpent".'[113]

Bely may have resented being seen as a 'Siegfried' figure on
this occasion, but he was certainly not averse to perceiving his
friends in Wagnerian terms at other times. This happened in
July 1904, for example, during a disastrous visit that he and his
friend Aleksey Petrovsky made to Shakhmatovo, the Blok
family estate. To Bely, it seemed that he was not just travelling
to visit friends, but to worship at the shrine of the 'Divine
Sophia', in keeping with the Solovyovian mystical ideal which
he and Blok had devoted themselves to serving.[114] Bely could
therefore not resist seeing Shakhmatovo at this time as a temple
of holy art like Bayreuth, at the centre of which was Blok as the
Wagner figure at the head of their cult.[115] Throughout their
stay, Bely and Petrovsky attempted to maintain the cult of
Blok's wife that her husband had inaugurated, by finding
portentous and mystical significance in her every gesture, but
Blok himself felt unable to live up to the expectations of his
friends. He now saw something false and theatrical in their
veneration of his wife, and Bely was forced to admit that his
erstwhile 'spiritual brother' now more closely resembled the
disillusioned Nietzsche in his concerted attempts to argue that
he was not mystical, rather than Wagner. In truth, Bely too
had become slightly disenchanted with the mystical ideal. He
was not ready, however, to face up to certain harsh truths that

Blok felt he could no longer ignore, and was content for the time being to continue to maintain the myth of this 'Russian Bayreuth'.[116]

Bely next saw Blok in January 1905 and his arrival in Petersburg coincided with the peaceful demonstration that came to be known as 'Bloody Sunday'. Revolutionary ferment was in the air and the symbolism of Wagner's *Ring* achieved new poignancy as Russian audiences began to interpret the work as political allegory.[117] Blok and his wife were amongst those in Petersburg who now began to throng to the Mariinsky Theatre to hear Wagner's music dramas, and were particularly captivated by Ershov's famed performance in *Siegfried*, which they went to see with Bely during his stay.[118] The three friends were swept away by the 'revolutionary fervour' aroused by the heroic atmosphere of that work, according to Bely, to the point of their inevitable identification with its characters: 'Yes, one of us was Wotan and one of us was Siegfried (obvious who); Lyubov Dmitrievna showed clear Valkyrie-like features.'[119]

Wagner's *Ring* was evidently still in Bely's mind when he made another, equally unsatisfactory, visit to Shakhmatovo in June 1905, this time accompanied by Sergey Solovyov, the other close friend who had made up the 'mystic triumvirate' with Blok.[120] Although their conviction that they could together create a new form of existence was proving to be an illusion, Bely was still feeling insulted and betrayed by Blok's abandonment of his earlier worship of the 'Divine Sophia' and his descent into the world of mundane reality.[121] It seemed to him that their pure ideal, the 'ideas' by which they had lived and which, they believed, were personified by Lyubov Blok, had (in a conflation of the mythology of Wagner's *Ring* with the St George legend) been kidnapped like Brünnhilde by an 'ominous Dragon' that had to be slain: 'I remember very clearly that precisely at that time, Lyubov Dmitrievna pointed to a picture hanging on the wall which depicted the bound Brünnhilde with a writhing dragon at her feet. "Free Brünnhilde!" she said. And I understood that she was summoning us to a final, decisive battle.'[122] The dragon, in Bely and Solovyov's eyes was the 'demon of despondency – disillusioned idleness', which symbolised the 'spirit of all that was bourgeois, and life without heroic deeds', and its victory they ascribed to Blok's current mood.[123] Solovyov, in particular, was irked by Blok's apparent unwillingness to remain true to his grandfather Vladimir Solovyov's precepts or even be drawn into explanation, when he had been the one who had always insisted on openness.[124] As a result, the 'literary talk at table degenerated into barely concealed duels' between Solovyov and the Bloks, with the 'points of their rapiers' hidden behind the bouquets of wild roses.[125] Incensed by Solovyov's constant hectoring, Blok's mother Aleksandra Andreevna (who, according to Bely, regarded her son as nothing less than an oracle)[126] took her revenge with the reproach that he was exhibiting various objectionable tendencies characteristic of the Kovalensky family, to whom they were both related. The implication was that the Kovalenskys were somehow a 'lesser species',[127] and Bely leapt at the Wagnerian connotations. In his estimation, however, it was Blok who was behaving more like a Kovalensky 'Nibelung', and he felt it was ignoble of him to respond to Solovyov's direct blows with evasion. Such behaviour, Bely felt, was consonant with the '"lesser species" of the dwarf Mime' rather than the noble race of which Siegfried was a member.[128]

Bely contrived to leave Shakhmatovo early and by the end of the year had made his peace with Blok. New problems quickly arose, however, when Lyubov, who had became the object of what was to prove an ill-fated infatuation, decided to respond to Bely's increasingly ardent professions of affection. In their own private version of the *Ring*, Blok was evidently finding it difficult to keep abreast of the gruelling demands of his role as Siegfried, and Bely, like an over-enthusiastic understudy, was longing to take over.[129] The Russian 'Brünnhilde' eventually decided she wished to be woken by a new 'Siegfried', and the most intense moments of their disastrous affair were conducted against a suitably Wagnerian background. At the beginning of 1906, *Parsifal* was performed for the first time in Russia at three concerts on consecutive Sunday afternoons, and the first concert was attended by Bely, Blok, his mother and Lyubov

Dmitrievna. Driven perhaps by the overpowering music they had just heard, Bely and Lyubov chose to declare their feelings for each other as they returned from the concert in the same sleigh.[130] A few days later, Bely wrote excitedly to his mother to tell her that he had heard the first act of *Parsifal* and would shortly hear the second and third acts.[131] In fact this never happened, because Bely decided to return to Moscow in order to prepare for his elopement with Lyubov Dmitrievna, who was now writing almost daily letters to him. She was convinced that Bely would return to Petersburg to attend the last *Parsifal* concert on 19 March: 'Today there was *Parsifal* and the whole time I had a mad idea that I would see you there.'[132] The affair ended somewhat tragically, however and Bely sought solace by travelling abroad.

At the end of September 1906, when Bely arrived in Munich, he was cheered by the news that Emil Medtner would be able to join him at the end of the year. Perhaps inspired by his proximity to the opera theatre, 'renowned throughout Europe, for its festival performances of Wagner's works during August, which hardly take second place to Bayreuth',[133] Bely felt a surge of renewed interest in his attempts to combine music and literature and took up his already finished fourth 'Symphony' again, hoping to bring together the disparate lines of his themes in a verbal equivalent of Wagner's 'endless melody'.[134] The experiment failed dismally, however, and Bely was finally resigned to the idea that a verbal 'symphony' was not feasible: the plot had divided into two different worlds and its final fragmented form resembled anything but counterpoint. Bely nevertheless wrote initially with fervour, 'dreaming the whole time of seeing Medtner and discussing the task with him'.[135] His manuscript had undergone some important changes since its original draft in 1902. The following passage in which the chief protagonist, Adam Petrovich, goes to consult a mystical anarchist, for example, was certainly a later addition, for 'mystical anarchism' had arisen as a reaction to the 1905 Revolution:

A mystical anarchist with golden hair and an ingratiatingly forked beard ran out to meet him.

His frock-coat, green as a bottle, was unusual . . .
He reminded one of Christ in Correggio's representation – it was
exactly the same image . . .
He loved music in a dumbfounded sort of way: he liked to listen to
Wagner most of all; his eyes shone green, like chrysolite . . .[136]

That Bely is here painting a satirical portrait of Vyacheslav
Ivanov, who together with Chulkov supported the doctrine of
'mystical anarchism' (reviled by Bely), is confirmed by his
description of the poet in his memoirs, where he likens him to
Correggio's picture of Christ (who is portrayed with a forked
beard).[137] Further on in the *Fourth Symphony*, the mystical
anarchist expresses his thoughts by drawing an analogy with
the *Ring*, and it cannot be pure coincidence that the one scene
he alights upon is that of Siegfried fighting the dragon:

He awakened hope. He talked of the impossible.
With his voice he created velvet tones as he clasped the proofs in his
hand: 'Are we not passing through the fiery zone of passion like
Siegfried?
Why has the ancient dragon bared its teeth to us? We will unsheath
our sword as if we were seeking Brünnhilde.
Look, she is flying from the dawns . . .'[138]

The fact that Adam Petrovich sees the woman he is obsessed
with as Brünnhilde, suggests, furthermore, that certain passages in the *Fourth Symphony* have a strongly autobiographical
flavour:

'I'm only going to think of her . . .'
He lay in his bed. His thoughts raced. He opened his eyes . . .
Other thoughts aroused him – thoughts of sorrow: 'I am the seeker,
and she is Brünnhilde, encircled by a ring of fire!'
'Brünnhilde from the flames . . .'[139]

An unexpected recriminatory letter from Lyubov Blok,
together with reports of sudden gaiety in Petersburg (after the
gloom of 1905), threw Bely once again into despair. Suddenly
feeling imprisoned in Munich, he felt an intense desire to
escape, and mistakenly he thought he could do so into the
mythical world of Wagner, as he had evidently done before:

'Where could I escape to? To Petersburg? No, that way was cut off – I had given her [Lyubov Blok] my word; to Moscow? No ... Where then? I sought escape in Wagner; but my ears were filled with some kind of rubbish and not Wagner; a fit of rage – my article "Against Music".'[140] In Bely's deranged state, not even music could calm his nerves or lift his spirits. At this ultimate low point, it seemed as if all his ideals had crumbled to dust and the desire to retaliate in some way was overwhelming. The result was his article, 'Against Music', which represented an inversion of everything he had previously stood for. Music was the obvious victim for attack, for it was the symbol of all Bely's early idealist aspirations, and Wagner's music, more than any other, had in some way always confirmed his utopian beliefs in the reality of the 'azure dawns'. It had also been an ever-present background to his romance with Lyubov Blok, and therefore qualified for especial excoriation.

In an article written at the end of 1906, Bely was still maintaining that music was the 'soul of all art'.[141] In 'Against Music' however, written and published shortly afterwards,[142] Bely railed against all the idealistic notions he had previously held about music (that it lay 'beyond the boundaries of art', and was 'more than art'), and his onslaught was also directed at people like Ivanov and Chulkov who still held such ideas. Music, Bely now argued, should not be identified with the 'soul of creativity' since it was (merely) 'a form of art'.[143] The meaning of life, in his view, was 'words, names and deeds', and since none of these were properties of music, music could not possibly be the 'main root of religion'.[144] It is in the second half of the article that Bely is more specific about what exactly now repulses him about music. He argues that music is a vampire which has drunk from the soul of the latent hero in each person, while real heroism has been 'as it were seduced by corresponding strains in music', and 'dissolved into the unrealisable'.[145] People are no longer filled with a desire to be real heroes, according to Bely, but are instead content to go to concerts, in order for music to 'loan' them 'greatness' while they are sitting comfortably in their seats. Far from then being inspired to carry out great deeds, he continues, these music lovers simply go home to drink tea, under the false impression that they are happy.[146]

What Bely is talking about here, of course, is his personal reaction to Wagner, in the light of the recent events of his life. If Beethoven had by some miracle sometimes managed to find a natural way out for his 'unnatural art', he writes, Wagner's music was unnatural throughout, and listening to much of it led undoubtedly to a softening of the brain: 'Wagner used the entire depth of his melodies only to show how the muscles of the non-existent hero tense in his non-existent fight with the dragon (it is impossible to see Wagner's attempt as a beginning of the union of words with music for this attempt is utterly false).'[147] Wagner's heroism was false, as 'behind the mask of borrowed heroism' there was only the 'false morality' and 'vacuous, self-satisfied callousness of the weak-willed bourgeoisie'. The music of the future, Bely concludes, must become only the 'means', rather than the 'end', and should return to 'words, names and deeds' that which it 'stole from them'. The Beethoven Symphonies will only constitute 'proper music', according to Bely, when they become just 'one of the means of adorning life'.[148]

Bely's 'Against Music' was not just an attack on Chulkov's doctrine of mystical anarchism and Ivanov's ideas about 'spiritual collectivism';[149] nor was it just a revolt against Medtner's incessant proclamations that music was 'everything'.[150] Most importantly it was a reaction to recent events. Bely drops the heaviest clue himself when he talks about Wagner in the article, for it cannot be without significance that the only work he specifically refers to is *Siegfried*. What seems to have really driven Bely to fulminate 'against music' (in a manner bearing more than a passing resemblance to Nietzsche's diatribes against Wagner) was surely the fact that he felt that he had been given a chance to be a 'Siegfried', but had failed dismally when he was finally spurned by Lyubov Blok. Wagner's heroic music had inspired him with the desire to be a hero in real life, but he had been cruelly deceived. Chastened by his experiences, it was not surprising that Bely was now filled with revulsion for what he had previously marvelled at. He had felt capable of the heroism necessary to win his heroine, but when his plans went awry, he seems to have felt that heroism in contemporary life could only ever be a pale shadow of its counterpart in music.

The publication of 'Against Music' in *Vesy* in March 1907 brought a swift response from Emil Medtner, who took it as a personal attack, according to Bely.[151] The two friends had never met in Munich, for by the time that Medtner arrived at the end of December, Bely had already left for Paris. In his riposte, which was published in *Zolotoe runo* in May 1907,[152] Medtner implied that Bely's sudden outburst against the art form he had previously hallowed was somewhat inevitable. Bely's notion about the theurgic purpose of art, he argued, combined with his endorsement of Schopenhauer's aesthetics of music was bound to end in disenchantment. Medtner also pointed out that it was somewhat disingenuous of Bely to criticise those who linked music to religion, for he himself had also taken Schopenhauer's philosophy of art to its furthest limit in earlier articles by describing music as religious. And it was Bely who had sought nothing less than a self-affirming, universal communion with God that would be achieved through the agency of art, principally music. Because of its being extolled to such an excess, Bely's aspirations were bound to remain aspirations, in Medtner's opinion.[153] Bely and other writers had erred in focussing exclusively on the side of music which Nietzsche defined as 'Dionysian', he argued, because by seeking only 'intoxication' in music, they never heard music as a whole. Medtner found Bely's sudden attack on Wagner 'inexplicable', and concluded that Bely's anger and disappointment stemmed from his inability to articulate why Wagner's music aroused in him such strong feelings. He recommended that those predisposed to softening of the brain should not listen to Wagner anyway, as few could withstand the 'temperature' of the ring of fire with which Wagner surrounded his muse Brünnhilde.[154] Bely was not content to let the matter drop, but his reply to Medtner's reply was decidedly feeble,[155] and brought the acrimonious exchange to an end.

Curiously, the dispute had not brought their correspondence to a halt, but it was probably a matter of some importance to him that his friendship with Medtner did not founder completely, now that he had alienated himself from Blok.[156]

In December 1907, Medtner returned to Moscow from his travels in Germany, and went almost straight from the station to hear a lecture Bely was giving on Nietzsche. For Bely, the reunion with Medtner (whom he had not seen since his visit to Nizhny Novgorod in 1904) was both a 'great joy' and 'the greatest spiritual gift'.[157] In their first meetings, 'everything was as before', in other words, endless discussion of 'Wagner and Schumann and Nietzsche',[158] although Bely thought that his friend had changed since the last time they had met; his eyes had somehow dimmed and become narrower, and a sarcastic frown had formed around his lips. Nevertheless he found that Medtner did much to lift the gloom of the 'bitter days' of 1908.[159] Despite everything that had gone before, Medtner was able once again to encourage Bely to be a 'Siegfried': 'He smoothed over the darkest years [of my life] and strengthened my courage . . . he gathered all the "gnomes" of Germany . . . to forge swords for his friends: it was as if he was saying to me: "Only with this sword will you impale the dragon, free Brünnhilde and become Siegfried" . . . These speeches inspired me.'[160] In Bely's eyes, only Medtner could fill the space in his life that Blok had until recently occupied: 'He was precisely the person who could help resolve the dissonance of my confused relationship with A. A. Blok into the necessary chord. He applied himself with great affection to harmonising the world of my consciousness with the help of music, philosophy and culture.'[161] It was perhaps to show his renewed solidarity with Medtner that Bely signed his review of Chulkov's *The Veil of Isis* (*Pokryvalo Izidy*) in *Vesy* in January 1909, as 'Siegmund' (otherwise known as 'Wölfing').[162]

Ruled over by Emil, who wished to be the conductor of his friends' aspirations, the Medtners' flat now became the Mecca for Germanophiles in Moscow, or as Bely put it, the 'centre for injecting of chaotic Muscovites with Germanism'.[163] Medtner's goal was to make his friends into Germans, although

Bely always maintained that his 'Germans' belonged to the epoch of Goethe, and could never be encountered in real life.[164] By a stroke of irony, the windows of the Medtners' flat in Gnezdikovsky Lane looked out onto the house inhabited by the cosmopolitan Pyotr d'Alheim, a great proselytiser of French culture. Thus while Medtner was preaching the ideas of 'Novalis, Hölderlin, Richard Wagner, Zimmel and Christiansen', d'Alheim would be extolling the merits of 'Corneille and Lamartine, Villiers de l'Isle-Adam and François Villon'.[165] Cultured Moscow at that time was sharply divided into two spheres of influence, according to Bely,[166] since people were enjoined to be either 'with Medtner' or 'with d'Alheim', but not with both.[167] The conflict of cultures was inevitably seen by Medtner in Wagnerian terms, and the clashes of the *Ring* were transposed almost wholesale to the battlefield of Gnezdikovsky Lane. Bely threw himself into the fray: 'The pavement of Maly Gnezdikovsky Lane seemed to be the Rhine, in which splashed the Rhine daughters – the Turgenev mermaids.[168] From the d'Alheim fortress one could hear the song of the Lorelei enchantress; here appeared the perfidious Loge himself in the guise of Bryusov; the Moscow Wotan was active, his physiognomy thoroughly changed since the time of the Wanderer (he appeared as Rachinsky) ... our Brünnhilde, M. A. Morozova, also came here [once] ...'[169] A myth now grew up that was no longer about the 'Golden Fleece' [*Zolotoe runo*] which the Argonauts had sought, but about the 'Rhine gold' [*zoloto Reina*], which the 'evil gnomes' had stolen. Medtner was still obsessed by his *The Wibelungen*-inspired notion that the characters of the *Ring* were inextricably linked to medieval German history, and, 'baring his teeth, felt that the destruction of Valhalla, and the Wolfs, the Welfs, the Guelphs and the Ghibellines were all joined together'. In the myth of Medtner, according to Bely, 'the era of Attila was linked by the twentieth century to the era of Friedrich Barbarossa and centred in Gnezdikovsky Lane'.[170]

In the time which had elapsed since their last meeting, Medtner had become 'more of a viking, a trouble-maker, an ideological swordsman who had declared war against the

Nibelungs: the perfidious Mime (d'Alheim, perhaps), the perfidious Alberich (the composer Reger), the critic Karatygin
above all and those who supported the destruction of the
"Wohltemperierte klavier"'.[171] Liszt and Reger were the
oldest 'enemies' of the Medtner household,[172] while d'Alheim's
cult of Liszt made him 'Mime' in Medtner's eyes, but also
'Hagen', for promoting his 'poisonous mixture of music by
Grétry, Musorgsky and Liszt'.[173] To complicate matters
further, Liszt was also seen by Medtner as 'Mime', according
to Bely.[174] Karatygin, meanwhile, was condemned, like the
composer Reger he idolised, as 'Alberich'. Even Medtner's
own brother Nikolay was cast as 'Alberich' for patronising the
House of Song, which often performed his music. The 'House
of Song' [*Dom pesni*] had been founded by d'Alheim and his
wife, the singer Mariya Olenina in 1908. A venture which
sought to explore the link between poetry and music in the
performance of songs, with accompanying lectures, it was an
enterprise which involved many notable Moscow critics, trans-
lators and composers and resulted in a considerable raising of
musical standards in the city. Seven or eight concerts were
given each year, with lectures on both specialised and general
topics.

The 'House of Song' was seen by Medtner as a 'trap for
twentieth-century Siegfrieds' who had to compete with the
French 'Rolands' in order to win the hand of the Russian
'Brünnhilde' (the 'future culture of Russia')[175] by preaching
the culture of Goethe, Beethoven and Kant.[176] Both
'Germany' and 'France' had laid claim to 'Russia', he
declared, and had raised their swords ('Nothung' versus
'Durandal') for her.[177] Strangely enough, the goal of the
'House of Song' was to 'promote the work of Wagner', albeit
through song, not opera.[178] D'Alheim's belief that 'only art
could revolutionise life'[179] certainly brought him into line with
Wagner's ideas, and he would go into great detail to back it up
with 'magnificent quotations' and 'demonstrations' in front of
Bely and his friends to show 'how important it was to remember the ideas of Wagner and Schumann'.[180] For Bely, Nikolay
Medtner and numerous others, it was just not possible to make

a choice between the 'Gothic-Germanic' and the 'Celtic-Romanesque'.[181] In November 1908, Bely actually gave a lecture at the 'House of Song', and began to spend a great deal of time with Mariya Olenina's niece Asya. As a consequence, his free time was divided between his two sets of friends.[182] Medtner, with some justification, saw Bely's relationship with Asya as a threat to their friendship (it was she who encouraged Bely's interest in Rudolf Steiner) and vainly tried to persuade his friend that his place was not with the d'Alheims, who embodied the 'spirit of darkness' for him. Waving his hands in the air, he would preach all the more passionately 'Beethoven, Wagner, Brahms and his brother'.[183]

The lectures d'Alheim gave at his wife's concerts enjoyed great popularity. Unlike Medtner, he would leave nothing to chance and his talks were always painstakingly prepared.[184] Furthermore, he enjoyed talking to an audience. Medtner, on the other hand, only felt happy when he was at home, at his friends the Morozovs' house, or out on a walk with the company of just two or three people, but then, writes Bely, he would be peerless.[185] Margarita Morozova, the above-mentioned Russian Brünnhilde, was the beautiful and talented wife of the millionaire and art patron Mikhail Morozov and hostess to an artistic salon during the Symbolist period. Bely had idolised Morozova from afar as the heroine of his second 'Symphony' since 1901, but had only begun to visit her regularly after 1905, when they became firm friends, forming a triumvirate with Medtner once the latter had returned to Moscow. 'We three often spent evenings together', Morozova writes in her memoir of Bely; 'Our talks stretched into the early hours and in spring, when it became light early, we used to go out into our garden and walk around, inhaling the fragrance of the lilacs and listening to the chatter of the birds.'[186] It was no coincidence that Morozova was seen by Medtner and Bely as a Russian Brünnhilde, for she had visited Bayreuth in 1901 with her husband,[187] and seemed to shared her two friends' passionate interest in Wagner. The composer, indeed, seems to have been a constant topic of discussion, according to Bely, who maintains that their 'conversations "en trois"' about 'the rhythm of culture, the culture of music, Nietzsche-Wagner, Russia, Germany' helped him worked out his ideas about 'the genesis of our culture'.[188]

BELY, MEDTNER, ELLIS AND MUSAGET

At the beginning of January 1909, a meeting with the Theosophist and follower of Rudolf Steiner, Anna Mintslova, had marked Bely's first serious foray into the occult world, and the replacement of the *Ring* with *Parsifal* as a prism through which to see the world.[189] Mintslova proposed to Bely that they form a secret 'Brotherhood of Knights of Truth', and, as Maria Carlson points out, certain themes which recurred in their conversation, including 'Eastern occultists', 'enemies systematically poisoning Russia', 'knighthood', 'the medieval motif' and 'the role of Russia', were later to find an echo in Bely and Ivanov's writings.[190] Some of these themes were not of course new to Bely. The 'medieval motif', and the theme of 'knighthood' had appeared in his first 'Symphony', in his early poetry and in the anonymous letters he sent to Margarita Morozova. The idea of 'enemies, systematically poisoning Russia', moreover, was almost a fixation with Bely, and manifested itself most frequently, as we have seen, in the identification of real-life events and situations with the various conflicts of the *Ring*. Medtner's habit of seeing life in terms of the struggle between Siegfried and the dragon or the Nibelungs naturally appealed to a writer whose own life was fraught with conflicts of one kind or another, and who tended to see predicaments in black and white terms. As a student, for example, Bely had become obsessed with this idea of 'destroying the enemies', and would gather stones to throw every day at their invisible images in the well at his family's country estate, thinking he was somehow bringing about their destruction.[191] Medtner, the 'master swordsman' who 'loved getting into fights', had accompanied Bely on his last visit to the estate in May 1908 before it was sold, and found Bely's 'strategy' an excellent way of venting his rage against the Nibelung enemies who he thought were poisoning Russian culture: 'he would pick up a stone, and having first weighed it in the air, quivering with some sarcastic words directed at the Nibelungs (d'Alheim or the critic Karatygin), he would then throw it and listen to see if it fell to the bottom of the well'.[192]

In May 1909, Bely had met with Mintslova again. This time she explained that the new order of knights arising was the resurgence of Rosicrucianism and that Bely was to form with her and an unnamed individual in Petersburg (Vyacheslav Ivanov) a mystical triumvirate to co-ordinate a Russian lodge. They were to 'group together those who join in brotherhood', 'to become the standard of the spiritual world; those individuals would prepare themselves by doing exercises; exercises are armament . . . the armed KNIGHTS would form a circle of knights (the ROUND TABLE at which the Grail appears, first kept by the Knights of the Grail, later by the Knights Templar and finally by the Rosicrucians)'.[193] The link with Wagner's *Parsifal* here is an obvious one, and Medtner was the first person whom Bely thought of involving in this enterprise. When Medtner returned from a trip abroad in the spring of 1909, Bely went immediately to see him at his dacha and at dawn recounted all that had passed between him and Mintslova. It is hardly surprising that Medtner 'was appreciatively thrilled by the magnificent Wagnerianism of the whole',[194] for as Maria Carlson points out, Mintslova brought together many timely factors.[195] Medtner did indeed respond positively to the idea of this knightly order (even if *Parsifal* was not his favourite work by Wagner), and for two main reasons, according to Bely:

The enemies were spreading like mushrooms; without the knighthood, without taking up arms, we would probably run into difficulties; secondly, knights, lodges, yes, yes: the musical leitmotif of that theme; Siegfried, the theme of Nothung, Friedrich Hohenstaufen, the knights of the Grail; here after all was Lohengrin, Parsifal: 'Ti-te-ta! Ti-te-ta!' . . . and illumined by the dawn, he was already conducting. In a word, he perceived the idea about the order like he perceived everything else in the world, in a totally musical way.[196]

Ellis, another close friend from the Argonaut days, was also eager to be involved, but Mintslova considered him too unstable to be initiated into the 'Brotherhood'. His injured pride did not stop him becoming an active mouthpiece for Rosicrucian ideas, however. Much to the consternation of Bely (and presumably also Medtner) who had been bound to secrecy, Ellis turned the sculptor Konstantin Krakht's studio into a 'noisy platform' from which he proclaimed the necessity for organising an expedition to seek the Grail.[197]

As well as 'preparing for a cosmic battle with the secret enemies' in the spring of 1909,[198] Bely and Medtner also discussed the rather more down-to-earth idea of setting up a publishing house. Medtner had long dreamed of there being a platform for the younger generation of Russian Symbolists who had first grouped together as Argonauts, for he was convinced that he, Bely and Ellis could 'achieve a great deal' if they worked together.[199] It was only through the financial generosity of Medtner's German friend Hedwig Friedrich, however, that Musaget came into being.[200] Medtner had previously excelled at bringing together 'triads' of people with different qualities, but in forming Musaget, he now had to bring together 'sextets and dectets', envisaging himself as a violin, Bely as a 'cello and the impetuous Ellis as the brass in its 'editorial symphony'.[201] Musaget was the name the friends eventually chose for their new publishing house, because Apollo Musagetes was the 'leader of all the muses, representing the choral dance [*khorovod*] of the arts, philosophy and myth'.[202]

The main Symbolist publishing house Skorpion and its journal *Vesy* (which closed at the end of 1909) had presented Symbolism more as an 'artistic school', according to Bely, whereas for himself, Ellis and Medtner, Symbolism was more a 'world view'.[203] The declared purpose of Musaget, therefore, was to focus on the 'problem of culture' and to 'throw bridges across movements and schools in art to the wider horizons of philosophical problems'.[204] Wagner was to feature prominently in the new enterprise, for in providing funds for Musaget, Hedwig Friedrich made the sole stipulation that the proposed journal should be Germanophile in its outlook and 'by no means hostile to Wagner'.[205] This was not a problem to Bely and Medtner, of course, whose affiliations had always been Germanic and Wagner-orientated. Only Ellis amongst the proposed editorial triumvirate felt any real sympathy towards the French tradition, but within a year he not only became convinced of the superiority of German culture, but also had transformed himself into a fanatical Wagnerian.

At first, energies were focussed on the publication of a journal, and at the end of August 1909, Bely wrote to Medtner outlining its possible contents, proposing that there should definitely be articles on German culture, particularly on Wagner and Goethe.[206] The following month, Bely wrote again to Medtner about the proposed journal: 'If in the first year there are to be two articles on general cultural problems, two articles on Greek culture, two articles on Eastern culture, four on German culture (Goethe, Nietzsche, Wagner and others), two on cultural and religious problems, two on energy theory, two on ethics and aesthetics, then we *must* have an editorial team.'[207] Bely went on to suggest names of possible authors for each of those sections, and asked for Medtner's advice with regard to the articles on German culture: 'Who? Make use of your time in Weimar. Suggested topics: *Nietzsche* ..., *Wagner*: Medtner, who else? A. Ivanov (remember his two articles on Wagner in *Mir iskusstva*? They were interesting), Argamakov (a Wagnerian, can write well, is recommended by Krakht).'[208] In November 1909, however, plans for the Musaget journal were temporarily shelved,[209] and book publishing remained its chief activity for the next two years.

In 1910, the year that Russian Symbolism underwent its greatest crisis, leading to its collapse as a coherent movement, seven books were published by Musaget, including Bely's collection of essays *Symbolism* (*Simvolizm*), and Ellis' monograph *The Russian Symbolists* (*Russkie simvolisty*), which ends with the following words: 'We believe in the great, universal future of Symbolism! ... Then, and only then [when we serve the supreme symbol, the Eternal Feminine], will our darkened and impoverished altar be illumined again, and amongst us will appear the teacher so long awaited, the servant and knight whom we will meet in the name of the new Parsifal! He shall come!'[210] Clearly Ellis had undergone his conversion to

Wagnerism by the time he submitted the final manuscript, and in July 1910, he wrote to Medtner from Germany (where he had now become Anthroposophy's most recent neophyte) to assure him of his belief in Musaget and also, *inter alia*, to admit defeat in their dispute. What that dispute was about becomes only too clear when Ellis confesses to being won over:

(1) in the acknowledgement of the supremacy of the Germans over the French, (2) in the indisputable acknowledgement of the supremacy of R. Wagner over all Symbolism, with Baudelaire at the head; on the other hand, I believe that in time you will bow down to the absolute personality of Steiner . . . In my Wagnerisation, which is still progressing, I feel even closer to you personally . . . Huge changes are going on inside me . . . Steiner's influence on me is all powerful. Only Wagner with his *Tristan* and the classic Middle Ages are now acceptable to me because of that. I will never be a Goethean, and with Nietzsche I have parted forever. But I love *Parsifal* like Dante's *Paradiso*. There is no Dionysianism there . . .[211]

Under the influence of Steiner, Ellis had come to believe that the only way out of the crisis that Symbolism was undergoing (of which the impulse towards 'Dionysianism' was a salient feature, in his view) lay in the subordination of art to religion. Accordingly, his letter ends: 'I await Parsifal',[212] for Wagner's last opera, he felt, manifested this tendency to a supreme degree (although as far as Wagner was concerned, the exact opposite was in fact the case).

For Ellis, Bely and others of their circle, the move to occultism and Anthroposophy from Symbolism was a natural one, and the fervent admiration Ellis developed for Wagner is not surprising, for the composer was a key figure to both movements. Rudolf Steiner had given many lectures on Wagner in 1905,[213] and as Colin Wilson notes, he was 'an artist for whom he felt profound sympathy, since Wagner had laboured to create his own "Mystery Centre" in Bayreuth, and had subsequently crowned his career with a celebration of the Christian mystery in *Parsifal*'.[214] Steiner believed that there was 'a deep connection between the artistic work of Wagner and the spiritual movement of the present day known as Theosophy',[215] and that this connection was especially strong

1. Mikhail Vrubel, 'Val'kiriya', portrait of Princess Mariya Tenisheva (1899)

2. Vladimir Tatlin, set design for *Der Fliegende Holländer* (1915–18)

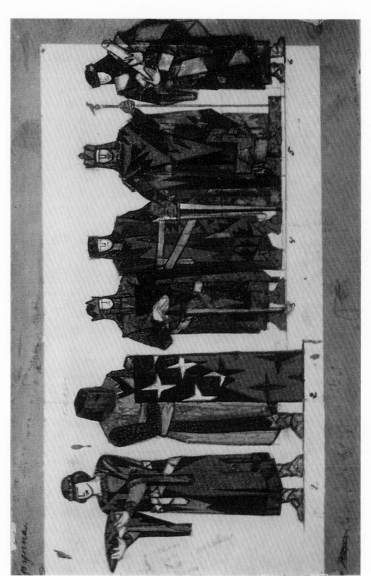

3. Ivan Fedotov, costume designs for *Lohengrin* (1918)

4. Georgy Yakulov, set design for Mayakovsky's *Mystery Bouffe* (1920), which became the set design for *Rienzi* (1923)

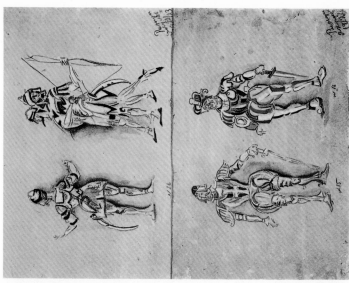

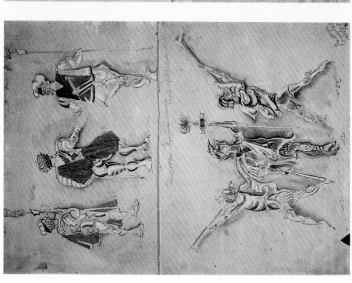

5. Georgy Yakulov, costume designs for *Rienzi* (1923)

6. G. Kosyakov, illustration for the Society of Wagnerian Art's chamber performance of *Das Rheingold* (1925)

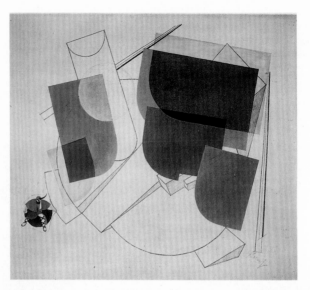

7.   Aleksandr Khvostenko-Khvostov, design for act one of *Die Walküre* (the Hunding theme) (1929)

8.   Aleksandr Khvostenko-Khvostov, design for act one of *Die Walküre* (the Sieglinde theme) (1929)

9. Aleksandr Khvostenko-Khvostov, costume designs for *Lohengrin* (1932)

10. Aleksandr Khvostenko-Khvostov, costume designs for *Lohengrin* (1932)

in *Parsifal*, since Wagner's last opera, he contended, had direct links (through the secret of the Holy Grail) with the esoteric tradition of Rosicrucianism, which was of crucial importance to the 'spiritual science' of Anthroposophy: 'Richard Wagner knew in his soul that he must send forth into the world this secret of the Holy Grail, [and that] he must send it out into the world in music.'[216] From his letters to Medtner, it is obvious that Ellis absorbed all Steiner's ideas about Wagner and *Parsifal* unquestioningly, believing like his mentor, for example, that 'Wagner's creative work consists, in its essence, of a religious deepening of art',[217] and that Wagner was 'not merely' a musician, but one 'whose desire it is to resuscitate for the people of modern times the mysteries of the Holy Grail'.[218] Ellis became increasingly convinced that through Wagner, Russian Symbolism could emerge from its present impasse into a new form of existence, that 'a new form of Symbolism' was emerging from two central points of concentration, 'the link between Wagner and Schopenhauer' (which was 'the most important point of culture') and 'the link between Goethe and Schiller'.[219]

Ellis returned to Moscow in autumn 1910 to disseminate the teachings of Steiner and also to preach the great truths embodied in *Parsifal*. Musaget had officially begun its activities in March of that year and three different circles had formed under its aegis. One group was committed to the exploration of verse rhythm (and was led by Bely), another concentrated on the discussion of philosophical issues (and was attended frequently by Bely), while the third was devoted to the study of Symbolism. This last group was run by Ellis and Krakht. Bely was not a regular habitué of this group, as its real interest, he claimed, lay in the reading of papers that called for the 'search for Monsalvat and Kitezh'[220] (in other words, the Grail).[221] Ellis was now preaching Rosicrucianism together with his new-found Wagnerism with even greater fanaticism than in 1909. At this point, Bely did not want to hear about Rosicrucianism from Ellis, however. Having initially placed great hopes in Mintslova and the mission of the 'Brotherhood' (to the point of convincing himself that the entire Musaget enterprise was part of it) he had gradually become disillusioned and had broken permanently with Mintslova in May 1910. Yet, despite his affected disdain for the style in which Ellis preached his new-found beliefs, Bely was apparently still entranced by the idea of Rosicrucianism, and had become fascinated by *Parsifal*.

Bely spent five months abroad between November 1910 and May 1911 with Asya Turgeneva on a quasi-honeymoon, and his *Travel Notes* (*Putevye zametki*) contain numerous references both to Wagner and his last work, although it must be borne in mind that Bely's habit of revising his texts means that the Wagnerian allusions were possibly inserted after Bely's conversion to Anthroposophy. After travelling initially to Venice, the couple went to Sicily via Naples, and in a manner reminiscent of Medtner, who labelled people as either 'Siegfried' or 'Mime', allowing for no intermediate state, Bely cast Naples as 'Klingsor'.[222] During his stay in Sicily, as Boris Christa points out, Bely felt alternately like a knight in search of the Grail (of whom sexual chastity was demanded) and Amfortas, under the power of the evil Klingsor: 'I heard the sounds of the great Wagner and the Knights Templar before me. Monreale drew me on, Florence and Rome repulsed me. During those years I was in suspense over the secret of Klingsor, whose powers bent me to the earth. I was Amfortas – my terrible wound awaited healing. The Grail drew me on.'[223] In Palermo, Bely and Asya stayed in the hotel where Wagner had spent several months finishing the score of *Parsifal*, and this evidently made a great impression on Bely, as he asked to see the rooms that Wagner had stayed in and talked at length to the hotel owner about his German guest. Not only does Bely remark on the fact to Blok and his mother in the letters he wrote at the time,[224] but he devotes several pages of his *Travel Notes* to recounting his conversations with the hotel owner about Wagner's behaviour.[225]

Although the legendary Monsalvat was held to be in Spain, Bely located it in Sicily, seeing the island's geographical position in relation to Italy as comparable to the *Parsifal* scenario:

From Calabria, Klingsor throws his spear menacingly through the strait to the land of Sicily; and the soil of Sicily shudders from the spear's blow; its red, bleeding wound is Etna. Sicily is Amfortas, suffering a terrible wound for bearing the secret purpose: to bring the grace hidden in the Grail to earth; the smile of the mosaic is the divine prototype of the possibilities of earthly life . . . taken captive by the black Klingsor, it awaits the deliverer.[226]

One might not necessarily leap to the conclusion that there was an explicit link with Wagner when Bely asks where 'Perceval' is, given his informed references to Chrestien de Troyes and Wolfram von Eschenbach, the authors of the original legend of *Parsifal*, yet he clearly did also consider Wagner as central to the mystery of the Grail: 'Wolfram's lines depict [Perceval] as the bearer of light; and as gentle as a dove; he is Wagner's music, I have overheard this music; it sounds out over Palermo.'[227] Over the centuries, claims Bely, figures as diverse as Pythagoras, Empedocles, Friedrich II and Count Cagliostro had all tried to solve the mystery of the Grail (in other words, the workings of the volcano, Mount Etna), but had been driven back by the 'blows of Klingsor's spear': 'Then came Goethe and Wagner from the north to solve the riddle. The former found that "here was the key to everything",[228] while the latter caught the sound of Pythagorean fractions in the air; unity in multiplicity . . . in the mystery drama the riddle of Sicily stands once again. Here he completed Perceval.'[229] Like Ellis, Bely declares that the future lies 'in Perceval' and in Rosicrucianism:

Wagner, the precursor of the Future heard this future . . . the sounds of the mystery drama are a ripe, succulent fruit . . . 'Perceval' blossomed with a legend that was nurtured by the juices of both the East and the West . . . two cultures collide within it and it shudders from the age-old struggle . . . Beneath the struggle is the ripening symbol of Sicily: music, or Saint Cecilia . . . it was she who must have summoned the great Wagner, whom life endowed with wisdom, so that he could speak in sounds: the mystery of the wild rose, will blossom in a new way; the cross, outlined on the old cathedral with a clear circle is the cross within the rose.[230]

Whilst Bely continued his travels with Asya Turgeneva in the Middle East, plans to publish a Musaget journal were being

revived. Vyacheslav Ivanov (who had affiliated with Musaget
shortly before its launch) had written to Blok in January 1911,
suggesting that they join forces with Bely to publish a 'Diary of
Three Poets'. Bely greeted the idea with great enthusiasm upon
his return to Russia, as he was keen to draw Blok into the fold
of Musaget.[231] By September 1911, the putative 'Diary of
Three Poets' had become *Trudy i dni* ('Works and Days'),[232]
and was to be published under the general editorship of Bely
and Medtner.[233] The first issue appeared in January 1912, and
contained an affirmation by Bely of Musaget's strong allegiance to Wagner, in which he declared that culture should
strive for 'organic wholeness' (the ever elusive goal in his own
work), as the two 'great artists and sages of our recent and
turbulent past', Nietzsche and Wagner, had done. Nietzsche
had sought this 'organic wholeness' by attempting to create
culture 'anew', according to Bely, whilst Wagner strove to find
'the eternal' in pre-existing forms. 'And it is in the latter
method', writes Bely 'that we perceive greater significance.'
Following Wagner's precepts, then, could lead to the 'religious
culture longed for by our epoch'.[234] In the second issue of
Trudy i dni, Bely again invoked Wagner and Nietzsche as the
spiritual forbears of the particular brand of Symbolism prom-
ulgated by Musaget: 'We remain Russian Symbolists. But we
bow down with deepest reverence before the great geniuses
Wagner and Nietzsche. Bowing down before the past is not a
sign of subordination to the past.'[235] Thus for Bely, at least,
Wagner was a key figure, the cynosure in a constellation of
great artists who had been drawn into the orbit of Russian
Symbolism, which, in its idealistic aspirations towards organi-
cism and universalism, was rapidly spiralling out of the realm
of art. As A. V. Lavrov has commented, 'the names which the
Trudy i dni theoreticians used to support their ideas about
Symbolism appeared with varying frequency and in different
combinations, but they all without fail brought Symbolism out
of the confines of an historically developed literary movement.
Homer, Dante, Shakespeare, Goethe, Tyutchev, Gogol,
Nietzsche and Wagner all served to affirm the supra-historical
conception of Symbolism as a sort of super-art that was

emerging from the greatest artistic achievements of mankind.'[236]

The 'Wagneriana' section of *Trudy i dni* was inaugurated by Emil Medtner with the publication of a translation of an article about Wagner's autobiography by the ultra-conservative Houston Stewart Chamberlain in the second issue of the journal.[237] In 1913, when *Trudy i dni* ceased to exist as a periodical publication, the composition of the journal changed to comprise two sections, the first of which consisted exclusively of materials under the rubrics 'Goetheana' and 'Wagneriana' (in 1914 'Danteana' was added to this section). Most of the space in 'Wagneriana' was initially taken up by Medtner's 'Sketches for a Commentary' (*Nabroski k kommentariyu*), although the major study of Wagner's music dramas which Medtner dreamed would arise from these sketches never materialised, and as A. F. Losev has pointed out, these articles, for all their occasional insights and promise, were ultimately rather disappointing.[238] The article on *Parsifal* by Ellis, meanwhile, says considerably more about the author's preoccupations with medieval religious art and spiritual 'knighthood' than it does about its supposed subject.[239] It cannot therefore be said that any of these articles made a significant contribution to Russian Wagner scholarship. The same, unfortunately, must be said of Sergey Durylin's *Wagner and Russia* (*Vagner i Rossiya*), published by Musaget in 1913.[240] Durylin considered that Rimsky-Korsakov's last opera was a triumphant vindication of his claim that Wagner was closer to Russia than any other country in his aspiration towards religious art, and in his deliberate use of folk sources (that is to say, myth) as the substance of his art: 'Wagner came to Russia along [the] path of Christian myth creation, and Russia will meet him with joy and acknowledgement, for that has been our national and religious path from time immemorial – the path to the invisible city.'[241] The publication of Sergey Shenrok's translation of Wagner's essay *Die Wibelungen* by Musaget in 1913 would appear to be something of a curiosity were it not for the fact that, as we discovered earlier, Medtner had something of a fixation with Friedrich Barbarossa.

ELLIS AND THE 'RUSSIAN WAGNER'

In September 1911, Ellis moved permanently to Germany to devote himself to the cause of Anthroposophy. Despite his absorption with the personality of Rudolf Steiner, he was also working frenetically on translations of all Wagner's librettos for Musaget, a task he saw as wholly consonant with his new calling. These translations, referred to generically as the 'Russian Wagner', were envisioned by Ellis as nothing less than the key to Russia's salvation. *Parsifal* was the first work he attempted (under commission by Medtner) and by the end of October that year, Ellis claimed to have translated half of the *Ring*, as he wrote jubilantly to Medtner:

I translated both *Rheingold* and *Die Walküre* during August and Kiselyov and even Petrovsky and Rachinsky[242] found my translations above average. I'm working on *Siegfried* now in my spare time . . . The whole of the *Ring* will be issued in Russian in a luxurious edition. It will be important for young people in Russia and you will be able to feel that I first came to Wagner under your influence from the French [Symbolists], whom I have abandoned once and for all.[243]

The following month Ellis wrote again to Medtner to thank him for making corrections to his translation of *Parsifal*, and to inform him that he had obtained permission from Steiner to publish his lecture on *Parsifal*[244] as an accompaniment to his translation. Meanwhile, he awaited an 'official answer' from Musaget as to whether it was permissible for him to write a 'Symbolist' preface to his translation.[245]

Medtner wanted nothing to do with Anthroposophy and was to lead a bitter and increasingly solitary struggle against the rising tide of occultism as gradually more and more of the associates of Musaget became disciples of Steiner. He had evidently tried to remonstrate with Ellis, for in a letter of December 1911, the latter retorted that 'talking about the doctor without having lived with him, read his works and experienced the revival of the best ideals of Christianity' was 'utter dilettantism', like 'judging Wagner having only heard *Tannhäuser* at the Zimin Theatre[246] or by leafing through the score of the *Ring*'.[247] Ellis' relations with Medtner were to become increasingly fraught, a situation compounded by the rather large discrepancy between the extent of his aspirations and his talent as a translator. The initially ebullient and over-confident tone in his letters was gradually to give rise to one of desperation as Musaget started to default on the small stipend it was paying him to carry out the Wagner translations, and it slowly dawned on Ellis that Medtner did not find his work acceptable for publication. In December 1911, however, he was still full of faith in his messianic belief that Wagner would lead the Russian people to a new form of existence: 'The Wagner cult has taken fire, it is the salvation of present-day Russia from all evils, I feel within myself an endless number of ideas ... about *Wagner*. I am ready to translate *all* his works and write a major monograph on him.'[248] In his euphoria, Ellis proposed to Medtner a whole series of other books on Dante, Byron, Wagner, Baudelaire, Goethe and theosophy. 'Of course not everything will be acceptable to Musaget', he admits, 'but Musaget will certainly publish the book on Wagner. I can already hear the voice dictating it. I will write a part of it as an introduction to [my translation of] *Parsifal*.' 'You already know that I am *not* a writer', he continues, 'but an orator, and not a man of letters but a preacher and disseminator of ideas ... In one year I managed to get Moscow interested in Steiner and Wagner (as I once got Moscow interested in Baudelaire) without having seen Steiner or knowing any German ....'.[249]

When Ellis informs Medtner that Steiner had advised him to 'concentrate on Wagner', we can begin to surmise to what extent his zeal was fuelled by the inspiration of his teacher. Steiner, according to Ellis, had advanced the idea that there could be no art without theosophy, and had privately confessed to him that *all* modern art was false and exclusively concerned with the imagination (the so-called 'astral plane'), with the sole exceptions of works by Goethe and Wagner. Steiner's advice, writes Ellis, had given him the 'strength to translate *Götterdämmerung* as well', in a way he had 'never translated anything else':

I think I will spend a minimum of ten years on Wagner and then will present him to Russia – translations and commentaries. Definitely Wagner – he is the only bridge from Symbolism to theosophy, from paganism to Christianity, from individualism to knighthood, from madness to wisdom, from passion to purity, from pessimism to 'resurrection', from redemption to messianism, from *art* to art, from the stage to the mystery, from the cult of the feminine to the cult of the masculine ... from fantasy to the more real ... from demonism to seraphism, from the all-human to the super-human. I adore Wagner ...[250]

In another letter written in December 1911, Ellis wrote to inform Medtner of his rapid progress with the 'Russian Wagner':

In two weeks time, I'll be sending [the translation of] *Götterdämmerung*, which will be given to Bugaev for his expert advice as is only fair and desirable. After the same amount of time I will send *Lohengrin*, three quarters of which I did in Hannover. I'm personally more pleased with it than I am with my *Parsifal* translation; it was easier to translate and besides, theosophy strengthens artistic creativity a thousand times, creating an *ethical* uplift which is essential in Wagner ... The manuscript of *Lohengrin* will be given to you and you alone, otherwise it will take centuries ...[251]

In February 1912, Ellis wrote to ask Medtner again to agree to his conditions for the publication of his *Parsifal* translation and to ask whether his translation of *Der fliegende Holländer* for Musaget should be accompanied by a biographical and literary introduction without, he was tactful enough to add, any 'occultism and theosophy'.[252] Demanding also an answer on whether monographs, translations of books on Wagner and articles by him would be needed by Musaget, Ellis proposed to Medtner that a forum be held by the Musaget editors to discuss their Wagner plans, and offered articles for *Trudy i dni* on the following topics:

1. Wagner's pessimism (Wagner and Schopenhauer)
2. The sources of Wagner's *Parsifal*
3. Wagner's symbolism and aesthetics
4. Wagner's writings on [musical] drama
5. The Bayreuth enterprise – history, biography ...
6. Wagner's first works

I await a prompt response! I could do a decent monograph on Wagner *in a year* and then go on to Baudelaire. What would be best? *I am engrossed in Wagner from every point of view!*[253]

By now, Ellis was virtually penniless, as the payments from Musaget had become extremely infrequent,[254] and by March 1912 he had reached desperation point: 'Surely my translations of Wagner (approved by the whole of Musaget) give me the right to at least a fleeting existence?',[255] he appealed to Medtner in a letter advising him that he was writing articles on 'Wagner and his Lohengrin' and 'Demonism in Wagner'.[256] Struck by a wave of deep despondency, Ellis confided in Medtner his fear that Symbolism would soon founder if it did not concentrate its energies on Wagner, Goethe, Schiller and Novalis. Everything had failed, according to Ellis, except Musaget, which alone could redeem the situation. Medtner's only hope, in Ellis' evaluation, was sexual abstinence, Christianity and conversion to Rosicrucianism.[257]

An ecstatic reunion with Bely after his meeting with Steiner in May 1912 fired Ellis with a new energy, however, and he felt a renewed allegiance to Musaget. His presentiment that Rosicrucianism would fail in Russia without 'Romanticism, art and music' compelled him to return to Musaget 'like a prodigal son', he wrote to Medtner that month, yet he was frustrated that the first issue of *Trudy i dni* had been published and his *Parsifal* translation had still not appeared:

For me there is no Christianity without Romanticism, without Dante, without the Grail legend, the tears of Elisabeth and Tannhäuser, without the Gothic style, the cult of the Madonna ... Wagner, whom I have learned to love even more, has brought us together ... Hurry up and publish *Parsifal* and my verses soon. I have already translated the 'Dutchman', now *Tannhäuser*. Tell me if I need to translate *Rienzi* or even *Das Liebesverbot* and *Jesus von Nazareth*. The slow publication horrifies me ...[258]

Medtner had obviously not yet abandoned the idea of publishing Ellis' translation of *Parsifal*, for advance notice of its publication was given in the Musaget catalogue printed at the back of the first issue of *Trudy i dni*: 'This translation of R. Wagner's most significant work constitutes the first attempt to provide a comparatively close transcription in Russian (making the libretto of the musical mystery drama into an independent literary work). In striving to convey more or less the rhythm of Wagner's original verse, the Russian translation always uses rhyme, ignoring the irregular use of rhyme in the original ...'[259] Only Parsifal, writes the author of this catalogue entry (probably Ellis himself), is capable and worthy of becoming the 'central figure of Christian mystery, the ultimate form of the development of Symbolism'.[260] In June 1912 Ellis sent a further plea for his article about *Parsifal* to be published in *Trudy i dni*. He declared that he found the journal 'interesting', but felt that it needed a new slogan. 'From Symbolism to the Occultism of Rosicrucianism', however, was something to which Medtner and Vyacheslav Ivanov, who were now feeling the onslaught of 'Steinerism' from all sides (by now, Bely, Ellis, Petrovsky and Sizov were all Anthroposophists), would never agree. Ellis also informed Medtner that he was now translating *Tannhäuser* in this letter. 'Wagner in Russia is essential at the moment', he wrote worriedly, 'I believe that Musaget will agree to publish the *entire* Russian Wagner, but it must be done soon. I fear that some crude, cheap translations will appear.'[261]

Ellis was slowly coming to realise, however, that all his Wagner projects were coming to nothing. A sudden insight into the deficiencies of his translations led to a massive loss of confidence. 'It is clear to me', he wrote on 17 June 1912, 'that neither my poems, nor the commissioned translations of all Wagner's dramas can be published ... because they are basically bad ... It is clear that I am not necessary to Musaget!'[262] Ellis now began to face up to the reality that his Wagner translations were not good enough to be published, but he was not willing to acquiesce without a fight, as the following passage from his next hysterical and deluded letter to Medtner shows. The publication of his Wagner translations had evidently become a matter of life or death importance to him:

> I protest against the categorical refusal to publish my Wagner translations, considering that *only* I can translate Wagner in Russia now, but am prepared under your competent supervision, as a pupil, to re-do my translations 100,000 times because I am working on behalf of Wagner and Musaget and not Ellis ... I request that *Parsifal* and *Lohengrin* (Krakht has it) are accepted *on principle*. I am ready to subject any other Wagner translation to your criticism ...[263]

Ellis was also still determined that Musaget should become the mouthpiece of Rosicrucianism and Steinerism since he steadfastly believed that Symbolism's transition to occultism was its only natural course. The downfall of Musaget, according to Ellis, would not only be a 'blow to the whole of Russian literature', but would also 'have a demoralising effect on Russia' as a whole. Wagner, he maintained, held the key to Musaget's survival, since it was precisely his works which represented the transition from Symbolism to the mystery dramas of Steiner (i.e. occultism):

> With this in mind, I formed a Wagner circle, translated Wagner and made commentaries. It is vital to publish a 'Russian Wagner' as soon as possible, for otherwise the chance will be lost. In order not to perish, Musaget must publish a Russian translation of Steiner's mysteries after Wagner. If Musaget does not do this, the mysteries will be published elsewhere and the most vibrant ... currents of modernity and of the future will pass it by ...[264]

Bely joined Ellis in the campaign to propagate Anthroposophical ideas on the pages of *Trudy i dni*, and by the middle of 1912, editorial unity was already destroyed. Medtner reassured Vyacheslav Ivanov that the 'preaching of occultism, particularly of a certain [Steinerian] slant' was 'inadmissible',[265] and that without maintaining its allegiance to Kant, Goethe and Wagner, the existence of *Trudy i dni* would be 'a lie, a fiction'.[266] Yet, as A. V. Lavrov points out, 'a certain leaning towards Anthroposophy' nevertheless became noticeable,[267] particularly in Ellis' 'Munich Letters' (*Myunkhenskie pis'ma*), which were the first articles by him to be published in the journal.[268]

In putting forward his theory that there was a close link
between the occultism of Steiner and Symbolism, Ellis
inevitably found it necessary to refer to Wagner: 'From the
very beginning, [the Symbolist movement] strove towards the
synthesis of all elements in culture and even semi-consciously
gravitated towards its origins, i.e., towards the region lying
beneath the concept of "culture". In Wagner it came directly
into contact with the origins of religious esotericism and with
messianism.'[269] In the second part of his article, Ellis returned
to the question of Wagner's importance to the Symbolist movement. He claims that forgetting Wagner ('or to be more
precise, the insufficient understanding of his works and the
proximity of his ultimate goals to the goals of the "first knights
of Symbolism"') and the exaltation in his stead of playwrights
such as Ibsen, Hamsun and Maeterlinck 'was from the very
beginning Symbolism's greatest mistake':[270]

It is time to come into the open about it! Along with other mistakes,
that was the most serious one!
    And from a theoretical point of view, Wagner will always be close
to the Symbolists! In so far as he deliberately destroyed all the
conventional limits of the classification of the arts and preached a
single super-art, he is close to every one of us ultimately. In so far as
he believed more than anyone else in higher worlds ... in so far as he
stressed with unprecedented temerity the religious foundation of all
art and in *Parsifal* went right up to the question of the sacred nature
of the mystery, he is close to us all precisely now ...[271]

Ellis concluded that the 'general idea of Symbolism' and the
'general messianic and prophetic meaning and pathos of the
Symbolist movement' found 'complete and beautiful expression in the work of Wagner'.[272]

    The publication of Ellis' 'Munich Letters' unfortunately did
nothing to diminish the flow of his incriminatory and hurt
letters to Medtner. In November 1912 Ellis once again
broached the subject of his Wagner translations:

About Wagner
I have a letter from you in which you ask me to translate *all* of
Wagner ... And I am translating the whole of Wagner! Are you
prepared personally ... to read through all my translations as a

rough draft and tell me categorically, without sentimentality, and without fearing to hurt me,

1. what will do
2. what will not do
3. what needs re-working?

Your opinion about Wagner I take as an authority. I am prepared to translate the whole of *Parsifal* again, prepared to stake my whole life for Wagner's sake, *but there must be a Russian Wagner and* Musaget *must be the publisher*. Do you agree with the latter? You must surely know how little vanity I have, how I value criticism and am ready to make compromises where necessary . . .[273]

In this letter we find a strange mixture of humility and arrogance, for on the one hand Ellis admits that he finds the translations very difficult, yet on the other he now asserts that the poetry in Wagner's librettos is second-rate and that his translations are even superior to the original at some points. The letter ends with a plaintive cry for help, however:

Understand my friend, that I have to convey verbally that which Wagner could convey in three different ways. I am prepared to see faults in my translation, but you must appreciate the huge task before me. There must, of course, be a Russian Wagner at all costs, but . . . help me and don't waste all your energy on criticising my translation – that's easy to do. Stefan George, the translator of Dante and Baudelaire, chose the pieces he liked best of all, but I have to translate the whole of Wagner . . .[274]

At the end of November 1912 Ellis again wrote to Medtner about Wagner at great length, asking for 'everything possible' to be done to put (another) advance notice of his *Parsifal* translation in the Musaget catalogue, and professing now to revere the *Ring* above *Parsifal* as the most perfect work of art in all respects, and claiming to be the first Russian to dare to place it 'above Shakespeare, almost on a level with Dante'. He could still not relinquish the idea that Musaget's great mission was to publish the 'Russian Wagner', however:

In Berlin I received a letter from you at around the time when I got back the draft of my manuscript of *Parsifal*, where you said that 'every line of Wagner must be translated, *Die Feen, Das Liebesverbot* and *Jesus von Nazareth*'. I believe in the possibility of my creating a complete 'Russian Wagner' ... There must be a 'Russian Wagner' and Musaget (who else?) must help. There is a Russian Shakespeare, Goethe, Schiller, Dante – why should there not be a Russian Wagner? ... There should not be introductions. I am not planning to write any, except for *Parsifal*. Let Wagner speak for himself ...[275]

Two days later, Ellis raised the question of the 'Russian Wagner' yet again;[276] but his translations were never published. He had to content himself with the publication of the article he wrote on *Parsifal*, which was presumably intended as the introduction to his translation in the sixth issue of *Trudy i dni* in 1913 (the only issue for that year) under its rubric of 'Wagneriana'.

Ellis began to become disillusioned with Steiner and Anthroposophy at the end of 1912, and by March 1913, Bely realised that the close-knit Anthroposophical group he had formed with Ellis and others was about to fall apart.[277] Later that year, Bely broke off relations with Ellis when he discovered Musaget was to publish his denunciation of Steiner's ideas,[278] and in February 1914, Ellis wrote to Medtner to confirm that his break with Steiner was final. 'We must all destroy Steinerism or be spiritually destroyed ourselves' he declared, for Germany's tragedy, he believed, had been to 'turn culture into religion' – Lohengrin had departed, Siegfried had turned into a Nibelung and Alberich, under his guise as Bismarck, had put the Rhine gold into Spandau. That, in Ellis' view, was the sum of German history.[279] Although he abandoned occultism for good in 1914, Ellis' allegiance to Wagner remained.[280] At some later point he made the acquaintance of Hans von Wolzogen, the editor of *Bayreuther Blätter*, and in 1932, his article 'The Temple of the Holy Grail as Poetry and Truth' (*Der Tempel des Heiligen Grales als Dichtung und Wahrheit*) appeared on the journal's pages.[281] Ellis presented Wolzogen with a copy of the Musaget edition of Wagner's *Die Wibelungen* as a token of his 'deep respect', writing the following dedication: 'This Russian version of R. Wagner's *Die Wibelungen* is a literary and cultural relic of the Wagner movement in Russia at the great Russo-German music [*sic*] publishing house Musaget, which was wiped out by the barbaric Revolution.'[282]

BELY, ANTHROPOSOPHY AND THE SEARCH FOR THE GRAIL

No doubt one of Medtner's worst nightmares became reality when Bely too converted to Anthroposophy. After preparing the first issue of *Trudy i dni*, which appeared in March 1912, Bely had left Russia for Brussels with Asya Turgeneva, and by May, he had met Steiner and been won over to the Anthropo-sophist cause. Like his affair with Lyubov Blok, the events leading up to Bely's involvement with Steiner were strangely connected with Wagner. Having met Steiner, Bely became convinced of the mystical significance of a series of strange happenings, alternately benign and threatening, which began at the end of 1910. Significantly, the first of these took place in Monreale in Sicily, 'the locality where Wagner finished *Parsifal*', and where Bely himself experienced, it will be recalled, intense feelings about the Grail legend.[283] The second took place in Brussels. After a bout of feverish illness, in which he dreamed about Steiner, Bely and Asya went to the opera to hear *Lohengrin*, *Tristan und Isolde* and *Die Walküre* performed by Bayreuth artists. These days, wrote Bely to Blok, 'were coloured by the *Ring*,'[284] and were accompanied by an intense feeling of expectancy, and the conviction that the series of strange incidences that befell him and Asya had been no coincidence: 'We realised that the game, the puzzle was turning into something else, and that we had to cross some kind of Rubicon ... We decided to wait a bit, for something told us there would be a continuation of the mystery on the day that *Götterdämmerung* was to be performed.'[285] On that day, writes Bely, they received one letter from Ellis, telling them their 'time had come' and another from Aleksey Petrovsky, enclos-ing various Steiner addresses and the information that Steiner was shortly to lecture in Cologne. Bely had by now decided that a meeting with Steiner was inevitable, but was positive he had to let events first take their course: 'We were very sure that something important would happen on Saturday at the theatre':[286] 'But at the theatre there was nothing, no one: only Wagner, Wagner and more Wagner; and – *Götterdämmerung*.

But we had to go on – Valhalla could not go up in flames!!!'[287] There was nothing for it but to go immediately to Cologne to seek a meeting with Steiner. After arriving in the city, Bely and Asya took a cab along the Rhine. Wagner yet again came to Bely's mind as they travelled down the river bank and he imagined he saw 'the Rhine daughters asking for the fateful ring from Siegfried'.[288] Since Bely's defection from the editorial board of *Trudy i dni* in the middle of 1912 due to the conflict over the journal's bias towards Steiner, his relations with Medtner had been strained. In September 1913, however, the two friends met in Dresden where Medtner was staying with Hedwig Friedrich. Friendly feelings were re-established and the reunion was celebrated by a visit to the opera to hear *Tristan und Isolde*.[289] A month later, however, Bely learned of Medtner's intention to publish Ellis' 'pasquinade' against Steiner, and, with characteristic impulsiveness, wrote to Medtner to inform him he was breaking off all relations with him and Musaget.

When Bely decided to dedicate himself to Anthroposophy in September 1913 and live amongst Steiner's followers in Germany, he considered the course of lectures that Steiner gave in Leipzig on the mystery of the Holy Grail at the end of that year (and a dream he had about the Grail afterwards) to be his 'initiation'.[290] It was here that Bely received profound spiritual illumination and, significantly, it was here also that 'once Richard Wagner and Goethe (during his illness) had received their initiation into life'.[291] On 6 January 1914, Steiner read a lecture about 'Parzifal' in Berlin,[292] which contained an interpretation of Wolfram von Eschenbach's version of the legend. Wagner's *Parsifal* could not have been far from Bely's mind, however, as he started hallucinating in April 1914 that Asya Turgeneva's sister Natasha was actually Kundry in disguise. Amongst other factors, the asceticism demanded by Anthroposophy was leading to Asya's gradual estrangement from Bely, and in his frenzied state, he imagined Natasha had been sent by Steiner to seduce him and thus lure the young 'Parsifal' away from his search for the 'Grail'.[293]

During the years in which Bely spent as an acolyte of Steiner, he wrote comparatively little. Yet nearly all the writings belonging to this period contain at least a passing reference to Wagner,[294] and his novel *Petersburg*, begun at the end of 1911 and largely written between 1912 and 1913, is no exception. The character of Sofiya Petrovna Likhutina, for example, idolises Isadora Duncan (who danced in *Tannhäuser* at Bayreuth in 1904) and Arthur Nikisch (particularly noted for his interpretations of Wagner). She wants to perform the 'Ride of the Valkyries' at Bayreuth, and it is this particular piece of music which the 'tin throat' of her gramophone would 'belch' out at her guests.[295] The second obvious link with Wagner in *Petersburg* is contained in Bely's depiction of Peter the Great as the 'Flying Dutchman'.[296] As Robert Maguire and John Malmstad point out, Peter the Great spent a great deal of time in Holland,[297] and this Wagnerian association subtly suggests the diabolic nature of the city's continuing existence (Peter the Great was seen by some as the Antichrist), for the Dutchman is condemned to sail the seas eternally for having invoked the devil. The third thematic link with Wagner in *Petersburg* has to do with *Parsifal*, but will only be deciphered by those acquainted with Bely's *On the Pass* (*Na perevale*) and his *Notes of an Eccentric* (*Zapiski chudaka*). It is none the less an important one. As we have seen, whereas previously Bely had grafted the symbolism of the *Ring* on to his perception of events, seeing the struggle of 'good' and 'evil', as Medtner did, in terms of 'Siegfrieds' doing battle with the 'Nibelungs', the majority of Bely's references to Wagner after his conversion to Anthroposophy pertain to *Parsifal*, where the evil Mime is remodelled as Klingsor. In the second part of *On the Pass*, which was written in 1916 and 1917, Bely refers directly to Apollon Apollonovich Ableukhov, the main character of *Petersburg*, as Klingsor, and does so as the result of his belief in certain Anthroposophical ideas.

In Anthroposophy, the spirit's journey to self-knowledge is threatened by two opposite paths of demonic temptation: the cerebral path of Ariman and the Luciferian path of the heart, leading to an existence lacking the necessary influence of one or the other. In *Petersburg*, explains Bely in *On the Pass*, Apollon

Apollonovich Ableukhov constantly escapes into the cerebral world of his brain (hence his love of 'cerebral games' (*mozgovye igry*), which is the kingdom of Klingsor, behind whom 'stands Ariman'.[298] Bely also identifies Ableukhov with Klingsor in his *Notes of An Eccentric*, in which he describes himself as a figure akin to Parsifal, banished from Monsalvat for killing a swan and under attack from an evil magician he knew very well: 'In previous years I tried to depict him clearly in *Petersburg*; he is Apollon Apollonovich Ableukhov, the famous bureaucrat . . .'[299] It is clear from the allusions to *Perceval* in the second part of *On the Pass* that Bely was inspired by Wolfram and de Troyes' versions of the legend, but Wagner's music drama was also in his mind: 'Before us stands Perceval, who responds to our epoch. Our epoch responds to him; with Wagner's mystery it becomes one with him.'[300]

Amongst all the impenetrable Anthroposophical ideas in *On the Pass*, a basic leitmotif of 'We await Perceval' (who will make it possible for 'brain' and 'heart' to be united) can be discerned.[301] Until 'Perceval' comes to deliver her, writes Bely, Kundry (the soul) will be trapped in the tower of Klingsor (the skull), thus preventing the dove (the spirit) from entering the repository of the Grail (the heart).[302] Klingsor warns that the striking of Perceval's spear against the walls of the tower will bring death, but the skull must be split, according to Bely. The spirit must be allowed to descend to unify the head and the heart, for only then will Perceval be 'with us': our new body will be 'Monsalvat', and the 'cognition' of our new body will be 'Perceval'.[303] Without 'true admiration for the Heavenly Kingdom', asserts Bely, our struggle for freedom will either result in the emasculation of our heart 'in union with Klingsor' (behind whom stands 'Ariman, Mephistopheles and darkness') or in 'the drowning of the mind by the heart' (behind whom stands Lucifer).[304] According to Bely, *Petersburg* demonstrates the first of these impulses, since Nikolay Apollonovich is constantly aware of the inevitability of the explosion within himself.

Bely illustrates the 'struggle for freedom' by quoting from his ballad 'The Jester' (*Shut*). Written in 1911, it is the centrepiece of his collection *The King's Daughter and her Knights* (*Korolevna i rytsary*), published in 1919, and depicts a king's daughter imprisoned in a castle by a hunch-backed jester. Awaiting deliverance by a spear-bearing knight 'flying from the darkness of ages', the King's daughter is told to await her salvation, for 'The spear has struck/At the iron gates!'[305] In *On the Pass*, Bely explains that the King's daughter 'is the soul of our life, like Kundry imprisoned by Klingsor; the hunch-backed jester is Klingsor',[306] thus confirming that the poem is an allegory of man's Anthroposophical journey constructed using the symbolism of Wagner's *Parsifal*. It is important to recognise, then, that not only does *The King's Daughter and her Knights* represent 'the most concentrated manifestation of the medieval element in Bely's poetic world',[307] but that this medieval element is of a very specific kind.[308] The dates of composition of these poems range from 1909 to 1911, that is to say they post-date Bely's acquaintance with Mintslova, before which time he never talked about *Parsifal* in his writings.

Becoming a fervent disciple of Steiner did not mean that Bely was necessarily blind to the potentially negative consequences of the cult that surrounded his teacher. Earlier we have seen that Bely and Sergey Solovyov saw Blok as a Wagner figure, and his estate as a kind of Russian Bayreuth, to which they had come to participate in their own festival of holy art. Although Bely did not see Steiner as a Wagner figure, he nevertheless considered in 1914 that the 'court' which surrounded him, and which was ruled by his wife, exhibited unwholesome features characteristic of the Bayreuth atmosphere during its worst years. In the published extracts from his *Intimate Biography*, Bely describes reading Nietzsche's *Wagner in Bayreuth* at this time, and transmuting the philosopher's arguments against Wagner into criticisms of Steiner's wife.[309] That same year, Medtner published (through Musaget) a critique of Steiner's ideas about Goethe.[310] For Bely, it was more than their friendship could withstand, and incensed by Medtner's book, he wrote *Rudolf Steiner and Goethe* in reply, as an attempt to refute the charges against his mentor. It was inevitable that a reference to Wagner's *Ring* would creep in somewhere. Bely claims that Medtner's logic had proceeded not from Logos, but from 'Loge', the treacherous intermediary between Valhalla and Nibelheim in the *Ring*:[311] 'Loge devours logic, and from it is hatched an involuntary lie; lying comes from Loge; genuine logic from Logos. The author has not followed Logos, but Loge ...'[312] It was a blow calculated to hurt and marked an ignominious end to a once intense and important friendship.[313]

Bely's penchant for constructing elaborate and complex charts and diagrams to provide graphic representations of his ideas was not neglected during his Steiner years. Amongst the unpublished items in Bely's archive are nineteen 'Tables and Diagrams of Intellectual Heredity (a Metaphysical Conception)' (*Tablitsy i skhemy ideinoi priemstvennosti (metafizicheskaya kontseptsiya)*) which are dated 1912 to 1916, precisely the years in which Bely was a pupil of Steiner. These tables have an undeniable link with Bely's 'History of the Becoming of the Soul's Self-Knowledge' (*Istoriya stanovleniya samoznayushchei dushi*),[314] another unpublished manuscript which was begun in 1913, but mostly written between 1924 and 1926, and intended, according to D. Pines, to be a 'study of the history of the philosophy of culture'.[315] Wagner features prominently in this work which contains Bely's 'most extensive and detailed interpretation of West European culture, commencing with the first years of Christianity and extending up to the first decades of the twentieth century'.[316] Nineteenth-century culture for Bely is characterised by Hegel, Goethe, Kant, Schopenhauer, Nietzsche, Wagner, Gogol, Dostoevsky and Tolstoy, to each of whom Bely grants separate chapters. Wagner, moreover, is granted the distinction of being the only composer to whom Bely devotes an entire chapter out of the thirty-two that comprise the second volume of this work,[317] which tells us much about Bely's recognition of the scale of Wagner's contribution to the development of European culture. In his notes for this work, Bely remarks upon the 'short period of time' in which Darwin, Liszt, Wagner and Ibsen were born, and also sees significance in the span of approximately forty years marking the deaths of Feuerbach, Darwin,

Turgenev, Wagner, Liszt, Hartmann, Pasteur, Solovyov, Blavatskaya, Nietzsche, Ibsen and Tolstoy.[318]

Since the 'History of the Becoming' is written in the decidedly dense language of Anthroposophy (the chapter on Wagner being no exception), the tables and diagrams are of immense value, for Bely's presentation of man's cultural evolution in graphic terms means that his ideas can be conveyed (in the first tables at least) in an entirely lucid way. Through his obsessive interest in establishing lines of intellectual heredity, the tables provide conclusive evidence that Bely did indeed view Wagner's connection to the Symbolist movement as a crucial one. In Table One (the most straightforward of the diagrams), we find Bely trying to show the immediate provenance of the main philosophical and literary influences on the Russian Symbolist movement. By means of myriad arrows pointing in different directions, Bely's argument is that the emergence of Symbolism was directly indebted to Gogol, Schopenhauer, Nietzsche, Solovyov, Rückert and Merezhkovsky, but also indirectly to Wagner.[319] In the second table, Bely ranges more widely, reaching back in his genealogical tree of European culture to the sixteenth-century forebears of Russian Symbolism, and Wagner has a much more prominent role here along with Nietzsche as the 'father' rather than the 'grandfather' of Symbolism.[320] The influence of Steiner can already be seen clearly in the second table (in the form of numerous arrows emanating from 'occultism' and 'Mysticism'), for as Julia Crookenden observes, in 'The History of the Becoming', Bely was using 'Anthroposophy's schema of the microcosmic evolution of man's awareness of his seven-fold being to describe stages of historical evolution over the last 2,000 years'.[321] Anthroposophical concepts can be seen even more clearly in the third table, which is already a highly elaborate and esoteric affair filled more with terms, rather than names of individuals. That notwithstanding, it is nevertheless most interesting to see that Bely makes a direct link between Rosicrucianism and Wagner, thus substantiating our earlier findings that Wagner's *Parsifal* was very much in Bely's mind in the numerous references to 'Perceval' and the 'Grail' in his writings. The third table concentrates largely on general trends rather than individual figures, which renders his evolutionary grouping of Schopenhauer, Wagner, Nietzsche, Solovyov, Symbolism and the 'Doctor' (Steiner) all the more significant.[322] Bely's subsequent tables get progressively more tangled and complex, as he tries to plot a map of ever more ambitious and arcane dimensions. Table Seventeen, however, despite the multiple arrows and dotted lines, is clearly another attempt to trace the roots of ideas to their source, although this time with a different slant. Wagner, Nietzsche and Schopenhauer again occupy central positions, but in this table they actually seem to be the most important figures in the whole diagram, to judge from the rings around their names and the arrows leading directly from them to 'Symbolism', suggesting these three individuals were its chief precursors. It is interesting to note, moreover, that there is again a direct arrow leading from the 'Grail legends' to Wagner. What also distinguishes this particular table is Bely's belief that the East, the Middle Ages and Classicism had all contributed in creating the amalgam that was Symbolism, the 'end product', as it were, of centuries of cultural dialogue.[323]

CHAPTER 6

Wagner and the Russian Symbolists: Aleksandr Blok

WAGNER IN BLOK'S LIFE

Like Bely and Ivanov, Blok was of a mentality which made him particularly receptive to German culture, and to German Romanticism above all. In fact, as far as Blok's younger contemporary Nikolay Gumilyov was concerned (and he was not alone in perceiving peculiarly Germanic qualities in Blok's poetry), Blok was more a Romantic than a Symbolist: 'Blok is a Romantic. A Romantic of the purest water, and a German Romantic moroever. It was not for nothing that his father was German [*sic*] ... The German blood in him is very strong and it is reflected in his appearance. Yes, Blok is a Romantic with all the virtues and insufficiencies of Romanticism. For some reason no one seems to understand that, but it is the key to his work and to his personality too.'[1] Blok shared Ivanov's and Bely's passionate interest in Wagner, but almost none of their ambivalence. Indeed, while Ivanov adored the music of Beethoven more than than any other, and Bely worshipped Schumann, Blok would have unhesitatingly declared that Wagner was his favourite composer. When Bely began to ponder Blok's personality in detail shortly after his death, musing on which particular artists and thinkers had been important to him, it is interesting to note that one of his first observations was that Blok had 'loved Wagner very, very much'.[2] Blok had always maintained that he did not understand music, and before a performance of *Die Meistersinger* in January 1913, had regretted that he could only 'swim in Wagner's musical ocean'.[3] Such statements have usually been considered somewhat disingenuous, since Blok's powers of musical perception were clearly acute, but perhaps all he is doing here is lamenting his lack of theoretical knowledge, and his inability to explain the reason for the hypnotic effect that Wagner's music had on him. His protestations of being tone-deaf certainly do not seem to have interfered with his capacity to enjoy music in any way.

Felicitously, Blok's devotion to Wagner was shared not only by his immediate family, but also by his close friend Evgeny Ivanov and his respective family, and so there were often joint excursions to hear the *Ring* at the Mariinsky Theatre. The performance of *Siegfried* on 14 January 1905, for example, was attended not only by Evgeny's entire family, who had bought a box for the evening, but also by Blok and his wife (who had seats in the stalls), and by Bely, who was visiting from Moscow.[4] Evgeny and his brother Aleksandr (who published an article on the *Ring* in *Mir iskusstva* in 1904) were renowned in Petersburg intellectual circles for their knowledge of Wagner, and the composer must have been a frequent subject of their conversations with Blok. Such was the intensity of Wagner's hold over Blok and his family that phrases from the texts of his operas even became woven into the fabric of their daily lives. Echoing Wotan's words to Alberich from the second act of *Siegfried*, Blok's mother wrote to Evgeny's sister Mariya in March 1913, for example: 'All things go their appointed way [*Alles ist nach seiner Art*]. Yes, that's what we all repeat after Wagner – I, and Sasha, and Lyuba, and Manya, my sister . . .'[5] Three years earlier, Blok had even called his country house 'Valhalla' as he undertook major renovation work in the summer of 1910,[6] a jocular appellation which proved rather prophetic in view of the fact that the house was later burned down during the Revolution. Blok not only knew Wagner's poetic texts extremely well, and quoted from them regularly in his writings (his aunt M. A. Beketova maintained that the texts of Wagner's works were as much a part of Blok's 'inner life' as their scores),[7] but he also was well acquainted with the composer's theoretical writings, which proved to be extremely influential when he began writing about the theatre himself. In

1918, he wrote a preface to his wife's new translation of *Art and Revolution*, a work which he found highly topical.

The first work by Wagner which Blok saw performed on stage was *Die Walküre*, the work which began the Mariinsky Theatre's first production of the *Ring* in 1900; and after 1907, when the tetralogy began to be performed as a complete work, Blok bought an annual subscription whenever he was able. As Evgeniya Knipovich's memoirs of the poet have revealed, Blok knew the work very well indeed. At one point during a walk she took with Blok during the summer of 1920, he decided to sit down under a tree to rest for a while, and as Knipovich sat beside him, watching the shadows of the leaves flitting across his face, she could not help but remember a certain famous scene from the *Ring*. When she sang out 'Hey, Siegfried! Kill the evil gnome!' to him, however, Blok 'opened his eyes and replied: "E. E. Knipovich, in Wagner the bird sings that from a tree." '[8] Blok was evidently considered by many people to be something of an expert on the *Ring*, as in 1919 he was appointed by the publishing house *Vsemirnaya literatura* to edit Sofya Sviridenko's new translation of the work. Since he did not consider the translation fit for publication at that time, Marietta Shaginyan was later commissioned to revise it, and the advice given to her by Blok in the last few months of his life provides further testimony of his intimate knowledge of Wagner's texts, both in their Russian and German versions.[9] While he was checking Shaginyan's corrections, he made a note in his diary of the final words of the Rhinemaidens in *Das Rheingold*, which he perhaps considered an eloquent expression of his feelings at the time:

> Traulich und treu
> ist's nur in der Tiefe
> falsch und feig ist,
> was dort oben sich freut!

Although the *Ring* remained Blok's favourite work by Wagner, he enjoyed hearing *Tristan und Isolde* when it was revived in 1909, as well as *Die Meistersinger*, and *Parsifal*, which were not performed in St Petersburg until 1912 and 1913 respectively. Like Bely and Ivanov, Blok seems to have been considerably less interested in *Lohengrin, Tannhäuser* and the other operas from Wagner's early repertoire. This is hardly surprising, of course, since the elements of Wagner's works which principally attracted the Russian Symbolists (the endless melody, the interest in inner experience and the use of leitmotif, for example) were exclusively features of the music drama. That notwithstanding, Blok was often seen as possessing a 'Lohengrin-like melancholy'.[10]

THE FORGING OF THE SWORD: WAGNERIAN IMAGES IN BLOK'S POETRY

The twenty-year-old Blok had been writing poetry seriously for three years when he heard *Die Walküre* in December 1900,[11] and the experience was such a powerful one that it inspired him to write a poem about it.[12] Composed in the form of a brief dialogue between Siegmund and Sieglinde, 'The Valkyrie (On a Motif from Wagner)' (*Val'kiriya (Na motiv iz Vagnera)*) depicts and alludes to the main events in the first act of *Die Walküre*. In the space of twenty-five lines, Blok manages to evoke the wounded Siegmund's arrival at Hunding's dwelling ('I am wounded! Open up!'), his meeting with Sieglinde and their instant attraction to each other ('This is the voice of a friend'), their realisation that Hunding is their enemy ('Black Hunding is not with me'), and the sighting of the sword in the ash-tree which Siegmund is to extract ('the sword glints in the tree trunk'). In Blok's interpretation of the myth, Siegmund and Sieglinde seem instantly to recognise their shared destiny, whereas of course this takes place considerably later in Wagner's version of events. The theme of love appears early on in the orchestral score, however, even if it does not arise until later in the libretto, as D. M. Magomedova has pointed out,[13] and Blok was conceivably speaking in this poem with the voice of the Wagnerian orchestra; re-telling the story of the first act of *Die Walküre* in terms of the unconscious feelings of its characters. The line 'Wälse! Wälse! Where is your sword?' is the only one quoted verbatim from Wagner's text. Blok may have been recalling these words from memory, but it should be pointed out that he possessed the libretto to *Die Walküre* both in its German original, and in its Russian translation.[14] Blok's 'Valkyrie' ends on a note of radiant expectancy ('Dear traveller, come and rest!/(She opens the door)'), rather than with the physical passion which concludes the first act of Wagner's opera, but a state of unfulfilment and longing is characteristic of the general mood of the poetry he composed at this time. Indeed, what seems to have inspired Blok to write this poem was not simply the passionate music of the score of *Die Walküre*, but the fact that Wagner's moving tale of love and heroism, replete with all its rich symbolism, struck a chord with the themes of his own work. The verses of Blok's first cycle 'Ante Lucem', which contains poems composed between 1898 and 1900, typically feature two main protagonists: the lyric hero (closely aligned with the poet himself) and the female object of his worship and adoration, who is usually idealised and portrayed in abstract terms. In some poems, however, such as in 'The Valkyrie', there is also an 'other', in this case personified by Hunding. Blok's 'The Valkyrie' is thus not so much a simple re-telling of Wagner's story (which would obviously be a pointless exercise), but rather a variation on the central theme of his poetry, in this case seen through the prism of Wagnerian imagery, with Sieglinde embodying his mystical ideal. The chaste and religious nature of Blok's poetry at this time also made it unlikely that his version of *Die Walküre* would end in the consummation of incestuous love, which is, of course, how the first act of Wagner's opera is concluded. This may be partly why it was not included in the 'canonical' text of 'Ante Lucem', and was only published in a later collection. But the concluding scene of the first act of *Die Walküre* clearly made a great impression on Blok, for he was to mention it in the first letter he wrote to Bely in January 1903. Although Blok's involvement with Wagner's music was in general far less critical than that of his fellow poets, he was not unaware of a possible 'demonic' side to Wagner. As we have seen in the previous chapter, the idea that the incestuous love of Siegmund and Sieglinde in the first act of *Die Walküre* could also be 'hallowed' (by applying Merezhkovsky's ideas about the sanctification of all human achievement) was something he found difficult to countenance. Despite Wagner's seductive music, he believed, these scenes belonged firmly to the 'hell' of art, and had nothing to do with religion. Precisely because of its seductive powers, however, Blok often found Wagner's music difficult to resist. Many years later, in March 1914, for example, he could not stop himself from going to hear *Die Walküre*, which was perhaps his favourite work by Wagner, even though he knew beforehand that the standard of performance would be low. 'Despite the cast, there's always the *music*' was the comment in his diary.[15]

That Wagner's music did indeed have a hypnotic effect on Blok quite unlike any other is confirmed by his powerful response to a concert he went to in January 1901 (a month after hearing *Die Walküre*) at which excerpts from *Parsifal* were performed. Hearing Wagner's music again inspired Blok to compose a poem, this time about the links between music and memory. Although Blok 'never understood before/The art of holy music', hearing excerpts from *Parsifal* provoked a surge of involuntary memory, 'So that all former beauty/Came back from oblivion in a wave'.[16] Even without seeing the work performed on stage, Blok appears to have intuitively perceived the function of Wagner's leitmotifs as instruments of remembrance, a key concept to both artists.

Over the next few years, Blok continued to write mystical verse in homage to the divine female being who was the subject of most of his poetry, and whom he addressed as 'The Beautiful Lady'. Under the influence of Vladimir Solovyov, Blok had come to identify his radiant vision with the Divine Sophia, but in June 1903, he discovered there were affinities with another of Wagner's heroines when he heard the final scenes of *Tristan und Isolde* performed at a concert in Bad Nauheim during a stay in Germany. In a letter to his fiancée Lyubov Mendeleeva (whom he regarded as the Divine Sophia incarnate), he described what exactly drew him to liken Isolde to his 'Beautiful Lady':

I liked Tristan and Isolde's *Liebestod* very much. First Tristan *mouru* [*sic*] *pour son amour* – great wails, titanic cries. Then *la belle Isolda* began to mourn. It became very quiet and 'A Great Silence Descended'. Then she started to sing, and again the violins began to scream and titanic cries resounded. And that is how she died, but it was still quiet. *Elle mouru pour le pur tendresse* [*sic*]. That is what I understood, because Isolde was a woman, and probably did not believe in either her own or Tristan's death. She loved the wild, heavenly 'lie' of passion, which never dies and never will die. That's what I understood, and I liked it. My Lady would like it in the same way. She must know and sympathise more with the feeling of strong passion than with German *Akkurat-Liebe* (if such a term exists, I didn't invent it anyway) – naive and uncultured, ultra-German passion, i.e., the German passion of the Valkyries and the Gods (gods). That is what my Lady is like. She is always with me, but never speaks. I suspect that she generally does not like to speak much, and prefers listening, although when she listens, she understands much more than the person talking. I mean, the person talking to Her understands, but at the time he is in seventh heaven and is totally absorbed with her contemplation.[17]

The Wagnerian heroine with whom Blok most frequently identified his 'Beautiful Lady', however, whom he often portrayed in his verse symbolically asleep on a mountain crag, was Brünnhilde. Lyubov Blok, who personified his poetic ideal, has confirmed that the third act of *Die Walküre* does indeed lie behind Blok's poetic depictions of his heroine asleep or encircled by a ring of flames. Before her marriage to Blok in August 1903, they had often attended performances of *Die Walküre* at the Mariinsky Theatre,[18] and later she realised that 'everything was in a fog' because Blok had deliberately seen her as the sleeping Brünnhilde:

Before my eyes there was always a 'romantic haze', especially when it came to Blok and the objects and space that surrounded him . . . This is what the ring of fire and the swirling smoke around Brünnhilde are all about; their meaning became clear to me at a performance at the Mariinsky Theatre. They not only protect the Valkyrie, but also separate her from the world and her hero; whom she sees through this fiery, hazy curtain.[19]

From the increasing number of references to the forging of swords in the poetry he wrote at this time, it also becomes clear that Blok himself identified with the heroic aspirations of Wagner's Siegfried. *Siegfried* was first performed at the

Mariinsky Theatre in February 1902, and there were a further five performances later that year. Blok certainly heard the work in January 1905, but it is highly probable that he had been to one of the 1902 performances, for he mentions Siegfried's conversation with the woodbird in the letter he wrote to Bely in January 1903.

The important symbol of the sword recurs like a leitmotif throughout the early phase of Blok's verses to 'The Beautiful Lady' to denote, like Wagner's *Nothung*, 'integrity of the spirit'.[20] Its connotations are not exclusively Wagnerian, for Blok had always been prone to clothe his worship of the Eternal Feminine in the medieval imagery of chivalrous love, finding it suitably ethereal for his evocation of communion with the Divine.[21] But it is interesting to note that the sword symbol appeared in his poetry for the first time in December 1900,[22] just after he had been to see *Die Walküre*, which suggests that Blok was more than conscious of the Wagnerian associations of this image. The image of the sword in Blok's poetry symbolises both the spiritual fidelity and asceticism demanded of service to the Divine Sophia (qualities not far removed from the symbolism of the Cross), and, somewhat paradoxically, the virility and strength linked to Wagner's *Nothung*. It is possible, however, that Blok did not see any contradiction here. Wagner was certainly cognisant of the legends which equated Siegfried with Jesus Christ,[23] and Solovyov had made a similar juxtaposition in a poem written in June 1900 entitled 'The Dragon', which Blok undoubtedly knew. Dedicated to 'Siegfried', the last lines of this poem read: 'But before the dragon's jaws/You have understood that cross and sword are one'.[24]

The first act of Wagner's *Siegfried* is quite clearly the inspiration of a poem written in July 1904, in which the lyrical hero is depicted standing over a forge, being served by a stooping, Mime-like dwarf dressed in black.[25] Another Wagnerian sub-text can be found in a poem written in December 1904, in which the act of actually forging the sword is introduced.[26] It was approximately at this time that the image of Blok's feminine Ideal was now occasionally surrounded in his poetry by 'a halo of red fire' like Wagner's Valkyrie.[27] Further proof that

Siegfried was indeed in Blok's mind when he composed these poems has been provided by Bely's memoirs. As we have seen in the previous chapter, the atmosphere of heroism in *Siegfried* inspired Blok and his wife to identify themselves with Wagner's heroes after going to a performance of the work days after the 'Bloody Sunday' events of January 1905, when revolutionary ferment was still in the air.

After 1905, the Wagnerian imagery in Blok's poetry inevitably changed its hue, however. For a combination of reasons, including increasing self-doubt, the realisation that art had nothing to do with religion, the shock and disillusionment which followed the 1905 Revolution and his wife's resistance to being made into a deity, Blok began to find it increasingly difficult to see himself as the self-assertive and fearless hero of *Siegfried*. After the composition of his last poem about the 'Beautiful Lady', written in June 1904, Blok began to see himself instead as the all too human and weak Siegfried of *Götterdämmerung* who had betrayed Brünnhilde, and also as the doomed Siegmund. He had already mocked his pretensions as a knight 'standing watch' in a poem of 1902, in which he portrayed himself as 'only a fancy-dress knight, a ridiculous figure with a cardboard sword',[28] and in July 1905, he again parodied his former religious fervour with a description of himself as a puppet-knight with a wooden sword.[29] Scenes from *Götterdämmerung*, which was first performed in St Petersburg in January 1903, also now began to filter through into Blok's poetry. 'Fever' (*Bred*), for example, a poem written in October 1905, evokes the moment when Siegfried's memory returns to him and he suddenly realises his betrayal of Brünnhilde.[30] In the next troubled years, Blok continued to see himself from time to time as a knight fighting the powers of darkness, but the defiance and bravado of poems such as 'You Awoke Early in the Morning' (*Ty probuzhdalas' utrom rano*), written in April 1907,[31] with its image of the splintered *Nothung* and Wotan's spear glimmering in the mist, cannot mask the pervading spirit of failure and despondency. In other poems, the atmosphere is totally desolate. In the poem 'Voices' (*Golosa*), for example, written in January 1907, we find that the 'iron sword' is now lost in a 'silver blizzard', the line 'Where is my sword? Where is my sword!' feebly echoing Siegmund's heroic call to Wälse in the poem of 1900.[32] 'Beyond the Hill Came the Sound of Resilient Armour' (*Za kholmom otzveneli uprugie laty*), another poem written a few months later reinforces the sense of doom by depicting a scene on the eve of a battle, in which the hero already knows he is to perish.[33] When Blok describes his hero preparing to meet his ghastly fate, he has obviously drawn from the *Todesverklärung* scene in the second act of *Die Walküre*, in which Brünnhilde comes to tell Siegmund that he must die in his battle with Hunding. In *Die Walküre*, Brünnhilde is in fact so moved by Siegmund's concern for Sieglinde that she decides to protect him in the battle, but in Blok's poem, it is as if he has dispensed with Siegmund's temporary reprieve, knowing already that he will die anyway at the hands of Wotan, who will direct his 'midnight spear/At the joyous sun-god's breast'.[34] In the first draft of this poem, the final four lines had made its Wagnerian associations explicit, by alluding to Brünnhilde's pledge to lead Siegmund to Valhalla:

> And then, sending the mists to the hills,
> You – Valkyrie, Maiden, Snake,[35]
> Will tend to my burning wounds with passion
> Beneath the faithless glint of the spear.[36]

According to Evgeniya Knipovich, Blok felt that those like Siegmund, who were capable of heroic deeds, but were doomed, had to suffer 'an unhappiness of a particular kind; a hero's unhappiness, which denies only the hero's personal right to a happy fate and life'.[37] To illustrate this, she draws attention to the notes Blok made for his 1912 article 'From Ibsen to Strindberg' (*Ot Ibsena k Strindbergu*), in which he likens Strindberg to Siegmund: 'Strindberg is an example of a strong mind not afraid of contradiction. Strindberg's laboratory is merry, but he himself is sad, "unhappy" (*Wälsung*).'[38] In fact, Blok thought that *all* deeds carried a certain sadness within them, according to Knipovich; the waking of Brünnhilde by Siegfried '*always* seemed to him to be a sad and unecessary event',[39] since far from being the prelude to happiness, it was 'merely the prologue to tragedy and universal destruction'.[40] This is perhaps why the symbolic image of the 'ring of fire' continued to recur in Blok's poetry, reflecting his desire to leave his 'Brünnhilde' deep in slumber,[41] and why Russia, which from 1906 became a new poetic ideal of a different kind, also appears in his poetry as Brünnhilde, 'deep in sleep'.[42] In the final draft of 'From Ibsen to Strindberg', where Blok compares Ibsen to Siegfried, we find him expressing exactly this idea: 'So Siegfried reaches the top of the crag, having understood the voice of the bird; he overcomes the ring of fire and brings himself love and destruction at the hands of the daughter of Chaos, whom he awakened.'[43] A discussion of the scene of Brünnhilde's awakening, interestingly enough, is how Aleksandr Ivanov begins his article 'Loge and Siegfried', which was published in *Mir iskusstva* in 1904.[44] The fact that the other episodes from the *Ring* which Ivanov chooses to discuss (Siegmund's death, the forging of the sword, Siegfried's betrayal) are precisely those which are reflected in Blok's poetry is not all that surprising, however, since the article no doubt represents the fruits of the Ivanov brothers' long conversations about Wagner with Blok.[45]

When Blok compromised on his religious ideal, he regarded himself as a failure, and, like Siegmund, saw himself as *Wehwahlt*, an unhappy creature destined by virtue of his race to suffer. It will be remembered that this is precisely how Emil Medtner saw himself, and the kinship Blok immediately felt with Medtner when he met him in 1910 may have been partly to do with the fact that he too saw himself as a Wälsung, and shared his tendency towards self-destruction.[46] Blok also intuitively felt that destruction would be the fate of the Russian intelligentsia if it persisted in not heeding the warning signs of impending cataclysm, which he often saw poetically in terms of the destructive but cleansing fire which ends Wagner's *Ring*. According to Evgeniya Knipovich, Blok accepted and respected the revolutionary impulse with which the *Ring* was conceived, and was convinced that a new 'Siegfried' would be born from the ashes of the old world.[47] The first occasion on which the ending of *Götterdämmerung* is alluded to in Blok's poetry had occurred in his 1904 poem 'They Arose from the

Darkness of Graves' (*Podnimalis' iz t'my pogrebov*), which speaks not only of a 'frenzied dragon' but a 'last twilight of fire'.[48] It was after 1906, however, when Blok surrendered for a time to the rebellious and hedonistic lifestyle that went with the doctrine of 'Mystical Anarchism', that his poetry frequently began to contain images of snowstorms, whirlwinds and leaping flames. These images were consonant with his vision of the hell of art (which he felt he was descending into deeper and deeper as his spiritual crisis worsened) and were also intimately connected with Blok's perception of Wagner's *Ring*, as Evgeniya Knipovich deduced. When she challenged Blok about his 1907 poem 'On the Snowy Bonfire' (*Na snezhnom kostre*),[49] for example, maintaining that she could perceive echoes of the 'Flight of the Valkyries' and Siegfried's funeral march from *Götterdämmerung* in its 'rhythm, sound and music', his only response was 'How did you guess?'[50]

In 1910, when Blok began once again to believe himself capable of heroic deeds, the image of *Nothung* reappears in his writings. In his essay 'On the Contemporary State of Russian Symbolism', he analysed the movement's evolution by describing his own poetic journey in terms of the Hegelian dialectic, and dressing it in the recondite symbolic imagery of his verse. By describing the 'thesis' of the religious vision of the Divine Sophia as a 'golden sword' piercing the heart of the poet or theurgist, and the 'anti-thesis' of the 'hell' of art as a time when the 'golden sword' has become tarnished,[51] the 'link with Wagner, with Nothung and Siegfried', as Knipovich has remarked, lay right on the surface.[52] Blok's remedy to the crisis that Russian Symbolism found itself in was sobriety, a 'return to life' and social commitment.[53] The choice was either 'death through submissiveness, or a self-sacrificing deed of courage. The golden sword was given to smite blows.'[54] Opting to take the latter path, Blok felt, was the only way to find the 'golden sword' which had been lost, and thereby reach the state of 'synthesis'.

It was in his long narrative poem 'Retribution' (*Vozmezdie*), begun in 1911, that Blok took the first major step along this path. The central idea of this poem – punishment for a fatal error – is a Wagnerian one, and Blok reinforces the connection with the *Ring* by introducing the sword-forging image once more.[55] Over the years, Blok had gradually committed himself to escaping from the subjective world of his early lyrics in order to devote himself to the theme of Russia's destiny, and perhaps it was part of his attempt to achieve greater objectivity that he actually names the sword as the 'faithful Nothung' for the first time, by openly comparing the artist's purpose with Siegfried's great deed. Only someone as fearless as Siegfried, suggests Blok, might have the strength to fight the metaphorical 'dragon' of the old world hovering over Europe, 'its jaws gaping open, parched with thirst'.[56] Mime, for whom Blok always maintained a 'strange pity' (because despite his perfidy, he was 'still the person who raised Siegfried')[57] is pictured cowering at the hero's feet. Yet Blok still felt himself to be 'helpless and weak'; he did not yet possess the strength to fulfil his duty as a poet and carry out the self-sacrificing deed of heroism he so often talked about in his essays.[58]

The appearance of images from the *Ring* in Blok's poetry was the direct result of his seeing the work performed on stage, and the same is true of the images from *Tristan und Isolde* which appear in his 1910 poem 'The Hours, Days and Years Go By' (*Idut chasy i dni i gody*). As a close acquaintance of the director, Blok had been invited to the dress rehearsal of Meyerhold's new staging of *Tristan und Isolde* at the end of 1909. In the end, Lyubov Dmitrievna went in his place, and it was perhaps due to her disappointment with the production[59] that he decided only to catch the last few bars of its fourth performance from behind the doors one night, for there is no evidence of Blok actually hearing the work from beginning to end on this occasion. To judge from a letter he wrote to his mother afterwards, however, even hearing those few bars had been a profound experience: 'Each time I hear it, it excites me more and more; music is a most dangerous and influential thing. Its influence does not go through me without effect.'[60] The 'influence' of *Tristan* in 'The Hours, Days and Years Go By' is manifest in its last two lines ('So fall, coloured bandage!/Gush forth, blood, and turn the snow crimson!') which replicate the dying Tristan's call (*Hahie! Mein Blut, lustig nun fliesse!*) as he casts away his bandage to die.[61] Note too, that the sword in Blok's poem is first 'unnecessary' (since, as James Forsyth has commented, 'its bearer's arm has been rendered powerless by a woman's love'),[62] and then falls from a shaking hand, as Tristan drops his sword when struck by Melot in the second act of Wagner's opera.

Themes from *Parsifal* also do not emerge in Blok's poetry until a relatively late stage, since full stage performances of the work were officially banned until the copyright expired at the end of 1913. It was staged at the first opportunity in St Petersburg, however, and Blok heard the work at least twice during 1914, although it must be said that he was as much driven by his desire to see his current paramour (appearing as a flower maiden) as he was by his love of Wagner. The stamp of *Parsifal* certainly seems to be unmistakably imprinted on Blok's narrative poem 'The Nightingale Garden' (*Solov'inyi sad*), which he composed in 1915. Boris Solovyov has explored the similarities between the two works in some detail: 'Both heroes are called on to perform heroic deeds and carry out their duty, and dangerous temptations lure them; next door to the world they live in is a charmed garden where beautiful enchantresses live, embodying all conceivable pleasures and enticements ... Having succumbed to evil, they try to trap the hero in their nets, and make him forget about his duty and heroic deeds so that he stays forever in the sultry, poisoned air of the garden.'[63] Solovyov contends that Blok's hero is ultimately taking issue with Wagner's concept of heroism in this poem by choosing to strengthen 'ties with life' rather than escape from it, as he supposes Parsifal does. Yet the real heroic deed of sacrifice surely lies in the fact that both heroes turn their back on the 'Garden of Eden', rather than in the nature of their subsequent actions, in which case Blok's hero does have much in common with Parsifal.[64] Like Parsifal, Blok's hero cannot stay in the 'Garden of Eden' forever, for not only does he subconsciously realise that it is in reality a *paradis artificiel*, representing moral passivity, but that 'it is not given to nightingale song to drown out the sea'.[65] His duty is not to return to 'fine comforts' but to 'vanish in the freezing wastes' of creative hardship, since for the poet there can be no comfort or rest.[66] There can be either artistic creativity, or happiness, but not both. D. M. Magomedova has categorised the kinship between the two works as 'purely formal', since Solovyov, in her view, overlooks the Christian overtones of the concepts of 'heroic deed', 'duty' and 'temptation' in *Parsifal*.[67] But to those who do not see *Parsifal* as a Christian work,[68] this is not a very convincing counter-argument. It is generally acknowledged that 'The Nightingale Garden' is an autobiographical work which is partly about Blok's relationship with Lyubov Andreevna-Delmas, who sang Carmen at the Theatre of Musical Drama at the same time as she was singing the role of a flower maiden in *Parsifal*, and Blok's linking of the names of Kundry and Carmen in his notebooks provides further evidence of the connection between the two works.[69] In passing, it is also worth mentioning that Blok was sometimes seen as a Parsifal-like figure by his contemporaries.[70]

Blok had always considered the ultimate theme of the *Ring* to be the inevitable arrival of a new 'Siegfried',[71] and it is thus not surprising that he saw the Russian Revolution in 1917 as a kind of *Götterdämmerung* writ large. The images of an all-enveloping fire in his poetry reached their apotheosis in January 1918 when Blok composed his masterpiece 'The Twelve' (*Dvenadsat'*), which Boris Solovyov has described as the Nothung whose creation Blok had dreamed about in 'Retribution', 'cast in a fire of great rage':[72] 'To the sorrow of all the bourgeois/We will fan a fire throughout the world' (*My na gore vsem burzhuyam/Mirovoi pozhar razduem*).[73]

WAGNER AND THE REGENERATION OF RUSSIAN THEATRE

The 1905 revolution was the catalyst which forced Blok to reconsider all his previously held notions about society and the role of the artist. The upsetting of all these former values opened Blok's eyes for the first time to questions of ethics and morality as he struggled to come to terms with his nascent feelings of guilt before the Russian 'people'. The struggle was made all the more difficult by Blok's overwhelming sense of sadness and despair over the culture of the 'old world' whose painful death throes he was now witnessing. This was only natural, as he was its offspring, and part of the pain he experienced was undoubtedly the prescience of his own doom.

Yet in some areas of his life, Blok remained an uncompromising idealist, and his commitment to the revolution – his heroic act of sacrifice – partly expressed itself in a new-found interest in the regeneration of Russian theatre. In his concern about the contemporary artist's isolation and the need to reach wider audiences, Blok reflected the interests of his fellow-Symbolists, and Wagner, not surprisingly, was an iconic figure in his vision of a new Russian theatre. But unlike Ivanov, for example, who was attracted to all Wagner's most utopian fantasies about the brotherhood of man, and the need for a ritualistic, communal theatre, Blok was far more realistic.

Blok had acquired copies of the librettos of all Wagner's works that most interested him, namely the *Ring*, *Tristan und Isolde* (in both German and Russian) and *Parsifal*, whose Russian translation was published in 1909.[74] An inventory of 1921 also lists Blok as possessing a fourteen-volume Leipzig edition of Wagner's writings.[75] These volumes have not been included in the more detailed inventory of Blok's library recently published, however, and although Blok certainly knew German well, there is reason to suggest that he was more inclined to read Wagner's writings in Russian translation, as references to them only occur in his own writings after these translations were published. Blok possessed copies of the Russian translations of both *Art and Revolution* and *Opera and Drama*, both of which were published in 1906, and later on acquired translations of *Beethoven*, published in 1911 and *The Wibelungs*, published in 1913. The underlinings and markings in his copies of *Art and Revolution* and *Opera and Drama* demonstrate that he read these works very carefully, and reveal that he found Wagner's analysis of contemporary theatre very topical, despite the fact that it was written over fifty years before. He was clearly not interested, however, in the more musical side of Wagner's writings,[76] since the first and third parts of *Opera and Drama* (headed 'Opera and the Essence of Music' and 'Poetry and Music in the Drama of the Future'), in which the composer addresses the history of operatic develop-ment, and outlines how emotional expression can be enhanced musically, are almost devoid of underlinings. What interested Blok was the second part: 'The Play and the Essence of Poetry', and it is intriguing to note that in its Russian translation, Wagner's turgid prose becomes almost a model of pellucidity. Perhaps this may account for the fact that Wagner's writings on the theatre, usually derided and ignored elsewhere, found their most receptive audience in Russia.

Blok had turned to the theatre in a sincere attempt to achieve greater objectivity in his work, and this drew him immediately to Wagner's claim in *Opera and Drama* that a 'true work of art can only be born through transition from the world of the imagination to actuality, i.e. the world of the senses'.[77] He also found salient Wagner's view that literary drama owed its beginning to the 'egoistic spirit of our artistic development' and needed 'living human speech'. Underlining Wagner's explanation that modern drama had originated from the Romance and Greek tragedy, Blok made a particular note of the composer's emphasis on 'the direct presentation to the senses' which had made possible the development from romance to drama. Another page on, and Blok once more makes note of Wagner's argument for an 'intelligible lan-guage'.[78] Blok was bound to share Wagner's respect for Shake-speare, since the latter occupied a special position in his own affections, and he was clearly interested in the passage in *Opera and Drama* in which Wagner describes the dilemma faced by those who wish to see the 'fantasy' of Shakespeare's dramas embodied on stage, but are disillusioned by the mechanical reality. Wagner viewed Goethe's *Faust* as a watershed in the development of drama, and Blok was moved to underline what Wagner pinpointed as the reason for Goethe's innovation, namely *Das Drängen des Gedankens in die Wirklichkeit*,[79] in which he believed that the future content of drama lay. Blok was less interested in Wagner's analysis of Greek drama than in his interpretation of Christian art. It is interesting to note that he drew a line in the margin by Wagner's declaration that the power of the 'Christian myth' lay in its 'transfiguration through death', which he defines as the sole content of Christian art, and wholly characteristic that Blok should also draw a line by Wagner's discussion of chivalresque Romances, with whose medieval spirit he empathised so strongly.

Blok's subsequent markings and underlinings demonstrate how much he drew on Wagner in the formulation of his new, realistic attitude to art, and how much he was indebted to Wagner for providing him with a model of an artist who stressed the indivisibility of art and politics. It is telling, for example, that he found Wagner's remark that 'he who still avoids politics at the present time is deceiving himself in thinking he exists' apposite, for it is a sentiment he had begun to voice himself.[80] It is also intriguing that Blok drew a line in the margin by Wagner's statement that the 'fall of the state' could be called nothing other than 'the society's religious consciousness materialising in its purely human essence' (*Das sichverwirklichende religiöse Bewusstsein der Gesellschaft vor ihrem rein menschlichen Wesen*), for his mystical view of revolution as the emanation of the spirit of music (which embodied the voice of the people coming to the fore) is not all that far removed from it. In fact, Blok's attitude to revolution was markedly similar to Wagner's, for neither were at all interested in politics at ground level.[81] Wagner's view of revolution was essentially mystical too.

Out of all Wagner's writings, *Art and Revolution* made the greatest impression on Blok, to judge from the sheer volume of underlinings in his copy, and he refers to it directly in his articles from 1908 onwards. Blok had called for reform in the theatre since 1906, when he claimed that individualism was undergoing a 'crisis', and that the 'elemental downpours' of Wagner's music and Ibsen's dramas had prepared the way for theatre's resurrection.[82] Blok was particularly interested by Wagner's discussion of the defects of Christian art in *Art and Revolution*, and in his article 'About the Theatre' (*O teatre*), written in 1908, he quotes from the passages he had underlined in *Art and Revolution* to back up his arguments, supporting, for example, Wagner's view that 'the honest artist must confess from the beginning that Christianity was never art and in no way could it give life to genuine art'.[83] Blok then goes on to describe the state of Russian theatre by quoting two subsequent paragraphs from *Art and Revolution*, in which Wagner deplores the 'industry' of an art form whose moral aim was 'profit' and whose artistic aim was merely preventing the audience from becoming bored. Far from symbolising the flourishing of civilisation, which theatre pretends to do, writes Wagner in the passage quoted by Blok, this 'flourishing' is merely the flourishing of a 'corrupt, empty, soulless and artificial social structure'.[84] In fact, with his condemnation of the contemporary theatrical public and his call for a proper 'people's theatre', with his glorification of drama as the highest conceivable form of art, and his optimistic prediction that theatres would soon be filled by a new, attentive public (the main points of Wagner's treatise), Blok's 'About the Theatre' is, in the last analysis, little more than a Russian version of *Art and Revolution*, but one addressing the conditions of early twentieth-century dramatic theatre in Russia, rather than mid-nineteenth century opera in Germany. It is thus particularly poignant that the metaphor Blok picks to depict the inevitability of upheaval in the Russian theatre comes from the *Ring*. Making an analogy with Siegfried's separation from the hunting party in *Götterdämmerung*, which precedes his death and the destruction of Valhalla, Blok writes that 'The longer this fateful and universal strike against the flesh[85] which characterises our times lasts ... the more audible will be in the night-time fields, swiftly rid of winter's snow, the distant, agitated horn of the hero who has lost his way.'[86]

Blok made a concerted attempt to put into practice what he preached with the composition of his own plays, through which he hoped to communicate with a wider audience. Most would argue that he failed miserably in this particular task, but *The Rose and the Cross* (*Roza i Krest'*), ironically one of his most obscure works, is deserving of study here on the strength of the links it seems to have with Wagner's music dramas, an issue which has not been fully explored. Viktor Zhirmunsky first tackled the topic in 1964, when he drew a tentative parallel between Bertran's death in *The Rose and the Cross* and the *Liebestod* of *Tristan und Isolde*, noting that Blok had put the last scene of the play into verse 'to the melodies of Wagner', and had decided on 'his' Wagner when contemplating possible musical accompaniment.[87] It was *Die Meistersinger* that Blok went to see on 15 January 1913 before finishing his play, however. R. D. B. Thomson has therefore argued that if there are Wagnerian parallels in *The Rose and the Cross*, then they are with *Die Meistersinger* and not with *Tristan*, although there is no evidence to suggest that Blok was 'well acquainted' with *Die Meistersinger*, as Thomson claims.[88] In fact, it seems most likely that Blok had never heard the work before, for its first performance in Petersburg had taken place only on 21 December 1912, and Blok was probably attending only its third or fourth performance. As we have seen, Wagner's music dramas only seem to have influenced Blok's writings after he had seen them performed on stage, but here he was already finishing *The Rose and the Cross*. Blok makes no other reference to *Die Meistersinger* in his writings, moreover, nor does he appear to have ever acquired a copy of its libretto. The coincidence between the significance of Gaetan's song in *The Rose and the Cross* and Walther von Stolzing's 'Prize Song' is indeed striking, but it is difficult to see any real resemblance between the characters of Gaetan and Hans Sachs, for example, and the prevailing mood of Blok's play hardly matches the fundamentally optimistic spirit of *Die Meistersinger*. Thus in general one is more inclined to agree with Robert Hughes that 'the three stages of Bertran's death and transfiguration (wherein Joy and Sorrow – his physical suffering – do indeed become one) are very like the long dying of Tristan as he awaits the arrival of Isolde', since Tristan's death is also 'accomplished in three stages of reminiscence and a final transfiguration in which the joy of understanding becomes at one with his suffering'.[89] The parallels with *Tristan* do not stop there. Blok situated his play in thirteenth-century France (having studied numerous sources concerning medieval legends in which the Tristan legend must have been prominent), as Gottfried von Strassburg had done for his version of the legend of *Tristan*, and also as Meyerhold had done for his production of Wagner's work in 1909. Blok, as we know, knew about this production, and he probably also knew about Meyerhold's next production of Hardt's *Tantris der Narr* at the Aleksandrinsky Theatre (with music by Kuzmin), which was based on the same legend. Perhaps it was Hardt's example that led him to conjure up the names of Bertran and Izora, that are so reminiscent of Tristan and Isolde. It is also known that Blok planned this work as an opera initially. His use of the 'free rhythms in poetic monologues and dialogues so characteristic of Wagner's music dramas' may indeed imply that he initially conceived *The Rose and the Cross*, as Zhirmunsky has suggested, on precisely those lines. This supposition gains further weight with S. Burago's observation that Blok's 'symphonic principle of combining the poetry of folk legend with a structure based on leitmotif' is precisely that of the music drama, and also with Blok's note in 1916 that he wanted to explain the significance of alliteration in the play to the actors of the Moscow Art Theatre:[90] alliteration was a device Wagner used extensively to give his verse its maximum emotional load.[91]

A further link with Wagner's *Tristan* is revealed by the fact that in 1919, Blok planned to construct a drama on the Tristan theme, and again started compiling a bibliography including 'Bédier, Wagner, E. Hardt, Meyerhold's article on the production of *Tristan*'.[92] He had planned seven scenes, but stopped at the last scene of the first act ('The deck of the ship'), unable to decide whether to follow Wagner's or Gottfried von Strassburg's version of the legend at this point.[93] Another connection is provided by Mikhail Tereshchenko, who had originally commissioned Blok to write *The Rose and the Cross*. On 2 November 1912, Blok read him what he had written, and later noted in his diary the fact that Tereshchenko had pointed out that the ending was 'like the ending of "Kurwenal", which I didn't know (I have not read or heard the Wagner)'.[94] This is a strange remark to make, yet R. D. B. Thomson is rash to assume that Blok must definitely have seen *Tristan und Isolde* before 1912. Despite its improbability, there is no evidence of him seeing the work, beyond our knowledge that he heard a concert performance of part of the work in 1903, and also heard its concluding scenes through the doors of the Mariinsky Theatre in 1909. The copies of the libretto he possessed, moreover, may have been acquired in 1919, when he was planning his 'Historical Picture' of the Tristan legend. Thomson is perhaps also misguided in thinking that 'Blok took "Kurwenal" for an unfamiliar Wagner opera.' Tereshchenko was probably pointing out (quite reasonably) the similarity between the deaths of Kurwenal and Bertran, who are both faithful servants who die tragically and needlessly, and what Blok may have been saying here is that he had never specifically looked at or remembered this particular part of *Tristan*. This is quite a plausible notion if Blok really had not seen the work in full, particularly if one remembers that Tereshchenko had actually brought *Tristan* into his conversation with Blok a few weeks earlier.[95]

Despite all the apparent links with *Tristan*, it might, however, be rash to pinpoint any one particular work by Wagner that might have influenced the composition of *The Rose and the Cross*. S. Burago has justifiably likened Gaetan, for example, to the 'Flying Dutchman', 'condemned to eternally wander in the ocean of life',[96] and the Wagnerian influence on the play was perhaps a synthesis of all Blok's unconscious and conscious appropriations from the composer's works. There is one small clue that has so far been overlooked by commentators which points to such a conclusion. It is an addendum to an entry in Blok's diary of 27 January 1913, where, in the summary of his conversation with Stanislavsky about the play, he describes the director's ideas for the staging: 'The wounded [Bertran] enters (he is carried). He says to the audience that he received the blow from the sword from the one who has been the cause of all his sufferings.'[97] Underneath, Blok subsequently noted down Evgeny Ivanov's interpretation of Bertran: 'Bertran – unhappy because Wotan's spear hangs over him all the time – was not supposed to and not able to carry out murder. He could wipe away the insult only through being wounded – the fact of the murder did not exist.'[98] Blok's reaction to Ivanov's perception of Bertran as a Siegmund type was 'I'll think about it', but the very fact that Ivanov could see features of the 'unhappy hero' in Bertran proves that this was not an implausible interpretation. Given that the play was highly autobiographical, in fact, mythology from the *Ring* (which had played such an important role hitherto in the development of Blok's conception of 'heroism') was almost bound to make an appearance in a play about failure, albeit in a veiled and distorted form.

PART 3

Wagner and Soviet Russia

CHAPTER 7

Reception and performance history, 1917–1941

THE RENAISSANCE OF WAGNER

With the exception of Meyerhold's staging of *Tristan und Isolde* in 1909, pre-revolutionary Wagner productions in Russia tended to be unexciting from a scenic point of view. The 1917 Revolution paved the way for theatrical experimentation of all kinds, however, and some of the early Soviet Wagner stagings were amongst the most radical Soviet opera productions of the time, with designs by leading avant-garde artists. A key figure here was the founder of Russian Constructivism, Vladimir Tatlin, who created some strikingly original designs for *Der fliegende Holländer* between 1915 and 1918. Tatlin had spent several years in the navy, and clearly retained a deep love of the sea, for it was the nautical setting which principally drew him to Wagner's opera, to judge from the numerous sketches he made of masts, decks, sails and rigging.[1] Dominating Tatlin's final design for the set (which he hoped would be made out of construction materials) were several large masts which he intended members of the cast to climb up and down during performances, in order to exploit the full potential of both the vertical as well as horizontal space of the stage. Tatlin had thus not just produced a simple set design, but had worked out a radical conception for producing the work. As Mikhail Kolesnikov has commented, with these designs, Tatlin was the first 'to break up the surface of the stage, building several planes tilted at different angles and intersecting each other at different levels, which opened up new and promising possibilities for the actors' dynamic and plastic movement'.[2] Tatlin's conception

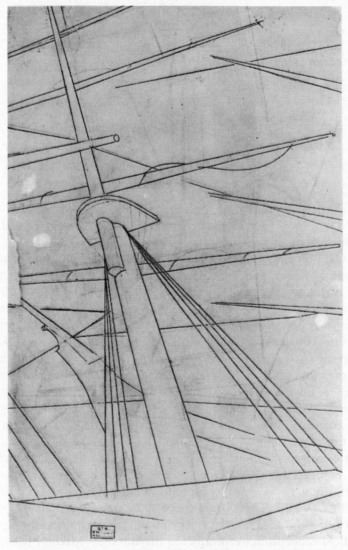

10. Vladimir Tatlin, design for *Der fliegende Holländer* (1915–18).
Compare with illustration 11.

for *Der fliegende Holländer* thus occupies an important position in the development of Constructivist stage design in Russia, but it was also of relevance to his own art, for it was his mathematically precise sketches of masts (rather than the Eiffel Tower, the Baku oil derricks, or works by Boccioni, Bruegel or Rodin, as some critics as have suggested) which were undoubtedly the chief inspiration for the shape of his famous Tower, the utopian 'Monument to the Third International' of 1920, the first sketches for which he began in early 1919.[3]

The end of World War I in March 1918 meant that the ban forbidding the performance of German music in Russia could finally be lifted, thus making it possible for new productions of Wagner's works to take place, but Tatlin's innovative ideas for producing *Der fliegende Holländer* were sadly never realised. The swiftness with which Wagner's works returned to the repertoires of the newly nationalised Petrograd and Moscow opera houses, however, is testament to the intensity of Russian enthusiasm for Wagner, which had somehow survived the four-year moratorium and a major revolution: *Parsifal* was revived at the Theatre of Musical Drama within days of the signing of the Brest-Litovsk peace treaty. To judge from a four-line verse which had become familiar during the War, the ban on Wagner had been particularly unpopular:

> Wagner is loved by you and us
> Why should we offend him in this way?
> It's time to bring back the good old days
> And give Siegfried back to us today![4]

'In countries where they think clearly and soberly, they do not confuse Apollo with Mars', wrote Vyacheslav Karatygin scathingly in April 1918, when he reported that the performances of *Parsifal* were drawing capacity audiences: 'The situation is different here. Tsarist Russia declared that all German art was to be forbidden because of the war with Germany ... Wagner's name was absent from concert and theatre posters for a long time. But *tempora mutantur*. Wagner has been restored and is free once again to affect the hearts and minds of our musicians as profoundly as before.'[5] The revival of *Parsifal* was swiftly followed by a concert of Wagner's music (conducted by Albert

Coates), and revivals of *Die Meistersinger* at the Theatre of Musical Drama and *Die Walküre* at the Mariinsky Theatre, which also played to packed houses.[6]

The first new Wagner staging after the Revolution was a 'futuristic' production of *Lohengrin*, staged by Fyodor Komissarzhevsky at the former Zimin Theatre in Moscow (now renamed the *Teatr Soveta rabochikh deputatov*). Komissarzhevsky was a romantic idealist whose interest in the Revolution extended only as far as it affected the creative freedom of the artist. His dream was to create a cosmic 'mystery' theatre, and his opera productions, including *Lohengrin*, tended to be universalised, highly symbolic affairs which had little or no reference to contemporary reality. Lohengrin in Komissarzhevsky's production thus appeared as a 'mystical knight' and emissary of the Holy Grail, rather than as a medieval warrior, as suggested by his costume, which was reminiscent of a priest's robes. In an endeavour to bring the Lohengrin legend out of its historical confines and emphasise its universal content, the designer Ivan Fedotov constructed a futuristic-looking three-dimensional set filled with cubes and cones (such as Malevich had used for the revolutionary Cubo-Futurist staging of *Victory Over the Sun* in 1913), thus breaking sharply with the naturalism of conventional opera production. The abstract, timeless quality of the production was further enhanced by Komissarzhevky's impressionistic and stylised treatment of the chorus, whom he arranged in static groups on different levels to create a 'moving harmony of colours', presumably under the inspiration of Aleksandr Tairov, who had experimented with choreographing the movements of his actors in the production of Annensky's *Famira Kifared* he staged at the Kamerny Theatre in 1916. The première of Komissarzhevsky's *Lohengrin* opened the second Soviet operatic season in Moscow on 5 September 1918, and was prefaced by a speech by Anatoly Lunacharsky, the new Commissar of Enlightenment, who spoke to the packed and enthusiastic auditorium about the role of opera in the new society, and about Wagner in particular. The critic for *Izvestiya* responded positively to Komissarzhevsky's decision to replace the traditional naturalistic sets with 'austere, majestic forms' and a stage broken into different levels,[7] but others felt his production of *Lohengrin* was too abstract and modern, and thus unable to convey the austere majesty of Wagner's score.[8] The virtual absence of document-ation about the production, however, makes it impossible to judge how far those criticisms were valid. Komissarzhevsky's attempts to fuse music and drama in his productions to achieve his avowed goal of 'synthetic theatre', show yet again how potent Wagner's ideas were for Russian artists, even after the Revolution, for they undoubtedly lay behind Komissar-zhevsky's belief that 'perfection in theatrical art', could be achieved by a 'synthetic union of drama, opera and ballet'.[9]

After presenting Lohengrin primarily as an emissary of the Holy Grail, it was inevitable that Komissarzhevsky should next want to tackle *Parsifal* (which had never been staged in Moscow), and it was due to his insistence that the work was rehearsed at the end of 1918 at the Bolshoi Theatre, where he had became artistic director. When the board of directors at the Bolshoi drew up a list of works to be performed in the 1919–20 season in April 1919, it is interesting to note that works by Wagner (*Parsifal*, the *Ring* and *Lohengrin*) headed the list of foreign operas whose staging was desirable at all costs, 'regardless of the availability of performers, inclusion in the repertoire in previous seasons, absence of good sets etc.', and surprisingly took precedence over *La Traviata*, *Carmen* and *Il Barbiere di Seviglia*.[10]

The production of *Parsifal* never reached completion.[11] Komissarzhevsky decided to emigrate and no one else was prepared to champion a work whose spirit of resignation was so 'remote from the spirit of the revolutionary times' and there-fore devoid of interest for the 'new audience' of workers filling Soviet opera houses, who received free tickets.[12] New Soviet operas with revolutionary content would have been the ideal material for the post-1917 repertoire, but in their absence, Wagner's works were evidently judged a good substitute. *Parsi-fal* may have been considered ideologically unsuitable for the new Soviet repertoire because of its absence of positive heroism and the religiosity of its subject, but *Das Rheingold*, *Tannhäuser* and *Die Walküre* had all passed muster and these three works were revived at the Bolshoi Theatre in October 1918, February and April 1919 respectively. Emil Kuper (who had now become chief conductor at the former Mariinsky Theatre), Ershov and other avid Wagnerians were responsible for the revival of Wagner's works in Petrograd. In an interview of September 1920, Kuper declared that he was planning the production of no less than seven Wagner operas at the former Mariinsky,[13] and a special commission was set up to ensure the tetralogy had a 'permanent place in the repertoire'.[14] Despite the theatre's freezing temperatures (there being no heating during the winter months in the early years after the Revolution), the revival of Wagner's works at the Mariinsky was greeted with 'jubilation', according to the critic P. Konsky, who later maintained that Wagner's music sounded at that time 'particularly poignant' and 'made everything worthwhile'.[15] The legendary pianist Mariya Yudina was amongst those for whom Wagner's music had a particular resonance just after the Revolution: 'It was a cold and hungry time, but it was a time full of hope and inspiration. It was the renaissance of Wagner. His music embodied the spirit of the first revolutionary years.'[16]

WAGNER AND ART FOR THE PEOPLE

During the first revolutionary years there was a great deal of controversy about exactly what sort of culture should be created for the new audience, and what the official attitude to the cultural legacy of the past should be. Particular attention was paid to the debate about the creation of Soviet theatre since drama was thought to be an effective weapon in the battle to win over a largely illiterate population to the new ideas of Communism. Although politically radical, figures like Lenin and Lunacharsky were actually quite conservative when it came to the debate about the theatre. Unlike the leaders of the militant Proletarian Culture movement *Proletkul't*, who were deeply hostile to all pre-revolutionary culture, and who advocated the formation of a new mass culture created exclusively for and by the workers, Lenin and Lunacharsky voted to retain the old repertoires, arguing that revolutionary art and new forms of expression could only be created by drawing on the lessons of the past. The case for preserving institutions like the Bolshoi and the Mariinsky was more complicated, since they were such obvious symbols of the old culture, but opera proved remarkably popular with the new mass audiences and actually became, as Boris Schwarz has pointed out, 'the ideal medium by which to introduce the untutored listener to "serious" music'.[17]

Wagner was an important figure to the debates about theatre on a practical as well as a theoretical level, and was endorsed enthusiastically by Lunacharsky, who promoted him as an ideal revolutionary artist. An immensely cultured and erudite man, and the author of many perceptive articles on literature and music, Lunacharsky had first written about Wagner (whom he considered 'one of the greatest artists of the last century')[18] in 1906.[19] What attracted Lunacharsky most to Wagner (and what, incidentally, also drew the 'father of Russian Marxism' Georgy Plekhanov to Wagner)[20] was the composer's socialist vision in *Art and Revolution* of an ideal art form that would be for the people. Wagner's condemnation of bourgeois theatre as a profit-making institution and place of light entertainment, and his dream of a theatre which would be reminiscent of that of ancient Greece in terms of its role in socially educating the masses made *Art and Revolution* for Luna-charsky an 'almost classic expression of the theory of theatre' he hoped would emerge in Bolshevik Russia.[21] Believing that in the artistic sphere *Art and Revolution* was as important a document as the 'Communist Manifesto', which was also a product of the 1848 Revolutions of course, Lunacharsky undertook to disseminate its ideas to a wider audience by ensuring that a new edition of the 1906 translation, with a preface he had specially written for it, was one of the first titles issued by the literary publications department of *Narkompros* in 1918.[22] Lars Kleberg has maintained that this new edition of *Art and Revolution* was the 'first significant publication on theatrical theory to appear in Soviet Russia'.[23] Since the other most important works of the period were Romain Rolland's *Théâtre du Peuple*, first published in 1910 and re-issued in 1919 with an introduction by Vyacheslav Ivanov,[24] and the *Proletkul't* leader Platon Kerzhentsev's *Creative Theatre* (*Tvorcheskii teatr*), first published in 1918,[25] this theory would seem to hold water, as both Rolland's and Kerzhentsev's advocacies of mass festivals were themselves inspired by Wagner.[26]

While Romain Rolland openly acknowledged his debt to Wagner in *Théâtre du Peuple*, Wagner's influence on Kerzhentsev was rather more indirect. In *Creative Theatre*, Kerzhentsev called for an ideally open-air, proletarian theatre which would cease to be a place for people's 'entertainment and amusement' and which would involve the active participation of the audience,[27] as Greek tragedy had done.[28] It is no coincidence that the ideas Kerzhentsev was putting forward bear a strong resemblance to the Wagner-influenced theories for a new communal art based on myth that Vyacheslav Ivanov had begun to develop in 1905, and which he now returned to in 1919 in his official capacity as an employee of *Narkompros*. There was obviously a major difference between them, since Ivanov still envisaged a theatre with a mystic and religious, rather than political and ideological base, such as Kerzhentsev was proposing. Both, however, were seeking a unifying art that would abolish the boundary between artist and audience, and the fact that Kerzhentsev actually quotes from Chulkov's 1908 essay on the subject ('Principles of the Theatre of the Future'), which is itself full of Wagner and Ivanov-inspired ideas about an ideal communal art,[29] confirms Wagner as a major, if indirect, source of his ideas. Ivanov's ideas were surprisingly influential after the Revolution. The collapse of Symbolism as a coherent movement in 1910 had led to a hiatus in his theorising on the theatre of the future, yet after the 1917 Revolution, he once again turned to Wagner, maintaining that his music dramas represented a prototype on which Soviet art should model itself. He did so now from a position of authority. In autumn 1918, Ivanov started working for the theatre department (TEO) of *Narkompros* in Moscow, and between February to June 1919, he gave several lectures which were published as articles for *Vestnik teatra*, the journal of the *Narkompros* theatre administration.[30] Two articles in particular would seem to contain strong evidence that Wagner's ideas had not lost their potency for Ivanov.

Ivanov had constantly maintained in his writings before the Revolution that culture was in a situation of crisis, and that an era of synthesis was imminent. Now again he predicted a new cultural era, when intimate art, which was refined but isolated, would be replaced by collective creation on a large scale. Man was living in a period of sterile individualism, Ivanov believed, but the new 'organic epoch' would bring about the reintegration of culture and spiritual synthesis. There would be no more theatre in the sense of spectacle (*sozertsanie*) since spectators would become participants (*deyateli*) as they had been for the religion of Dionysus. They would unite into one body in the rebirth of the chorus, which would break down the barriers between the stage and the auditorium.[31] The art of the new age would be a collective ritual and an expression of the community, but above all it would be *sobornoe*.

To create this new, post-revolutionary synthetic art, Ivanov advocated the formation of large choirs throughout the country and the organisation of festivals, which should be developed along dramatic principles with the active participation of all present. During the summer, he advocated that works from the current repertoire should be performed on large stages and circular arenas erected in the open air. These outdoor performances, combining visual, orchestral and choreographic elements would present heroic deeds, myth, fairytale and legend.[32]

Ivanov unambiguously names Wagner as one of the progenitors of the new, synthetic art he was once again prophesying in a subsequent lecture he gave before a performance of *Die Walküre* at the Bolshoi Theatre, which was later published as an article.[33] Here Ivanov places Wagner as the vital link in (what he sees as) the natural chain of musical evolution from Beethoven and Skryabin:

Three musical geniuses are especially dear to us, the people at the beginning of a new era ... Wagner was conscious of being

Beethoven's successor and the executor of his behests ... Skryabin, unresponsive to Beethoven's music, saw his predecessor as Wagner. But all three are perhaps only precursors of the art which will accomplish their greatest aspirations ... fusing the masses into a single spiritual body ... it could not until now be achieved ... because it requires another culture than that through whose soil it had to push its shoots until today. It will not tolerate the culture of solitary and isolated [people], but the culture of those joined by a common great idea and common will.[34]

Ivanov had not really modified his views in the fifteen years separating his two Wagner articles. When he writes, for example, that the 'collective voice of humanity is contained within the harmonies of the orchestra'[35] he is essentially restating an idea he had expressed in 'Wagner and the Dionysian Rite'. And while applauding Wagner's music dramas for being 'conceived as national festive performances', he is nevertheless still critical of Wagner's preoccupation with the individual fates of his heroes: 'In the world epic unfolding before us we see only heroes; there is no place for crowds of people and the many-mouthed voice of the living chorus as we know it in the 9th Symphony of Beethoven and Skryabin's symphony, "Prometheus, Poem of Fire".'[36] Ivanov had placed great hopes in Skryabin, for he believed that with him, 'the truth of Nietzsche's idea about the birth of tragedy being out of the spirit of music was confirmed before our very eyes', since 'the element of music possessing him drew him irresistibly to forms of action'.[37] Ivanov believed that Skryabin could pick up where Wagner had left off, as it were, and complete the journey to the ultimate Mystery. 'The Mystery acted like a magnet in his creative life', wrote Ivanov. Its participants 'would take part in the performance of sacred drama, sing in the chorus or walk in celebratory processions. Collectivism had to be realised in art and art turned to the events of life. With this Skryabin expressed the most profound idea of our time.'[38] Yet Skryabin's death precluded him from achieving his goals and in the end only Wagner could provide Ivanov with any concrete justification for his prophecies. The Revolution had suddenly made all Ivanov's ideas about collectivism in art and the birth of a new age very topical. Like many of his contemporaries, he saw the *Ring* as allegorical of the contemporary situation. The death of Siegfried', he wrote, 'carries with it the ruin of all Valhalla, the whole world of the first gods; but a new mankind will rise on the ruins of Valhalla.'[39] In the mean time, he continued, we await 'the action of the choral multitude and its human voice of many mouths, real human heroism rather than magic, symbolic heroism'.[40]

Of the three second-generation Symbolists, only Bely did not nurture any utopian ideas about the future of a people's theatre in Russia (proletarian or otherwise) at the time of the Revolution. But even he could not but think of Wagner as the most obvious revolutionary artist in his essay 'Revolution and Culture', written in June 1917, in which he puts forward the idea that artistic creativity is impossible in times of revolutionary upheaval, and that the artist must therefore use the temporary hiatus to abandon himself to the times and 'transform his own soul'.[41] During the revolutionary period, Bely believed that the artist should make the gesture of 'giving himself up, the gesture of forgetting himself as an admirer of beauty' and surrender to the feeling of being 'just another citizen caught up in the whole process'.[42] And it was Wagner that Bely had in mind as his model:

Remember the great Wagner: when he heard the singing of the revolutionary crowd, he broke off the symphony [he was conducting] with a wave of his baton and tore from the conductor's rostrum to run to the crowd and speak to them, and escape by fleeing from Leipzig [*sic*]. Wagner could have written magnificent dithyrambs and could have conducted them in Switzerland, but he did not write dithyrambs; he broke off the symphony . . .[43]

Wagner may have forgotten about being an artist in his zeal to join the revolutionary cause, writes Bely, but this is not to say that the revolution had no effect on his creativity. On the contrary, the revolution had such a cataclysmic impact on Wagner, according to Bely, that it silenced him and only later found resonance in his work, when it exploded 'in great bursts' with the *Ring*, and was 'reflected in the exorcising blaze of fire enveloping Valhalla'.[44]

Like Ivanov, Blok also surrendered to a utopian idealism about Russia's new future after the Revolution, fervently believing in the imminent and inevitable arrival of a new 'Siegfried'. And like Lunacharsky, Blok was also keen to promote Wagner as the ideal artist-revolutionary after 1917. In order fully to understand the Revolution, Blok believed it was necessary to see beauty in it, and this beauty, according to Evgeniya Knipovich, was intimately connected for him with Wagner's works.[45] In March 1918, he wrote a brief but enthusiastic article about *Art and Revolution* (which he linked to the Communist Manifesto) to accompany his wife's new translation of the work, which Lunacharsky and Gorky discussed using for their new 'people's edition'.[46] The following year, Blok wrote a lengthy and Wagner-inspired article on the collapse of humanism, in which he follows Wagner's general line of thought in *Art and Revolution* almost exactly, describing the 'development' of art as a process of disintegration, then calling for a rejection of 'civilisation' and a return to nature.[47] Like Wagner some seventy years before him, in 'The Collapse of Humanism' (*Krushenie gumanizma*), Blok also aspires to the ideal of artistic synthesis as a remedy to the disintegration of contemporary art, and places his hopes in the people as the artists and audience of the future. He further betrays the source of his ideas when he alights particularly on the achievements of Goethe and Schiller. Examination of Blok's copy of *Opera and Drama* reveals that he found Wagner's discussion of these two writers' contribution to the development of European drama particularly noteworthy.[48]

The music critic Leonid Sabaneev was another prominent figure who found Wagner's works highly germane to the foundation of mass art after the Revolution, as can be ascertained from the ideas expressed in the preface to his unpublished study of Wagner, which he completed in 1923:

The revelation of the essential and profound aspect of this brilliant artist-revolutionary *is now particularly important*, precisely because his monumental but at the same time versatile devices of symbolising ideas in images are very contemporary and exceedingly suitable for those new forms of art which the liberated mass consciousness is now seeking here in Russia. *Wagner is now the closest to our consciousness*, to our spiritual needs ... closer than anyone else ... One need not close one's eyes to the fact that far from everything in Wagner's ideology is acceptable to us today ... But that monumentalism which he achieves in expressing ideas through *symbols* must inevitably serve as the example and *prototype* for the style which is proclaimed today and which is awaited in art transformed by the revolution. In this respect the study of Wagner's methods is particularly important and neces-sary ... His art *holds the key to developing the organisation of the masses*, his attitude is organically revolutionary and *agitational*. His great ... powers of expression, his rich *symbolism* present brilliant *methods for agitation*, regardless of whom they are addressed to ... In the pantheon of composers there is not one more revolutionary than Wagner ...[49]

Initially it seemed that the new Soviet theatre would fulfil the idealistic prophesies of Kerzhentsev, Ivanov, Sabaneev and Blok, for during the early Bolshevik years 'mass festivals' were organised by *Proletkul't* on a huge scale, often involving thou-sands of people.[50] With their roots in Greek drama, the medi-eval mystery plays and the pageants of the French Revolution, these mass festivals combined dance, rhythmic declamation, fragments from operas and the decorative arts in a synthesis on a scale Wagner could never have dreamed of.[51] That there was indeed a distinct Wagnerian flavour to these mammoth mythicisations of recent events is borne out by the testimony of foreign witnesses, some of whom, as Robert C. Williams has pointed out, actually assumed that 'Soviet Russia had fulfilled the cultural prophesies of Friedrich Nietzsche and Richard Wagner, bringing about a rebirth of Greek antiquity, where the arts were again a festive religion that integrated man with nature and society, purifying him through periodic drama and spectacle'.[52] Although the the Proletkul'tists would never admit to naming Wagner as a major source of their inspiration (since all past culture was anathema to them), the composer's ideas were nevertheless extremely influential, as James von Geldern has shown.[53] Not only were some members of *Prolet-kul't* romantic idealists like Wagner, perceiving the revolution 'less as a political than as a spiritual movement' (the actor Aleksandr Mgebrov, for example),[54] but others, like the

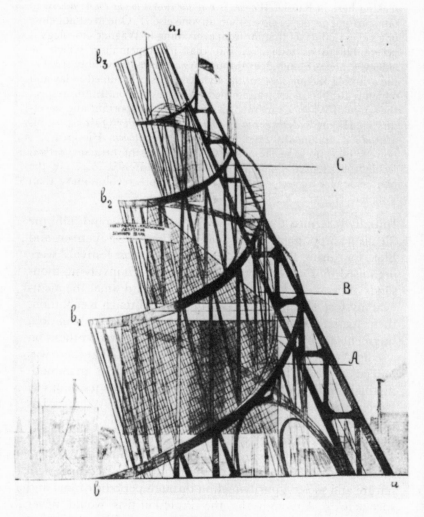

11. Vladimir Tatlin, drawing of the *Monument to the Third International* (1920).

peasant playwright Pyotr Kozlov, borrowed from the subject matter of his music dramas for their own works. It was not for nothing that Viktor Shklovsky described Kozlov's *Legend of the Communard* (*Legenda o kommunare*) (1919) as 'Wagner interpreted according to the libretto',[55] since the play not only features a Siegfried-like hero whose heart is forged out of iron, but an evil dragon-like Vampire, a symbolic ring and a forest which murmurs.[56] Wagner's music itself was also featured in the mass festivals. In 'The Mystery of the Liberation of Labour' enacted in Petrograd on 1 May 1920, for example, music from *Lohengrin* was employed to represent the workers' unrest,[57] and a few months later it was used again to symbolise the rise of the proletariat in the 'Towards a World Commune', a mammoth event which took place in July 1920, after the opening of the second congress of the Communist International in Petrograd in July 1920.[58] Ironically enough, Wagner's music was also chosen to commemorate the heroes of the Revolution. After the opening of the Congress in the Tauride Palace on 19 July, Lenin laid a wreath at the recently unveiled Monument to the Victims of the Revolution in the Field of Mars, and it was the funeral march from *Götterdämmerung* (performed by a 500-strong brass band) which was chosen to accompany the canon salute from the Peter and Paul Fortress. 'Could it ever have occurred to the genius Richard Wagner', wrote a correspondent at the time, 'that his music . . . would be the first to honour the memory of those whom the whole of mankind have a duty to revere? But it is as if this music was created for this moment. In it there is the sadness of loss, the sadness of death; in it is also the joy of achievement, the joy of life.'[59] Wagner had always occupied a special place in the hearts of the people of Petrograd, but the fact that 'Siegfried's Funeral March' was performed again after Lenin's death at the concert held in his memory at the Bolshoi Theatre in 1924,[60] suggests that it might actually have been the Bolshevik leader himself who had chosen that particular piece of music in 1920. Lenin's passion for Beethoven is well known, but Nadezhda Krupskaya revealed that the Soviet leader also had a great fondness for Wagner when she filled in a questionnaire about her late

12. V. Shukhaev, set design for *Das Rheingold* (1920).

husband for the Institute of the Brain.[61] That this revelation was not ideologically a very palatable one is indicated by the rather horrified tone of the Soviet musicologist Simon Dreiden who wrote a book about Lenin's artistic interests in 1970: 'One after the other they rise up before us, captivating images of the music which found a response in Lenin's soul ... But the chain of associations – up to this point so wide-ranging and full of facts providing indisputable evidence of Lenin's musical tastes – suddenly breaks off, and one is scarcely able to read as far as the words "was very fond of Wagner". Could this not be a misprint?'[62] A misprint this certainly was not, for Dreiden further reveals that Lenin used to enjoy going to hear Wagner performed in Europe during his years of exile before the Revolution from the 1900s onwards, and was apparently extremely knowledgeable about his works.[63]

WAGNER PRODUCTIONS IN THE AGE OF
CONSTRUCTIVISM

It was not only the theorists who espoused Wagner's populist ideas after the Revolution. Those actually working in the theatre, including the great directors Vakhtangov, Tairov, Stanislavsky and Meyerhold, also drew inspiration from them. Vakhtangov, head of the People's Theatre which opened in Moscow in December 1918, quoted enthusiastically from Wagner's *Art and Revolution* in an article of 1919, in which he proclaimed that 'the artist must create "together" with the people'.[64] References to Wagner's writings crop up in Stanislavsky's articles,[65] and it is also difficult not to see the shadow of Wagner behind Tairov's ideal of 'synthetic' theatre.[66] Meyerhold, who for a short time was head of Soviet theatre administration, also continued to take an active interest in Wagner after the Revolution, and in 1921 he chose *Rienzi* to be the third production in his flagship theatre, the RSFSR No. 1, which he founded in autumn 1920 to stage plays of revolutionary tragedy and buffoonery. Meyerhold, the most important figure in Soviet theatre in the 1920s, was perhaps not quite as extreme in his artistic views as the Proletkul'tists, who wanted nothing

13. Georgy Yakulov, set design for *Rienzi* (Teatr RSFSR No. 1, 1921).

to do with anything created before 1917. Nevertheless, he had now become a director with an aggressive political agenda, and he envisioned his RSFSR Theatre No. 1 to be a·'model of the new proletarian theatrical collective',[67] the first in a string of theatres all over the country with revolutionary repertoires celebrating the overthrow of the old order. Artistically, Meyerhold had always been an innovator, forever experimenting with new techniques and ways of presenting drama and opera. Now, in a decisive break with the past, he decided to abolish scenery, costumes, and all other illusionary props which would be reminiscent of the pre-revolutionary bourgeois theatre that had entertained the ruling classes. A large problem remained, however, which was the shortage of socialist dramas suitable for this radical treatment. Meyerhold's solution was to revolutionise the 'classical' repertoire by turning familiar dramas from the old repertoire into militant agitprop, and this was the treatment meted out to *Rienzi*. Meyerhold's intention was to show that there was a work in the opera repertoire 'with great revolutionary content', worthy not only of being shown at his theatre, but also at the nation's most important operatic showcase, the Bolshoi Theatre.[68]

The production, directed by Meyerhold's associate Valery Bebutov, but with his collaboration, was indeed revolutionary in many ways. A new 'Bolshevised' text (which included the creation of two new roles) was constructed by Bebutov and the Imagist poet Vadim Shershenevich out of fragments of Bulwer-Lytton's novel, and was to be performed with Wagner's score as an accompaniment. This meant that each now heavily politicised role had to be performed by both an actor (or 'tragi-comedian', to use Meyerhold's term) and a singer. The production not only incorporated both drama and singing, but also some mime scenes developed by Meyerhold. The set designs, which were to be based on the model which the avant-garde artist Georgy Yakulov had originally designed for the RSFSR's first production of Mayakovsky's *Mystery-Bouffe*, promised to be highly original.[69] It was also one of the first productions to be performed without theatrical costumes.[70] On 8 July 1921, a concert performance was given at the Conserva-

14.   Georgy Yakulov, model of set for *Rienzi* (former Zimin Theatre, 1923).

toire's Great Hall, with the orchestra of the Bolshoi Theatre, conducted by A. I. Orlov, and a military band. One further performance was given, but although the production was greeted by one critic as an event of exceptional significance with regard to the 'creation of revolutionary theatre',[71] it was never completed. Lunacharsky thought that the 'revolutionising' of *Rienzi* would have been the theatre's greatest achievement to date,[72] but Meyerhold's attempts to turn the traditional repertoire into pieces of propaganda had been highly controversial. Very little of the original works remained after they had received his treatment, and his abstract stagings were not deemed truly proletarian. With the beginning of NEP and the partial return to the capitalist system, the theatre's subsidy was withdrawn, forcing it to close in September later that year, before *Rienzi* was ready for its première.

Wagner continued to be a popular composer in the twenties in Soviet Russia. In Petrograd, the former Mariinsky Theatre repertoire for the 1922–3 season, for example, included *Lohengrin*, *Tannhäuser*, *Die Walküre* and *Siegfried*. In an interview given in October 1922, I. V. Ekskuzovich, who had become the theatre's director in 1920, spoke of the plans to complete a new production of the *Ring*, using Kolomiitsov's translation (rather than Tyumenev's), and at an open meeting a few weeks later, he also mentioned the theatre's intention of performing *Tristan* that season, although neither of these plans ever came to fruition.[73] The following season, a new, openly experimental production of *Rienzi* was staged by the radical young theatre director Nikolay Petrov, with designs by Vladimir Shchuko, another leading member of the theatrical avant-garde. Not only was this the first time that Constructivist-style sets had appeared on the stage of the former Mariinsky theatre,[74] but it was Petrov's first full operatic production (after reviving *Tannhäuser* the previous year), and was premièred on 7 November 1923 as a highlight of the festivities marking the sixth anniversary of the Revolution.[75] Despite Petrov's attempts to interpret *Rienzi* as a work of revolutionary content (in the continuing absence of new revolutionary operas in the repertoire), the production was not considered a great success, and was removed from the repertoire after only five performances.[76]

It was the Bolshoi Theatre in Moscow, the new capital, that continued to take centre stage in the sphere of theatrical experimentation in Russia at this time. The disappearance of the huge tsarist subsidies meant that staging new productions was a costly exercise, and therefore only infrequently attempted, but in March 1923, after stagings of *Carmen* and *Aida* in previous years, a lavish new production of *Lohengrin* was premièred. The production, produced by Vladimir Lossky, was staged in honour of the twenty-fifth anniversary of the great Russian tenor Leonid Sobinov's career on the stage, and survived in the Bolshoi Theatre repertoire until the end of the

15. Fyodor Fyodorovsky, costume design for *Lohengrin* (Bolshoi Theatre, 1923).

1935–6 season. Premièred on 29 March 1923, it was designed by Fyodor Fyodorovsky, and the colourful extravagance of this 'spectacle of mass heroic theatre', involving a cast of 300, embodied the utopian optimism of the early revolutionary years.[77] Like Komissarzhevsky, Lossky and Fyodorovsky decided not to interpret *Lohengrin* historically, feeling such an approach went against the grain of Wagner's music.[78] All references to the old German legends that had originally inspired the work were therefore excised, and attention was focussed instead on the struggle between good and evil forces in the work. Scenically, the production was a stylised, non-representational one, with columns, long curtains and geo-metrically shaped constructions replacing scenery and painted sets, and the choreographed gestures of the chorus following the overall monumental architectural style. Sets of steps resem-bling the raked seating of an amphitheatre broke up the stage into different levels, the aim being to enable the chorus to move together as a single unit. Positioned in the centre of the stage was a rectangular platform on which the soloists stood to perform their solos, like statues on pedestals. For the Bolshoi Theatre, which had never previously been known to be in the vanguard of theatrical innovation, this production, which was only its second experimental staging, was a radical departure from tradition. The costumes for *Lohengrin* were also highly stylised, the futuristic-looking, spiky outfits with their elabor-ate head-dresses surely the most unconventional ever designed for the opera at that time. But the helmets and huge shields were also rather heavy, which made moving and singing at the same time something of a challenge, as the male chorus found to their cost, and in 1925 they finally petitioned to have the march from the last act removed. The soloists' costumes were also cumbersome: the singer performing the role of Ortrude complained that her costume for act one weighed twenty kilograms.[79]

Lighting and colour also played important roles in the production and were used in an innovative way. White, silver and gold were chosen to symbolise the qualities of goodness, innocence and purity associated with Lohengrin and Elsa,

16. Fyodor Fyodorovsky, costume model for *Lohengrin* (Bolshoi Theatre, 1923).

while the sharply contrasting black and dark gold colours used for the costumes of Telramund, Ortrude and their retinue, were supposed to represent the powers of darkness. This colour symbolism was foreshadowed by a specially designed curtain which was hung in front of the stage during the overture. In the top right-hand corner it showed Lohengrin and the swan descending to earth from the heavens in colours of silver and gold, with Elsa reaching up towards them, while a glowering Telramund and Ortrude were depicted on the left-hand side of the curtain in red, black and violet colours against a dark background. While the overture was performed, the curtain was illuminated by beams of light projected on to it in varying shades and intensities in an attempt to express the musical leitmotifs in a visual way. Thus the curtain was flooded with a pure silver-coloured light during the motif of the Swan-Knight, for example, 'drowning out' the knights of darkness, but became suddenly ablaze with shades of crimson and violet at the appearance in the score of the motif of the evil Telramund, causing the image of Elsa to grow dim.[80] By making light become an active element in the production, rather than using it merely as a method of illuminating scenery and soloists, Lossky and Fyodorovsky were seeking to create a symphony of light and colour which could merge with the symphony of sound in Wagner's score. It is hard not to see behind their ideas the shadow of Meyerhold, who had first been inspired by Adolphe Appia to experiment with stage lighting in Russia in 1907. The attempt to subordinate the music to the overall general conception of the production was not universally approved; the conductor Nikolay Golovanov in particular was very hostile to Fyodorovsky's dazzling sets, and complained that they distracted attention from Wagner's score.[81] According-ing to Huntly Carter, a contemporary observer, *Lohengrin* was a huge success with the public, however. 'It was an excellent example of the grandiose or monumental manner in opera', he wrote:

The production was certainly the most picturesque, even gorgeous, one from the realistic-expressionist point of view that I had seen. It was a magnificent example of stage pageantry designed to reproduce

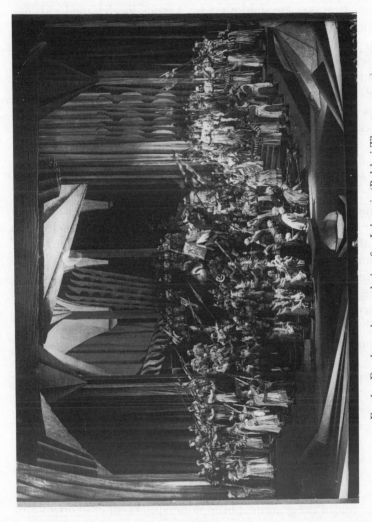

17. Fyodor Fyodorovsky, set design for *Lohengrin* (Bolshoi Theatre, 1923).

the legendary atmosphere of the opera. I marvelled at its richness of effect and wondered how a nation that had gone through, and was still going through unparalleled vicissitudes, could provide such a banquet of costume and colour, and how the performers working under extreme difficulties of shortage of food, inadequate housing, lack of proper everyday clothing and so on, could still give of their very best. I was struck by the reverent enthusiasm of the audience of common folk that completely filled the immense auditorium ... The scenes of the opera passed before one like a succession of old German paintings ... To heighten the effect, the characters were made to move against a rayonnist background, that is, a background resembling the multi-coloured rays of the sun.[82]

Carter's praise was not entirely unqualified, for in general he found the production rather too 'kaleidoscopic' and 'diffuse', and he also had mixed feelings about the platform at the centre of the stage, since it made the soloists resemble 'political speakers occupying a soap box'.[83] There were no such criticisms from the German medical specialists who had come to Russia to treat the ailing Lenin, however. According to Dr Nikolay Semashko, they attended every performance, claiming that 'they had never seen anything like it in Germany'.[84] Amongst Russian critics, only Yury Sakhnovsky had any serious reservations.[85] Boris Gusman, the critic for *Pravda*, considered that the production represented a major step forward for the Bolshoi, and claimed that the 'monumentality' of Wagner's works corresponded more than ever before to the heroic scale of the epoch.[86] Khrisanf Khersonsky, writing for *Izvestiya*, felt that *Lohengrin* was hardly an appropriate opera for the new repertoire with its monarchist and German nationalist spirit, but he had to concede that it was nevertheless a very good production.[87]

It was at the 'Free Opera of S. I. Zimin', which operated between 1922 and 1924, that the most radical productions were taking place in Moscow. The set for I. Prostorov's 1923 production of *Rienzi*, premièred on 3 April 1923 in a version which censored all the tragic elements by dropping the last two acts, was another model of scenic experimentation. It was designed by Georgy Yakulov, who now had the opportunity to

see to fruition the radical ideas he had initially explored for
Meyerhold and Bebutov's abortive production of the work two
years earlier. Leonid Sabaneev was impressed by Yakulov's
'symphony of colour and light',[88] and by the stylised grouping
of the singers on the many different levels that the stage had
been broken up into.[89] Sergey Chemodanov was also full of
praise for Yakulov's imaginative staging,[90] but O. Litovsky was
rather more ambivalent. While acknowledging the production's good intentions (including the employment of live
horses and large crowds of people on stage), and its timely
appearance in the repertoire, Litovsky condemned the lighting
effects as an 'ensemble of tastelessness' which had nothing to do
with Wagner and were more in keeping with the style of
Ambroise Thomas' comic opera *Mignon*. He was also scathing
about the 'salon compositions' of the Studio of Synthetic Dance
led by the dancer Inna Chernetskaya, who had trained with
Isadora Duncan, and was a leading figure in the Russian
avant-garde dance world of the time.[91] It is perhaps not
surprising that Chernetskaya became involved in the production of a Wagner opera, for as Nicoletta Misler has commented, her ideal of 'synthetic dance'[92] was still very much
indebted to the 'symbolist idea of the synthesis between music,
painting, and dance', which of course hailed from Wagner's
idea of the *Gesamtkunstwerk* in the first place. Huntly Carter
made no comment about the dancing in *Rienzi*, but found
Yakulov's designs highly iconoclastic. 'If stage-craft advance in
the form of realistic-expressionism set its mark on *Lohengrin*', he
wrote, 'something even more revolutionary appeared in the
scenery for *Rienzi*. Here a treatment that was more left-wing
[i.e. avant-garde] than the home of classic opera had ever
known, presented itself in the form of the circus ideas with
which the *Proletkul't* theatre had definitely associated itself. The
scenery, as designed by Yakulov, was shaped like a circus
arena, with steps at all angles and all levels, with suggestions of
a trapeze and hoops and the rest of the objects and agents of
circus representation.'[93] Introducing elements from the circus
was perhaps the most extreme way in which left-wing directors
and artists attempted to revolutionise the theatre after 1917.

Amongst the many forms of popular entertainment incorporated into productions between 1918 and 1923, the circus had
perhaps the greatest appeal, due to its emphasis on impro-
visation and physical movement, which made it an effective
means with which to liberate the theatre from its bourgeois,
literary past and ridicule its pretensions. It was also traditionally closer to the people than the dramatic theatre, an art
form which had originally been imported from the West. Not
surprisingly, Meyerhold was a chief innovator in this area. He
employed acrobatics in both his productions of *Mystery Bouffe*
in 1918 and 1921, and went even further in this direction the
following year in his productions of *The Magnanimous Cuckold*
and *Tarelkin's Death*, where Stepanova's Constructivist sets
were little more than circus props. Many other avant-garde
theatrical figures also experimented with 'circusation' (*tsirki-
zatsiya*) at this time, including Sergey Radlov, a pupil of
Meyerhold's who actually employed circus artistes in his
troupe (and who would later produce *Das Rheingold* at the
former Mariinsky Theatre), and Yury Annenkov, who was the
first to revolutionise a play from the 'classical' repertoire by
adding clowns and trapeze artists. *Proletkul't* drew on these
examples in its quest to find new forms when it set up its first
experimental Workers Theatre in Moscow in 1920, and it was
Sergey Eisenstein, Meyerhold's most gifted pupil, who took
these ideas to their limit. Eisenstein had used various circus
techniques in his production of *The Mexican* for the *Proletkul't*
theatre in 1921, and in 1922, when he returned to the theatre
after leaving Meyerhold's workshop, he took them even further
by turning an Ostrovsky play into a circus revue, where the
stage was replaced with a ring, and acting with acrobatics and
clowning. It is in this context, then, that we must understand
Yakulov's set for *Rienzi*, with all its multi-storey terraces and
vertiginously positioned trapeze apparatus. As John Bowlt has
pointed out, Yakulov's interest in spontaneity and the element
of chance led him to regard all theatre as a circus experience,
and in his productions, including presumably *Rienzi*, he
employed a chaotic system of contraptions and machines in
order to enhance the dynamic element.[94]

Fyodorovsky's and Yakulov's non-objective designs for *Lohengrin* and *Rienzi*, with their bright colours and geometrical structures, were two of the most interesting experimental opera productions in the early Soviet years, although their concern with architecture and three-dimensional space actually represented a revival of the methods used in baroque theatre, albeit using solid forms rather than painted sets. As J. Gregor has commented, Yakulov's *Rienzi* was 'nothing else than an architectural design of Piranesi, translated from a drawing in perspective into the modern style of flat surfaces' by 'elaborating architectural details, stairs, bridges, pillars till the whole stage is covered with them, in order to bring out the spatial value of every point'.[95] To a certain extent, the productions of *Lohengrin* and *Rienzi* also betray features of what Aleksandr Fevralsky described as 'decorative Constructivism', the vulgarisation which by 1923 had already began to pollute the purity of the first austere and functional Constructivist stagings.[96]

Despite the popularity of *Lohengrin* with the public, V. Blyum, the head of the *Narkompros* repertoire commission (*Glavrepertkom*) was concerned that greater effort had not been made to select a politically more suitable opera for production. In a lecture he gave in September 1923, he acknowledged the fact that the subject-matter of most Russian operas made it somewhat inevitable that the Bolshoi was still 'celebrating a tsar every night', but thought that *Rienzi* would have been a better choice than *Lohengrin*, which he described as a 'model of monarchic propaganda'.[97] In his notes to the Central Control Commission investigating the Bolshoi Theatre's activities, I. Trainin, president of *Glavrepertkom*, also wondered why *Lohengrin*, the 'least acceptable' of Wagner's works, had been selected for performance over the 'revolutionary' *Ring*, and *Die Meistersinger*, which was about the people, and recommended that the theatre's artistic management should be given the sack.[98] The negative preliminary conclusions drawn by the Commission and the exacerbation of the tension between the theatre management and *Glavrepertkom* (which deplored the fact that the theatre's repertoire had not essentially changed since the Revolution) led Lunacharsky to call a meeting of the academic-artistic section of the State Academic Council in December 1923. Since the Bolshoi was now the Soviet Union's premier showcase theatre, it was obviously a matter of some importance that it projected the right image to the world. At the meeting Trainin once again insisted that the theatre should reform itself by producing the *Ring* and *Die Meistersinger* (a work Lunacharsky also wished to see performed), while E. M. Beskin, head of the cultural department (*Kul'totdel*) of the All-Russian Union of Art Workers (*Vserabis*), and deputy head of the Main Political-Educational Committee of *Narkompros* (*Glavpolitprosvet*), condemned the choice of the 'Catholic' and 'mystical' *Lohengrin* and demanded that the theatre's current policy of preserving the past be radically changed. It also emerged during the meeting that efforts had been made by Beskin and his colleagues earlier in the year to arrange for a production of *Rienzi*, but that plans had been thwarted by the shortage of money needed to stage the work.[99]

Rienzi's theme of popular rebellion certainly made it an extremely popular work in the early 1920s, but the opera was apparently still not revolutionary enough. In 1924, the dramatist N. Vinogradov was commissioned to create new subjects for old scores in an attempt to 'solve the problem of revolutionary opera', and *Rienzi* was one of four works earmarked by the former Mariinsky Theatre to receive this treatment. Meyerbeer's *Les Huguenots* became 'The Decembrists', his *Prophet* became the 'Paris Commune', *Sleeping Beauty* became the 'Sunny Commune', and *Rienzi* was turned into 'Babouef', which would depict a series of 'triumphant and bloody pictures of the Great French Revolution and the heroic fate of Babouef, the leader of the communists'.[100] Besides revolutionising operas from the old repertoire, the theatre also decided its productions would seek to bring out the 'real' meaning of operas which were ahead of their time, and had been distorted by incorrect contemporary interpretations. The *Ring*, for example, was described as a work which clearly expressed 'the revolutionary aspirations of its time', and put into practice the ideas expressed in *Art and Revolution*, but which had been 'deliberately distorted by the Germans and by democratic absolutism in the

18. Ivan Kozlovsky as Lohengrin (Bolshoi Theatre, 1927).

name of nationalist and imperial demands'. In a similar vein, *Die Meistersinger* was now viewed as 'propaganda for living, independent art' and a satire of 'stagnant formalism'.[101] It was planned, therefore, for the first two parts of the *Ring* to be staged during the 1925–6 season, and for work to begin on a new staging of *Die Meistersinger* and the rest of the tetralogy. The new production of *Die Meistersinger* received its première in November 1926, and Shchuko started making designs for *Das Rheingold* in 1925, but the new production of the *Ring* was a failure, since all that resulted were a few performances of *Die Walküre* in 1927, and *Götterdämmerung* in 1931.[102]

Without Emil Kuper, who emigrated in 1924, the former Mariinsky Theatre had lost its greatest champion of the Wagnerian cause, but fortunately, a group of Wagner devotees had formed the previous year with the aim of propagandising Wagner's works (particularly the *Ring*). Led by Konstantin Khmelnitsky, an enthusiastic engineer who had visited Bayreuth before the Revolution, the group of some thirty musicians decided it would strive to 'bring the treasures of Wagner's musical legacy closer to the broad masses of workers' by giving chamber performances (there being no national radio service yet).[103] Their first concert took place on 11 June 1924, when *Das Rheingold* was performed with a piano as sole accompaniment. After Professor A. V. Sapozhnikov brought back Cosima Wagner's greetings following a meeting he had with her in Germany, the circle registered officially with *Narkompros* in April 1925, when it became the 'Society of Wagnerian Art'. By this time there were fifty-one singers, five pianists and six conductors amongst its members, as well as advisors such as Mariya Yudina and Ivan Ershov, and the veteran Wagnerians Karatygin and Kolomiitsov, who sat on the board. The society hoped to acquaint 'thousands of workers'[104] with the *Ring* through its chamber performances and thus prepare the proletariat for full performances of these 'complex' works. After increasing the ensemble to two pianos, two performances of *Das Rheingold* and *Die Walküre* were given in May 1925, with colour slides as 'scenery'. 'We should welcome the organisation of a group whose aim is to bring Wagner's works to the masses',

19. G. Kosyakov, male costume design for the Society of Wagnerian Art's chamber performances (Leningrad, 1925).

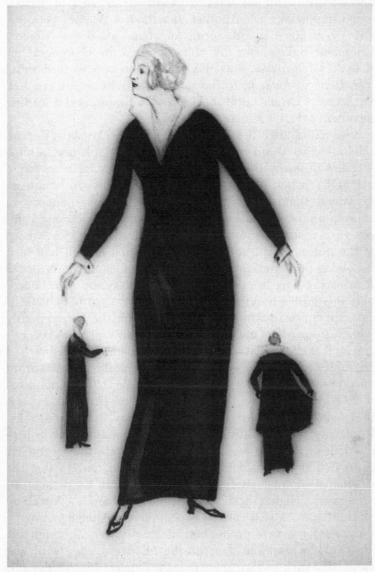

20.   G. Kosyakov, female costume design for the Society of Wagnerian Art's
      chamber performances (Leningrad, 1925).

declared the critic for *Rabochii i teatr*; it was work of 'serious social importance'.[105] Another unorthodox Wagner performance took place in the spring of 1924, when the Moscow Chamber Ballet, run by the avant-garde choreographer Kasyan Goleizovsky, staged a production of a work entitled *The Death of Isolde* featuring a constructivist set by Anatoly Petritsky, a former pupil of Aleksandra Ekster, and a leading member of the Ukrainian avant-garde.[106]

Two years after the repertoire crisis, the Bolshoi Theatre celebrated its 100th anniversary. Evidently still under some pressure to justify the theatre's existence, Lunacharsky wrote a lengthy article to commemorate the event. Although he explained that the Bolshoi had to be preserved mostly in expectation of the time when there would be poets and composers to create new musical tragedies, Lunacharsky's defence of the Bolshoi was also based on the vision he still had of it becoming the sort of theatre Wagner dreamed about in *Art and Revolution*. Apart from the former Mariinsky, he maintained, only the Bolshoi had the capacity to create a synthetic theatrical experience in which all the arts would be harmoniously joined to present operas depicting man's greatest experiences.[107] As far as Wagner was concerned, the Bolshoi had certainly learned its lesson following the politically disastrous mistake of staging *Lohengrin*, and in response to the criticisms of the GUS commission, a new staging of *Die Walküre* was premièred in December 1925, produced by Vladimir Lossky. Replacing the naturalistic scenery traditionally used in productions of the *Ring* was an assortment of abstract geometric constructions designed by Mikhail Sapegin, one of the first graduates of the openly experimental (and Constructivist-orientated) Higher State Artistic and Technical Workshop (Vkhutemas). A year earlier, Sapegin had created a Constructivist set for a new production of *Scheherezade*, although the 'bow' of the ship-like structure he filled the stage with was inclined at such a sharp angle that the dancers found it difficult to perform on it.[108] Evgeny Braudo greeted this attempt to move away from the 'visual falsity of conventional Wagnerian realism' with enthusiasm, noting that the revival of even one part of *Ring* had to be considered a major artistic event in Moscow.[109] Boris Asafiev, on the other hand, found it difficult to enthuse about the black sheets of fabric hanging down obliquely against a 'cosmic' backdrop supposed to represent the sky. Neither was he impressed by the slippery wooden slope which the artists had to perform on, looking as if they were about to fall over at any moment. Although the stark setting ('I don't see any scenery; All I can see is a timber yard' was the conductor V. Suk's response)[110] suggests the production might in fact have been rather interesting, in Asafiev's eyes Wagner's 'world tragedy' had been reduced to a puppet show, which reminded him strongly of Tolstoy's impressions of *Siegfried*. Asafiev had more positive things to say about Lossky's attempt to interpret *Die Walküre* scenically by changing the intensity and colour of the lighting, but failed to see whether the lighting effects were supposed to be connected to the dynamics of the music, the falls and rises of emotion, or with the development of the stage action, since they did not seem to be organically linked to anything.[111] Leonid Sabaneev, writing for *Izvestiya*, felt that the sets belonged more to the sphere of geometry than theatre, and although he reacted positively to the ideas experimented with in the production (such as the attempt to make the backdrop change colour and tone according to the intensity of the music), it seemed to him that they had not been fully thought out, and resulted in too much that was stationary.[112]

The fact that the next three new Wagner productions in the Soviet Union were all stagings of *Die Meistersinger* reflects the gradual regimentation of the arts which began to happen from 1926 onwards as a result of the nation's deepening economic problems. *Die Meistersinger* was chosen for production at the former Mariinsky to mark the ninth anniversary of the October Revolution in 1926, and was accorded this honour because of the 'agitational' scenes which occur in the work 'precisely at those moments when the people are brought on to the stage and Wagner puts forward his ideas'.[113] It was produced by Viktor Rappaport and designed by Vladimir Dmitriev, a young member of the avant-garde who had been responsible for the striking Cubo-Futurist sets in Meyerhold's iconoclastic pro-

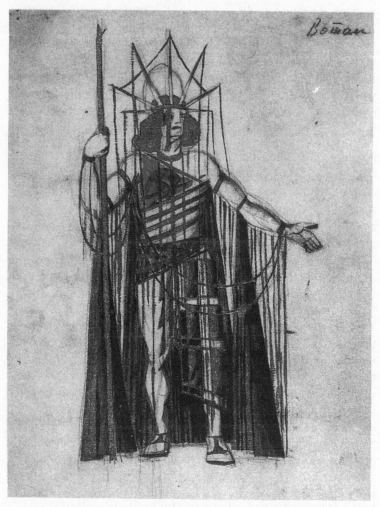

21. Vladimir Shchuko, costume design for Wotan in a projected production
of *Das Rheingold* (1925).

duction of *The Dawn* for the RSFSR Theatre No. 1 in 1920,
and who was later to design many important opera productions, including the world premières of Prokofiev's *A Love
for Three Oranges* and Shostakovich's *Lady Macbeth of Mtsensk*.
Despite Rappaport's efforts to play down Walther von

Stolzing's aristocratic origins,[114] the resulting production was not a success, however.[115] Musing later that year on why the most recent Wagner productions in Moscow and Leningrad had failed, Rappaport laid the blame on Wagner's theatrical techniques themselves: the idea of basing dramas on myth, for example, the 'superhuman scale' of his characters' feelings, and the system of leitmotifs, which led (a heinous sin) to 'abstract thought'. 'Obviously I don't want to say that Wagner has outlived his time for us', he concluded, 'but I think that the topicality of his works has now significantly declined, and we can now boldly ascribe him to the classics.'[116]

WAGNER AND THE CULTURAL REVOLUTION: THE PROBLEM OF IDEOLOGY

One anomaly of the early Soviet attitude to Wagner is that while Wagner the 'revolutionary' was extolled as a paragon for Soviet artists, Wagner the 'reactionary' was summarily and conveniently overlooked. In an article of 1924, for example, a critic reported an attack on Wagner by a German musicologist and observed that it was no coincidence that opposition to Wagner should have arisen precisely at this time: 'The bourgeoisie has now become completely reactionary and the old operatic forms designed for amusement are closer to it than the austere and majestic form of the music drama. The class which is now entering the heroic phase of its development [i.e. the proletariat] is the true executor of Wagner's ideas.'[117] By the end of the first decade of Soviet rule, however, Wagner began to disappear altogether from repertoires, as the doctrinaire Marxist views which were now playing an increasingly important role in Soviet culture prompted a change in attitude towards the composer hitherto seen as a model revolutionary. Stalin had emerged victorious from the struggle for power amongst the Bolshevik leadership which followed Lenin's death in 1924, and in 1928, NEP was replaced with the first five-year plan, centring on accelerated industrialisation and the collectivisation of agriculture. In order to fulfil Stalin's unrealistic goal of outstripping the technological achievements

22. Vladimir Shchuko, set design for *Das Rheingold* (1925).

of the West, the country had to be plunged into almost wartime conditions of austerity, which spelled a swift end to the relatively liberal atmosphere of pluralism and experimentation which had prevailed under NEP, and the beginning of the so-called 'cultural revolution'. Lunacharsky resigned in 1929, leaving the Party free to subject the 'cultural front' to its primitive ideas about the role of art, while an aggressive 'class war' was launched against the intelligentsia and all left-wing, avant-garde artists, whose work was now denounced as 'anti-Soviet' and 'unintelligible to the masses'. Militant proletarian groups assumed ever greater control in the cultural sphere, as art was increasingly forced to come under the conservative guidelines of the party, and support Stalin's policies in a realistic and accessible manner. This new shift in cultural policy also affected the performance of Wagner's works. In his article 'Music and the Cultural Revolution' published on 6 November 1928, Nikolay Malkov summarised the new position:

The very change of artistic tastes among the most progressive circles of the musical world is already proof of the influence of the revolutionary epoch, which is perceived as the air which we breathe. What is characteristic in this respect is a fundamental shift in the evaluation of Wagnerian art, which not long ago was belived to be the height of attainment in operatic theater, but which now is qualified as the ideologically unacceptable product of bourgeois pan-Germanism, invested, moreover, with a static stage form, which does not at all meet our contemporary requirements for an operatic performance. Does this mean that our appraisal of the purely artistic merits of the great music of Wagner has changed? Have we moved from praise to abuse? Not at all. But the social criteria have changed. The mode of our perception of life has changed, and Wagner's art, with its mysticism, which hypnotizes consciousness, with its fantastic heroism, in which the self-affirming aspirations of the bourgeoisie of imperialistic Germany were embodied, is at variance with our artistic worldview . . .[118]

The Party's greater concern with literature meant that changes in cultural policy took slightly longer to filter through to the Russian musical world (the experimental conductorless orchestra *Persimfans* devoted a whole concert to Wagner's works in

23. Vladimir Dmitriev, set for act one of *Die Meistersinger* (GATOB, 1926).

November 1928, for example), but when the question of Wagner's place in the repertoire was raised at a meeting of the Bolshoi Theatre's artistic committee in April 1928, only *Die Meistersinger*, his sole 'realist' work, could be recommended for performance as it was thought most 'suitable ideologically'. There was a 'wonderfully optimistic finale', for example, that was 'bright, jolly, and full of fun'.[119] The ensuing production, designed by Fyodorovsky and staged in a new translation by the former Acmeist poet Sergey Gorodetsky, reflected the new pressures to conform, as scenically it was traditional in character, although vestiges of the Constructivist craze for steps and platforms can be seen in Fyodorovsky's set designs. The production was certainly not conservative in the political sense, however, and here a decisive role was played by Evgeny Braudo, who revealed the work's 'ideological significance' by interpreting it from a sociological point of view. By emphasizing the 'mass scenes' and the satirical elements in the work and by portraying the chorus of apprentices as a 'strong force rebelling against the stagnant urban life and the rules of the Guild', he maintained that the production could demonstrate that *Die Meistersinger* was a 'genuine opera for the masses, both necessary and desirable in the contemporary Soviet operatic repertoire'.[120] Despite 'the innovation of a social approach to the staging *Die Meistersinger*', the resulting production was condemned as 'clichéd', 'trite' and 'pretentious', and disappeared from the repertoire after two seasons.[121]

The first signs of real repression appeared when the 'Society of Wagnerian Art' was forced to cease functioning in 1930 on the orders of Party functionaries, and an unsigned article calling for 'greater vigilance on the artistic front' appeared in the Leningrad newspaper *Smena* which castigated the ideological incorrectness of several Leningrad musical associations. Under the heading 'Marxism is not applicable to Wagner' (Khmelnitsky's response to being asked how his activities fitted into Soviet musical culture), the Society of Wagnerian Art was roundly condemned for its lack of engagement with proletarian artistic principles.[122] In the Ukraine, however, political pressure had evidently not yet been stepped up. In the

24. Fyodor Fyodorovsky, set design for act three of *Die Meistersinger* (Bolshoi Theatre, 1929).

same year that the Bolshoi Theatre opted for a conservative staging of Wagner's most ideologically acceptable work, Aleksandr Khvostenko-Khvostov, who had graduated from the Moscow School of Art in 1917, and who had studied with Aleksandra Ekster in Kiev in 1918, was producing some highly original ideas for a new staging of *Die Walküre* in Kiev. These abstract designs, by one of the most interesting Constructivists working in the Ukraine, were by far the most radical ever attempted in the Soviet Union at that stage, but were sadly never put into practice. Khvostov (who believed artists should do more than design costumes and sets) had studied the old German legends from which *Die Walküre* arose, and the ash tree in his interpretation was not just support for a dwelling, but Igdrazil, the tree of life, a holy totem at the centre of a temple. The stage was to be turned into a revolving circular platform, at the centre of which would stand a grey cylinder, representing the ash tree. To accentuate the drama, Khvostov's innovation was to use different coloured mobiles to convey the emotional experiences of the protagonists, an idea no doubt inspired by Ekster, who had used coloured fabrics in a similarly interactive way in the production of *Salome* she designed for Tairov's theatre in 1917.[123] Thus a 'crescendo' of tulle, satin, flannel and velvet in six shades of brown fabric, and shaped like a blunt rectangle (reminiscent of the shape of a shield) would bring out the 'Hunding theme' in the first act, for example, while mobiles made out of gauze, tulle, satin and silk in six shades of red would bring out those moments in the action linked to Sieglinde. The Sieglinde mobiles were circular-shaped (therefore less aggressive than the harsh lines of the Hunding mobiles) and were designed to suggest feminine qualities. The director F. Lopatinsky's innovatory idea was to place the soloists immobile at the front of the stage, as if taking part in a ritual, whilst their 'retinues' would express their feelings through mime.[124] Three years later, Khvostov made designs for a production of *Lohengrin*, but his markedly less adventurous sketches make it clear that the era of experimentation was over even in the Ukraine by then.[125]

In 1932, it was the turn of the experimental Maly Opera

25. Vladimir Dmitriev/Tatyana Glebova, set for act three of *Die Meistersinger* (Maly Theatre, 1932).

Theatre in Leningrad to stage *Die Meistersinger*, this time with E. Kaplan as producer, Tatyana Glebova and Vladimir Dmitriev (once again) in charge of design, and the imaginative Goleizovsky as choreographer. In the spirit of the times, however, the work had to be ideologically reconceptualised, after which Walther emerged as a sea-faring captain representing the newly emerging class of the bourgeoisie. In the new Marxist version of Wagner's opera, Walther defeats the old feudal structure of the Meistersinger, but is ultimately discredited by his materialist acquisitiveness. The production was not considered a success,[126] and was later criticised for the concessions it had made to 'vulgar sociological slogans' and to the 'formalist ideas' fashionable at the time.[127]

The last real manifestation of Soviet interest in Wagner occurred in 1933, the 50th anniversary of the composer's death. After reviving *Götterdämmerung* in 1931, a new, progressive production of *Das Rheingold* was staged at the former Mariinsky Theatre, which was to be followed by productions of the three remaining parts of the tetralogy in the spirit of a 'critical assimilation of the artistic legacy of the past', a phrase which recurred in many articles written about Wagner during that year. The main task was to make a decisive break with pre-revolutionary Wagnerism, which was now condemned outright as a 'reactionary' feature of imperialism, and to liberate Wagner from the 'harmful' and 'alien' associations that had clung to his name in the previous era due to the 'sectantist cliquishness' of the 'so-called Wagnerians'. Pre-1917 productions of the *Ring* were now seen as a 'distortion of Wagner's aims' and vehicles for 'imperialist ideology', while Wagnerian mythology was now seen as manifesting the 'tragic contradictions of social reality', its ideological centre being Wagner's supposed affirmation of the inevitability of the destruction of the capitalist old world.[128] Soviet Wagnerians now had to focus exclusively on Wagner as the 1848 revolutionary, the creator of Siegfried, in order to win the battle to keep Wagner in the repertoire. Despite the sociological approach, the new production of *Das Rheingold* was scenically not without interest, for the noted designer Isaak Rabinovich, who had collaborated on

26.   N. Kovalsky as Walther in *Die Meistersinger* (Maly Theatre, 1932).

many noted avant-garde theatrical productions in the twenties, was keen to develop further Lossky's experiments with lighting effects. His aim was to erase the gap between the dynamism of the musical score and the immobility of the visual spectacle on stage by creating a constantly changing multi-coloured symphony of light which would synthesise with the music, and act as the link drawing the soloists into its development. The lighting was to become a protagonist almost, uniting all the constituent elements in an organic synthesis which would overcome the previous static nature of Wagnerian drama.[129] The producer Sergey Radlov (sadly no longer the tireless innovator he had been in the early twenties) had different ideas, however, and wished to create a stylised atmosphere of 'monumental simplicity' by placing the performers like statues amongst 'the architecture of mountain scenery'.[130]

Although the critic Roman Gruber felt the 'majestic spaciousness' and 'stately simplicity' of the sets went a long way in overcoming the 'stuffy, oppressive confines' of traditional productions, he was disappointed overall by the experiments with the stage lighting. Not only did he feel that the effects had no organic link to the music, at times they actually conflicted with it, and seemed to have been introduced only for 'entertainment' value. Gruber also was critical of the producers' decision to raise the curtain early, in order to show shoals of fish swimming backwards and forwards and strips of white light pulsating out of time with the music, in a 'crude' and 'primitive' attempt to evoke the waters of the Rhine. But his chief criticism was directed at the attempt to focus all attention on the lighting and other decorative effects, for while he believed such effects could enhance the expressive gestures of the performers, they certainly could not replace them. As a result, he wrote, the singers remained largely static throughout the performance, acting merely as targets for the various spotlights directed on them.[131]

Other commemorative events in 1933 included a lecture and concert series, the publication of a collection of Wagner's essays,[132] and a new monograph by Gruber, with chapter headings such as 'Wagner and the Period of Revolutionary

Ferment', 'Wagner the Artist and Reformer' and 'Wagner's Path to Reaction'.[133] Both *Rabochii i teatr* and *Sovetskoe iskusstvo* printed special Wagner issues,[134] and Boris Asafiev contributed an article about Wagner to the Vienna music journal *Anbruch*.[135] On 13 February 1933 (the anniversary of Wagner's death), Lunacharsky contributed a lengthy article on Wagner to *Izvestiya*,[136] which was reprinted two months later in the Soviet Union's premier music journal *Sovetskaya muzyka*, founded in January of that year.[137] The increasingly critical attitude to Wagner forced Lunacharsky to speak now of the composer as a 'problem'. Reiterating Lenin's view that work on the future was impossible without work on the past, Lunacharsky refused to conform to political pressures entirely, however: 'What should our attitude be towards Wagner? Perhaps we should cast him aside, since he is a reactionary? Perhaps we should say: Only from this point to that point? Accept the early Wagner uncritically, forgetting how immature he was? ... Or should we discard the later Wagner completely, forgetting the powerful music, the passionate emotions, the shining artistry of this genius, a prisoner of reaction? ... An understanding of Wagner from a socialist point of view is a very intricate affair.'[138] Lunacharsky even managed to hold Wagner up as an example in a lecture he gave on Socialist Realism to the Organising Committee of the Union of Writers on 12 February 1933, in which he declared that the theatre was important in times of class war because of its ability to affect people's emotions. While acknowledging that art was a living mirror of life, he reminded the committee that fantasy was also important, and that Wagner, despite being a 'renegade', was a great teacher in this sphere.[139]

After Hitler rose to power in 1933, and it became known who his favourite composer was, Wagner's name began to disappear from Soviet theatre posters and concert programmes. In his memoirs of cultural life in the 1930s, the violinist Yury Elagin overstates the case somewhat when he maintains that Wagner was never performed, since he recalls attending a performance of Shostakovich's 5th Symphony in November 1937, at which Evgeny Mravinsky (who was appointed chief conductor of Leningrad Philharmonic in 1938, and later became world-renowned for his interpretations of Wagner) also conducted excerpts from the *Ring* and *Tristan und Isolde*.[140] Concerts with music by Wagner were also occasionally held in Moscow, usually conducted by Nikolay Golovanov or Aleksandr Gauk (one was attended by the writer Mikhail Bulgakov and his wife at the Conservatoire on 26 March 1935).[141] Nevertheless, the situation was grave enough for the young musicologist Dmitry Gachev to decide to 'resurrect the real truth about Wagner' in an article in *Izvestiya* which appeared in September 1937, underneath a photograph of beaming Kolkhoz farmers.[142] Gachev was not only angered by the disappearance of Wagner's music from concert posters, opera repertoires and radio broadcasts, but by the fact that this had taken place with the apparent approval from the authorities. In his article (which was almost his last publication before his arrest and untimely death), Gachev set out to unmask the 'falsification' which Wagner's works were made subject to in 'fascist Germany', arguing that he was one of the great revolutionary composers.[143] Gachev's complaints were evidently heard somewhere, as a cycle of Wagner concerts took place in 1938 to celebrate the 125th anniversary of the composer's birth,[144] accompanied by a commemmorative article by the critic Arnold Alshvang in *Pravda*, in which he also argued for Wagner to be perceived as a revolutionary:

German fascism sees Wagner as a forerunner of national-socialist theories ... But the fascists pass over significant facts which show Wagner to be a genuine revolutionary, both as an artist and as a man ... In our struggle for Wagner's musical legacy we must expose this foul lie. Despite all the contradictions into which this great artist fell ... from his work *Art and Revolution* to the gloomy Catholic mysticism of *Parsifal* ... Wagner continues to live for us in the great people's image created by him of Siegfried, the fighter and revolutionary ...[145]

WAGNER AND THE NAZI–SOVIET PACT: EISENSTEIN'S
DIE WALKÜRE

The last and most important avant-garde Soviet Wagner staging took place by chance in 1940, when Sergey Eisenstein was suddenly invited to produce *Die Walküre* at the Bolshoi

Theatre as part of the pro-German musical politics which followed the signing of the Nazi–Soviet pact in August 1939 by Molotov and Ribbentrop. It was the first time Eisenstein had worked in the theatre since his experiments at the *Proletkul't* theatre in the early 1920s, and the first time he had ever worked in opera. But Wagner proved to be a composer with whom he had a number of affinities, and the experience was a fruitful one. Eisenstein found Wagner's music particularly visual in its imagery and not surprisingly, since he was a film maker, it was the search to find the visual equivalent of the score to *Die Walküre* which preoccupied him most during work on the production. Traditional productions of the *Ring*, he considered, contained a fundamental contradiction between form and content, in that the stagings were far removed from the spirit of myth and prehistory he believed were embedded in Wagner's music. This flaw, Eisenstein contended, was caused by the isolation of bourgeois man in the nineteenth century, which was in stark contrast to the natural harmony between man and his surroundings which prevailed in prehistoric times and which he was trying to convey in his production. In his production, therefore (which was designed by Pyotr Vilyams), his goal was to revive the syncretic unity of prehistoric society in which everything, as he saw it, was linked to everything else. This was achieved, for example, by involving the scenery in the action as much as possible, in the belief that this was in the spirit of ancient tribes who saw the participation of the forces of nature in all their behaviour and actions. Thus not only did the leaves of the ash tree (interpreted by Eisenstein as a symbol of the creation of the world) rustle and change colour in his production, but the cliffs on which Siegmund and Hunding do battle were made to rise and fall according to the intensity of the music. Eisenstein also made the tall trees flanking the stage bow to the ground and rise again as Brünnhilde was carried towards Valhalla on her rocky ledge, as if disappearing into thin air. To achieve the syncretism of colour and sound, Eisenstein experimented with creating a spectacular multi-coloured light display which amalgamated with the *Feuerzauber* music, and paved the way for his future work in colour film.

Eisenstein also introduced, deviating radically from Wagner's score, much mime action to reinforce further the idea of the organic links between man and nature at a time when man did not yet perceive himself as an independent unit. Wotan, for example, was made to emerge from the ash tree when Sieglinde told the story of her father in the first act, Hunding and Fricka were both surrounded by so-called 'pantomimic choruses', and Wotan's chorus, the eight Valkyries, was supplemented by a further set of warrior-maidens riding air-borne on horses made out of papier-mâché. As a further means of achieving audio-visual unity, Eisenstein had wanted to relay the music of the *Ritt der Walküren* throughout the theatre by means of loudspeakers, but this unfortunately proved too difficult. He had also wanted to show a piece of specially shot film while Siegmund told his story of his life in act one, but again this was technically too difficult to engineer.

This brief overview of Eisenstein's scenic experiments does not even begin to do justice to the far-reaching structuralist ideas about myth which lie behind them,[146] but it must already be clear that many of his innovations were in fact a continuation, albeit a distinctly more successful one, of some of the ideas explored in the Wagner productions of the twenties and thirties. More poignantly, they also lead directly back to his own productions for the *Proletkul't* theatre and also to the innovations of Meyerhold, Eisenstein's former teacher and Russia's greatest theatrical pioneer, who, in February 1940, shortly before the first rehearsals for *Die Walküre* began, was shot in a Moscow prison as an 'enemy of the people', having been denounced for refusing to abandon his modernist experiments. It was Meyerhold who had first introduced the idea of a *mise-en-scène* consisting of concrete structures rather than painted sets which could actually become a 'participant' in the action, and it was Meyerhold who had first experimented with mime and the possibilities of stage lighting in Russia in 1907 after reading Appia's famous work. In 1936, Meyerhold declared that all Eisenstein's work had originated in the 'laboratory' where they had 'once worked together as teacher and pupil',[147] and he was intensely proud of this former pupil who

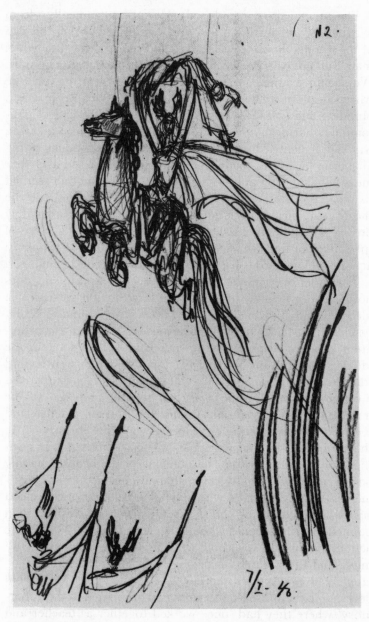

27.   Sergey Eisenstein, sketch for *Die Walküre*, (Bolshoi Theatre, 1940).

28. Sergey Eisenstein, sketch for *Die Walküre* (Bolshoi Theatre, 1940).

29. Sergey Eisenstein/Pyotr Vilyams, act one of *Die Walküre* (Bolshoi Theatre, 1940).

30. Sergey Eisenstein/Pyotr Vilyams, act two of *Die Walküre* (Bolshoi Theatre, 1940).

31. Sergey Eisenstein/Pyotr Vilyams, act three of *Die Walküre* (Bolshoi Theatre, 1940).

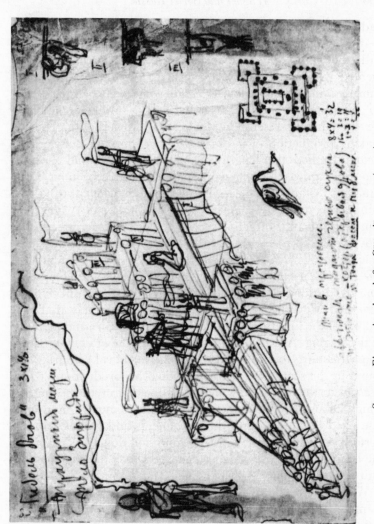

32. Seregey Eisenstein, sketch for *Götterdämmerung* (1940).

had already become a 'master'.[148] Prior to *Die Walküre*, Eisenstein's last practical work in the theatre had been bound up with the pantomime and circus techniques he had experimented with at the *Proletkul't* theatre, and the 'pantomimic choruses' and flying Valkyries can in some ways be considered an extension of those experiments. It is unlikely that the eleven-year-old Eisenstein had seen Meyerhold's epoch-making production of *Tristan und Isolde* in 1909, but he had clearly studied the lengthy article Meyerhold had written about his approach to the work with some care, for in his own, equally substantial article, 'The Embodiment of Myth', containing an outline of *his* ideas for the production of Wagnerian music drama, he directly refers to it by counterposing the movement and physicality of the *Ring* with the 'unreality and inaction' of *Tristan*'s internalised drama.[149] His production of *Die Walküre* itself, however, seems nevertheless to have been conceived along the same lines of 'theatrical realism' which governed Meyerhold's approach to *Tristan*, namely that the score, not the libretto should determine the nature and method of the staging. As Meyerhold set *Tristan* in the era of Gottfried von Strassburg to correspond with the medieval colouring he found in the score, so Eisenstein rooted his production of *Die Walküre* in the period to which the Nibelung myths belonged, which he also believed best suited Wagner's music. Eisenstein also tried to choreograph the movements and gestures of the performers using mime, as Meyerhold had done in *Tristan*, in the belief that such movements could 'embody the content and unity of the drama'.[150]

Wagner proved to be an important figure, not just as a composer, but also as theorist to both Meyerhold and Eisenstein in their search for artistic synthesis in their work, the elusive goal they pursued throughout their respective careers. Meyerhold claimed to have read Wagner's theoretical writings from start to finish, and he was the first to acknowledge their importance and relevance to his work.[151] Eisenstein also found Wagner's essays absorbing reading, as can be judged from the numerous citations in his article 'The Embodiment of Myth', and it is tempting to speculate that it may have been Meyerhold who had first introduced him to them. Eisenstein may have later even acquainted himself with the extensive notes Meyerhold made from Wagner's writings for his production of *Tristan*, for it is he we have to thank for taking the risk of saving these materials for posterity by hiding his friend's entire archive in his dacha in August 1941 to avoid it being confiscated by the authorities.[152] For obvious reasons Eisenstein could not acknowledge his debt to Meyerhold openly, or even mention his name, but the very fact that he even dared to mention the *Tristan* production in his article suggests that this was perhaps the only way he could find of publicly paying homage, however obliquely, to the beloved teacher whose tragic death had robbed the Russian theatre of its greatest genius. The first performance of Eisenstein's production of *Die Walküre* took place in November 1940, and was well attended by diplomats and prominent figures from the artistic and scholarly world, according to Yury Shaporin. Like most critics, Shaporin had mixed feelings about the production. While acknowledging that the introduction of pantomime helped bring movement into most static scenes of the first two acts, he felt that the 'cinema tempos' used by Eisenstein were not applicable to the epic flow of a Wagnerian music drama.[153] Other criticisms included David Rabinovich's doubts about the wisdom of Eisenstein's decision to interpret *Die Walküre* as primeval myth, and A. Shavedryan's questioning of the 'obscure symbolism' in the production (a complaint frequently made about Eisenstein's films).[154] Despite its extravagance, *Die Walküre* was only performed six times, and although Eisenstein had harboured hopes of producing the other parts of the *Ring*, the Nazi invasion in June 1941 precluded those hopes from becoming reality. It is a strange irony that Eisenstein's production of *Die Walküre* immediately followed his highly anti-German film *Aleksandr Nevsky*, and the speed with which both became political embarrassments is remarkable.

In March 1940, Shostakovich's close associate, Ivan Sollertinsky, had made (on behalf of an enthusiastic public) an appeal for Wagner's works to be revived in Leningrad.[155] His call was answered, but the première of the new production of

Lohengrin on 17 June 1941 (produced by V. Lassik, designed by S. Virsaladze and sung in a new translation by Gorodetsky)[156] preceded the arrival of Hitler's troops by only five days and only one performance of the work was given.[157] With the Nazi invasion, all Wagner's works were once again proscribed from the repertoire.

WAGNER AND RUSSIAN LITERATURE DURING THE PRE-WAR SOVIET PERIOD

By the time of the Revolution, Wagner's influence on Russian writers had not exactly ceased, but was already on the wane. Wagnerian images continued to surface in the writings of Andrey Bely after 1917, however. The Revolution brought an end to his references to *Parsifal* in his work; now it was once more the *Ring* which provided him with a source of imagery. Siegfried makes an undisguised appearance in his 'poem about sound' *Glossolaliya*, for example, which constitutes 'an attempt to depict in sounds the cosmology of anthroposophy'.[158] In describing the birth of consonants, Bely deftly manages to liken the conflict of the tongue with the exhalation of warm breath emanating from the throat to the fight between Siegfried and the evil serpent: '"Ha-hi" flies out [of the throat]; *serpent* in Sanskrit is *ahih*; an outrage of suffocation and wheezing threatens; but the tongue rising upwards boldly steps into the unknown and closes the gap; the serpent *ahih* crawls out of the hole and threatens to strangle us, but the tongue, like Siegfried, strikes the serpent with the sword "R". "R" is the first action: the tongue's victory.'[159] Bely's cosmic journey in *Glossolaliya* proceeds through four stages of evolution, each of which he illustrates with sounds he considers germane to their composition. Bely identifies the word *Newelung*, for example, with the fluid lunar state; it contains the root *li* (signifying something which flows), *volna* (meaning wave) and *Nebel* or *Newel* (meaning mist), thus leading inevitably, in his view, to the word *Nibelung*. Further on, Bely declares that the word *mime*, which means 'spirit' in Lithuanian, ceases to be such when 'frozen' into concepts, leading to words such as *Meinung* (opinion), *mashina* (machine or mechanism), or even the Nibelung 'Mime'.[160]

Mime reappears in the opening lines of Bely's poetic masterpiece, *The First Meeting* (*Pervoe svidanie*), which he completed in 1921, significantly, in view of the above, as a gnome crumbling the crunches of consonants into tomes.[161] The fact that Bely's use of the word 'gnome' is associated with Wagner's Nibelungs has been pointed out by Nina Berberova, who has also noted the undisputable link with the prologue of Blok's 'Retribution', where Mime is depicted cowering at Siegfried's feet.[162] The poem contains another conspicuous Wagnerian reference in the evocation of a concert conducted by Vassily Safonov, where Bely draws a parallel between the chorus of bassoons, the collective prophecy of the Norns (weavers of destiny) and Wotan's 'cawing raven' [*sic*] from *Götterdämmerung*.[163] The third Wagnerian reference is a less obvious one, however, and has not been commented on. In line 840, Bely declares himself to be a 'godforsaken Ghibelline', cowering at the feet of the Guelfs like Mime, and Berberova's explanation of Ghibelline and Guelf as, respectively, 'a member of the aristocratic party in medieval Italy, and a member of the papal party, opposed to the authority of the German emperors',[164] needs amplification. As noted earlier, in Wagner's essay *The Wibelungs*, which was his attempt to identify the historical roots of the Nibelung legends, he explains that Ghibelline and Guelf are Italian renditions of the German dynasties of Wibelung and Welf.[165] The proximity of 'Wibelung' to 'Nibelung' is, as Wagner is at pains to point out, no coincidence, and when Bely describes himself as a Ghibelline in *The First Meeting*, he was perhaps deliberately inverting the opening image of Blok's 'Retribution' to portray himself as Mime, with Wagner's *Wibelungs* in mind. Wagner's *The Wibelungs* was, of course, a favourite work of Emil Medtner, who is noticeably absent from the roster of Bely's friends who pass in and out of *The First Meeting*. Evidently the rancour of Bely's separation with Medtner was still intensely felt, and this reference to the Ghibellines and the Guelfs, whom Medtner 'would often talk about to those close to him',[166] is perhaps the nearest Bely could muster to an acknowledgement of the close friendship that had once united them.

The final Wagnerian reference to appear in Bely's writings can be found in the introduction to his last novel *Masks* (*Maski*), published in 1932, in which he describes himself deprecatingly as a 'pitiful Wagner' in his attempts to create new forms of expression by combining rhythmic and graphic elements with colour and sound.[167] Ada Steinberg has looked at the ways in which Bely went about his synaesthetic experiments, noting that Bely specifically calls his repetition of colours 'musical leitmotifs'.[168] Although she does not elaborate on Bely's purpose in employing these devices, it is precisely his statement that they are to 'illuminate the inner state of the characters'[169] which confirms that Wagner, the composer who first consciously used musical leitmotifs, was indeed still his model. As we saw earlier, illuminating the inner state of his characters was essentially what Bely had tried, and failed, to do in his 'Symphonies'. Although he might have abandoned the attempt to produce 'musical' works using verbal syntax, we can see that his concept of the leitmotif had not undergone any essential revision since the composition of the 'Symphonies' some thirty years earlier. In his earlier works, Bely had tried to use the repetition of images and the rhythm of their recurrence as a way of suggesting the meaning lying behind the logical surface of words. The preface to *Masks* reveals that even at the very end of his creative life Bely was still wrestling with ways of giving meaning to colour and sound (and colour and sound to meaning) in order to create a *Gesamtkunstwerk* in prose that had all the psychological depth of the Wagnerian music drama.

Other Russian writers who continued to be inspired by Wagner after the Revolution include Eduard Bagritsky, whose 1922 poem 'Wagner' evokes a performance of *Der fliegende Holländer* in which the Dutchman is seen 'flying' over the orchestra stalls,[170] and Georgy Adamovich, whose second collection *Purgatory* (*Chistilishche*), also published in 1922, contains three poems linked to *Tristan und Isolde*, two of which are are also entitled 'Wagner'.[171] Wagner was apparently a frequent subject of Adamovich's conversations with Mikhail Kuzmin, who, as Gennady Shmakov has revealed, experienced mingled feelings of hatred and adoration towards the composer.[172] Although repelled by Wagner's personality, in 1909 (the year he lived with Vyacheslav Ivanov) Kuzmin remarked on the favourable impression that the poetry in Wagner's librettos had made on him, and in the 1920s he spent a prolonged period studying the score of *Lohengrin*, when the Maly Theatre commissioned him to make a new translation of the libretto. This led him to make the highly original assertion that there was more philosophy in *Lohengrin* and *Tristan und Isolde* 'than in any of Nietzsche's books'.[173] Kuzmin might have been embarrassed about his 'hidden passion' for Wagner, but much of the imagery which permeates the cycles 'Sea Idylls' (*Morskie idillii*), written in 1921 and 1922, 'The Trout Breaks the Ice' (*Forel' razbivaet led*), written between 1925 and 1928, and the unpublished 'Tristan' (written in the late 1920s and early 1930s), is, as Shmakov has shown, unashamedly Wagnerian.[174] It almost exclusively concerns *Tristan und Isolde*, which he saw as a 'grandiose metaphor of passion and love', a correlation he had apparently long been interested in.[175] 'Tristan' was the title Vladimir Nabokov gave to a poem he composed in 1921 in emigration,[176] and *Tristan und Isolde* is a work referred to in Pasternak's early poem 'Definition of Creation' (*Opredelenie tvorchestva*), written in 1919, in which the poet explores the mysteries of creativity.[177] Although Pasternak retained a deep love of Wagner's music from the beginning to the end of his life, he nevertheless belonged to a generation for whom the composer was firmly associated with the nineteenth century (in other words, the past).[178] Despite his deep-rooted affinities with German culture, Pasternak's musical tastes were eclectic, and references to Wagner in his verse therefore jostle with those to a whole host of other composers. A typical example is the comparatively late 'Music' (*Muzyka*), written in 1957, in which the poet muses on the compositional processes of Chopin and Tchaikovsky as well as evoking a flight of the Valkyries above city roofs.[179] In 1932, Pasternak was commissioned to make a new translation of the *Ring* for the former Mariinsky Theatre (evidently with the new production in mind), but nothing came of the project.[180] Marina Tsvetaeva also had a deep involvement with German culture and music, but like Pasternak, she also belonged to a younger generation than that of her elder contemporaries the Symbolists, and Wagner was no longer such a potent figure. Pasternak nevertheless saw Tsvetaeva's use of leitmotifs in her poem 'The Pied Piper' (*Krysolov*) as essentially Wagnerian.[181] Tsvetaeva agreed with Pasternak about her use of leitmotifs, and responded that musicians had also on occasion made the same observation about the Wagnerian flavour of her poetry.[182] Tsvetaeva's contemporary Akhmatova was also a poet with musical associations, but with the exceptions of two poems of 1936 and 1940,[183] her work has no real connection with Wagner.

CHAPTER 8

Reception and performance history, 1941–1991

The critic Eduard Stark had watched Wagner's works disappear from the repertoire one by one in the thirties. Before he learned of the unexpected decision to stage *Die Walküre* at the Bolshoi in 1940 (which was of course entirely due to political reasons), he had expressed a quiet optimism about the fate of the Wagnerian repertoire in Russia, confident that another chapter in the history of Russian productions of Wagner had yet to be written:

There will be a new time, other singers will maybe arrive and revive the majestic muse of Wagner ... Now, while these lines are being written, the Valkyrie Brünnhilde is sleeping peacefully beneath the canopy of a hundred-year-old fir tree, in a ring of wild fire, awaiting the time when her sun-blessed youth Siegfried, lover of victory, will come and wake her. But this will already be a new phase in the history of Wagner on the Russian stage. It *will* come; it must without fail come, for this is the real task of the Soviet stage – to master once again the whole creative heritage of the greatest artist of the operatic theatre.[1]

That prediction was sadly never fulfilled, however, for the reappearance of Wagner's works in the Soviet repertoire after World War II was – again for political reasons – highly sporadic. Only three new Soviet Wagner productions were staged in Moscow and Leningrad in the forty-six-year period between 1945 and 1991, but this was not for lack of enthusiasm on the part of the opera-going public, for Russian affection for Wagner certainly seemed to linger after the war. In Moscow, barely a month had passed after the peace declaration had been signed when three Wagner concerts were held in quick succession.[2] Those under the illusion that the end of the war would usher in a new era of artistic tolerance and freedom, were sadly mistaken, however, as cultural policy under Andrey Zhdanov proved even more repressive than it had been in the 1930s, and brought with it a new wave of purges. Stalin's new five-year plan initiated to rebuild the country after the ravages of war was accompanied by renewed regimentation of the arts, an intensification of the Party's control of intellectual life and a mounting xenophobia which manifested itself in a particularly vicious campaign against all forms of 'reactionary bourgeois' Western decadence.

In the atmosphere of terror brought about by Zhdanov's infamous resolution of 1948,[3] decisions to include music by Wagner in a concert programme were not taken lightly. After a concert of his music conducted by Samosud which took place in Moscow in January 1946, and another in February 1947 conducted by Golovanov, Wagner's name disappeared almost completely from Soviet concert posters in Moscow and Leningrad.[4] Writing about Wagner during the *Zhdanovshchina* was also out of the question, particularly after Tikhon Khrennikov, the newly appointed head of the Union of Composers, launched a series of attacks on Soviet musicologists during a three-day meeting in February 1949, accusing them of either 'servility to the West' or 'formalism'.[5] Due to the fascist stigma which rendered Wagner even more ideologically incorrect than he had become anyway after the cultural revolution, there had been a dearth of books and articles written about his music and ideas since the 1930s, but all those critics who had showed an interest in the composer before, including leading musicologists such as Roman Gruber and Mikhail Druskin, and who did not spend their time exclusively writing insipid tributes to the achievements of Russian and Soviet 'socialist realist' music, were now publicly condemned for their unpatriotic activities.[6] In 1950 it was decided that Soviet musicology should be rebuilt 'on the basis of Marxist-Leninist methodology', obliterating 'all formalist and cosmopolitan tendencies as well as traces of bourgeois ideology'.[7] Although Zhdanov died in 1948, a few months after drawing up his last infamous resolution, his policies remained intact until the death of Stalin, in March 1953. It is interesting to note the speed with which Wagner returned to concert repertoires after Stalin's death, however: a Wagner concert conducted by Nebolsin was held in April 1953, and was followed by another the following month, conducted by Gauk.[8] Leopold Stokowsky included music by Wagner at two of his concerts when he visited Russia on a US–USSR cultural exchange in 1958, and became the first American to conduct a Soviet orchestra. Once again, Wagner was a very accurate barometer of the political climate in the Soviet Union. It was also not until after Stalin's death and the beginning of the 'Thaw' in the late 1950s that Wagner's name began to reappear once more on the pages of *Sovetskaya muzyka* with any regularity. There had been one article about Wagner in *Sovetskaya muzyka* between the end of the war and Stalin's death (the publication of an article Tchaikovsky had written in 1891, which contained some sharp criticisms of Wagner); three articles were published immediately afterwards in 1953.[9] Mikhail Druskin was the first to challenge the Stalinist view of Wagner in a courageous article of 1955, in which he discussed the realism of *Die Meistersinger*:

The question arises: could Wagner have created such an outstanding and essentially national work ... if in his dramaturgy he proceeded from false, reactionary aesthetic principles? After all, according to a still widespread perception, it is customary to consider that the ideas and artistic content of Wagner's works became consistently and steadily degraded, beginning approximately in the middle of the 1850s, when he rejected his former revolutionary convictions ...[10]

Druskin continued this line of argument in his review of the new staging of *Der fliegende Holländer* at the Maly Theatre in Leningrad in 1957, in which he surveyed recent Soviet criticism of Wagner:

Basing their arguments on a few very uncharacteristic, and sometimes random pronouncements made by major figures in Russian music, Wagner's critics declared that he was no opera composer at all, but a great, although largely unsuccessful, symphonist. Taking umbrage behind such pronouncements, as if behind a shield, their selection of which was not distinguished by scholarly objectivity, musicologists did not analyse Wagner's works (with all their inherent cruel contradictions) so much as expose them. It hardly needs saying that this method of 'picking holes' in the classics of German (and world) music has harmed both our theoretical thinking and our operatic and concert life . . .[11]

The year 1958 marked the 75th anniversary of Wagner's death, which was celebrated in the Soviet Union with the publication of a short monograph about Wagner by Druskin, the first book-length study of the composer to appear since 1933, and articles by N. Vieru, A. Kenigsberg and B. Levik in *Sovetskaya muzyka*. Kenigsberg also took advantage of the new cultural freedom by publishing a book on the *Ring* in 1959, which was followed by a more general study of Wagner in 1963. Short studies on *Lohengrin* and Wagner's overtures were also published by Georgy Krauklis in 1963 and 1964. The 'Thaw' also resulted in Wagner's return to the Russian stage. Several concert performances of Wagner's operas were given in Moscow during the 1950s, conducted by Samosud, and the huge success of the semi-staged performance of *Lohengrin* given at the Bolshoi Theatre on 28 June 1956 showed that the hunger to see Wagner performed on stage had not diminished during the terrible Zhdanov years, as K. Ptitsa's memoirs make only too clear: 'On the evening of the performance, the public burst through all twenty doors of the Bolshoi Theatre, sweeping aside all human and mechanical barriers. I'm not exaggerating when I say that there were one and half times more people than there were seats . . .'[12] The first new full-scale Wagner production since World War II finally took place when the Maly Theatre staged *Der fliegende Holländer* in 1957, conducted by Kurt Sanderling and produced by S. Lapirov, with designs by A. Konstantinovsky. Five years later, in 1962 (the year in which Shostakovich's *Lady Macbeth* was revived in a revised version), the ill-fated production of *Lohengrin* was revived at the Kirov. 'Our attitude to Wagner's works is so changeable! It's either unrestrained apologetics or complete rejection', commented the two musicologists assessing the performance.[13]

Despite the relative liberalism of the Krushchev years, a certain degree of political caution is evident in the Bolshoi Theatre's decision also to choose *Der fliegende Holländer* for its first new Wagner production there since 1940. Not only was it the first time that particular work had been heard at the Bolshoi since the 1904–5 season, it was also one of Wagner's early and more traditional works, and thus presented fewer ideological problems. The new staging, produced by Joachim Herz and designed by Reinhard Zimmerman from the DDR, was conducted by Boris Khaikin and premièred on 14 May 1963 to celebrate the 150th anniversary of Wagner's birth. Despite Mikhail Druskin's valiant efforts to free Soviet writing about Wagner from politics, it is clear from I. Nestiev's review of the production that the 'vulgar sociological' approach was still affecting music criticism: 'Wagner's legacy is perceived in different ways in the West – bourgeois-idealist aesthetics fetishise the weak, reactionary sides of Wagner's work, and see him as forefather of contemporary modernism. Progressive musicians see in him a musician-innovator, a fighter for new mass art, calling for a revolutionary transformation of life.'[14]

FROM THE BREZHNEV YEARS TO *GLASNOST*

After Krushchev's removal from power at the end of 1964, the Central Committee made a concerted attempt to re-impose ideological control on Soviet intellectual life, particularly after the arrests of Sinyavsky and Daniel in 1966 and the events in Czechoslovakia in 1968, which resulted in a renewed effort to stamp out dissidence and experimentation. In a statement published in *Pravda* on 17 December, the Party exhorted 'workers of Soviet music' in this period of 'sharp aggravation of the class struggle between Socialism and Capitalism' to 'come forth even more actively against bourgeois ideology, to convey even more consistently the ideas of Socialist humanism, Soviet patriotism, and proletarian internationalism'.[15] Naturally this new mood was not particularly conducive to the performance of Wagner's works, and the curtailment of the promising revival of his operas in Leningrad and Moscow begun during the 'Thaw' was no doubt directly due to the new militancy in Soviet cultural policy. While there were no new Wagner productions between 1963 and 1979, when a disappointing new staging of *Das Rheingold* (produced by V. Milkov, designed by V. Volsky and conducted by Yury Simonov) was finally premièred at the Bolshoi Theatre, the large numbers of Wagner enthusiasts in Moscow were nevertheless able to enjoy the performances given by several touring companies, whose visits were probably arranged during the 'Thaw' years. In 1969, the State Opera from East Berlin arrived to give a series of performances of *Die Meistersinger*, followed in 1971 by the Vienna State Opera's visit to perform *Der Rosenkavalier*, *The Marriage of Figaro* and *Tristan und Isolde* (conducted by Karl Boehm and Heinrich Hollreiser), and the Royal Swedish Opera's performances of the *Ring* in 1975. Opera, as Boris Schwarz has commented, 'is the lifeblood of the Russian musical scene', and the Vienna Opera (its performances of *Tristan* in particular) was received with 'rapt attention'.[16] It is hardly surprising that the performances were discussed with the 'sort of detail usually accorded premières', however, for astonishingly these actually were the very first performances of *Tristan* to take place in Moscow. Further tours by foreign companies included visits from the Hamburg Opera in 1983, who performed *Lohengrin*,[17] and the Deutsche Staatsoper in 1986, who brought to Moscow their production of *Tannhäuser*.[18] A year later, the Komische Oper gave further performances of *Tannhäuser* and also brought their production of *Die Meistersinger* (by Harry Kupfer).[19] During the 'stagnation' years of the Brezhnev era there was predictably a reduction in the publication of materials about Wagner that was particularly marked after 1968. A. Kenigsberg produced a study of *Der fliegende Holländer*, *Tannhäuser* and *Lohengrin* in 1967, and S. Markus devoted a substantial section to Wagner in his history of musical aesthetics published in 1968, but by far the most important writing on Wagner published that year was a lengthy article by the highly respected scholar Aleksey Losev, in which he examined the attitudes of major writers, philosophers and composers towards Wagner's work.[20] Losev was the first to explore seriously Wagner's impact on Russian culture. He not only dared to suggest that Wagner's music and ideas had been widely influential in Russia (when the question of foreign influence was expressly avoided in Soviet scholarship), but he also declared outright that earlier Marxist interpretations of Wagner were primitive and fallacious. After Losev's article appeared, no serious criticism of Wagner was published in the Soviet Union until 1972, when Nina Vieru's study of *Die Meistersinger* was published, which was followed in 1974 by a collection of essays by and about Wagner edited by Georgy Krauklis. In 1978 a further selection of Wagner's writings was published in Russian translation, accompanied by another important article by Losev, and a major new biography of the composer by Boris Levik appeared. The centenary of Wagner's death in 1983 was marked by a substantial two-part article about Wagner's links with Russian culture in *Sovetskaya muzyka* by Abram Gozenpud, and the participation of Soviet musicologists at an international symposium held in Leipzig.

It was only during the period of *glasnost* and *perestroika* during the late eighties, however, that music critics began to write more freely about Wagner. The policy of *glasnost* meant that the collection of critical articles on Wagner by Soviet and East German musicologists which appeared in 1987 (the first for thirteen years) was marked by an unprecedented degree of objectivity. Lyudmila Polyakova, of the Moscow Institute of Arts History, not only alluded to Wagner's comparatively recent rehabilitation from the ranks of *personae non gratae* in Soviet scholarship in her article on Wagner and Russia, but spoke frankly of the period of 'complete rejection of Wagner' after World War II, admitting that 'the inertia of that period' was 'very difficult to overcome even now'.[21] Now that it had become permissible to talk freely of Wagner's influence on Russian culture, Anna Porfirieva, a musicologist at the Leningrad Institute of Theatre, Music and Cinematography, was able to publish two articles; the first a study of Meyerhold and Wagner which appeared in 1986, and the second a comparison of Wagner's and Vyacheslav Ivanov's dramatic theories, which was published the following year. Abram Gozenpud, from the same institute, was also now able finally to publish on a subject which had clearly occupied him since the publication of his history of opera in Russia, in which he devoted a substantial amount of attention to pre-revolutionary Wagner productions. His biography of the great Russian Wagnerian tenor Ivan Ershov appeared in 1986, and was followed by his book-length study about Wagner's influence on Russian culture in 1990. By the time that Mikhail Gorbachev came to power and Soviet society began to open up, however, it was already too late for old traditions to be revived at the country's two main bastions of operatic conservatism, the Bolshoi and Kirov Theatres, and although Russia's fascination with Wagner had persisted far longer than that of other European countries, it was now something which definitely belonged to the past. It was extra-ordinary enough that a nineteenth-century composer could exert a hold over Russian creativity as late as 1940, but it was only natural that Wagner's influence should diminish once it became clear that the utopian dreams of an ideal art for the masses which would transform the new socialist society would never become reality. It is no coincidence that Russian Wag-nerism died with the end of Stalinism.

WAGNER AND RUSSIAN LITERATURE DURING THE POST-WAR SOVIET PERIOD

Naum Korzhavin's poem 'At a Wagner Concert' (*Na kontserte Vagnera*) appears to be the only work of Russian literature to have been directly inspired by Wagner after World War II.[22] Written under the impact of a concert Korzhavin attended during the 'Thaw' in 1963, it is hardly the work of a fervent Wagnerian, however. To Korzhavin, Wagner's music is a 'riot of cold passions', whose thunder reminds him of the sound of tanks advancing on people, while the composer himself is a 'demon' who wishes to 'drown' his audience with the ethereal, 'glassy beauty' of his music:

> He knows neither passion, nor God
> Neither pain, nor even insult . . .
> Which is why he makes so much noise,

Frightens you
    and makes your blood run cold.[23]

Aleksey Remizov also found Wagner's music rather over-powering. The text of Wagner's *Tristan und Isolde* was one of a number of sources that the 74-year-old emigré writer studied while writing his own version of the legend in 1952, and he was troubled by the similarities with his own work when he heard Wagner's score performed on the radio. Although he resolved to construct his story differently, Wagner's work still cast a shadow over it, as can be detected from a letter he wrote in February 1953, in which he commented that in his and other versions of the legend, Isolde was a character who remains silent, in contrast to Wagner's opera, in which 'she sings a lot'.[24] 'After the music of Richard Wagner which cuts right through you philosophically, no other music will ever be able to drown it out', Remizov concluded in the preface he wrote to his story in March 1953: 'but if you have picked up a pipe, you should just get on and play it and not pay any attention. The shadows of Tristan and Isolde themselves speak musically anyway, and it was not for nothing that I summoned them to torture my restless soul.'[25] In writing his *Tristan and Isolde*, Remizov had found Veselovsky's translation of Bedier's version of the legend particularly useful, and it was Bedier's rendition which inspired the poet Olga Sedakova's 'series of impro-visations' on the subject of Tristan and Isolde, which, although not dated, were probably written at some point in the 1970s.[26] Unlike Remizov, she makes no mention of Wagner in the preface to her 'Tristan and Isolde' (*Tristan i Izolda*), but, as Remizov had discovered earlier, it was impossible to write a new version of the legend in the twentieth century without being at least conscious of the imposing presence of Wagner's opera.

Appendices

The programmes of Wagner's concerts in Russia

19 FEBRUARY 1863 (PETERSBURG)

Beethoven Symphony No. 3
Wagner   *Der fliegende Holländer*: Matrosenchor, Ballade der
           Senta mit Chor, Ouvertüre
           Lohengrin: Vorspiel
           Tannhäuser: Marsch und Chor, Lied an den
           Abendstern, Ouvertüre

26 FEBRUARY 1863 (PETERSBURG)

Beethoven Symphony No. 5
Wagner   *Tristan und Isolde*: Vorspiel, Verklärung
           Die Walküre: Siegmunds Liebesgesang
           Die Meistersinger: Versammlung der Meister-
           singerzunft, Pogners Anrede, Ouvertüre

6 MARCH 1863 (PETERSBURG)

Wagner   *Tannhäuser*: Ouvertüre, Arie der Elisabeth, Duett,
           Tannhäuser und Elisabeth, Marsch und Chor
           Lohengrin: Vorspiel, Elsas Gesang an die Lüfte
           Die Walküre: Siegmunds Liebesgesang, Ritt der
           Walküren, Wotans Abschied und Feuerzauber
           Siegfried: Schmelzlied, Hämmerlied

           (Soloists: Valentina Bianchi, Sobolev, Setov,
           Radkovsky)

13 MARCH 1863 (MOSCOW)

Beethoven   Symphony No. 5
Wagner   *Lohengrin*: Vorspiel, Elsas Gesang an die Lüfte
             Tannhäuser: Marsch und Chor, Lied an den
             Abendstern, Ouvertüre

15 MARCH 1863 (MOSCOW)

Wagner   *Tannhäuser*: Ouvertüre, Marsch und Chor
             Lohengrin: Elsas Gesang an die Lüfte, Vorspiel
             Die Meistersinger: Ouvertüre, Evas Liebesgesang
             [*sic*]
             Die Walküre: Ritt der Walküren
             Siegfried: Schmelzlied, Hämmerlied
             Lohengrin: Einleitung zum 3. Akte

17 MARCH 1863 (MOSCOW)

Beethoven   Symphony No. 7
Wagner   *Tannhäuser*: Ouvertüre
             Lohengrin: Elsas Gesang an die Lüfte, Vorspiel
             Die Meistersinger von Nürnberg: Evas Liebesgesang
             [sic]
             Die Walküre: Ritt der Walküren

             (Soloists: Irina Onore, Mikhail Vladislavlev,
             Finocchi)

21 MARCH 1863 (PETERSBURG)

Beethoven   Symphony No. 6
Wagner   Eine Faust-ouvertüre
             Die Walküre: Ritt der Walküren
             Siegfried: Hämmerlied

2 APRIL 1863 (PETERSBURG)

Wagner Eine Faust-ouvertüre
Tannhäuser: Duett, Tannhaüser und Elisabeth
Lohengrin: Einleitung zum 3. Akte, Elsas Gesang
an die Lüfte
Die Walküre: Siegmunds Liebesgesang, Ritt der
Walküren, Wotans Abschied und Feuerzauber
Tristan und Isolde: Vorspiel, Liebestod

5 APRIL 1863 (PETERSBURG)

Beethoven Symphony No. 8
Wagner *Tannhäuser*: Ouvertüre
Lohengrin: Vorspiel

(Soloists: Bianchi, Setov, Radkovsky)

Dates of the first performances of Russian productions of Wagner's operas in Petersburg and Moscow

Day and month given where information is available

Lohengrin	4 October 1868, Mariinsky Theatre, St Petersburg
Tannhäuser	13 December 1874, Mariinsky Theatre
Rienzi	3 November 1879, Mariinsky Theatre
Lohengrin	1887, Mamontov and Krotkov Private Operas, Moscow
Lohengrin	1889, Bolshoi Theatre, Moscow
Siegfried	27 January 1894, Bolshoi Theatre
Tannhäuser	4 September 1898, Bolshoi Theatre
Tristan und Isolde	5 April 1899, Mariinsky Theatre
Die Walküre	24 November 1900, Mariinsky Theatre
Tannhäuser	1901, Mamontov Private Opera, Moscow
Siegfried	4 February 1902, Mariinsky Theatre
Die Walküre	24 February 1902, Bolshoi Theatre
Der fliegende Holländer	19 November 1902, Bolshoi Theatre
Götterdämmerung	20 January 1903, Mariinsky Theatre
Das Rheingold	27 December 1905, Mariinsky Theatre
Die Meistersinger	30 August 1909, Zimin Theatre, Moscow
Tannhäuser	1909, Zimin Theatre, Moscow
Götterdämmerung	10 October 1911, Bolshoi Theatre
Der fliegende Holländer	11 October 1911, Mariinsky Theatre
Das Rheingold	14 March 1912, Bolshoi Theatre

Die Meistersinger	December 1912, Theatre of Musical Drama, Petersburg
Parsifal	21 December 1913, Ermitazh Theatre/ Theatre of Musical Drama
Die Meistersinger	20 March 1914, Mariinsky Theatre

Wagner in the Russian repertoire 1890–1914

The following table gives a breakdown of the repertoires of the Mariinsky and Bolshoi Theatres between 1890 and 1914 as published in the *Ezhegodnik imperatorskikh teatrov*. Two sets of figures are shown for each season. The top figures relate to the Mariinsky Theatre in St Petersburg and the lower figures relate to the Bolshoi Theatre in Moscow.

KEY

A *Number of operas in repertoire in the given season*
B *Number of performances during the given season*
C *Number of operas by Wagner in repertoire of given season*
D *Number of performances of operas by Wagner in the given season*
E *Number of Russian operas in the repertoire in the given season*
F *Number of French operas in the repertoire in the given season*
G *Number of German/Austrian operas in the repertoire in the given season*
H *Number of Italian operas in the repertoire in the given season*
I *Number of operas by Wagner (C) as percentage of A.*
J *Number of performances of operas by Wagner (D) as percentage of B.*

	A	B	C	D	E	F	G	H	I	J
1890–91 season										
Mariinsky	21	123	1	6	12	4	1	4	04.7	04.8
Bolshoi	23	125	1	2	8	6	2	7	04.3	01.6
1891–92										
	20	120	0	0	12	4	0	4	00.0	00.0
	24	124	1	6	12	5	1	6	04.1	04.8

	A	B	C	D	E	F	G	H	I	J
1892–3										
	23	139	1	2	11	6	1	4	04.3	01.4
	23	118	1	3	10	7	1	5	04.3	02.5
1893–4										
	24	119	2	8	8	8	2	6	08.3	06.7
	24	118	2	5	10	5	2	7	08.3	04.2
1894–5										
	19	80	1	4	8	4	1	6	05.2	05.0
	20	75	0	0	11	3	1	5	00.0	00.0
1895–6										
	28	143	2	8	13	6	2	7	07.1	05.5
	19	68	1	2	9	2	3	5	05.2	02.9
1896–7										
	29	139	1	6	13	6	2	8	03.4	04.3
	25	121	1	1	11	7	3	3	04.0	08.0
1897–8										
	32	141	7	27	9	9	3	5	21.8	19.1
	23	112	0	0	12	7	2	2	00.0	00.0
1898–9										
	32	162	2	4	16	6	4	6	06.2	06.1
	25	159	2	10	13	6	1	4	08.0	02.5
1899–1900										
	23	135	3	15	12	4	3	3	13.0	11.1
	33	158	2	3	16	8	2	7	06.0	01.8
1900–1										
	21	137	4	28	9	5	4	3	19.6	20.4
	31	161	2	6	16	2	6	5	06.4	03.7
1901–2										
	24	138	4	19	11	4	7	1	16.6	13.7
	33	155	2	8	18	8	2	5	06.0	05.1
1902–3										
	23	137	4	15	11	5	5	2	17.3	10.9
	32	169	3	15	17	7	3	4	09.3	08.8

	A	B	C	D	E	F	G	H	I	J
1903–4										
	25	139	4	24	13	6	4	2	16.0	17.2
	34	135	4	13	16	9	4	5	11.7	09.6
1904–5										
	24	134	4	18	10	6	5	3	16.6	13.4
	35	123	2	6	19	9	2	5	05.7	04.8
1905–6										
	28	142	4	19	12	5	7	4	14.2	13.3
	22	119	0	0	12	6	1	3	00.0	00.0
1906–7										
	28	159	5	15	12	7	6	3	17.8	09.4
	23	165	0	0	12	7	1	4	00.0	00.0
1907–8										
	30	156	6	29	13	7	7	3	20.0	18.5
	23	166	0	0	14	5	0	4	00.0	00.0
1908–9										
	27	154	6	24	12	5	7	3	22.2	15.5
	22	165	1	5	12	5	1	3	04.5	03.0
1909–10										
	28	154	7	31	13	5	7	3	25.0	20.1
	23	168	2	7	13	4	2	4	08.6	04.1
1910–11										
	28	167	7	25	12	6	7	3	25.0	14.9
	25	180	2	9	10	7	3	4	08.0	05.0
1911–12										
	30	166	7	34	13	7	7	1	23.8	20.4
	23	174	5	20	10	5	5	3	21.7	11.4
1912–13										
	32	170	7	27	12	7	8	4	21.8	15.8
	22	175	3	11	11	6	3	2	13.6	06.2
1913–14										
	32	138	8	33	12	6	8	5	25.0	23.9

No figures published for the 1913–14 season at the Bolshoi Theatre

Breakdown of works by Wagner in the repertoire
1890–1914

Figures in square brackets indicate number of performances given.

	Mariinsky Theatre	Bolshoi Theatre
1890–1	*Lohengrin* [6]	*Lohengrin* [2]
1891–2		*Lohengrin* [6]
1892–3	*Lohengrin* [2]	*Lohengrin* [3]
1893–4	*Tannhäuser* [5]	*Siegfried* [3]
	Lohengrin [3]	*Holländer* [2]
1894–5	*Lohengrin* [4]	
1895–6	*Tannhäuser* [7]	*Siegfried* [2]
	Lohengrin [1]	
1896–7	*Tannhäuser* [6]	*Lohengrin* [1]
1897–8	*Lohengrin* [8]	
[German Touring Company]	*Lohengrin* [3]	
	Holländer [3]	
	Die Meistersinger [3]	
	Die Walküre [3]	
	Siegfried [4]	
	Tristan und Isolde [3]	
1898–9	*Lohengrin* [1]	*Lohengrin* [3]
	Tristan und Isolde [3]	*Tannhäuser* [7]
1899–1900	*Tristan und Isolde* [4]	*Siegfried* [1]
	Tannhäuser [8]	*Lohengrin* [2]
	Lohengrin [3]	

	Mariinsky Theatre	Bolshoi Theatre
1900–1	*Tannhäuser* [9] *Die Walküre* [10] *Lohengrin* [6] *Tristan und Isolde* [3]	*Tannhäuser* [3] *Lohengrin* [3]
1901–2	*Lohengrin* [4] *Tannhäuser* [6] *Die Walküre* [5] *Siegfried* [4]	*Lohengrin* [4] *Die Walküre* [4]
1902–3	*Lohengrin* [4] *Tristan und Isolde* [3] *Götterdämmerung* [3] *Siegfried* [5]	*Lohengrin* [4] *Holländer* [8] *Die Walküre* [3]
1903–4	*Tannhäuser* [4] *Die Walküre* [9] *Lohengrin* [5] *Götterdämmerung* [6]	*Lohengrin* [3] *Holländer* [4] *Die Walküre* [2] *Siegfried* [4]
1904–5	*Die Walküre* [5] *Siegfried* [3] *Götterdämmerung* [4] *Tannhäuser* [6]	*Tannhäuser* [3] *Holländer* [3]
1905–6	*Tannhäuser* [2] *Lohengrin* [5] *Das Rheingold* [9] *Die Walküre* [2]	
1906–7	*Lohengrin* [3] *Das Rheingold* [3] *Die Walküre* [3] *Siegfried* [3] *Götterdämmerung* [3]	
1907–8	*Tannhäuser* [12] *Lohengrin* [7] *Das Rheingold* [3] *Die Walküre* [3] *Siegfried* [3] *Götterdämmerung* [3]	

	Mariinsky Theatre	Bolshoi Theatre
1908–9	*Tannhäuser* [7] *Lohengrin* [1] *Das Rheingold* [3] *Die Walküre* [6] *Siegfried* [3] *Götterdämmerung* [4]	*Lohengrin* [5]
1909–10	*Tannhäuser* [4] *Lohengrin* [3] *Das Rheingold* [3] *Die Walküre* [9] *Siegfried* [3] *Götterdämmerung* [3] *Tristan und Isolde* [6]	*Lohengrin* [6] *Die Walküre* [1]
1910–11	*Tannhäuser* [4] *Lohengrin* [4] *Tristan und Isolde* [1] *Das Rheingold* [4] *Die Walküre* [4] *Siegfried* [4] *Götterdämmerung* [4]	*Lohengrin* [7] *Die Walküre* [4]
1911–12	*Holländer* [9] *Lohengrin* [2] *Tristan und Isolde* [2] *Das Rheingold* [4] *Siegfried* [5] *Die Walküre* [8] *Götterdämmerung* [4]	*Lohengrin* [5] *Das Rheingold* [5] *Die Walküre* [2] *Siegfried* [2] *Götterdämmerung* [6]
1912–13	*Lohengrin* [3] *Tannhäuser* [2] *Tristan und Isolde* [5] *Das Rheingold* [4] *Die Walküre* [5] *Siegfried* [4] *Götterdämmerung* [4]	*Lohengrin* [2] *Das Rheingold* [6] *Die Walküre* [3]

	Mariinsky Theatre	Bolshoi Theatre
1913–14	*Tannhäuser* [2]	No information
	Lohengrin [5]	available
	Tristan und Isolde [1]	
	Die Meistersinger [4]	
	Das Rheingold [4]	
	Die Walküre [6]	
	Siegfried [4]	
	Götterdämmerung [7]	

Wagner in the Soviet repertoire 1917–1991

Number of performances given, where information is available. Works in square brackets indicate performances by foreign touring companies. Figures in square brackets indicate number of performances given.

Abbreviations:

TMD	Theatre of Musical Drama
GATOB	State Academic Theatre of Opera and Ballet (formerly Mariinsky)
Kirov	Kirov Theatre (formerly GATOB)
Maly	Maly Theatre
BT	Bolshoi Theatre
Zimin	former Zimin Theatre

	Petrograd/Leningrad	Moscow
1917–18	*Parsifal* (TMD) *Die Walküre* (GATOB) [3] *Die Meistersinger* (TMD)	
1918–19	*Die Walküre* (GATOB) [4]	*Lohengrin* (Zimin) *Das Rheingold* (BT) [9] *Tannhäuser* (BT) [3] *Die Walküre* (BT) [3]
1919–20	*Die Walküre* (GATOB) [7]	*Die Walküre* (BT) [4]

	Petrograd/Leningrad	Moscow
1920–1	*Die Walküre* (GATOB) [8]	*Rienzi* (RSFSR 1/Conservatoire)
1921–2	*Die Walküre* (GATOB) [3]	
1922–3	*Lohengrin* (GATOB) [9] *Siegfried* (GATOB) [2] *Tannhäuser* (GATOB) [5] *Die Walküre* (GATOB) [3]	*Lohengrin* (BT) [12] *Rienzi* (Zimin)
1923–4	*Tannhäuser* (GATOB) [7] *Rienzi* (GATOB) [5]	*Lohengrin* (BT) [14]
1924–5	*Siegfried* (Acts 1 and 3) (GATOB) [1] *Götterdämmerung* (3rd Scene, Act 1) (GATOB) [1]	*Lohengrin* (BT) [3]
1925–6		*Die Walküre* (BT) [6] *Lohengrin* (BT) [10]
1926–7	*Die Meistersinger* (GATOB)	*Lohengrin* (BT) [3]
1927–8	*Die Walküre* (GATOB)	*Lohengrin* (BT) [8]
1928–9		*Die Meistersinger* (BT) [18] *Lohengrin* (BT) [3]
1929–30		*Die Meistersinger* (BT) [7] *Lohengrin* (BT) [12]
1930–1	*Götterdämmerung* (GATOB)	*Lohengrin* (BT) [8]
1931–2	*Die Meistersinger* (Maly) [13]	*Lohengrin* (BT) [5]
1932–3	*Rheingold* (GATOB) *Die Meistersinger* (Maly)	*Lohengrin* (BT) [5]

	Petrograd/Leningrad	Moscow
1933–4	*Rheingold* (GATOB) *Götterdämmerung* (GATOB) *Die Meistersinger* (Maly)	*Lohengrin* (BT) [5]
1934–5		
1935–6		*Lohengrin* (BT) [5]
1936–7		
1937–8		
1938–9		
1939–40		*Die Walküre* (BT) [6]
1940–1	*Lohengrin* (Kirov) [1]	
1941–2		
1942–3		
1943–4		
1944–5		
1945–6		
1946–7		
1947–8		
1948–9		
1949–50		
1950–1		
1951–2		
1952–3		
1953–4		
1954–5		
1955–6		
1956–7	*Holländer* (Maly)	
1957–8		
1958–9		
1959–60		

	Petrograd/Leningrad	Moscow
1960–1		
1961–2	*Lohengrin* (Kirov)	
1962–3		*Holländer* (BT)
1963–4		
1964–5	*Lohengrin* (Kirov) [7]	
1965–6		
1966–7		
1967–8		
1968–9		[*Die Meistersinger*] (BT)
1969–70		
1970–1		[*Tristan*] (BT)
1971–2		
1972–3		
1973–4		
1974–5		[*Ring*] (BT)
1975–6		
1976–7		
1977–8		
1978–9		*Das Rheingold* (BT)
1979–80		
1980–1		
1981–2	*Lohengrin* (Kirov)	
1982–3		[*Lohengrin*] (BT)
1983–4		
1984–5		
1985–6		[*Tannhäuser*] (BT)
1986–7		[*Tannhäuser*] (BT)
1987–8		
1988–9		
1989–90		
1990–1		

Notes

1 RECEPTION AND PERFORMANCE HISTORY, 1841–1863

1 R. Vagner, 'Ob uvertyure', tr. Sh., *Repertuar russkogo teatra*, 5 (6 June 1841), pp. 10–15.

2 It is possible that hiding behind the Russian letter 'Sh', which is how the translation was signed, was the German-born 'cellist, composer and conductor Carl Schuberth [Karl Shubert], who had been resident in St Petersburg since 1835. It was Schuberth who conducted the first performance of the overture to *Tannhäuser* in St Petersburg, the first time that music by Wagner was publicly performed in Russia. One of the concerts that Wagner conducted in 1863, moreover, was a benefit for Carl Schuberth, whose help and advice the composer acknowledges (albeit grudgingly) in his memoirs. Schuberth's brother Ludwig had been first 'cellist under Wagner's baton in the orchestra at Magdeburg in 1834 and preceded Wagner as kapellmeister in Königsberg.

3 See T. N. Livanova, *Muzykal'naya bibliografiya russkoi periodicheskoi pechati XIX veka*, 6 vols. (Moscow, 1960–74), III, p. 70.

4 See D. V. Stasov, 'Muzykal'nye vospominaniya 1840–1860', *Russkaya muzykal'naya gazeta*, 11 (1909), p. 289.

5 For more information on the state of opera in mid-nineteenth-century Russia, see the introductory chapter of Robert Ridenour's *Nationalism, Modernism and Personal Rivalry in 19th-Century Russian Music* (Ann Arbor, 1981), pp. 5–24.

6 John Deathridge, Carl Dahlhaus, *The New Grove Wagner* (London, 1984), p. 31.

7 It was Bakunin who perhaps influenced Wagner to end the *Ring* with universal conflagration. The argument has also been put forward that Bakunin was the model for Siegfried, Wagner's man of the future.

8 See A. I. Gertsen [Herzen], *Polnoe sobranie sochinenii v 30kh tomakh* (Moscow, 1950–64), XXIV, p. 297.

9 See Evgeny Albrekht, *Obshchii obzor deyatel'nosti vyshochaishe utverzhdennogo S-Peterburgskogo Filarmonicheskogo Obshchestva s prilozheniyami i s proektom izmeneniya ego ustava* (St Petersburg, 1884), p. 18.

10 See Albrekht, *Obshchii obzor*, pp. 19–21.

11 See N. F. Findeizen, *Ocherk deyatel'nosti Sankt-Peterburgskogo otdeleniya Imperatorskogo Russkogo Muzykal'nogo Obshchestva (1859–1909)* (St Petersburg, 1909), p. 1.

12 See L. Barenboim, *A. G. Rubinshtein*, 2 vols. (Leningrad, 1957–62), I, pp. 179, 290 and II, p. 13, and A. Rubinshtein, *Muzyka i ee predstaviteli* (Moscow, 1891, reprinted 1921), pp. 43–6. It is interesting to note that Rubinstein (to whom belongs one of the few recorded objections to Wagner's notorious *Judaism in Music* (*Das Judenthum in der Musik*) in Russia) had a project to write a dramatic oratorio to accompany the Bible, and believed a special theatre (not entirely dissimilar from the *Festspieltheater* in Bayreuth) would have to be built for its performance.

13 See Findeizen, *Ocherk deyatel'nosti: prilozhenie*, pp. 1–8.

14 See N. Manykin-Nevstruev, *Imperatorskoe Russkoe Muzykal'noe Obshchestvo. Moskovskoe otdelenie. Simfonicheskie sobraniya 1–500. Staticheskii ukazatel'* (Moscow, 1899).

15 See Yury Kremlyov, *Russkaya mysl' o muzyke*, 3 vols. (Moscow, 1954–60), I, p. 230.

16 L. Korabelnikova, 'Iskusstvo i predmetnaya sreda v dukhovnoi zhizni Rossii vtoroi poloviny XIX veka': 'muzyka', in *Russkaya khudozhestvennaya kul'tura vtoroi poloviny XIX veka*, ed. G. Y. Sternin (Moscow, 1988), p. 112.

17 See N. F. Findeizen, 'Ocherki russkoi muzykal'noi kritiki', *Russkaya muzykal'naya gazeta*, 51 (1901), p. 1283.

18 This was Nikolay Kashkin, who wrote for *Moskovskie vedomosti* (See V. Yakovlev, *Izbrannye trudy o muzyke*, 3 vols. (Moscow, 1964–83), III, p. 183).

19 See A. D. Oulibicheff [Ulybyshev], *Beethoven, Ses Critiques et Ses Glossateurs* (Leipzig, 1857).

20 See Kremlyov, *Russkaya mysl' o muzyke*, I, p. 230.

21 See B. Volman, *Russkie notnye izdaniya XIX–nachala XX veka* (Leningrad, 1970), p. 90.

22 See V-a, O. [A. V. Ossovsky], 'Pervyi russkii vagnerianets', *Russkaya muzykal'naya gazeta*, 15–16 (1913), p. 411.

23 See P. A. Vyazemsky, *Polnoe sobranie sochinenii*, 12 vols. (St Petersburg, 1878–96), X, p. 210.

24 See K. Zvantsov, 'O Rikharde Vagnere. Po sluchayu novogo sochineniya A. D. Ulybysheva', *Syn otechestva*, 25 (1857), p. 4.

25 See Richard Taruskin, *Opera and Drama in Russia As Preached and Practised in the 1860s* (Ann Arbor, 1981), p. 39.

26 See A. N. Serov, *Izbrannye stat'i*, ed. G. N. Khubov, 2 vols. (Moscow-Leningrad, 1950–7), I, p. 71.

27 See *Muzykal'nyi i teatral'nyi vestnik*, 13 (1856), p. 473. Cited in Kremlyov, *Russkaya mysl' o muzyke*, I, p. 232.

28 See Evgeny Braudo, 'Vagner i Serov (dva neopublikovannikh pisem)', *Severnye zapiski*, 5–6 (1913), p. 64.

29 For its full implications, see Taruskin, *Opera and Drama in Russia*, pp. 40–1.

30 See Serov, *Izbrannye stat'i*, I, pp. 71–2.

31 See Braudo, 'Vagner i Serov', p. 65.

32 See Braudo, 'Vagner i Serov', p. 68.

33 See Serov, *Izbrannye stat'i*, I, p. 446.

34 K. Zvantsov, 'A. N. Serov v 1857–1871 gg. Vospominaniya o nem i ego pis'ma', *Russkaya starina*, 59 (1878), pp. 665–6.

35 See M. Pekelis, *A. S. Dargomyzhsky i ego okruzhenie*, 3 vols. (Moscow, 1966–83), III, p. 82.

36 See, for example, N. A. Rimsky-Korsakov, 'Vagner i Dargomyzhsky (1892)', *Sovetskaya muzyka*, 3 (1933), p. 137.

37 Pekelis, *Dargomyzhsky i ego okruzhenie*, III, p. 83.

38 See A. S. Lyapunova and E. B. Yazovitskaya, eds., *Mily Alekseevich Balakirev: Letopis' zhizni i tvorchestva* (Leningrad, 1967), p. 343.

39 See Tsezar Kyui [Cui], *Izbrannye stat'i*, ed. I. L. Gusin (Leningrad, 1952).

40 See A. N. Sokhor, *Aleksandr Porfirievich Borodin: zhizn', deyatel'nost', muzykal'noe tvorchestvo* (Moscow, 1965), p. 107.

41 See N. D. Kashkin, 'Iz vospominanii o A. P. Borodine' in N. D. Kashkin, *Stat'i o russkoi muzyke i muzykantakh*, ed. S. I. Shlifstein, (Moscow, 1953), pp. 35–44.

42 P. D. Boborykin, *Vospominaniya v dvukh tomakh*, 2 vols. (Moscow, 1965), I, p. 306.

43 For an informed account of this controversy, see Taruskin, *Opera and Drama in Russia*, pp. 1–32.

44 See A. Gozenpud, *Rikhard Vagner i russkaya kul'tura* (Leningrad, 1990), pp. 25–9, 39–45.

45 Friedrich Roesch, 'Richard Wagner, Franz Liszt und Hans von Bülow in ihren Beziehungen zur Philharmonischen Gesellschaft in St. Petersburg', *Allgemeine Musik-Zeitung*, 22–3 (1896), p. 292.

46 See Roesch, 'Richard Wagner, Franz Liszt und Hans von Bülow', pp. 293–4.

318 *Notes to pages 18–25*

47 Although Riga was part of the Russian Empire at this time, Wagner's two-year sojourn in the Latvian capital does not fall under the purview of this study, since the composer fraternised exclusively with his fellow-countrymen. For details, see Elmar Arro, 'Richards Wagners Rigaer Wanderjahre: Über einige baltische Züge im Schaffen Wagners', *Musik des Ostens*, 3 (1965), pp. 123–68.

48 See Richard Wagner, *My Life*, tr. Andrew Gray (Cambridge, 1983), p. 711.

49 See Arkhivist [Evgeny Braudo], 'Rikhard Vagner pod nadzorom III otdeleniya', *Vestnik teatra i iskusstva*, 2 (1922), p. 4.

50 Evgeny Braudo, *Rikhard Vagner i Rossiya (Novye materialy k ego biografii)* (Petrograd, 1923), p. 41.

51 See Wagner, *My Life*, p. 712.

52 R. Wagner, letter to Josef Standhartner, 15 February 1863, Nationalarchiv der Richard-Wagner-Stiftung, Bayreuth.

53 Wagner, letter to Standhartner, 15 February 1863.

54 For the programme of this and all subsequent concerts conducted by Wagner in Russia, see Appendix 1.

55 Braudo, *Vagner i Rossiya*, p. 44.

56 See the original of this letter in the Manuscripts Department of the Russian State Library (RGB), *fond* 175, *ed. khr.* 2, fol. 6. The extract cited was censored when the letter was published in *Sovetskaya muzyka*, 1 (1960), pp. 73–8.

57 The hall's capacity was in fact 2,200.

58 R. Wagner, letter to Mathilde Maier, 20 February 1863. See *Richard Wagner an Mathilde Maier*, ed. H. Scholz (Leipzig, 1930), pp. 71–2.

59 See John Deathridge, Martin Geck, Egon Voss, *Wagner Werk-Verzeichnis* (Mainz, 1986), p. 487.

60 Wagner, *My Life*, p. 715.

61 P. Tchaikovsky, letter to Nadezhda von Meck, 28 March 1879. See P. I. Chaikovsky, *Polnoe sobranie sochinenii. Literaturnye proizvedeniya*, vols. V–XVII (Moscow, 1959–81), VIII, pp. 114–15.

62 See Tsezar Kyui, *Izbrannye pis'ma*, ed. I. L. Gusin (Leningrad, 1955), p. 55.

63 Lyapunova and Yazovitskaya, *Balakirev: Letopis' zhizni i tvorchestva*, p. 88.

64 Y. Kremlyov, A. Lyapunova, E. Frid, *Mily Alekseevich Balakirev: Issledovaniya i stat'i* (Leningrad, 1961), p. 31.

65 Wagner, *My Life*, p. 714.

66 Compare Kremlyov et al. *Balakirev: Issledovaniya i stat'i*, p. 31 and Wagner, *My Life*, p. 714.

67 Letter to Josef Standhartner, 15 February 1863.
68 R. Wagner, letter to Mathilde Maier, 27 February 1863. See Scholz, *Richard Wagner an Mathilde Maier*, pp. 72–3.
69 R. Wagner, letter to Mathilde Maier, 24 March 1863. See Scholz, *Richard Wagner an Mathilde Maier*, pp. 81–3.
70 R. Wagner, letter to Mathilde Maier, 6 April 1863. See Scholz, *Richard Wagner an Mathilde Maier*, pp. 83–6.
71 B. A. Fitingof-Shel, *Mirovye znamenitosti. Iz vospominanii* (St Petersburg, 1899), p. 153.
72 Fitingof-Shel, *Mirovye znamenitosti*, p. 187.
73 Verdi travelled to Russia in September 1862 for the première of his opera *La Forza del Destino* (10 November) which had been specially written for St Petersburg.
74 See Wagner, *My Life*, p. 715. M. Montagu-Nathan is mistaken in attributing this disparaging description to Aleksey Lvov, Leonid's more famous brother, who composed the music for the Russian national anthem (see his *A History of Russian Music* (New York, 1969), p. 60).
75 See Nikolay Kashkin, 'Vagner v Moskve (Po lichnym vospominaniyam)', *Muzyka*, 131 (1913), p. 376.
76 R. Wagner, letter to Josef Standhartner, 15 February 1863. Nationalarchiv der Richard-Wagner-Stiftung, Bayreuth.
77 R. Wagner, letter to Mathilde Maier, 19 February 1863. See Scholz, *Richard Wagner an Mathilde Maier*, pp. 70–1.
78 R. Wagner, letter to Minna Wagner, 22 February 1863. See *Richard Wagner an Minna Wagner*, ed. Hans von Wolzogen (Berlin, 1908), pp. 315–17.
79 R. Wagner, letter to Mathilde Maier, 9 March 1863. See Scholz, *Richard Wagner an Mathilde Maier*, pp. 78–9.
80 See Kashkin, 'Vagner v Moskve', p. 374.
81 Wagner, *My Life*, p. 716.
82 Tarnovsky later wrote articles on *Die Meistersinger* and *Die Walküre* for *Russkie vedomosti* in 1869 and 1870 (see Livanova, *Muzykal'naya bibliografiya*, v, part one, pp. 87 and 90).
83 See Kashkin, 'Vagner v Moskve', p. 377.
84 Wagner, *My Life*, p. 717.
85 See G. Bernandt, 'Vagner i Odoevsky', *Sovetskaya muzyka*, 6 (1953), p. 72.
86 R. Wagner, letter to Josef Standhartner, 27 March 1863. Nationalarchiv der Richard-Wagner-Stiftung, Bayreuth.
87 R. Wagner, letter to Mathilde Maier, 6 April 1863. See Scholz, *Richard Wagner an Mathilde Maier*, pp. 83–6.
88 R. Wagner, letter to Josef Standhartner, 27 March 1863.

89 Wagner, *My Life*, p. 718.

90 R. Wagner, letter to Minna Wagner, 8 April 1863. National-archiv der Richard-Wagner-Stiftung, Bayreuth.

91 R. Wagner, letter to Editha von Rhaden, 9 May 1863. See Wilhelm Altmann, 'Briefe Wagners an Editha v. Rhaden', *Die Musik*, 16 (1924), p. 714.

92 R. Wagner, letter to Editha von Rhaden, 15 July 1863. See Altmann, 'Briefe Wagners an Editha v. Rhaden', pp. 716–18.

93 R. Wagner, letter to Editha von Rhaden, 14 September 1863. Altmann, See 'Briefe Wagners an Editha v. Rhaden', pp. 719–22.

94 R. Wagner, letter to Editha von Rhaden, 2 February 1864. See Altmann, 'Briefe Richard Wagners an Editha v. Rhaden', p. 724.

95 R. Wagner, letter to Editha von Rhaden, 14 March 1863. See Altmann, 'Briefe Wagners an Editha v.Rhaden', pp. 726–8.

96 Roesch, 'Richard Wagner, Franz Liszt, Hans von Bülow', p. 298.

97 Rostislav, [F. Tolstoy] 'Pervyi kontsert Filarmonicheskogo obshchestva pod upravleniem Rikharda Vagnera', *Severnaya pchela*, 52 (1863), p. 1.

98 Rostislav, 'Pervyi kontsert Filarmonicheskogo obshchestva', p. 1.

99 Rostislav, 'Vtoroi kontsert Filarmonicheskogo obshchestva', *Severnaya pchela*, 58 (1863), p. 1.

100 Rostislav, 'Vtoroi kontsert Filarmonicheskogo obshchestva', p. 1.

101 Odin iz publiki, 'Kontserty Vagnera i ego muzyka', *Golos*, 59 (1863). Cited in Braudo, *Rikhard Vagner i Rossiya*, p. 37.

102 M. R. [M. Y. Rappaport], 'Muzykal'naya letopis'', *Syn otechestva*, 45 (1863), p. 345.

103 M. R., 'Muzykal'naya letopis'', *Syn otechestva*, 59 (1863), pp. 458–9.

104 A. N. Serov, 'Rikhard Vagner v Peterburge' and 'Kontserty Filarmonicheskogo obshchestva pod upravleniem Rikharda Vagnera', *Sankt-Peterburgskie vedomosti*, 40 and 52 (1863), re-printed in A. N. Serov, *Izbrannye stat'i*, 1, pp. 550–9.

105 A. Serov, 'Rikhard Vagner i ego kontserty v Peterburge', *Yakor'*, 2 (1863), pp. 33–4.

106 See Serov, *Izbrannye stat'i*, 1, pp. 550–3.

107 See Serov, *Izbrannye stat'i*, 1, p. 555.

108 Serov, 'Rikhard Vagner i ego kontserty'. Cited in Braudo, *Rikhard Vagner i Rossiya*, p. 39.

109 O. O. O. [V. Odoevsky], 'Pervyi kontsert Vagnera v Moskve', *Nashe vremya*, 57 (1863), p. 225.

110 Odoevsky, 'Pervyi kontsert Vagnera v Moskve', p. 225.
111 N. A. Melgunov, 'Kontserty gg. Rubinshteina i Vagnera', *Nashe vremya*, 72 (1863), p. 285.
112 Melgunov, 'Kontserty gg. Rubinshteina i Vagnera', p. 286.
113 Melgunov, 'Kontserty gg. Rubinshteina i Vagnera', p. 286.
114 Melgunov, 'Kontserty gg. Rubinshteina i Vagnera', p. 286.
115 N. Stepanov, *Iskra*, 12 (1863), p. 166.
116 See *Iskra*, 12 (1863). Reproduced in Pekelis, *Dargomyzhsky i ego okruzhenie*, III, p. 84.
117 The Russian admirer is of course Serov. See N. Stepanov, *Iskra*, 13 (1863), p. 191.

2 RECEPTION AND PERFORMANCE HISTORY, 1863–1890

1 Richard Wagner, letter to Karl Klindworth, December 1873, Nationalarchiv der Richard-Wagner-Stiftung, Bayreuth.
2 See K. Zvantsov, 'A. N. Serov v 1857–1871 gg. Vospominaniya o nem i ego pis'ma', *Russkaya starina*, 59 (1878), pp. 665–6.
3 See A. A. Gozenpud, *Russkii opernyi teatr XIX veka*, 3 vols. (Leningrad, 1969–73), II, p. 193.
4 See Gozenpud, *Russkii opernyi teatr*, II, p. 194.
5 *Lohengrin* was first performed in Prague, for example, in 1856, and in Vienna in 1858, although its Russian première actually preceded those in London (1875), Paris (1887) and New York (1871). See Alfred Loewenberg, *Annals of Opera*, 3rd edn (London, 1978), cols. 884–8.
6 See *Sovremennaya letopis'*, 35 (1868), pp. 14–15. Cited in Gozenpud, *Russkii opernyi teatr*, II, p. 195.
7 N. A. Rimsky-Korsakov, *Letopis' moei muzykal'noi zhizni* (Moscow, 1955), p. 61.
8 See Lyapunova and Yazovitskaya, *Balakirev: Letopis' zhizni i tvorchestva*, p. 148.
9 See *Sankt-Peterburgskie vedomosti*, 64 (1864), p. 23. Cited in Kremlyov, *Russkaya mysl' o muzyke*, II, p. 210.
10 See *Sankt-Peterburgskie vedomosti*, 278 (1868), p. 1.
11 See *Journal de St Pétersbourg*, 234 (1868). Cited in Kremlyov, *Russkaya mysl' o muzyke*, II, p. 82.
12 See *Sankt-Peterburgskie vedomosti*, 332 (1868). Cited in Kremlyov, *Russkaya mysl' o muzyke*, II, p. 126.
13 See Serov, *Izbrannye stat'i*, I, p. 447.
14 See *Syn otechestva*, 227 (1868), pp. 3–4.

15 See *Sovremennaya letopis'*, 35 (1868) pp. 14–15. Cited in Gozenpud, *Russkii opernyi teatr*, II, p. 195.

16 See A. Famintsyn, *Rikhard Vagner i ego opera 'Loengrin'* (St Petersburg, 1868).

17 Mikhail Stanislavsky, *Vagner i Rossiya* (St Petersburg, 1910), p. 38.

18 Stanislavsky, *Vagner i Rossiya*, pp. 38–9.

19 Stanislavsky, *Vagner i Rossiya*, p. 40.

20 See V. G. Karatygin, 'Obzor sezona: opera', *Ezhegodnik imperatorskikh teatrov*, 7 (1914), p. 136. Loewenberg incorrectly dates the month and the year of the production as February 1873 (see *Annals of Opera*, col. 850). The opera was sung in Russian, using Zvantsov's translation.

21 See Stanislavsky, *Vagner i Rossiya*, p. 41.

22 A. I. Volf, *Khronika peterburgskikh teatrov s kontsa 1855 do nachala 1881 goda* (St Petersburg, 1884), p. 134.

23 See Livanova, *Muzykal'naya bibliografiya*, VI, part one, p. 81. See also A. Gozenpud, 'Vagner i russkaya kul'tura', part I, *Sovetskaya muzyka*, 4 (1983), p. 84.

24 Stanislavsky, *Vagner i Rossiya*, p. 41.

25 See Livanova, *Muzykal'naya bibliografiya*, VI, part one, pp. 82–6.

26 See 1876 *Fremdenliste*, Richard-Wagner-Gedenkstätte der Stadt Bayreuth for a complete list of foreign visitors to the festival.

27 See E. Bortnikova, K. Davydova, G. Pribegina, eds., *Vospominaniya o P. I. Chaikovskom*, 2nd edn, (Moscow, 1973), p. 51.

28 P. I. Chaikovsky, *Muzykal'no-kriticheskie stat'i*, ed. A. A. Shcherbakov, 4th edn, (Moscow, 1986), p. 30.

29 G. Larosh [H. Laroche], ed., *P. I. Chaikovsky: Muzykal'nye fel'etoni i zametki* (Moscow, 1898), p. 111.

30 See M. I. Chaikovsky, *Zhizn' P. I. Chaikovskogo*, 3 vols. (Moscow, 1900–3), I, pp. 290, 494.

31 Chaikovsky, *Muzykal'no-kriticheskie stat'i*, p. 283.

32 See Modest Tchaikovsky, *The Life and Letters of Peter Ilich Tchaikovsky*, edited and abridged by Rosa Newmarch (London, 1906), p. 119.

33 See, for example, V. A. Zhdanov, N. T. Zhegin, eds., *P. Chaikovsky: perepiska s N. F. fon Mekk*, 3 vols. (Moscow, 1934–6), I, pp. 98–9.

34 See, for example, his letter to S. I. Taneev, 18 March 1878 in V. A. Zhdanov, ed., *Pis'ma P. I. Chaikovskogo i S. I. Taneeva* (Moscow, 1951), p. 31.

35 P. Tchaikovsky, letter to Nadezhda von Meck, 20 September 1884, in Modest Tchaikovsky, *The Life and Letters of Peter Ilich Tchaikovsky*, pp. 461–2.

36 See, for example, Vladimir Volkoff, *Tchaikovsky* (London, 1974), p. 279.

37 For an exposition of these reviews, see Kremlyov, *Russkaya mysl' o muzyke*, II, pp. 214–16.

38 See Larosh, *Izbrannye stat'i*, III, p. 213.

39 See Livanova, *Muzykal'naya bibliografiya*, VI, part one, pp. 84–5.

40 See the preface to Larosh, ed., *P. I. Chaikovsky: muzykal'nye fel'etony i zametki.*

41 See Larosh, *Izbrannye stat'i*, III, p. 52.

42 Larosh, *Izbrannye stat'i*, III, p. 257.

43 See *Bayreuther Blätter*, 9 (1878), p. 306.

44 'Spezialstatistik des Auslandes', *Bayreuther Blätter*, 1 (1887), p. 22.

45 Wladimir Iznoskow, 'Lettre sur la Musique Russe', *La Revue Wagnérienne*, 2 (1886), p. 13.

46 See Volf, *Khronika peterburgskikh teatrov*, p. 140.

47 Volf, *Khronika peterburgskikh teatrov*, p. 139.

48 See Larosh, *Izbrannye stat'i*, III, p. 366.

49 See V. P. Rossikhina, *Opernyi teatr Mamontova* (Moscow, 1985), p. 224.

50 See S. Volkonsky, *My Reminiscences*, tr., Mary Chamot, 2 vols. (London, 1924), I, p. 160.

51 See Volkonsky, *My Reminiscences*, I, p. 170. See also Leopold Auer, *My Long Life in Music* (London, 1924), pp. 227–8.

52 Stanislavsky, *Vagner i Rossiya*, p. 42.

53 See Auer, *My Long Life in Music*, p. 227.

54 K. Klindworth, letter to Richard Wagner, 24 December 1871, Nationalarchiv der Richard-Wagner-Stiftung, Bayreuth.

55 See *Muzykal'nyi mir*, 3 (1882), p. 4.

56 See 1882 *Fremdenliste*, and also 'Russischer Muziker und Bayreuth (zum 80 jährigen Bestehen der Festspiele)', clipping from *National-Zeitung* (Berlin), 15 August 1956, Richard-Wagner-Gedenkstätte, Bayreuth.

57 See Gerhard von Reutern, *Ein Freundschafts- und Familienkreis im 19. Jarhundert: Biographisches* (Berlin, 1981), pp. 80–3.

58 See Peer Baedeker, 'Aller Schmerzen Ende', *Bayreuth Programmheft (Parsifal)*, 1984.

59 See M. A. Ganina, ed., *A. K. Glazunov: Pis'ma, stat'i, vospominaniya*, (Moscow, 1958), p. 451.

60 See Alfred Loewenberg, *Annals of Opera*, 3rd edn (London, 1978), col. 1056.

61 See Angelo Neumann, *Erinnerungen an Richard Wagner* (Leipzig, 1907), p. 337.

62 See *Bayan*, 8 (1889), pp. 61–2.

63 Neumann, *Erinnerungen an Richard Wagner*, p. 334.
64 Stanislavsky, *Vagner i Rossiya*, p. 46.
65 Stanislavsky, *Vagner i Rossiya*, p. 47.
66 See Rimsky-Korsakov, *Letopis' moei muzykal'noi zhizni*, p. 169.
67 See N. A. Rimsky-Korsakov, 'O Vagnere (iz pis'ma Rimskogo-Korsakogo k synu)', *Muzyka*, 133 (1913), pp. 419–20.
68 See Kremlyov, *Russkaya mysl' o muzyke*, ii, p. 147.
69 See Sokhor, *Borodin: zhizn', deyatel'nost'*, pp. 326–7.
70 See M. P. *Musorgsky: Literaturnoe nasledie*, ed. Mikhail Pekelis and Aleksandra Orlova, 2 vols. (Moscow, 1971–2), i, p. 95. It is interesting to note, in this light, that Musorgsky was later called the 'Russian Wagner' (see 'Muzykal'nyi dnevnik', *Vestnik teatra*, 31–2 (1919), p. 9).
71 See Kyui, *Izbrannye pis'ma*, ed. I. L. Gusin (Leningrad, 1953), p. 272.
72 Neumann, *Erinnerungen an Richard Wagner*, p. 335.
73 M. Wolkenstein, letter to Cosima Wagner, 19 March 1889, Nationalarchiv der Richard-Wagner-Stiftung, Bayreuth. I am grateful to Hannelore Teuchert for bringing this letter to my attention.
74 Neumann's troupe and the Mariinsky Theatre orchestra left for Moscow on 4 April and presented the *Ring* at the Bolshoi Theatre on 6, 7, 9 and 10 April. A concert of Wagner's works was given on 8 April and *Die Walküre* was repeated on 11 April.
75 Neumann, *Erinnerungen an Richard Wagner*, p. 340.
76 Stanislavsky, *Vagner i Rossiya*, p. 50.
77 Stanislavsky, *Vagner i Rossiya*, p. 51.
78 See Agnes B. Murphy, *Melba: A Biography* (London, 1909), p. 60.
79 S. K-verina, 'Vosem' dnei v Baireite (muzykal'noe prazdnestvo Vagnera)', *Russkoe bogatstvo*, 8 (1889), p. 104.
80 K-verina, 'Vosem' dnei v Baireite', p. 103.
81 See Gozenpud, *Russkii opernyi teatr*, iii, pp. 111–13 for an account of the production, which was sung in Russian.
82 Henry-Louis de la Grange, *Mahler*, vol. i (London, 1970), p. 402.
83 Literally 'men of the soil': a term applied to Grigoriev, Strakhov and the Dostoevsky brothers in the 1860s in view of their beliefs, which combined both Slavophile and Westerniser ideas.
84 Apollon Grigoriev, 'Russkii teatr', *Epokha*, i, 2 (1864), reprinted in T. N. Livanova, *Opernaya kritika v Rossii*, 4 vols. (Moscow, 1966–73), ii, part 4, p. 322.
85 See Taruskin, *Opera and Drama in Russia*, p. 82.
86 Taruskin, *Opera and Drama in Russia*, p. 82.

87 Livanova, *Opernaya kritika v Rossii*, II, part four, pp. 322–3.
88 See A. Gozenpud, *Rikhard Vagner i russkaya kul'tura* (Leningrad, 1990) pp. 97–8.
89 See N. G. Chernyshevsky, *Polnoe sobranie sochinenii*, 16 vols. (Moscow, 1939–53), XV, p. 340.
90 F. M. Dostoevsky, *Pis'ma*, ed. A. S. Dolinin, 4 vols. (Moscow, 1928–59), IV, p. 394.
91 See Dostoevsky, *Pis'ma*, IV, p. 90.
92 A. Gornfeld, 'Vagner i Dostoevsky', *Russkie vedomosti*, 114 (1913), p. 2. Reprinted in *Boevye otkliki na mirnye temy* (Leningrad, 1924), pp. 42–53.
93 Gornfeld, *Boevye otkliki*, p. 42.
94 For a more detailed discussion, see Gornfeld, *Boevye otkliki*, pp. 45–53.
95 Malcolm V. Jones, *Dostoyevsky: The Novel of Discord* (London, 1976), p. 20.
96 Theodor Adorno, *In Search of Wagner*, tr. Rodney Livingstone (London, 1981), p. 81.
97 Gornfeld, *Boevye otkliki*, pp. 45–6.
98 From act one of *Parsifal* (See Richard Wagner, *Parsifal*, Opera Guide 21, ed. Nicholas John (London, 1986), p. 91.)
99 See Jones, *Dostoyevsky*, p. 100.
100 Thomas Mann, 'The Sorrows and Grandeur of Richard Wagner', in Thomas Mann, *Pro and Contra Wagner*, tr. Allan Blunden (London, 1985), p. 99.
101 See L. N. Tolstoy, *Polnoe sobranie sochinenii v 20x tomakh* (Moscow, 1963), X, p. 253.
102 See I. P. Matchenko, 'Pis'ma N. N. Strakhova k N. Y. Danilevskomu', *Russkii vestnik*, 3 (1901), p. 132.
103 See Z. L. Palyukh, A. V. Prokhorova, eds., *Lev Tolstoy i muzyka* (Moscow, 1977), p. 132.
104 See Palyukh and Prokhorova, *Tolstoy i muzyka*, p. 141.
105 See S. I. Taneev, *Dnevniki*, ed. L. Z. Korabelnikova, 3 vols. (Moscow, 1981–5), I, pp. 119–20.
106 Palyukh and Prokhorova, *Tolstoy i muzyka*, p. 161.
107 See entry for June 1896, Taneev, *Dnevniki*, I, p. 162.
108 Tolstoy, *Polnoe sobranie sochinenii*, XV, p. 85.
109 For a detailed discussion of Tolstoy's views on Wagner as expressed in *Chto takoe iskusstvo?*, see E. G. Babaev, 'K voprosu o printsipe narodnosti v estetike L. N. Tolstogo', *Uchenye zapiski (Tashkentskii vechernii pedagogicheskii institut)*, 4 (1957), pp. 103–40. See also Gozenpud, *Rikhard Vagner i russkaya kul'tura*, pp. 172–85.

110 See *Perepiska L. N. Tolstogo s N. N. Strakhovym, 1870–1894* (St Petersburg, 1914), p. 451.
111 See A. Khavsky, 'Tangeizer', *RMG*, 9 (1901), p. 267.
112 See Gozenpud, 'Vagner i russkaya kul'tura', part two, *Sovetskaya muzyka*, 5 (1983), p. 84.
113 Mann, *Pro and Contra Wagner*, pp. 93–4.
114 Mann, *Pro and Contra Wagner*, p. 94.
115 See Irene Masing-Delic, 'The Metaphysics of Liberation: Insarov as Tristan', *Die Welt der Slaven*, 1 (1987), p. 69.
116 See K-D Fischer, 'Turgenev und Richard Wagner', *Zeitschrift für Slawistik*, 31 (1986), pp. 229, 131.
117 Fischer, 'Turgenev und Richard Wagner', p. 229.
118 See Masing-Delic, 'The Metaphysics of Liberation', p. 68.
119 Fischer, 'Turgenev und Richard Wagner', p. 229.
120 See A. Kryukov, *Turgenev i muzyka* (Leningrad, 1963), p. 94.
121 Kryukov, *Turgenev i muzyka*, p. 94.
122 Kryukov, *Turgenev i muzyka*, p. 94.
123 See Masing-Delic, 'The Metaphysics of Liberation', pp. 59–77.
124 Masing-Delic, 'The Metaphysics of Liberation', p. 69.
125 Masing-Delic, 'The Metaphysics of Liberation', p. 69.
126 D. Tsertelev, 'Pamyati Vagnera' (1887), *Poety 1880–1890kh godov*, ed. G. A. Byaly (Leningrad, 1972), p. 218.
127 See B. Kats, *Muzyka v zerkale poezii*, 3 vols. (Leningrad, 1985–7), I, p. 103.

3 RECEPTION AND PERFORMANCE HISTORY, 1890–1917

1 S. A. Bazunov, *R. Vagner* (St Petersburg, 1891).
2 See 'Khronika', *RMG*, 1 (1894), p. 23.
3 'Khronika', *RMG*, 12 (1898), p. 113.
4 'Khronika', *RMG*, 3 (1896), p. 340.
5 'Khronika', *RMG*, 4 (1896), p. 630.
6 See *Teatral'nye izvestiya*, 442 (1896), p. 4.
7 See 'Khronika', *RMG*, 1 (1897), pp. 56–66.
8 See *RMG*, 2 (1898), pp. 134–56.
9 A. P. Koptyaev, *Putevoditeli k operam i muzykal'nym dramam R. Vagnera* (St Petersburg, 1898).
10 'Khronika', *RMG*, 2 (1898), p. 114.
11 Cutting from *Die Gesellschaft*, 9 (1898), Richard-Wagner-Gedenkstätte der Stadt Bayreuth.
12 H. Richter, letter to Cosima Wagner, 19 April 1898. Nationalarchiv der Richard-Wagner-Stiftung, Bayreuth.
13 Stanislavsky, *Vagner i Rossiya*, p. 52.

14 'Khronika', *RMG*, 4 (1898), p. 368.
15 See *Novosti i birzhevaya gazeta*, 78 (1898), p. 2.
16 *Novosti i birzhevaya gazeta*, 78 (1898), p. 2.
17 M. Yankovsky, ed., *I. V. Ershov: Stat'i, vospominaniya, pis'ma*, (Moscow, 1966), p. 350.
18 Volkonsky, *My Reminiscences*, I, p. 160.
19 Volkonsky, *My Reminiscences*, I, pp. 159–60.
20 See 'Khronika', *RMG*, 15–16 (1899), p. 471.
21 'Khronika', *RMG*, 15–16 (1899), p. 473.
22 'Khronika', *RMG*, 17 (1899), p. 508.
23 See A. Gozenpud, *Ivan Ershov* (Leningrad, 1986), p. 224.
24 'Khronika', *RMG*, 17 (1899), p. 508.
25 For an account of Ershov's interpretation of Tristan, see Gozenpud, *Ershov*, pp. 224–35.
26 'Khronika', *RMG*, 6 (1900), p. 175.
27 'Khronika', *RMG*, 7 (1900), p. 216.
28 'Khronika', *RMG*, 39 (1899), p. 946.
29 See Raymond Furness, *Wagner and Literature* (Manchester, 1982), pp. 32–68.
30 Alexandre Benois, *Reminiscences of the Russian Ballet*, tr. Mary Britnieva (London, 1941), p. 114.
31 Alexandre Benois, *Memoirs*, tr. Moura Budberg, 2 vols. (London 1960–4), II, p. 101.
32 See Bayreuth *Fremdenliste*, 1896, Richard-Wagner-Gedenkstätte, Bayreuth. Vladimir Nabokov's father visited Bayreuth also that year.
33 See N. Lapshina, *Mir iskusstva* (Moscow, 1977), p. 133.
34 Richard Buckle, *Diaghilev* (London, 1979), p. 13.
35 Buckle comments that this was rather late for a review to appear, but mistakenly equates the first performance by touring artists in 1898 with the first Russian production. See Buckle, *Diaghilev*, p. 53.
36 Buckle, *Diaghilev*, p. 537.
37 G. Likhtenberger, 'Vzglyady Vagnera na iskusstvo', *Mir iskusstva*, 7–8 (1899), pp. 107–28, 11–12 (1899), pp. 195–206.
38 See, for example, Aleksandr Ivanov, 'Loge i Zigfrid', *Mir iskusstva*, 6 (1904), pp. 128–45.
39 Although it contains a few inaccuracies, see Bernice Glatzer Rosenthal's pioneering 'Wagner and Wagnerian Ideas in Russia', in David C. Large and William Weber, eds., *Wagnerism in European Culture and Politics* (Ithaca, 1984), pp. 198–245, for a useful overview of Wagner's influence on the culture of Russia's 'Silver Age'.
40 E. P. Gomberg-Verzhbinskaya, Y. N. Podkopaev, eds., *Vrubel:*

Perepiska. Vospominaniya o khudozhnike (Leningrad-Moscow, 1963), p. 252.

41 S. Yaremich, *M. A. Vrubel: Zhizn' i tvorchestvo* (Moscow, 1911), p. 184.

42 See A. P. Ostroumova-Lebedeva, 'Vospominaniya o Serove', *Valentin Serov v vospominaniyakh, dnevnikakh i perepiske sovremennikov*, ed. I. Zilbershtein and S. A. Samkov, 2 vols. (Leningrad, 1971), I, p. 645.

43 Zilbershtein and Samkov, *Valentin Serov v vospominaniyakh*, I, p. 646.

44 L. V. Korotkina, *Rerikh v Peterburge-Petrograde* (Leningrad, 1985), p. 154.

45 See M. N. Pozharskaya, *Russkoe teatral'no-dekoratsionnoe iskusstvo kontsa XIX–nachala XX veka* (Moscow, 1970), p. 262.

46 David Burlyuk, *Rerikh: Zhizn' i tvorchestvo 1917–1930* (New York, 1930), p. 24.

47 L. V. Korotkina, 'Problema sinteza iskusstv v tvorchestve N. K. Rerikha (1890–1916)'. Unpublished dissertation (Leningrad, 1983), p. 128.

48 O. Y. Kochik, *Zhivopis'naya sistema V. E. Borisova-Musatova* (Moscow, 1980), p. 44.

49 See A. Rusakova, *V. E. Borisov-Musatov* (Moscow, 1966), p. 95.

50 Kenneth C. Lindsay, Peter Vergo, eds., *Kandinsky: Complete Writings on Art*, 2 vols. (London, 1982), I, p. 364. Kandinsky is vague with dates, but Lindsay and Vergo date the Monet exhibition as 1896. It so happens that there was one performance of *Lohengrin* at the Bolshoi in November 1896 (the first for three seasons and the last for three seasons), which is undoubtedly the one Kandinsky attended (he left Moscow for Munich later that year to study art).

51 Letter to M. F. Petrov-Vodkin, 23 March/5 April 1911, in *K. S. Petrov Vodkin: Pis'ma, stat'i, vystupleniya, dokumenty*, ed. E. N. Selizarova (Moscow, 1991), p. 141.

52 Furness, *Wagner and Literature*, p. 6.

53 See *Vesy*, 1 (1904), p. 1.

54 Of the first generation Symbolists, only Konstantin Balmont appears to have taken an active interest in Wagner (See L. L. Sabaneev, *Vospominaniya o Skryabine* (Moscow, 1925), pp. 165, 202–3).

55 See Volfing [E. Medtner], 'Vagnerovskie festshpili v 1907 g. v Myunkhene (zametki nevagnerista)', *Zolotoe runo*, 7–9 (1907), 10 (1907), 1 (1908), 2, 3–4, 5 (1908).

56 Ivan Konevskoy, *Stikhi i proza. Posmertnoe sobranie sochinenii* (Moscow, 1904), p. 27.

57 Innokenty Annensky, 'O net, ne stan', in *Stikhotvoreniya i poemy*, ed. Y. A. Andreev (Leningrad, 1990), p. 103.

58 As Vsevelod Setchkarev has pointed out, Annensky considered music to be the second most important art form after poetry, but '*O net, ne stan*', in which '*Parsifal* becomes a longing ... which will lead away from the alluring, singing sound of the waltz of life to Shadow and Death', is the only poem he wrote which mentions a specific musical work. See Vsevelod Setchkarev, *Studies in the life and Work of Innokentij Annenskij* (The Hague, 1963), p. 73.

59 See Venedikt Livshits, *Polutoroglazyi strelets: Stikhovoreniya, perevody, vospominaniya* (Leningrad, 1989), p. 46.

60 O. Mandelshtam, *Sobranie sochinenii*, ed. G. P. Struve and B. A. Filippov (New York, 1955), p. 63.

61 N. S. Gumilyov, 'Gondla', *Russkaya mysl'*, 1 (1917), pp. 67–97.

62 See Georgy Adamovich, *Oblaka* (Moscow-Petrograd, 1916), pp. 20–2.

63 See 'Memuary Kastorskogo', RGALI, *fond* 1922, *op.* 1, *ed. khr.* 10, fol. 62.

64 G. Larosh, 'O "*Val'kirii*"', Rikhard Vagner i vagnerizm', *Ezhegodnik imperatorskikh teatrov, prilozhenie 1-e*, (St Petersburg, 1900) p. 61.

65 See 'Khronika', *RMG*, 49 (1900), pp. 1204–5, 50 (1900), pp. 1243–4 and no. 52 (1900), pp. 1302–4.

66 See L. M. Kutateladze, ed., *E. F. Napravnik. Avtobiograficheskie, tvorcheskie materialy* (Leningrad, 1959), p. 42.

67 See 'Khronika', *RMG*, 37 (1899), p. 879. See also B. S. Shteinpress, ed., *Iz muzykal'nogo proshlogo. Sbornik ocherkov*, (Moscow 1965), pp. 276, 369–70.

68 See Rossikhina, *Opernyi teatr Mamontova*, p. 225.

69 See 'Khronika', *RMG*, 33–4 (1901), p. 836.

70 'Khronika', *RMG*, 5 (1901), pp. 149–50.

71 Kutateladze, *E. F. Napravnik: Avtobiograficheskie, tvorcheskie materialy*, p. 42.

72 See Gozenpud, *Ershov*, pp. 237–57 for further details.

73 Gozenpud, *Ershov*, p. 247.

74 'Khronika', *RMG*, 6 (1902), pp. 175–7.

75 'Khronika', *RMG*, 9 (1902), p. 268.

76 N. Salina, *Zhizn' i tsena. Vospominaniya artistki Bol'shogo teatra* (Leningrad-Moscow, 1941), pp. 99–100.

77 N. Dmitriev [N. Kashkin], *Imperatorskaya opernaya tsena v Moskve* (Moscow, 1898), p. 101.

78 Dmitriev, *Imperatorskaya opernaya tsena*, pp. 21–3.

79 Dmitriev, *Imperatorskaya opernaya tsena*, p. 108.

80 Salina, *Zhizn' i tsena*, p. 127.

81 Salina, *Zhizn' i tsena*, pp. 129–30.

82 Ivan Lipaev, 'Moskovskie pis'ma', *RMG*, 4 (1902), p. 118.
83 For further details, see L. M. Kutateladze, ed., *Artur Nikish i russkaya muzykal'naya kul'tura. Vospominaniya, pis'ma, stat'i* (Leningrad, 1975).
84 See Taneev, *Dnevniki*, I, p. 331.
85 Taneev, *Dnevniki*, II, pp. 372, 374.
86 See 'Khronika', *RMG*, 49 (1901), p. 1255.
87 See Peter P. Pachl, *Siegfried Wagner: Genie im Schatten* (Munich, 1988), p. 175. Siegfried Wagner later came to Russia in 1910 to conduct concerts of his and his father's music.
88 See 'Khronika', *RMG*, 5 (1902), p. 152.
89 Over the years, Russian visitors included a Princess Volkonsky, the Baronesses Korf, a Count Pushkin, Prince Vladimir Dolgorukov, Count Sergey Pahlen, a Princess Meshchersky, and Prince and Princess Trubetskoy, for example. See Bayreuth *Fremdenliste* 1901–1908, Richard-Wagner-Gedenkstätte, Bayreuth.
90 Ivan Lipaev, 'Baireit (putevye zametki)', *RMG*, 1902, no. 28–9, pp. 675–85, no. 30–1, pp. 705–13, no. 32–3, pp. 737–44, no. 34–5, pp. 769–79 and no. 36, pp. 801–11.
91 See Bayreuth *Fremdenliste*, 1902, Richard-Wagner-Gedenkstätte, Bayreuth.
92 See 'Vagneriana', *RMG*, 34–5 (1904), p. 350.
93 *Novoe vremya* review cited in *RMG*, 37 (1902), p. 851.
94 'Khronika', *RMG*, 37 (1902), p. 852.
95 M. N. Pozharskaya, *Russkoe teatral'no-dekorativnoe iskusstvo kontsa XIX–nachala XX veka* (Moscow, 1970), p. 209.
96 Pozharskaya, *Russkoe teatral'no-dekorativnoe iskusstvo*, p. 211.
97 'Khronika', *RMG*, 6 (1903), p. 181.
98 See I. Zilbershtein and V. A. Samkov, eds., *Sergey Dyagilev i russkoe iskusstvo*, 2 vols. (Moscow, 1982), I, pp. 167–73.
99 See Zilbershtein and Samkov, *Dyagilev i russkoe iskusstvo*, I, p. 364.
100 See A. N. Benua, *Moi vospominaniya*, 2 vols. (Moscow, 1980), II, pp. 373–5.
101 M. Ivanov, '"Gibel' bogov" R. Vagnera', *Novoe vremya*, 9662, 9669 (1903). Cited in 'Periodicheskaya pechat' o muzyke', *RMG*, 6 (1903), pp. 175–7.
102 See 'Khronika', *RMG*, 38 (1903), p. 840.
103 See 'Khronika', *RMG*, 19–20 (1903), p. 524.
104 'Khronika', *RMG*, 35 (1903), pp. 755–69.
105 'Khronika', *RMG*, 29–30 (1904), p. 694.
106 'Khronika', *RMG*, 10 (1904), p. 274.
107 'Khronika', *RMG*, 9–10 (1905), pp. 276–8.

108 'Khronika', *RMG*, 16 (1905), p. 480.
109 Anri Lishtanberzhe [Henri Lichtenberger], *Vagner kak poet i myslitel'*, tr. S. Solovyov (Moscow, 1905).
110 V. E. Cheshikhin, *Istoriya russkoi opery s 1674 po 1903 godu* (Moscow, 1905), p. 541.
111 'L', 'Itogi repertuara sezona 1904–5 v opernykh teatrakh v Rossii', *RMG*, 42 (1905), pp. 1011–14.
112 See 1904 *Fremdenliste*, Richard-Wagner-Gedenkstätte, Bayreuth.
113 See 'Khronika', *RMG*, 1 (1906), p. 14.
114 A. V. Ossovsky, 'Reingold', *Slovo*, 340 (1905). Reprinted in *A. V. Ossovsky, Muzykal'no-kriticheskie stat'i*, ed. Y. A. Kremlyov (Leningrad, 1971), pp. 128–30.
115 'Itogi repertuara opernogo sezona 1905–6', *RMG*, 40 (1906), p. 882.
116 V. Valter, 'Baireit v 1906 godu. Iz zapisok russkogo muzykanta', *RMG*, 37 (1906), pp. 769–75, 38 (1906), pp. 801–9, 39 (1906), pp. 482–8, 40 (1906), pp. 870–4, 42 (1906), pp. 929–4.
117 R. Vagner, *Iskusstvo i revolyutsiya*, tr. I. Ellen [I. M. Katsenelenbogen] (St Petersburg, 1906).
118 R. Vagner, *Opera i drama*, tr. A. Shepelevsky, A. Vinter (St Petersburg, 1906). Excerpts were also published by *RMG* during the year in its second, tenth, twelfth and thirteenth numbers.
119 'V. I.' [Vyacheslav Ignatovich], *Rikhard Vagner ('Kol'tso Nibelunga')* (St Petersburg, 1906).
120 V. P. Kolomiitsov, preface to V. I., *Rikhard Vagner ('Kol'tso Nibelunga')*, p. 1.
121 See E. V. Tomashevskaya, Y. A. Kremlyov, eds., *V. P. Kolomiitsov: Stat'i i pis'ma* (Leningrad, 1971). A portrait of Kolomiitsov painted in 1928 and reproduced in this publication, shows him sitting at the piano underneath a picture of Wagner.
122 See Ulrich Müller and Peter Wapnewski, eds., *Wagner Handbook*, translation edited by John Deathridge (Cambridge, Mass., 1992), p. 129.
123 'M': 'Sovremennye muzykal'nye deyateli: I. V. Ershov', *RMG*, 50 (1905), pp. 1209–14.
124 See Yankovsky, *Ershov: Stat'i*, p. 373. Ershov refused the invitation as he was not confident of his ability to sing in German.
125 E. Stark (Zigfrid), *Peterburgskaya opera i ee mastera* (Moscow 1940), pp. 238–9.
126 Stark, *Peterburgskaya opera*, p. 240.
127 Stark, *Peterburgskaya opera*, p. 230.
128 See Yankovsky, *Ershov: stat'i*, p. 58.
129 See Müller and Wapnewski, *Wagner Handbook*, p. 509.

130 For a more detailed discussion of Chaliapin's attitude to Wagner, see Victor Borovsky, *Chaliapin* (London, 1988), pp. 428–31.

131 'Khronika', *RMG*, 50 (1905), p. 1235.

132 See L. M. Kutateladze, L. N. Raaben eds., *A. I. Ziloti: vospominaniya, pis'ma* (Leningrad, 1963), p. 240.

133 'With all his pedantry, with all his inexorable dryness, he was an inspirer, he was a constructor ... He had no pose, he conducted his orchestra with his head slightly bent on one side. His hand moved like a metronome without volition, but under this seeming indifference there was an iron will. It made you dull to look at him, but it was pleasant to listen to him. He was always greeted with loud applause when he took his place on the conductor's chair, and this applause was a token not only of approbation but of gratitude', recalled Sergey Volkonsky. See Volkonsky, *My Reminiscences*, I, p. 177.

134 V. P. Shkafer, *Sorok let na tsene russkoi opery*, (Leningrad, 1936), p. 193.

135 Shkafer, *Sorok let na tsene*, p. 193.

136 'Khronika', *RMG*, 10 (1908), p. 238.

137 'Khronika', *RMG*, 10 (1908), p. 238.

138 'Khronika', *RMG*, 10 (1906), p. 245.

139 Prokofiev remembers that during one performance of *Siegfried*, Ershov had difficulty in dragging the dragon he had just killed into the cave. 'The music at this point is very quiet and every word spoken can be heard in the auditorium', writes Prokofiev. "Oh blimey, it's so heavy!" Ershov's angry whisper was heard from the cave ... and in answer came the cautioning remark: "Quiet Ivan Vasilievich! They can hear everything in the auditorium – it could be very embarrassing!."' See S. Prokofiev, *Avtobiografiya*, ed. M. G. Kozlova (Moscow, 1973), p. 377.

140 V. A. Telyakovsky, *Vospominaniya* (Leningrad-Moscow, 1960), p. 140.

141 A. V. Ossovsky, '"Kol'tso Nibelunga"', *Slovo*, 104 (1907), reprinted in Kremlyov, *A. V. Ossovsky*, p. 212.

142 Telyakovsky, *Vospominaniya*, p. 191.

143 M. Ivanov, 'Nitche i Vagner', *Novoe vremya*, 11148 (1907), p. 3.

144 M. Ivanov, 'Nitche i Vagner', *Novoe vremya*, 11155 (1907), p. 4.

145 See M. Ivanov, *Novoe vremya*, 11145 (1907), p. 3.

146 See Telyakovsky, *Vospominaniya*, p. 69.

147 N. V. Tumanina, 'Russkii opernyi teatr na rubezhe XIX i XX vekov', *Russkaya khudozhestvennaya kul'tura kontsa XIX nachala XX veka*, 4 vols. (Moscow, 1968–81), I, p. 335.

148 V. Valter, 'Vagner kak dirizher', *RMG*, 4 (1908), pp. 97–102.
149 Stark, *Peterburgskaya opera*, p. 250.
150 Stark, *Peterburgskaya opera*, pp. 251–2.
151 See, for example, Viktor Valter, 'R. Vagner (k 25-letiyu so dnya smerti)', *Russkaya mysl'*, 1 (1908), pp. 1–19, N. S. O., 'Cherti iz literaturnoi deyatel'nosti Vagnera', *Muzyka i zhizn'*, 1 (1908), pp. 8–11.
152 See 1888 *Fremdenliste*, Richard-Wagner-Gedenkstätte, Bayreuth.
153 See *Rech'*, 79 (1908), p. 5.
154 'Khronika', *RMG*, 14 (1908), p. 362.
155 Viktor Valter, *Obschedostupnoe posobie dlya slushatelei muzykal'noi dramy R. Vagnera 'Kol'tso Nibelunga'* (St Petersburg, 1908); Sofya Sviridenko, *Trilogiya 'Kol'tso Nibelunga' Rikharda Vagnera. Obschedostupnyi ocherk* (St Petersburg, 1908).
156 'Khronika', *RMG*, 10 (1908), p. 254.
157 S. A. Sviridenko, 'Itogi Vagnerovskikh spektaklei', *RMG*, 17 (1908), p. 416.
158 S. Sviridenko, *Vagnerovskie tipy. Trilogiya 'Kol'tso Nibelunga' i artisty peterburgskoi opery* (St Petersburg, 1908).
159 See Sviridenko, *Vagnerovskie tipy*, p. 229.
160 Sviridenko, *Vagnerovskie tipy*, p. 231.
161 Probably this was because Grand Duke Sergey died in 1905. Performances of Wagner had only been staged there, as we have seen, for his wife's benefit.
162 Y. Engel, 'Pis'mo o moskovskoi opere', *RMG*, 3 (1909), pp. 79–85.
163 See N. Vladykina-Bachinskaya, *Sobinov* (Moscow, 1958), pp. 174–82 and L. Sobinov, 'Sobinov o sebe. Avtobiografia (k 20-letnemu yubileyu)', *Muzykal'naya zhizn'*, 13 (1962), p. 14. Naturally this intensely lyrical interpretation did not appeal to a singer like Ershov for whom Wagner's roles were synonymous with heroism.
164 See *Leonid Vitalievich Sobinov. Pis'ma, stat'i, rechi, vyskazyvaniya*, ed. K. N. Kirilenko, 2 vols. (Moscow, 1970), II, p. 410.
165 See *Novosti sezona*, 1 September 1909, cited in V. Borovsky, *Moskovskaya opera S. I. Zimina* (Moscow, 1977), p. 113.
166 For a description of the visit and the production in Kiev see N. N. Bogolyubov, *Shest'desyat' let v opernom teatre* (Moscow, 1967), pp. 135–45.
167 'Eli', 'Posle Val'kirii', *RMG*, 10 (1909), pp. 267–71.
168 The production of *Die Meistersinger* opened the Zimin Theatre's season on 30 August 1909. It was sung in Viktor Kolomiitsov's specially commissioned translation, conducted by Emil Kuper

and directed by P. S. Olenin. For a full account of the production see Borovsky, *Moskovskaya opera S. I. Zimina*, pp. 111–23.

169 See 'Khronika', *RMG*, 45 (1909), p. 1040.
170 See Edward Braun, *Meyerhold on Theatre* (London, 1969), p. 58.
171 L. Arnshtam, 'Meierkhold i muzyka', *Sovetskaya muzyka*, 3 (1974), p. 56.
172 See Nikolay Volkov, *Meierkhold*, 2 vols. (Moscow-Leningrad, 1929), I, pp. 40, 72.
173 A. Gladkov, 'Vospominaniya, zametki, zapisi o V. E. Meierkholde', *Tarusskie stranitsy*, ed. V. Koblikov *et al.*, (Kaluga, 1961), p. 302.
174 B. Pokrovsky, 'Dva slova o mastere', *Sovetskaya muzyka*, 3 (1974), p. 59.
175 Edward Braun, *The Theatre of Meyerhold* (London, 1979), p. 33.
176 See V. Meyerhold, 'First Attempts at a Stylized Theatre', *Meyerhold on Theatre*, pp. 55–6.
177 See, for example, the essays by Sologub and Chulkov in *Teatr. Kniga o novom teatre*, ed. A. Lunacharsky and A. Benois (St Petersburg, 1908), pp. 179–98 and pp. 201–17.
178 Braun, *Meyerhold on Theatre*, p. 60.
179 See RGALI, *fond* 998, *op.* 1, *ed. khr.* 775, 838, 839, 842.
180 V. Meierkhold, 'K postanovke "Tristana i Izoldy"', *Ezhegodnik imperatorskikh teatrov*, 5 (1909), pp. 12–35.
181 A. L. Porfirieva, 'Meierkhold i Vagner', *Russkii teatr i dramaturgiya nachala XX veka. Sbornik nauchnykh trudov* (Leningrad, 1984), p. 135.
182 See V. E. Meyerhold, 'O Vagnere i muzykal'noi drame. Chernovye nabroski i vypiski (1909)', RGALI, *fond* 998, *op.* 1, *ed. khr.* 414.
183 See Volkov, *Meierkhold*, I, pp. 66–72; A. Matskin, *Portrety i nablyudeniya* (Moscow, 1973), pp. 232–6, Braun, *The Theatre of Meyerhold*, pp. 92–8; and Isaak Glikman, *Meierkhold i muzykal'nyi teatr* (Leningrad, 1989), pp. 41–52 for a discussion of its contents.
184 A Japanese theatre company had toured Russia in 1902, and their performances left a lasting impression on Meyerhold.
185 Porfirieva, 'Meierkhold i Vagner', p. 138.
186 Meyerhold, 'O Vagnere', fol. 54.
187 Adolphe Appia, *Die Musik und die Inszenierung*, cited in Braun, *The Theatre of Meyerhold*, p. 94.
188 See Meyerhold, 'O Vagnere', fol. 56, where he writes that 'musical and poetic art become understandable ... only through the art of dance (mime)'.
189 *Richard Wagner's Prose Works*, ed. and tr. W. A. Ellis, 8 vols. (London, 1892–9), I, pp. 101, 103.

190 Meyerhold, 'O Vagnere', fol. 59, cited in Porfirieva 'Meierkhold i Vagner', p. 141.

191 See Meyerhold, 'O Vagnere', fol. 57 (partially cited in Porfirieva 'Meierkhold i Vagner', p. 140).

192 See Meyerhold, 'O Vagnere', fol. 56.

193 See A. Potyomkin, 'Beseda s rezhisserom V. E. Meierkhold', *Peterburgskaya gazeta*, 296 (1909), p. 5, where the director explains that 'the dramatic content is born out of the feelings of normal people, and there are no abrupt movements or rapid crossings from one part of the stage to another. The actors are externally calm, and all their movements are gentle and lyrical.'

194 Braun, *Meyerhold on Theatre*, p. 89.

195 Lidiya Ivanova, 'Vospominaniya o V. Ivanove', *Novy zhurnal*, 148 (1982), p. 141

196 Meyerhold, 'K postanovke "Tristana i Izoldy"', cited in Braun, *The Theatre of Meyerhold*, p. 96.

197 Porfirieva, 'Meierkhold i Vagner', p. 128.

198 See 'Khronika', *RMG*, 45 (1909), pp. 1036–40.

199 See 'Khronika', *RMG*, 4 (1910), p. 110.

200 See Braun, *Meyerhold on Theatre*, p. 76.

201 See his review in *Rech'*, 304 (1909), p. 5. Benois believed that Meyerhold's production had nothing in common with Wagner's score, and thought that he strove too much for external effect.

202 See V. Meyerhold, 'Posle postanovki "Tristana i Izoldy"' (1910), reprinted in *V. E. Meierkhold: Stat'i, pis'ma, rechi, besedy*, ed. A. V. Fevralsky *et al.*, 2 vols. (Moscow, 1968), I, pp. 198–201.

203 Braun, *The Theatre of Meyerhold*, p. 190.

204 See Porfirieva, 'Meierkhold i Vagner', p. 138.

205 Paul Schmidt, ed., *Meyerhold at Work* (Austin, 1980), p. 141.

206 A. Gladkov, 'Meierkhold govorit', *Novy mir*, 8 (1961), p. 227.

207 See Y. Engel, 'Muzykal'nyi sezon v Moskve', *Ezhegodnik imperatorskikh teatrov*, 4 (1909), p. 203.

208 V. G. Valter, *Obshchedostupnoe posobie dlya slushatelei muzykal'noi dramy R. Vagnera 'Tristan i Izolda'* (Moscow, 1910); S. A. Sviridenko, *'Tristan i Izolda' R. Vagnera. Obshchedostupnyi ocherk dlya kratkogo oznakomleniya. V stikhotvornikh vyderzhkakh teksta*, tr. S. Sviridenko and I. Ershov (St Petersburg, 1910).

209 E. Shyure [E. Schuré], *Drama R. Vagnera 'Tristan i Izolda'*, tr. V. Kolomiitsov (Moscow, 1909).

210 'Bibliografiya', *RMG*, 5 (1910), pp. 148–51.

211 N. Rozen's translation of Schuré's *Richard Wagner: Son œuvre et son idée* was published in Moscow in 1909 as *Rikhard Vagner i ego muzykal'naya drama*.

212 N. Findeizen, 'Bibliografiya', *Ezhegodnik imperatorskikh teatrov*, 6 (1910), p. 174.

213 M. Ivanov, *Novoe Vremya*, 12208 (1910), p. 4.

214 M. Stanislavsky, *Vagner i Rossiya* (Moscow, 1910).

215 See S. Sviridenko. 'Khronika: novinki vagnerovskogo sezona', *RMG*, 18–19 (1910), pp. 467–70.

216 Coates, who was of English parentage although born in Russia, was chief conductor at the Mariinsky Theatre from 1911 until 1918, after which he returned to England. Like Emil Kuper, who *was* Russian, despite his English-sounding surname, he was an enthusiastic promoter of Wagner's music.

217 N. Bogolyubov, *Shest'desyat' let v opernom teatre* (Moscow, 1966) p. 157.

218 See 'Khronika', *RMG*, 16–17 (1910), pp. 436–8.

219 V. G. Karatygin, 'Itogi sezona 1909–1910 gg. Opera', *Ezhegodnik imperatorskikh teatrov*, 4 (1910), pp. 122–3.

220 'Muzykal'nyi 1910 god v Rossii', *RMG*, 1 (1911), pp. 1–5.

221 Bogolyubov, *Shest'desyat' let v opernom teatre*, p. 157.

222 S. Sviridenko, 'Vagnerovskii sezon 1910–1911', *RMG*, 18–19 (1911), pp. 456–8.

223 N. F. Findeizen, *Rikhard Vagner. Ego zhizn' i muzykal'noe tvorchestvo*, parts 1–2 (1813–1859), (St Petersburg, 1911).

224 R. Vagner, *Moya zhizn'*, vol. 1, ed. A. L. Volynsky (St Petersburg, 1911).

225 R. Vagner, *Betkhoven*, tr. V. Kolomiitsov (St Petersburg, 1911).

226 V. Valter, *Vagner, ego zhizn', tvorchestvo i deyatel'nost'* (Petersburg, 1911).

227 Y. Engel, 'Opernye novinki sezona 1911–12 g.', *Ezhegodnik imperatorskikh teatrov*, 4 (1912), p. 131.

228 Y. Engel, 'Obzor itogov moskovskogo opernogo sezona 1911–1912 g.', *Ezhegodnik imperatorskikh teatrov*, 5 (1912), p. 101.

229 See *Studiya*, 2 (1911), p. 24.

230 For its history, see G. Y. Yudin, ed., *Emil Kuper: Stat'i, vospominaniya, materialy* (Moscow, 1988), pp. 56–62.

231 See 'Khronika', *RMG*, 44 (1911), pp. 922–4.

232 See *Muzyka*, 46 (1911), pp. 992–5.

233 See *Studiya*, 3 (1911), pp. 16–17.

234 *Studiya*, 3 (1911), p. 25.

235 *Studiya*, 9 (1911), pp. 10–12.

236 See *Ezhegodnik imperatorskikh teatrov*, 4 (1912), p. 135.

237 See, for example, *Muzyka*, 74 (1912), pp. 379–80.

238 'Khronika', *RMG*, 50 (1911), pp. 1057–9.

239 'Khronika', *RMG*, 50 (1911), pp. 1057–9.

240 See A. Andreevsky, 'Vagnerovskie tsikli v Mariinskom teatre', *Studiya*, 34–5 (1912), pp. 6–9.

241 V. Kolomiitsov, ' "Nyurenbergskie mastera peniya' ". K pervomy predstavleniyu v Peterburge na tsene Teatra muzykal'noi dramy', *Den'*, 21 December 1912. Reprinted in Kremlyov, *Kolomiitsov: stat'i i pis'ma*, pp. 82–8.

242 They included a translation of J. Kapp's *Rikhard Wagner: eine Biographie* (Berlin, 1910), and A. Ilinsky's *Rikhard Vagner: ego zhizn' i tvorchestvo* (Moscow, 1913).

243 R. Vagner, *Vibelungi. Vsemirnaya istoriya na osnovanii skazanii*, tr. M. Shenrok (Moscow, 1913) and Sergey Durylin, *Vagner i Rossiya* (Moscow, 1913).

244 See *RMG*, 40 (1912), p. 825, and *Ezhegodnik imperatorskikh teatrov*, 2 (1913), p. 1.

245 K. Eiges, 'R. Vagner i ego khudozhestvennoe reformatorstvo', *Russkaya mysl'*, 6 (1913), p. 60.

246 Durylin, *Vagner i Rossiya*, p. 66.

247 V. Kolomiitsov, 'Rikhard Vagner i muzykal'naya drama v Rossii', *Muzykal'nyi kalendar' na 1913 god A. Gabrilovicha* (St Petersburg, 1913), p. viii.

248 Kolomiitsov, 'Vagner i muzykal'naya drama', p. xxxi.

249 See *Ezhegodnik imperatorskikh teatrov*, 4 (1913), p. 137.

250 See Yudin, *Emil Kuper: Stat'i*, p. 64.

251 For a full account of the Sheremetiev production of *Parsifal*, see A. B. Khessin, *Iz moikh vospominanii* (Moscow, 1959), pp. 205–13.

252 V. Karatygin, *'Parsifal'. Torzhestvennaya misteriya R. Vagnera. Tematicheskii razbor* (St Petersburg, 1914); M. Khopp, *'Parsifal'. Drama-misteriya v 3-x deistvakh. Istor.-tsenicheskii i muzykal'nyi razbor. Avtoriz. perevod R. Goldberg* (Moscow, 1913); S. Sviridenko, *'Parsifal'. Obshchedostupnoe posobie dlya oznakomleniya s vagnerovskoi misteriei* (St Petersburg, 1913). I. Korzukhin's *'Parsifal' R. Vagnera* (St Petersburg, 1914) and N. Taberio's *'Parsifal'. Istoricheskoe proiskhozhdenie skazanii o Parsifale. Soderzhanie i kratkii muzykal'nyi razbor dramy-misterii R. Vagnera* (St Petersburg, 1914) appeared the following year.

253 When Khessin had visited Bayreuth in 1904, accompanied by Valentin Serov and his mother, he was granted an audience with Cosima Wagner at 'Wahnfried'. See A. B. Khessin, *Iz moikh vospominanii* (Moscow, 1959) p. 184.

254 Khessin, *Iz moikh vospominanii*, p. 207.

255 Khessin, *Iz moikh vospominanii*, p. 207.

256 See *Teatr i iskusstvo*, 51 (1913), p. 1052.

257 See Khessin, *Iz moikh vospominanii*, p. 206.

258 Khessin, *Iz moikh vospominanii*, p. 210.

259 *Muzyka*, 176 (1914), pp. 295–6.

260 Y. V. Keldysh, 'Russkaya muzyka na rubezhe dvukh stoletii', *Russkaya khudozhestvennaya kul'tura*, I, p. 322.

261 B. Asafiev, 'O sebe', *Vospominaniya o B. V. Asafieve* (Leningrad, 1974), p. 442.

262 See Yudin, *Emil Kuper: Stat'i*, p. 51.

263 See *Muzyka*, 174 (1914), p. 258.

264 See A. V. Kashperov, ed., *A. N. Skryabin: Pis'ma* (Moscow, 1965), p. 531.

265 Skryabin's *Prometei: Poema ognya* (1908–10) was in some respects his answer to that work.

266 Sabaneev claims that it actually reduced him to tears. See L. Sabaneev, *Vospominaniya o Skryabine* (Moscow, 1925), p. 103.

267 L. Sabaneev, *A. N. Skryabin* (Moscow, 1922), p. 189.

268 See, for example, 'Khronika', *RMG*, 47 (1900), pp. 1149–50; O. Rizeman, 'Rakhmaninov i Skryabin', *Novoe vremya*, 9290 (1902), p. 4; *Studiya*, 12 (1911), p. 14; A. P. Koptyaev, *A. N. Skryabin* (Moscow, 1916), pp. 81–2; Igor Glebov, *Skryabin: Opyt kharakteristiki* (Petrograd, 1921), pp. 12–13; and M. Mikhailov, *A. N. Skryabin* (Leningrad, 1971), pp. 65 and 126–7.

269 See Ralph E. Matlaw, 'Scriabin and Russian Symbolism', *Comparative Literature*, I (1979), pp. 1–23.

270 See Sabaneev, *Vospominaniya o Skryabine*, p. 13.

271 See G. Katuar, letter to S. I. Taneev, 5 March 1895, RGALI, *fond* 880, *op.* 1, *ed. khr.* 266.

272 Sabaneev, *Vospominaniya o Skryabine*, p. 13.

273 See V. Bryantseva, *S. V. Rakhmaninov* (Moscow, 1976), pp. 71, 83, 312.

274 See S. I. Vasilenko, *Stranitsy vospominanii* (Moscow, 1948), p. 92.

275 See Taneev, *Dnevniki*, III, p. 340.

276 See Taneev, *Dnevniki*, III, pp. 70–3.

277 See Eric Walter White, *Stravinsky* (London, 1966), pp. 175, 179.

278 See Buckle, *Diaghilev*, p. 236.

279 I. Stravinsky, *Poetics of Music* (New York, 1947), p. 60.

280 See Prokofiev, *Avtobiografiya*, p. 378.

281 See Stanley Krebs, *Soviet Composers and the Development of Soviet Music* (London, 1970), p. 105. As Krebs shows, Wagnerian influence can be found in both Myaskovsky's 1st and 5th Symphonies (see p. 105 and 107).

282 See Detlef Gojowy, *Neue Sojwetische Musik der 20 Jahre* (Regensburg, 1980), p. 111.

283 S. I. Vasilenko, *Vospominaniya* (Moscow, 1978), p. 206.

284 Nicolas Nabokov, *Old Friends and New Music* (London, 1951), p. 37.

4 VYACHESLAV IVANOV

1 From an article Ivanov contributed on Symbolism to the *Enciclopedia Italiana* in 1936. See Vyacheslav Ivanov, *Sobranie sochinenii*, ed. D. V. Ivanov and O. Deschartes (Brussels, 1971–), II, p. 7.

2 Vyacheslav Ivanov, 'O Vagnere', *Vestnik teatra*, 31–2 (1919), p. 2.

3 Lydia Ivanova, 'Reminiscences', *Vyacheslav Ivanov: Poet, Critic and Philosopher*, ed. Robert Louis Jackson and Lowry Nelson, Jr (New Haven, 1986), p. 401.

4 V. I. Ivanov, 'Avtobiograficheskoe pis'mo', *Sobranie sochinenii*, II, p. 7.

5 A stanza of his autobiographical poem 'Infancy' (*Mladenchestvo*), for example, pays tribute to the Bolshoi Theatre. See Ivanov, *Sobranie sochinenii*, I, p. 246.

6 Ivanov, 'Avtobiograficheskoe pis'mo', *Sobranie sochinenii*, II, p. 18.

7 See, for example, 'Nitsshe i Dionis', 'Simvolika esteticheskikh nachal', 'Kop'e Afiny', 'Novye maski' and 'Vagner i Dionisovo deistvo', all published in *Vesy* between May 1904 and February 1905.

8 V. Pyast, *Vstrechi* (Moscow, 1929), p. 104.

9 Anna Tamarchenko, 'The Poetics of Vyacheslav Ivanov: Lectures given at Baku University' in Jackson and Nelson, *Vyacheslav Ivanov: Poet, Critic and Philosopher*, p. 84.

10 See N. V. Kotrelyov, 'Vyach. Ivanov: Professor Bakinskogo universiteta', *Uchenie zapiski Tartuskogo god. universiteta, Vypusk 209, Trudy po russkoi i slavyanskoi filologii, XI, Literaturovedenie* (1968), p. 335.

11 In 1912, he gave a lecture on the subject which was later published. See Vyacheslav Ivanov, 'Churlyanis i problema sinteza iskusstv', *Apollon*, 3 (1914), pp. 5–21.

12 N. Berdyaev, 'Ivanovskie sredy' in S. Vengerov, *Russkaya literatura XX veka*, 3 vols. (Moscow, 1916), III, pp. 97–8.

13 See Ivanov, *Sobranie sochinenii*, II, p. 784.

14 M. S. Altman, 'Iz besed s poetom Vyacheslavom Ivanovichem Ivanovym (Baku, 1921 g.)', *Trudy po russkoi i slavyanskoi filologii, XI, Literaturovedenie* (1968), p. 310.

15 See Lidiya Ivanova, *Vospominaniya. Kniga ob otse*, ed. John Malmstad (Paris, 1990), p. 129.

16 Vyacheslav Ivanov, 'Ellinskaya religiya stradayushchego boga', *Novyi put'*, 1 (1904), pp. 110–34; 2 (1904), pp. 48–78; 3 (1904),

pp. 38–51; 5 (1904), pp. 28–40; 8 (1904), pp. 17–26; 9 (1904), pp. 47–70.

17 Ivanov, 'Ellinskaya religiya', *Novy put'*, 3 (1904), pp. 50–1.

18 Ivanov, 'Ellinskaya religiya', *Novy put'*, 2 (1904), pp. 62–3.

19 Ivanov, 'Ellinskaya religiya', *Novy put'*, 2 (1904), p. 63.

20 The only obvious references to Dionysus in Wagner's writings can be found in *Art and Revolution, On the Destiny of Opera* (1871) (*Über die Bestimmung der Oper*), *The Name 'Musikdrama'* (1872) (*Über die Benennung 'Musikdrama'*), and *'On Poetry and Composition'* (1879) (*Über Das Dichten und Komponiren*).

21 Friedrich Nietzsche, *The Birth of Tragedy Out of the Spirit of Music*, tr. Francis Golffing (New York, 1956), pp. 119–20.

22 In *The Birth of Tragedy*, Nietzsche defines artistic creation as either Apollonian or Dionysian and advances the idea that music, in its capacity to engender myth and embody metaphysical reality, made possible 'the birth of tragedy', the highest form of artistic creation, since it was the product of an equal combination of the Dionysian and Apollonian principles.

23 Raymond Furness, *Wagner and Literature* (Manchester, 1982), p. 4.

24 Arthur Schopenhauer, *The World as Will and Representation*, tr. E. F. J. Payne, 2 vols. (New York, 1966), I, p. 256.

25 Nietzsche, *The Birth of Tragedy*, pp. 97–8.

26 Before succumbing to Wagner, it should be noted, Nietzsche's musical interests centred on Bach, Haydn and Schumann. See M. S. Silk and J. P. Stern, *Nietzsche on Tragedy* (Cambridge, 1981), p. 25.

27 See William Ashton Ellis, tr., *Richard Wagner's Prose Works*, 8 vols. (London, 1892–9), II, p. 126.

28 See Dieter Borchmeyer, 'Richard Wagner und Nietzsche', in Ulrich Müller and Peter Wapnewski, *Richard-Wagner-Handbuch* (Stuttgart, 1986), p. 118.

29 Ashton Ellis, *Richard Wagner's Prose Works*, V, p. 302.

30 A reference to *The Birth of Tragedy*.

31 Ivanov, 'Ellinskaya religiya', *Novy put'*, 3 (1904)), p. 51.

32 See Silk and Stern, *Nietzsche on Tragedy*, p. 40, and pp. 42–3.

33 Ivanov, 'Ellinskaya religiya', *Novyi put'*, 3 (1904) p. 63.

34 A case in point is Konstantin Rudnitsky's claim that Ivanov's ideal of 'collective action' [*sobornoe deistvo*] 'was undoubtedly inspired by Nietzsche's famous work *The Birth of Tragedy*', although the philosopher was not known for his populist ideas (see Konstantin Rudnitsky, *Russian and Soviet Theatre*, tr. R. Permar, ed. L. Milne (London, 1988), p. 9). See also Heinrich

Stammler, 'Ivanov and Nietzsche', in Jackson and Nelson, *Vyacheslav Ivanov: Poet, Critic and Philosopher*, pp. 297–312.

35 See Ivanov, *Sobranie sochinenii*, II, p. 796.

36 See V. Ivanov, 'Kop'e Afiny', *Po zvezdam* (St Petersburg, 1909), pp. 48–9.

37 Ivanov, *Po zvezdam*, p. 44.

38 See Nicholas Riasanovsky, 'Khomiakov on *Sobornost*'', *Continuity and Change in Russian and Soviet Thought*, ed. E. J. Simmons (Cambridge, Mass., 1955), pp. 183–96.

39 These ideas are expressed in Wagner's writings in *Art and Revolution* and *The Art work of the Future*.

40 V. Ivanov, letter to V. Bryusov, 28 December 1904, in S. S. Grechishkin, N. V. Kotrelyov and A. V. Lavrov, 'Perepiska s Vyacheslavom Ivanovym', *Literaturnoe nasledstvo*, vol. 85, *Valery Bryusov*, (Moscow, 1976), p. 468.

41 V. Ivanov, letter to V. Bryusov, 28 September 1904, *Literaturnoe nasledstvo*, vol. 85, p. 462.

42 See Viola Stephan, *Studien zum Drama des Russischen Symbolismus* (Frankfurt, 1980), p. 14.

43 See Ashton Ellis, *Richard Wagner's Prose Works*, II, pp. 347–8.

44 Ashton Ellis, *Richard Wagner's Prose Works*, II, pp. 329 and 330.

45 See Robert Louis Jackson, 'Ivanov's Humanism: A Correspondence from Two Corners', in Jackson and Nelson, *Vyacheslav Ivanov: Poet, Critic and Philosopher*, p. 350.

46 See Dmitry Ivanov, 'Motifs in Ivanov's Work' in Jackson and Nelson, *Vyacheslav Ivanov: Poet, Critic and Philosopher*, p. 383.

47 Jackson, 'Ivanov's Humanism', Jackson and Nelson, *Ivanov: Poet, Critic and Philosopher*, p. 350.

48 Ivanov, 'Nitsshe i Dionis', *Po zvezdam*, p. 5.

49 Max Hochschüler, 'Pis'mo iz Baireita', *Vesy*, 9 (1904), pp. 39–46. Ivanov assumed 'Max Hochschüler' to be a pseudonym of Maksimilian Shick, but a letter from M. N. Semyonov on the matter leaves the authorship ambiguous (see *Literaturnoe nasledstvo*, vol. 85, p. 464). Whoever Max Hochschüler was thus remains a mystery, but a clue to his identity can perhaps be found in the fact that he quotes verses by the young poet Aleksandr Bisk in the second part of his 'Letter from Bayreuth' (see *Vesy*, 10 (1904), pp. 49–58). Bisk coincidentally happened to be studying in Germany at the time, and that fact, combined with the manner in which Hochschüler quotes Bisk's poetry to support his arguments (Bisk only began to publish his verse in 1904, and in relatively obscure 'southern' publications, moreover) leads one to think that Hochschüler and Bisk may have been one and same person. Bisk's

son, the writer Alain Bosquet, has expressed doubt that his father was the author of the 'Letter from Bayreuth', but curiously recollects his father often mentioning someone by the name of Hochschüler (letter to present author, August 1990).

50 Hochschüler, 'Pis'mo iz Baireita', *Vesy*, 9 (1904), p. 45.
51 Hochschüler, 'Pis'mo iz Baireita', *Vesy*, 9 (1904), p. 40.
52 Hochschüler, 'Pis'mo iz Baireita', *Vesy*, 9 (1904), p. 42.
53 Hochschüler, 'Pis'mo iz Baireita', *Vesy*, 9 (1904), p. 44.
54 Hochschüler, 'Pis'mo iz Baireita', *Vesy*, 9 (1904), p. 43.
55 Hochschüler, 'Pis'mo iz Baireita', *Vesy*, 9 (1904), p. 44.
56 Hochschüler, 'Pis'mo iz Baireita', *Vesy*, 9 (1904), p. 46.
57 Hochschüler, 'Pis'mo iz Baireita', *Vesy*, 9 (1904), p. 46.
58 Ivanov was living near Geneva at the time.
59 V. Ivanov, letter to V. Bryusov, 19 October 1904, *Literaturnoe nasledstvo*, vol. 85, *Valery Bryusov* (Moscow, 1976), pp. 463–4.
60 V. Ivanov, letter to Bryusov, 16 November 1904, *Literaturnoe nasledstvo*, vol. 85, p. 468.
61 V. Ivanov, letter to Bryusov, 2 December 1904, *Literaturnoe nasledstvo*, vol. 85, pp. 469–70.
62 V. Ivanov, letter to Bryusov, 5 January 1905, *Literaturnoe nasledstvo*, vol. 85, p. 470.
63 See Ashton Ellis, *Richard Wagner's Prose Works*, II, p. 220.
64 Ivanov, *Po zvezdam*, p. 42.
65 Ivanov, *Po zvezdam*, p. 41.
66 Ivanov, *Po zvezdam*, p. 240.
67 Ashton Ellis, *Richard Wagner's Prose Works*, I, p. 47.
68 Ivanov, 'O Vagnere', *Vestnik teatra*, 31–2 (1919), p. 3.
69 See A. Porfirieva, 'Dramaturgiya Vyacheslava Ivanova (Russkaya simvolistskaya tragedia i mifologicheskii teatr Vagnera)' in *Problemy muzykal'nogo romantizma* (Leningrad, 1987), pp. 31–58.
70 Presumably Deschartes has in mind 'New Masks' (1904), 'Wagner and the Dionysian Rite' (1905) and 'Presentiments and Portents' (1906).
71 A quotation from 'Vagner i Dionisovo deistvo'. See Ivanov, *Po zvezdam*, p. 67.
72 Ivanov, *Sobranie sochinenii*, II, p. 671.
73 Ivanov, *Po zvezdam*, p. 65.
74 Ashton Ellis, *Richard Wagner's Prose Works*, I, pp. 183, 196, 201.
75 See part four of 'Novye maski', *Po zvezdam*, pp. 57–8. Wagner enlarges on this subject at length in *The Art-work of the Future*, where he writes, for example: 'The garment of religion, in which alone [Hellenic art] was the common art of Greece, and after whose removal it could only, as an egoistic, isolated, arts species,

fulfil the needs of Luxury ... this specific garb of the Hellenic religion we have to stretch out until its folds embrace the Religion of the future, the Religion of universal manhood and thus to gain already a presage of the Work of art of the future. The work of art is the living presentation of religion' (Ashton Ellis, *Richard Wagner's Prose Works*, I, p. 90).

76 Ivanov, *Po zvezdam*, p. 66.
77 Ashton Ellis, *Richard Wagner's Prose Works*, II, pp. 335–6.
78 Ashton Ellis, *Richard Wagner's Prose Works*, II, p. 336.
79 Ivanov, *Po zvezdam*, p. 66.
80 Ivanov, *Po zvezdam*, p. 67.
81 Ivanov, *Po zvezdam*, p. 67.
82 Ivanov, *Po zvezdam*, p. 67.
83 Ivanov, *Po zvezdam*, p. 69.
84 The fact that Ivanov talks of 'new populism' in his essay 'O russkoi idee' (see *Po zvezdam*, p. 315) shows that this was not coincidental.
85 Ivanov, *Po zvezdam*, p. 68.
86 Ivanov, *Po zvezdam*, p. 69.
87 Ivanov, 'Predchustviya i predvestiya', *Po zvezdam*, p. 194.
88 Ivanov, *Po zvezdam*, p. 209.
89 Ashton Ellis, *Richard Wagner's Prose Works*, II, p. 20.
90 Ashton Ellis, *Richard Wagner's Prose Works*, II, p. 353.
91 Ashton Ellis, *Richard Wagner's Prose Works*, II, pp. 107, 110–11.
92 Ivanov, *Po zvezdam*, p. 211.
93 Ivanov, 'Natsional'noe i vselenskoe v tvorchestve Skryabina (Skryabin kak natsional'nyi kompozitor)', in I. A. Mylnikova, 'Stat'i Vyach. Ivanova o Skryabine', *Pamyatniki kul'tury. Novye Otkrytiya. Ezhegodnik na 1983 god* (Leningrad, 1985), p. 99.
94 Ivanov, *Po zvezdam*, p. 208.
95 Ivanov, *Po zvezdam*, p. 217.
96 Ivanov, *Po zvezdam*, p. 196.
97 Ivanov, *Po zvezdam*, p. 285.
98 Ashton Ellis, *Richard Wagner's Prose Works*, II, p. 155.
99 Ashton Ellis, *Richard Wagner's Prose Works*, I, p. 52.
100 Ivanov, *Po zvezdam*, p. 219.
101 Ashton Ellis, *Richard Wagner's Prose Works*, I, p. 53
102 Ashton Ellis, *Richard Wagner's Prose Works*, I, p. 56.
103 G. Chulkov, 'O misticheskom anarkhizme' so vstupitel'noi stat'ei Vyacheslava Ivanova 'O nepriyatii mira' (St Petersburg, 1906).
104 G. Chulkov, 'Printsipy teatra budushchego', in Lunacharsky and Benois (eds.) *O teatre*, p. 209.
105 For more information, see Bernice Glatzer Rosenthal, 'The

Transmutation of the Symbolist Ethos: Mystical Anarchism and the Revolution of 1905', *Slavic Review*, 4 (1977), pp. 608–27.

106 D. Filosofov, 'Misticheskii anarkhizm (dekadentstvo, obshchest-vennost' i misticheskii anarkhizm)', *Zolotoe runo*, 10 (1906), republished in *Slova i zhizn'. Literaturnye spory noveishego vremeni (1901–1908 gg.)* (St Petersburg, 1909) p. 122.

107 Ivanov, *Po zvezdam*, p. 194.

108 'The highest conjoint work of art is the *Drama*', writes the composer in *The Art-work of the Future*: 'it can only be at hand in all its *possible* fullness, when in it each *separate branch of art* is at hand in *its own utmost fullness*'. See Ashton Ellis, *Richard Wagner's Prose Works*, I, p. 184.

109 Ivanov, *Po zvezdam*, p. 218.

110 Ashton Ellis, *Richard Wagner's Prose Works*, I, p. 77.

111 L. Zinovieva-Annibal, letter to M. M Zamyatina. See *Literatur-noe nasledstvo*, vol. 92, *Aleksandr Blok. Novye materialy i issledovaniya*, part III (1982), p. 238.

112 See L. Galich [Gabrilovich], 'Dionisovo sobornoe deistvo i misticheskii teatr "Fakely"', *Teatr i iskusstvo*, 8 (1906), p. 128.

113 See Gennady Shmakov, 'Mikhail Kuzmin i Rikhard Vagner', *Studies in the Life and Works of Mixail Kuzmin*, ed. John. E. Malmstad (Vienna, 1989), p. 32.

114 Sergey Averintsev, 'Poeziya Vyacheslava Ivanova', *Voprosy literatury*, 8 (1975), pp. 133–4.

115 Ashton-Ellis, *Richard Wagner's Prose Works*, II, pp. 254–5.

116 Ashton Ellis, *Richard Wagner's Prose Works*, II, pp. 254–5.

117 Ashton Ellis, *Richard Wagner's Prose Works*, II, p. 265.

118 K. Balmont, V. Ivanov, R. Ivnev, A. Kusikov, L. Nikulin, B. Pasternak, S. Rubanovich, I. Rukavishnikov, S. Tretyakov, V. Khlebnikov, V. Shershenevich, *My* (Moscow, 1920).

119 See Ivanov, *Sobranie sochinenii*, III, p. 737.

120 Two parts of his cycle 'Cor Ardens', for example, were headed 'Eros' and 'Love and Death'. See Ivanov, *Sobranie sochinenii*, II, pp. 223–533.

121 Ivanov, 'Natsional'noe i vselenskoe v tvorchestve Skryabina', in Mylnikova, 'Stat'i Vyach. Ivanova o Skryabine', *Pamyatniki kul'tury. Novye otkrytiya. Ezhegodnik 1983*, p. 99.

122 Ivanov, *Po zvezdam*, p. 204.

5 BELY, MEDTNER AND ELLIS

1 See Andrey Bely, *Na rubezhe dvukh stoletii* (Moscow-Leningrad, 1931), pp. 81, 182, 205, 208.

2 See S. A. Vengerov, *Russkaya literatura XX veka. 1890–1910* (Moscow, 1916), pp. 9–10.

3 Bely, *Na rubezhe dvukh stoletii*, p. 206.

4 Andrey Bely, *Nachalo veka* (Moscow-Leningrad, 1933), p. 4.

5 Bely, *Na rubezhe dvukh stoletii*, p. 183.

6 Andrey Bely, *Pochemu ya stal simvolistom i pochemu ya ne perestal im byt' vo vsekh fazakh moego ideinogo i khudozhestvennogo razvitiya* (Ann Arbor, 1982), p. 25.

7 Andrey Bely, 'Material k biografii (intimnyi), predznachennyi dlya izucheniya tol'ko posle smerta avtora' (1923), Central State Archive of Literature and Art, RGALI, *fond* 53, *op.* 2, *ed. khr.* 2, fol. 10.

8 Andrey Bely, 'Rakkurs dnevnika', cited in Roger Keys, 'Bely's Symphonies', in *Andrey Bely: Spirit of Symbolism*, ed. John E. Malmstad (Ithaca, 1987), p. 30.

9 Bely, *Na rubezhe dvukh stoletii*, p. 388.

10 Bely, *Na rubezhe dvukh stoletii*, p. 388.

11 References to *Tannhäuser* and *Lohengrin* in Bely's writings are very sparse indeed.

12 See Taneev, *Dnevniki*, II, pp. 372–4, 377–9, 381.

13 Bely, *Na rubezhe dvukh stoletii*, p. 28. Wagner makes no mention of Bugaev's libretto anywhere in his writings, but it is entirely plausible that he had indeed enthused about it. Buddhism was a subject of abiding interest for him, and he had himself written a sketch on a Buddhistic subject in 1856.

14 Anton Kovač, *Andrei Belyj: The 'Symphonies' (1899–1908). A Re-Evaluation of the Aesthetic-Philosophical Heritage* (Frankfurt/Munich, 1976), p. 54.

15 Bely, *Na rubezhe dvukh stoletii*, p. 389.

16 He had been composing poetry since 1895 and it is curious to note that amongst his unpreserved juvenilia was an incomplete long poem entitled 'Tristan', written in iambic pentameters. With no further information to hand, it is impossible to surmise what sort of a work this was and whether Wagner's *Tristan und Isolde* had anything to do with it.

17 Bely, *Nachalo veka*, p. 17.

18 Bely, *Nachalo veka*, p. 17.

19 Taneev, *Dnevniki*, II, p. 200.

20 See Keys, 'Bely's Symphonies', in Malmstad, *Spirit of Symbolism*, p. 20.

21 See Keys, 'Bely's Symphonies', Anton Kovač, *Andrej Belyj: 'The Symphonies'*, Ada Steinberg, *Word and Music in the Novels of Andrey Bely* (Cambridge, 1982) and Vladimir Alexandrov, *Andrei Bely:*

The Major Symbolist Fiction (Cambridge, Mass., 1985).

22 See A. V. Lavrov, 'Yunosheskie dnevnikovskie zametki Andreya Belogo', *Pamyatniki kul'tury. Novye otkrytiya na 1979* (Moscow, 1980), p. 135.

23 Schumann, Schubert, Haydn, Beethoven, Mozart, Tchaikovsky, Wagner, Brahms, Saint-Saëns and Skryabin are amongst the composers whose music he heard at the orchestral concerts he went to. See Bely, *Nachalo veka*, p. 130.

24 'Yunosheskie dnevnikovye zametki Andreya Belogo', cited in Keys, 'Bely's Symphonies', in Malmstad, *Spirit of Symbolism*, pp. 29–30.

25 See, for example, Gerald Janecek, 'Literature as Music: Symphonic Form in Andrey Belyi's *Fourth Symphony*', *Canadian-American Slavic Studies*, 8 (1974), pp. 501–12, Steinberg, *Word and Music Bely*, p. 35, and Kovač, *Andrei Belyj: The 'Symphonies'*.

26 E. [Emil Medtner], 'Simfonii Andreya Belogo', *Pridneprovskii krai*, 15 December 1903, p. 2.

27 Andrey Bely, *Mezhdu dvukh revolyutsii* (Leningrad, 1934), pp. 137–8.

28 Andrey Bely, 'O sebe kak pisatele', cited in Keys, 'Bely's Symphonies', in Malmstad, *Spirit of Symbolism*, p. 30.

29 Keys, 'Bely's Symphonies', in Malmstad, *Spirit of Symbolism*, p. 33.

30 Furness, *Wagner and Literature*, p. 7.

31 See Steinberg, *Word and Music*, p. 48.

32 See Keys, 'Bely's Symphonies', in Malmstad, *Spirit of Symbolism*, pp. 44–6 for a commentary on Bely's use of leitmotifs in these works.

33 See Steinberg, *Word and Music*, pp. 209–12 and pp. 238–44.

34 The German spelling of Medtner's name has been preferred here to the Russified version ('Emily Metner'); this was how he signed his copy of Bely's *Arabeski*, held at the Taylor Institution Library in Oxford.

35 See *N. K. Metner: Stat'i, materialy, vospominaniya*, ed. Z. A. Apetyan (Moscow, 1981), p. 297.

36 Bely, *Nachalo veka* p. 77.

37 Andrey Bely, 'Vospominaniya ob A. A. Bloke', *Epopeya*, 4 (1923), p. 82.

38 They thus did not meet at the concert itself, as A. V. Lavrov claims (See A. V. Lavrov, 'Andrey Bely: Khronologicheskaya kanva zhizni i tvorchestva', in *Andrey Bely, Problemy tvorchestva: Stat'i, vospominaniya, publikatsii*, ed. S. Lesnevsky and A. Mikhailov (Moscow, 1988), p. 776). Lavrov gives two possible dates for the meeting: 1 and 4 April. As Bely talks about Nikisch conducting a

Schubert symphony, it must have been the latter of the two dates, as no music by Schubert was performed at the concert of 1 April (See Taneev, *Dnevniki*, II, p. 422).

39 Andrey Bely, 'Nachalo veka. Vospominaniya. Tom Tretii, glavy 6–8, Berlinskaya redaktsiya (1922–23)', RGALI, *fond* 53, *op.* 1, *ed. khr.* 26, fol. 88. All subsequent references to 'Nachalo veka. B.R.', refer to chapters 6–8, except where otherwise stated.

40 Bely, *Nachalo veka*, p. 79.

41 See Bely, 'Vospominaniya ob A. A. Bloke', *Epopeya*, 4 (1923), p. 84 and Bely, *Nachalo veka*, p. 79.

42 Bely, 'Nachalo veka. B. R.', fol. 94.

43 Bely, *Nachalo veka*, p. 80.

44 Bely, 'Nachalo veka. B. R.', fols. 92–3.

45 See Bely, 'Vospominaniya ob A. A. Bloke', *Epopeya*, 4 (1923), p. 82.

46 See Georges Nivat, 'Histoire d'une 'tératogénèse' Biélyenne: Les rapports entre Emilij Medtner et Andrej Belyj', *Cahiers du Monde Russe et Soviétique*, 11 (1974), p. 94.

47 Bely, *Nachalo veka*, p. 25.

48 Bely, 'Nachalo veka. B. R.', fol. 85.

49 Bely, 'Material k biografii (intimnyi:)', fols. 31–2.

50 Bely, 'Nachalo veka. B. R.', fol. 96.

51 Bely, *Nachalo veka*, p. 83.

52 Bely, 'Nachalo veka. B. R.', fols. 96–7.

53 Bely, 'Nachalo veka. B. R.', fol. 98.

54 Bely, 'Nachalo veka. B. R.', fol. 88.

55 Bely, *Nachalo veka*, p. 87.

56 A. Bely, letter to E. K. Medtner, 24 January 1905. See *N. K. Metner: Stati'i, materialy, pis'ma*, ed. Z. A. Apetyan (Moscow, 1973), p. 69.

57 See Apetyan, *N. K. Metner: Stati*, p. 51.

58 Nikolay Medtner, letter to S. K. Saburova, 27 August 1912. See Apetyan, *N. K. Metner: Pis'ma*, pp. 134–5.

59 Bely, *Nachalo veka*, p. 77.

60 Bely, 'Nachalo veka. B. R.', fol. 93.

61 Bely, *Nachalo veka*, p. 86.

62 Bely, *Nachalo veka*, pp. 77–8.

63 Bely, 'Nachalo veka. B. R.', fol. 93.

64 *The Wibelungen* (1849) was the result of studies Wagner carried out into the link of myths with history when he was contemplating the creation of a drama based on Friedrich I, the prototype for Siegfried. The first Russian translation of this work was later published by Medtner in 1913.

65 Wotan in his mortal guise was Wälse or Wolf, hence his son
   Siegmund became the diminutive 'Wölfing'.
66 A German dynastic house, which ruled from 1138 to 1250.
67 The name 'Wibelung' denotes the Hohenstaufen dynastic house
   ('Waiblingen' was the name of a Hohenstaufen castle), as
   opposed to the 'Welfs', the rulers of Bavaria in the twelfth
   century. The Italians adopted these names in the thirteenth
   century, turning them into 'Ghibellini' and 'Guelphi' and applying them to their own political situation to denote pro- and
   anti-imperialists. The two houses were in conflict until the rule of
   Friedrich I 'Barbarossa' (1122–90), who was King of Germany
   from 1152, and a product of both dynasties through intermarry-
   ing. He tried to curtail Papal power in Germany and re-establish
   German power in Italy.
68 According to the legend, Friedrich I sits in the Kyffhäuser mountain in Thuringia, ready to come to Germany's aid in time of
   need.
69 Bely, 'Nachalo veka. B. R.', fol. 93.
70 Bely, 'Nachalo veka. B. R.', fol. 93. It need hardly be said that
   Medtner's political views were very reactionary indeed.
71 Boris Bugaev [Andrey Bely], 'Formy iskusstva', *Mir iskusstva*, 12
   (1902), pp. 343–61.
72 A. Bely, *Vospominaniya ob A. A. Bloke* (Letchworth, 1964),
   pp. 26–7.
73 See the 'kommentarii' in Andrey Bely, *Simvolizm. Kniga statei*
   (Moscow, 1910), pp. 519–20.
74 See Apetyan, *N. K. Metner: Stat'i*, p. 297.
75 Andrey Bely, *The Dramatic Symphony and The Forms of Art*, tr.
   Roger and Angela Keys and John Elsworth (Edinburgh, 1986),
   p. 165.
76 Bely, *The Dramatic Symphony and The Forms of Art*, p. 167.
77 Bely, *The Dramatic Symphony and The Forms of Art*, p. 181.
78 Bely, *The Dramatic Symphony and The Forms of Art*, p. 181.
79 *A. A. Blok–Andrei Bely: Perepiska*, ed. V. Orlov (Moscow, 1940),
   p. 3.
80 Bely, *The Dramatic Symphony and The Forms of Art*, p. 176.
81 Orlov, *Blok–Bely: Perepiska*, p. 3.
82 Merezhkovsky believed that art, via symbols, provided the sole
   means through which to perceive 'other worlds' and had thus
   turned all art into 'holy flesh', forgetting (or ignoring) its hellish
   side. Blok found this a contradiction in terms, as he saw art as
   necessarily part of the fallen world and the artist's task as the
   attempt to bring man back closer to God.

83 Orlov, *Blok–Bely: Perepiska*, p. 4.
84 Orlov, *Blok–Bely: Perepiska*, p. 8.
85 Orlov, *Blok–Bely: Perepiska*, p. 9.
86 See Orlov, *Blok–Bely: Perepiska*, p. 10.
87 See Orlov, *Blok–Bely: Perepiska*, p. 9.
88 Orlov, *Blok–Bely: Perepiska*, p. 10.
89 Bely, *Nachalo veka*, p. 111.
90 Bely, *Nachalo veka*, p. 111.
91 Bely, *Nachalo veka*, p. 111.
92 Bely, *Nachalo veka*, p. 307.
93 Bely, *Nachalo veka*, p. 307.
94 See, for example, his letters of 4 August, October–November 1904 and June and September 1905 (RGB, *fond* 167, *k.* 4, *ed. khr.* 42, 46, 54 and 61.)
95 E. Medtner, letter to A. Bely, 20 October 1903. See RGB, *fond* 167, *k.* 4, *ed. khr.* 23.
96 A. Bely, letter to E. Medtner, 29 December 1903. See RGB, *fond* 167, *k.* 1, *ed. khr.* 30.
97 RGB, *fond* 167, *k.* 4, *ed. khr.* 61.
98 See Bely, 'Nachalo veka. B. R.', fol. 94. See also Bely, *Nachalo veka*, p. 81.
99 Apart from a poem dedicated to Beethoven, and another entitled 'Minuet' (see A. Bely, *Stikhotvoreniya*, ed. J. Malmstad, 3 vols. (Munich, 1982–4), I, pp. 106–7, and pp. 136–7), none of Bely's early lyric verse has any obvious connection with musical form or musical concepts, Wagnerian or otherwise.
100 Bely, *Stikhotvoreniya*, I, pp. 231–2.
101 See Ernest Newman, *The Wagner Operas*, 2 vols. (New York, 1949), I, p. 120.
102 Bely, *Stikhotvoreniya*, I, pp. 183–4.
103 Bely, *Stikhotvoreniya*, I, p. 191.
104 For further poems featuring gnomes and giants possibly inspired by Wagner, see, for example, Bely, *Stikhotvoreniya*, I, pp. 175–80, 204–5, 213–17, 325 and II, pp. 62, 81–2, 204–10, 214, 221–3, and 229–30.
105 See Bely, *Stikhotvoreniya*, III, pp. 53–5 and 379–81.
106 Bely, *Nachalo veka*, p. 88.
107 Bely, 'Nachalo veka. B. R.', fol. 101.
108 Bely, *Nachalo veka*, p. 88.
109 Bely, 'Nachalo veka. B. R.', fol. 101.
110 Bely, *Nachalo veka*, p. 172.
111 Bely, *Nachalo veka*, p. 184.
112 Bely, *Nachalo veka*, p. 189.

113 Bely, *Nachalo veka*, p. 184.
114 For further details about this mystical ideal, see Avril Pyman, *The Life of Aleksandr Blok*, 2 vols. (Oxford, 1979–82), I, chapters 4–6.
115 See A. Bely, *Vospominaniya ob Aleksandre Bloke* (Letchworth, 1964), p. 145.
116 Bely, *Vospominaniya ob A. A. Bloke*, p. 145
117 Wagner's Russian audiences were of course not alone in perceiving the *Ring* as a politically charged work; George Bernard Shaw's famous sociological interpretation of the tetralogy, *The Perfect Wagnerite*, was published in 1898.
118 Bely maintains in his memoirs that they went to see *Die Walküre*, but that work was not performed during his visit. *Siegfried* was clearly the work they heard, particularly since Bely mentions its eponymous hero in the same breath (who of course does not appear in *Die Walküre*).
119 Bely, 'Vospominaniya ob A. A. Bloke', *Epopeya*, 2 (1922), pp. 275–6.
120 See Pyman, *The Life of Aleksandr Blok*, I, p. 224.
121 For Bely's account of their visit, see 'Vospominaniya ob A. A. Bloke', *Epopeya*, 2 (1922), pp. 240–65.
122 Bely, 'Vospominaniya ob A. A. Bloke', *Epopeya* 2 (1922), p. 249.
123 Bely, 'Vospominaniya ob A. A. Bloke', *Epopeya*, 2 (1922). p. 249.
124 Bely, *Mezhdu dvukh revolyutsii*, p. 22.
125 Bely, *Mezhdu dvukh revolyutsii*, p. 26.
126 Bely, *Mezhdu dvukh revolyutsii*, p. 23.
127 Bely, *Mezhdu dvukh revolyutsii*, p. 23.
128 Bely, *Mezhdu dvukh revolyutsii*, p. 26.
129 See Pyman, *The Life of Aleksandr Blok*, I, p. 225.
130 *Literaturnoe nasledstvo*, vol. 92 (Moscow, 1980–5), III, p. 239.
131 *Literaturnoe nasledstvo*, vol. 92, III, p. 239.
132 *Literaturno nasledstvo*, 92, III, p. 240.
133 Bely, *Mezhdu dvukh revolyutsii*, p. 107.
134 Bely, *Mezhdu dvukh revolyutsii*, p. 137.
135 Bely, *Mezhdu dvukh revolyutsii*, p. 138.
136 A. Bely, *Kubok metelei. Chetvertaya simfoniya* (Moscow, 1908), pp. 18–19.
137 Bely, *Nachalo veka*, p. 314.
138 Bely, *Kubok metelei*, pp. 19–20.
139 Bely, *Kubok metelei*, p. 28.
140 Bely, *Mezhdu dvukh revolyutsii*, p. 139.
141 Andrey Bely, 'Printsip formy v estetike. Pis'mo iz Myunkhena', *Zolotoe runo*, 11–12 (1906), p. 89.

142 Boris Bugaev, 'Protiv muzyki', *Vesy*, 3 (1907), pp. 57–60.
143 Bugaev, 'Protiv muzyki', p. 57.
144 Bugaev, 'Protiv muzyki', p. 58.
145 Bugaev, 'Protiv muzyki', p. 59.
146 Bugaev, 'Protiv muzyki', p. 59.
147 Bugaev, 'Protiv muzyki', pp. 59–60.
148 Bugaev, 'Protiv muzyki', p. 60.
149 Nivat, 'Histoire', p. 107.
150 Nivat, 'Histoire', p. 108.
151 Bely, 'Nachalo veka. B. R.', fol. 103.
152 Volfing [Emil Medtner], 'Boris Bugaev protiv muzyki', *Zolotoe runo*, 5 (1907), pp. 56–62.
153 Volfing, 'Boris Bugaev protiv muzyki', p. 58.
154 Volfing, 'Boris Bugaev protiv muzyki', p. 62.
155 B. Bugaev, 'Amicus Plato, magis amica veritas', *Pereval*, 10 (1907), pp. 58–60.
156 See Nivat, 'Histoire', p. 108.
157 Bely, 'Nachalo veka. B. R.', fols. 84–5. See also Bely, *Mezhdu dvukh revolyutsii*, p. 342.
158 Bely, 'Nachalo veka. B. R.', fol. 103.
159 Bely, 'Nachalo veka. B. R.', fol. 105.
160 Bely, *Mezhdu dvukh revolyutsii*, p. 345.
161 Bely, 'Nachalo veka. B. R.', fol. 105.
162 Zigmund [A. Bely], 'Chulkov. G. *Pokryvalo Izidy*. Kriticheskie ocherki (Moscow, 1909)', *Vesy*, 1 (1909), pp. 86–9.
163 Bely, *Mezhdu dvukh revolyutsii*, p. 343.
164 Bely, *Mezhdu dvukh revolyutsii*, p. 344.
165 Bely, *Mezhdu dvukh revolyutsii*, p. 343.
166 Bely, *Mezhdu dvukh revolyutsii*, p. 343.
167 Bely, *Nachalo veka*, p. 81.
168 The Turgeneva sisters were nieces of Maria Olenina. Asya was to become Bely's wife.
169 Bely, 'Nachalo veka. B. R.', fol. 127.
170 Bely, *Nachalo veka*, p. 81.
171 Bely, 'Nachalo veka. B. R.', fol. 105.
172 Bely, *Nachalo veka*, p. 84.
173 Bely, *Nachalo veka*, p. 78.
174 Bely, *Nachalo veka*, p. 78.
175 Bely, *Mezhdu dvukh revolyutsii*, p. 345.
176 Bely, *Nachalo veka*, p. 78.
177 Bely, 'Nachalo veka. B. R.', fol. 112.
178 Bely, *Nachalo veka*, p. 388.
179 Bely, *Nachalo veka*, p. 392.

180 Bely, *Nachalo veka*, p. 392.
181 Bely, 'Nachalo veka. B. R.', fol. 132.
182 Bely, See *Mezhdu dvukh revoluyutsii*, p. 343.
183 Bely, 'Nachalo veka. B. R.', fol. 126.
184 Bely, 'Nachalo veka. B. R.', fol. 112.
185 Bely, 'Nachalo veka. B. R.', fol. 112.
186 Margarita Morozova, 'Andrey Bely', in Lesnevsky and Mikhailov, *Andrey Bely: Problemy tvorchestva*, p. 529.
187 See the 1901 *Fremdenliste*, Richard-Wagner-Gedenkstätte der Stadt Bayreuth.
188 Bely, 'Vospominaniya ob A. A. Bloke', *Epopeya*, 4 (1923), p. 75.
189 For full details of Bely's relationship with Mintslova, see Maria Carlson, 'Ivanov–Belyj–Minclova: The Mystical Triangle', *Cultura e Memoria: Atti del terzo Simposio Internazionale dedicato a Vjaceslav Ivanov*, ed. Fausto Malcovati, 2 vols. (Florence, 1988), I, pp. 63–79.
190 Carlson, 'Ivanov–Belyj–Minclova', p. 70.
191 Bely, 'Nachalo veka. Berlinskaya redaktsiya', chapters 9–10 (1922–3), RGALI, *fond* 53, *op.* 1, *ed. khr.* 27, fol. 2.
192 Bely, 'Nachalo veka, Berlinskaya redaktsiya' (chapters 9–10), fol. 20.
193 Bely, 'Nachalo veka. Berlinskaya redaktsiya' (chapters 9–10), cited by Carlson, 'Ivanov–Belyj–Minclova', pp. 71–2.
194 Carlson, 'Ivanov–Belyj–Minclova', p. 72.
195 Carlson, 'Ivanov–Belyj–Minclova', p. 73.
196 Bely, 'Nachalo veka. Berlinskaya redaktsiya' (chapters 9–10), fols. 75–6.
197 Bely, 'Nachalo veka. Berlinskaya redaktsiya' (chapters 9–10), fol. 78.
198 Carlson, 'Ivanov–Belyj–Minclova', p. 73.
199 Bely, 'Nachalo veka. Berlinskaya redaktsiya' (chapters 9–10), fol. 76.
200 See A. V. Lavrov, 'Trudy i dni', *Russkaya kul'tura i zhurnalistika XX veka. 1905–1917: burzhuazno-liberalnye i modernistskie izdaniya*, ed. B. A. Byalik (Moscow, 1977), pp. 194–5 and Apetyan, *N. K. Metner: Pis'ma*, p. 125.
201 Bely, 'Nachalo veka. Berlinskaya redaktsiya' (chapters 9–10), fol. 89.
202 Bely, 'Nachalo veka. Berlinskaya redaktsiya' (chapters 9–10), fol. 91.
203 Bely, 'Nachalo veka. Berlinskaya redaktsiya' (chapters 9–10), fol. 89.
204 Bely, 'Nachalo veka. Berlinskaya redaktsiya' (chapters 9–10), fol. 89.

205 Emil Medtner, letter to L. Ellis, 26 August 1909, cited by Lavrov, 'Trudy i dni', p. 194.
206 A. Bely, letter to Emil Medtner, August/September 1909, RGB, *fond* 167, *k*. 2, *ed. khr*. 4.
207 A. Bely, letter to Emil Medtner, September 1909, RGB, *fond* 167, *k*. 2, *ed. khr*. 6.
208 A. Bely, letter to Emil Medtner, RGB, *fond* 167, *k*.2, *ed.khr*. 6.
209 See Lavrov, 'Trudy i dni', p. 193.
210 L. Ellis, *Russkie simvolisty* (Moscow, 1910), p. 336.
211 L. Ellis, letter to Emil Medtner, 9 July 1910, RGB, *fond* 167, *k*. 7, *ed. khr*. 24.
212 L. Ellis, letter to Emil Medtner, 9 July 1910, RGB, *fond* 167, *k*. 7, *ed. khr*. 24.
213 In 1907, he gave a lecture entitled 'Richard Wagner und die Mystik' (see *Die Drei. Monatschrift für Anthroposophie*, 10 (1929), pp. 713–31).
214 Colin Wilson, *Rudolf Steiner: The Man and His Vision* (Wellingborough, 1985) pp. 131–2.
215 R. Steiner, untitled lecture on *Parsifal* given at Laudin on 29 July 1905, (English translation) Rudolf Steiner House, London, p. 1.
216 Rudolf Steiner, lecture on *Parsifal*, p. 4.
217 Rudolf Steiner, lecture on *Parsifal*, p. 17.
218 Rudolf Steiner, lecture on *Parsifal*, p. 14.
219 L. Ellis, letter to Emil Medtner, autumn 1910, RGB, *fond* 167, *k*. 7, *ed. khr*. 26.
220 According to the legend, Monsalvat was the castle built to house the Grail. Kitezh is the mystical city in Rimsky-Korsakov's opera, *Skazanie o nevidimom grade Kitezhe i deve Fevronii*, often referred to as the Russian *Parsifal*. In 1913, *Musaget* published Sergey Durylin's *Vagner i Rossiya*, which compared the two works.
221 See Bely, 'Vospominaniya ob A. A. Bloke', *Epopeya*, 4 (1923), pp. 181–2.
222 A. Bely, *Putevye zametki* (Moscow-Berlin, 1922), pp. 48, 50.
223 Bely, *Putevye zametki*, cited in Boris Christa, *The Poetic World of Andrey Bely* (Amsterdam, 1977), p. 85.
224 See, for example, A. Bely, letter to A. Blok, end of November/beginning of December 1910, in Orlov, *A. A. Blok–Andrey Bely: Perepiska*, p. 243, and to A. D. Bugaeva, cited in S. D. Voronin, 'Iz pisem Andreya Belogo k materi', *Pamyatniki kul'tury: Novye otkrytiya. Ezhegodnik na 1986* (Leningrad, 1987), p. 71.
225 See Bely, *Putevye zametki*, pp. 58–9, 69–71.
226 Bely, *Putevye zametki*, p. 96.

227 Bely, *Putevye zametki*, p. 117.
228 A citation from Goethe's *Italienische Reise* (1816–17).
229 Bely, *Putevye zametki*, pp. 129–30.
230 Bely, *Putevye zametki*, p. 135.
231 See A. Bely, letter to Blok, end of May 1911, in Orlov, *A. A. Blok–Andrey Bely: Perepiska*, p. 257.
232 *Works and Days* was a principal work of Hesiod, one of the earliest Greek poets.
233 Lavrov, 'Trudy i dni', p. 197.
234 Andrey Bely, 'Orfey', *Trudy i dni*, 1 (1912), p. 67.
235 Andrey Bely 'O simvolizme', *Trudy i dni*, 2 (1912), p. 7.
236 Lavrov, 'Trudy i dni', p. 200.
237 See Volfing, 'Wagneriana', *Trudy i dni*, 4–5 (1912), p. 23.
238 See A. Losev, 'Problema Rikharda Vagnera v proshlom i nastoyashchem', *Voprosy estetiki*, 8 (1968), pp. 107–11.
239 Lavrov, 'Trudy i dni', p. 209.
240 See Losev, 'Problema Rikharda Vagnera', pp. 111–12.
241 Sergey Durylin, *Vagner i Rossiya* (Moscow, 1913), p. 66.
242 These three were all members of *Musaget*.
243 L. Ellis, letter to Medtner, 22 October 1911, RGB, *fond* 167, *k.* 7, *ed. khr.* 34.
244 This was possibly the lecture mentioned above which Steiner gave at Laudin on 29 July 1905.
245 See L. Ellis, letter to E. Medtner, 20 November 1911, RGB, *fond* 167, *k.* 7, *ed. khr.* 37.
246 The Zimin Theatre was privately run, and the implication is that its artistic standards were not of the highest order.
247 L. Ellis, letter to E. Medtner, 7 December 1911, RGB, *fond* 167, *k.* 7, *ed. khr.* 40.
248 L. Ellis, letter to E. Medtner, December 1911, RGB, *fond* 167, *k.* 7, *ed. khr.* 42.
249 L. Ellis, letter to E. Medtner, December 1911, RGB, *fond* 167, *k.* 7, *ed. khr.* 42.
250 L. Ellis, letter to E. Medtner, December 1911, RGB, *fond* 167, *k.* 7, *ed. khr.* 42.
251 L. Ellis, letter to E. Medtner, December 1911, RGB, *fond* 167, *k.* 7, *ed. khr.* 43.
252 L. Ellis, letter to E. Medtner, 5 February 1912, RGB, *fond* 167, *k.* 7, *ed. khr.* 51.
253 L. Ellis, letter to E. Medtner, 5 February 1912, RGB, *fond* 167, *k.* 7, *ed. khr.* 51.
254 L. Ellis, letter to E. Medtner, 13 February 1912, RGB, *fond* 167, *k.* 7, *ed. khr.* 54.

255 L. Ellis, letter to E. Medtner, 3 March 1912, RGB, *fond* 167, *k.* 7, *ed. khr.* 58.

256 L. Ellis, letter to E. Medtner, 3 March 1912, RGB, *fond* 167, *k.* 7, *ed. khr.* 58.

257 L. Ellis, letter to E. Medtner, 3 March 1912, RGB, *fond* 167, *k.* 7, *ed. khr.* 58.

258 L. Ellis, letter to E. Medtner, 6 May 1912, RGB, *fond* 167, *k.* 7, *ed. khr.* 59.

259 See Musaget catalogue, attachment to *Trudy i dni*, 1 (1912), p. 15.

260 Musaget catalogue, p. 15.

261 L. Ellis, letter to E. Medtner, 12 June 1912, RGB, *fond* 167, *k.* 7, *ed. khr.* 62.

262 L. Ellis, letter to E. Medtner, 17 June 1912, RGB, *fond* 167, *k.* 7, *ed. khr.* 63.

263 L. Ellis, letter to E. Medtner, 29 June 1912, RGB, *fond* 167, *k.* 7, *ed. khr.* 65.

264 L. Ellis, letter to E. Medtner, 4/17 August 1912, RGB, *fond* 167, *k.* 7, *ed. khr.* 68.

265 E. Medtner, letter to V. Ivanov, autumn 1912, cited by Lavrov, 'Trudy i dni', p. 205.

266 E. Medtner, letter to Bely and Ellis, 1/14 October 1912, cited by Lavrov, 'Trudy i dni', p. 205.

267 See Lavrov, 'Trudy i dni', p. 205.

268 See Ellis, 'Myunkhenskie pis'ma', *Trudy i dni*, 1, 4–5, (1912), pp. 46–50, 11, 6 (1912), pp. 49–62.

269 Ellis, 'Myunkhenskie pis'ma', 1, pp. 49–50.

270 Ellis, 'Myunkhenskie pis'ma', 1, pp. 58–9.

271 Ellis, 'Myunkhenskie pis'ma', 1, p. 59.

272 Ellis, 'Myunkhenskie pis'ma', 1, p. 59.

273 L. Ellis, letter to E. Medtner, 2 November 1912, RGB, *fond* 167, *k.* 7, *ed. khr.* 77.

274 L. Ellis, letter to E. Medtner, 2 November 1912, RGB, *fond* 167, *k.* 7, *ed. khr.* 77.

275 L. Ellis, letter to E. Medtner, 20 November 1912, RGB, *fond* 167, *k.* 7, *ed. khr.* 78.

276 L. Ellis, letter to E. Medtner, 22 November 1912, RGB, *fond* 167, *k.* 7, *ed. khr.* 79.

277 See John Malmstad, ed., 'Andrey Bely i Antroposofiya', *Minuvshee*, 6 (1988), p. 351.

278 See Ellis, *Vigilemus* (Moscow, 1914), and Malmstad, 'Andrey Bely i Antroposofiya', *Minuvshee*, 6 (1988), p. 357.

279 L. Ellis, letter to E. Medtner, 3 February 1914, RGB, *fond* 167, *k.* 8, *ed. khr.* 28.

280 After his departure for Italy in 1913, Ellis became a Jesuit priest and went to live in Locarno, Switzerland. In 1926, he published the first of a series of German translations and studies of Solovyov (Dr L. Kobilinski-Ellis, tr., *Gedichte W. Solowjews* (Mainz, 1926), *Monarchia St. Petri* (Mainz, 1929), *Christliche Weisheit (Sapienta Divina. Cosmologia perennis))* (Basel, 1929), *Der Heilige Wladimir und der Christliche Staat* (Paderborn, 1930)), which were followed by monographs on Zhukovsky and Pushkin in 1933 and 1948 respectively.

281 See *Bayreuther Blätter*, 1 (1932), pp. 21–8 and 2 (1932), pp. 94–108.

282 R. Vagner, *Vibelungi. Vsemirnaya istoriya na osnovanii skazanii*, tr. Sergey Shenrok, ed. and introd. E. Metner and M. Tsenker (Moscow, 1913), Richard-Wagner-Gedenkstätte der Stadt Bayreuth.

283 See Orlov, *A. A. Blok–Andrey Bely: Perepiska*, p. 295.

284 Orlov, *A. A. Blok–Andrey Bely: Perepiska*, p. 296.

285 Orlov, *A. A. Blok–Andrey Bely: Perepiska*, p. 298.

286 Bely, 'Nachalo veka. Berlinskaya redaktsiya' (chapters 9–10), fol. 249.

287 Orlov, *A. A. Blok–Andrey Bely: Perepiska*, p. 298.

288 Orlov, *A. A. Blok–Andrey Bely: Perepiska*, p. 298.

289 Malmstad, 'Andrey Bely i Antroposofiya', *Minuvshee*, 6 (1988), p. 355.

290 See Malmstad, 'Andrey Bely i Antroposofiya', *Minuvshee*, 6 (1988), pp. 363–5. The lectures (*'Christus und die geistige Welt'*) were given in Leipzig on 28–31 December 1913 and 1–2 January 1914.

291 Andrey Bely, *Na perevale*, (Berlin-Petersburg-Moscow, 1923), p. 149.

292 See Malmstad, 'Andrey Bely i Antroposofiya', *Minuvshee*, 6 (1988), p. 369.

293 See Malmstad, 'Andrey Bely i Antroposofiya', *Minuvshee* 6 (1988), p. 381.

294 See, for example, Bely, *Na perevale*, pp. 151 and 164, where Nietzsche is likened to Siegfried and Bismarck to Mime.

295 Andrey Bely, *Peterburg* ('Literaturnye Pamyatniki', Moscow, 1981), p. 62.

296 The 'Flying Dutchman' makes his first appearance in chapter 1. See Bely, *Peterburg*, p. 20.

297 See Andrey Bely, *Petersburg*, tr. Robert Maguire and John Malmstad (London, 1983), p. 304.

298 Bely, *Na perevale*, p. 141.

299 Andrey Bely, *Zapiski chudaka* (Moscow-Berlin, 1922), p. 82.
300 Bely, *Na perevale*, p. 62.
301 See, for example, Bely, *Na perevale*, pp. 140–2. Although, as we have seen, Bely tended to conflate the three major versions of the *Parsifal* legend, it is not appropriate to translate this as 'We wait for Parsifal' (See Rosenthal, 'Wagner and Wagnerian Ideas in Russia', p. 214) as he specifically uses de Troyes' spelling of 'Perceval'. Neither can 'Perceval' really be construed as the 'symbol of the poet's messianic hopes', for Anthroposophy was centred on the quest for individual self-knowledge.
302 Bely, *Na perevale*, p. 141.
303 Bely, *Na perevale*, p. 138.
304 Bely, *Na perevale*, p. 142.
305 Bely, *Na perevale*, p. 141.
306 See, for example, Bely, *Na perevale*, pp. 140–1.
307 G. S. Smith, 'Bely's Poetry and Verse Theory', in Malmstad, *Spirit of Symbolism*, p. 259.
308 Most of the other poems in the collection feature spear or sword-carrying knights, whilst 'Veshchii son' (1909), which would seem to be strongly linked to the cycle 'Starinnyi drug', contains images of *Götterdämmerung*-like conflagration. See Andrey Bely, *Stikhotvoreniya i poemy* (Moscow-Leningrad, 1966), pp. 353–4.
309 Malmstad, 'Andrey Bely i Antroposofiya', *Minuvshee*, 8 (1989), p. 420.
310 E. Metner [E. Medtner], *Razmyshleniya o Gete* (Moscow, 1914).
311 Froh tells Loge in Rheingold that he should be called 'not Loge but Lüge [lies]'. See Newman, *The Wagner Operas*, II, p. 465.
312 A. Bely, *Rudolf Shteiner i Gete v mirovozzrenii sovremennosti. Otvet Emiliyu Metneru na ego pervyi tom 'Razmyshleniya o Gete'* (Moscow, 1917), p. 271.
313 Medtner and Bely did not meet after their violent confrontation in Dornach in March 1915. Medtner remained in Zurich for the rest of his life, where he became a patient of Carl Jung. He embarked on a project to issue Jung's works in Russian in 1916, and the first of a projected four-volume series was published in 1929 under the name of *Musaget*, which Medtner obviously wished to revive. See K. Yung, *Psikhologicheskie tipy*, tr. S. A. Lorie; ed. and introd. E. K. Medtner (Zurich, 1929).
314 Also known as '*Istoriya stanovleniya samoznaniya dushi*'.
315 D. M. Pines, 'Literaturnoe nasledie A. Belogo: chernovyi avtograf', 28 January 1936. RGALI, *fond* 391, *op.* 1, *ed. khr.* 71.

316 Julia Crookenden, 'The chapter "Simvolizm" from Bely's "Istoriya stanovleniya samoznaiushchei dushi"', in *Andrey Bely Centenary Papers*, ed. Boris Christa (Amsterdam, 1980), p. 39.
317 D. M. Pines, 'Spisok proizvedenii Belogo unichtozhennye, propavshie, nenapechatennykh, sostavlenniyi Belym' (1927), RGALI, *fond* 391, *op.* 1, *ed. khr.* 67, fols. 6–10.
318 Andrey Bely, 'Istoria stanovleniya samoznaniya dushi: Chernovye nabroski i oglyavleniya knigi', RGALI, *fond* 53, *op.* 1, *ed. khr.* 71.
319 See Andrey Bely, '*Tablitsy i skhemy*', RGB, *fond* 25, *op.* 37, *ed. khr.* 1, fol. 1.
320 See Bely, '*Tablitsy i skhemy*', RGB, *fond* 25, *op.* 37, *ed. khr.* 1, fol. 2.
321 Crookenden, 'The chapter "Simvolizm"', p. 39.
322 See Bely, '*Tablitsy i skhemy*', RGB, *fond* 25, *op.* 37, *ed. khr.* 1, fol. 3.
323 See Bely, '*Tablitsy i skhemy*', RGB, *fond* 25, *op.* 37, *ed. khr.* 1, fol. 17.

6 ALEKSANDR BLOK

1 Irina Odoevtseva, *Na Beregakh Nevy* (Moscow, 1988), p. 172. See Avril Pyman, ed., *Aleksandr Blok: The Twelve* (Durham, 1989), pp. 21–33 for a discussion of this issue.
2 S. S. Grechishkin, A. V. Lavrov, 'Andrey Bely: Dnevnikovye zapisi', *Literaturnoe nasledstvo*, vol. 92, III, p. 800.
3 See Aleksandr Blok, *Sobranie sochinenii v vos'mi tomakh*, ed. V. N. Orlov *et al.* (Moscow-Leningrad, 1960–3), VII, p. 208.
4 See, for example, Blok, *Sobranie sochinenii*, III, p. 422 and E. P. Ivanov, 'Zapisi ob Aleksandre Bloke', *Blokovskii sbornik* (Tartu, 1964), pp. 389–90.
5 See *Literaturnoe nasledstvo*, vol. 92, III, p. 415. In June 1912, Blok used this phrase in his diary (see Blok, *Sobranie sochinenii*, VII, p. 150).
6 See VIII, p. 312.
7 See M. A. Beketova, ed., *Pis'ma Aleksandra Bloka k rodnym* (Leningrad, 1927–32), II, p. 429.
8 Evgeniya Knipovich, *Ob Aleksandre Bloke* (Moscow, 1987) p. 57.
9 See M. Shaginyan, 'Chetyre pis'ma Aleksandra Bloka', *Znamya*, 11 (1955), p. 191.
10 See N. S. Gumilyov, *Pis'ma o russkoi poezii*, ed. G. M. Fridlender and R. D. Timenchik (Moscow, 1990), p. 317 and Olga Forsh, *Sumashedshii korabl'* (Leningrad, 1988), p. 89.
11 Some critics have suggested that the inspiration for '*V zharkoi plyaske vakkhanalii*', an early poem of 1898 (See Blok, *Sobranie*

sochinenii, i, p. 373), was furnished by the opening *Bacchanale* from Wagner's *Tannhäuser* (see Rolf-Dieter Kluge, *Westeuropa und Russland im Weltbilds Aleksandr Bloks* (Munich, 1967), p. 89, and Robert P. Hughes, 'Nothung, The Cassia Flower and a "Spirit of Music" in the Poetry of Aleksandr Blok', *California Slavic Studies*, 6 (1971), p. 52). If that supposition is correct (and it is not implausible), then it would appear to be the first occasion on which Wagner exerted an influence on Blok's creative work. *Tannhäuser* had not been performed in St Petersburg (either in the concert hall and in the opera house) since the 1896–7 season, however, and was not a work that Blok was particularly captivated by.

12 See Blok, *Sobranie sochinenii*, i, pp. 349–50.
13 See D. M. Magomedova, 'Blok i Vagner', *Zbornik Radova Insituta za strane Jesike i knjizevnosti*, 6 (1984), p. 195.
14 See *Biblioteka A. A. Bloka*, ed. K. P. Lukivskaya, 3 vols. (Leningrad, 1984–6), i, p. 117 and iii, p. 158.
15 A. Blok, *Zapisnye knizhki*, ed. V. N. Orlov (Moscow, 1965), p. 210.
16 See Blok, *Sobranie sochinenii*, i, p. 465.
17 See *Literaturnoe nasledstvo*, vol. 78, *A. Blok: pis'ma k zhene* (Moscow, 1978), p. 142.
18 *Die Walküre* was performed on 24, 27 and 30 November and 8, 13, 21, 26 December 1900, as well as three times in early 1901 and five times in early 1902.
19 See Lyubov Mendeleeva-Blok, 'Facts and Myths about Blok and Myself', *Blok: An Anthology of Essays and Memoirs*, ed. and tr. Lucy Vogel (Ann Arbor, 1982), p. 23.
20 See Robert Donington, *Wagner's 'Ring' and its Symbols* (London, 1963), p. 142.
21 'I was born in the Middle Ages', Blok once claimed in his notebooks (see Blok, *Zapisnye knizhki*, p. 173).
22 See Blok, *Sobranie sochinenii*, i, p. 70.
23 See Ashton-Ellis, *Richard Wagner's Prose Works*, vii, p. 289.
24 V. S. Solovyov, *Stikhotvoreniya i shutochnye p'esy*, ed. Z. A. Mints (Moscow-Leningrad, 1974), pp. 136–7.
25 'The Bronze Sings as it Turns Red' (*Poet, krasneya, med*). See Blok, *Sobranie sochinenii*, ii, p. 42.
26 See Blok, *Sobranie sochinenii*, i, p. 540.
27 'Noch' (November 1904). See Blok, *Sobranie sochinenii*, ii, p. 48.
28 'Svet v okoshke shatalsya'. See Blok, *Sobranie sochinenii*, i, p. 210.
29 See Blok, *Sobranie sochinenii*, ii, pp. 67–8.
30 Magomedova, 'Blok i Vagner', p. 200.
31 See Blok, *Sobranie sochinenii*, ii, p. 333.
32 See Blok, *Sobranie sochinenii*, ii, pp. 232–4.

33 See Blok, *Sobranie sochinenii*, II, p. 429.
34 See Blok, *Sobranie sochinenii*, II, p. 260.
35 This is perhaps a reference to the 'gleissende Wurm' Hunding sees in both Siegmund's and Sieglinde's eyes, and which points to their kinship, as Brünnhilde was, after all, also a child of Wotan.
36 See Blok, *Sobranie sochinenii*, II, pp. 429-30.
37 See Knipovich, *Ob Aleksandre Bloke*, p. 95.
38 See Blok, *Sobranie sochinenii*, v, p. 687.
39 Knipovich, *Ob Aleksandre Bloke*, p. 94.
40 Knipovich, *Ob Aleksandre Bloke*, p. 97.
41 See, for example, 'Zaklyatie ognem i mrakom', Blok, *Sobranie sochinenii*, II, p. 272.
42 See 'Rus', written in September 1906 (Blok, *Sobranie sochinenii*, II, p. 106). See also Pyman, *The Life of Aleksandr Blok*, I, p. 212.
43 See Blok, *Sobranie sochinenii*, v, p. 458.
44 A. P. Ivanov, 'Loge i Zigfrid', *Mir iskusstva*, 4 (1904), pp. 128-45.
45 Magomedova, 'Blok i Vagner', pp. 201-2.
46 Although Blok somewhat feared Medtner, he wrote to Bely in June 1911: 'I deeply respect, value and feel a secret affection for E. K. Medtner (*Wölfing*)'. See Blok, *Sobranie sochinenii*, VIII, p. 345.
47 See Knipovich, *Ob Aleksandre Bloke*, p. 97.
48 See Blok, *Sobranie sochinenii*, II, pp. 153-4.
49 See Blok, *Sobranie sochinenii*, II, pp. 252-3.
50 Knipovich, *Ob Aleksandre Bloke*, p. 96.
51 Blok, *Sobranie sochinenii*, v, p. 427.
52 Knipovich, *Ob Aleksandre Bloke*, pp. 101-2.
53 Blok, *Sobranie sochinenii*, v, p. 431.
54 Blok, *Sobranie sochinenii*, v, p. 435.
55 See Blok, *Sobranie sochinenii*, III, p. 301.
56 Blok, *Sobranie sochinenii*, III, p. 302.
57 Knipovich, *Ob Aleksandre Bloke*, p. 94.
58 See Boris Solovyov, *Poet i ego podvig* (Moscow, 1964), pp. 418-22 and Hughes, 'Nothung, the Cassia Flower', pp. 49-50.
59 See *Literaturnoe nasledstvo*, vol. 92, III, p. 355.
60 See Beketova, *Pis'ma Aleksandra Bloka k rodnym*, ii, pp. 284-5.
61 Blok, *Sobranie sochinenii*, III, pp. 29-30.
62 James Forsyth, *Listening to the Wind: An Introduction to Aleksandr Blok* (Oxford, 1977), p. 71.
63 Solovyov, *Poet i ego podvig*, p. 612.
64 See S. Burago (who also makes a link with *Tannhäuser*), 'Blok i Vagner', *Izvestiya Akademiya Nauk*, 6 (1984), pp. 525-9.
65 Pyman, *The Life of Aleksandr Blok*, II, p. 201.

66 See Blok, *Sobranie sochinenii*, III, p. 95. Cited in Pyman, *The Life of Aleksandr Blok*, II, p. 200.

67 Magomedova, 'Blok i Vagner', p. 217.

68 See Mike Ashman, 'A Very Human Epic', *Parsifal*, Opera Guide 34 (London, 1986), pp. 7–14.

69 Solovyov, *Poet i ego podvig*, p. 613.

70 See Bely, *Vospominaniya ob A. A. Bloke*, p. 86.

71 Knipovich, *Ob Aleksandre Bloke*, p. 107.

72 *Poet i ego podvig*, p. 689.

73 iii, p. 351.

74 Lukivskaya, *Biblioteka A. A. Bloka*, I, p. 117.

75 Viktor Zhirmunsky, *Drama Aleksandra Bloka 'Roza i krest'* (Leningrad, 1964), p. 17.

76 Magomedova, 'Blok i Vagner', p. 207.

77 Lukivskaya, *Biblioteka A. A. Bloka*, I, p. 119 (subsequent references to Blok's underlinings in *Opera i drama* are cited from this page).

78 Lukivskaya, *Biblioteka A. A. Bloka*, I, p. 119.

79 Richard Wagner, *Oper und Drama*, ed. Klaus Kropfinger (Stuttgart, 1984), p. 149.

80 See, for example, A. Blok, 'Literaturnye itogi 1907 goda', in Blok, *Sobranie sochinenii*, V, pp. 209–32.

81 See Knipovich, *Ob Aleksandre Bloke*, p. 106.

82 Blok, *Sobranie sochinenii*, V, p. 95.

83 Blok, *Sobranie sochinenii*, V, p. 263.

84 Blok, *Sobranie sochinenii*, V, pp. 263–4.

85 Blok describes theatre as the 'flesh' of art.

86 Blok, *Sobranie sochinenii*, V, p. 270. The allusion to the lost hero, of course, relates to the beginning of the third act of *Götterdämmerung*, where Siegfried becomes separated from the hunting party and is shortly, by his own death, to cause the destruction of Valhalla.

87 See Viktor Zhirmunsky, *Drama Aleksandra Bloka 'Roza i krest'*, pp. 18–19.

88 R. D. B. Thomson, 'The Non-Literary Sources of "Roza i krest"', *Slavonic Review*, 45 (1967), p. 296.

89 Hughes, 'Nothung, the Cassia Flower', pp. 53–4.

90 Blok, *Zapisnye knizhki*, p. 286.

91 See Stewart Spencer, 'Language and Sources of the "Ring"', *The Rhinegold*, Opera Guide 35, ed. N. John (London, 1985), p. 31.

92 Zhirmunsky, *Drama Aleksandra Bloka*, p. 16.

93 See Pavel Medvedev, *Dramy i poemy Al. Bloka* (Leningrad, 1928), pp. 157–60.

94 See Blok, *Sobranie sochinenii*, VII, p. 173.

95 See Blok, *Sobranie sochinenii*, VII, p. 163.

96 See S. Burago, *Aleksandr Blok* (Kiev, 1981), p. 178.
97 See Blok, *Sobranie sochinenii*, VII, p. 244.
98 Blok, *Sobranie sochinenii*, VII, p. 244.

7 RECEPTION AND PERFORMANCE HISTORY, 1917–1941

1 Flora Syrkina, 'Tatlin's Theatre' in Larisa Zhadova *et al.*, *Tatlin* (London, 1988), p. 160.
2 Mikhail Kolesnikov, 'The Russian Avant-Garde and the Theatre of the Artist', in *Theatre in Revolution: Russian Avant-Garde Stage Design 1913–35*, ed. Nancy Van Norman Baer (London, 1991), p. 85.
3 See Kolesnikov, *Theatre in Revolution*, p. 86. and Christina Lodder, *Russian Constructivism* (New Haven, 1983), pp. 55–67.
4 Byl Vagner nam i vam rodnoi
Zachto emu ot nas obida?
Tryakhnite miloi starinoi
I vozvratite nam Zigfrida!
See S. Levik, *Chetverk veka v opere* (Moscow, 1970), p. 166.
5 See V. Karatygin, 'Vagneriana', *Nash vek*, 65 (1918), p. 4.
6 See V. Karatygin, '"Val'kiriya"', *Nash vek*, 85 (1918), p. 4.
7 [Anon], 'Teatr i muzyka', *Izvestiya*, 6 September 1918, p. 8.
8 See A. Gozenpud, *Russkii sovetskii opernyi teatr (1917–41)* (Leningrad, 1963), p. 33.
9 Theodore Komisarjevsky, *Myself and the Theatre* (London, 1929), pp. 143–4.
10 A. Z. Yufit, ed., *Sovetskii teatr: dokumenty i materialy. Russkii sovetskii teatr 1917–1921* (Leningrad, 1978), p. 89.
11 The same fate evidently befell the proposed production at the former Mariinsky Theatre (see V. Kolomiitsov, 'O "Parsifale" (k namechennoi postanovke dramy-misterii Vagnera v Mariinskom teatre)', *Biryuch Petrogradskikh gosudarstvennikh teatrov*, 7 (1918), p. 20).
12 See E. Grosheva, *Bol'shoi Teatr Soyuza S.S.S.R* (Moscow, 1978), p. 71.
13 Of these seven (*Rienzi*, *Tannhäuser*, the four parts of the *Ring* and *Tristan und Isolde*), only *Rienzi*, *Tannhäuser* and *Siegfried* took place (in 1923). See G. Y. Yudin, ed., *Emil Kuper: Stat'i, vospominaniya, materialy* (Moscow, 1988), p. 51.
14 See Yudin, *Emil Kuper*, p. 52. The members of this commission, apart from Kuper, included Glazunov, Benois, Golovin and Dobuzhinsky.

15 See Yudin, *Emil Kuper*, p. 66.
16 See Yudin, *Emil Kuper*, p. 52.
17 Boris Schwarz, *Music and Musical Life in Soviet Russia*, enlarged edition (Indiana, 1983), p. 27.
18 A. Lunacharsky, '[Eshche] ob iskusstve i revolyutsii', *Obrazovanie*, 12 (1906). p. 139.
19 A. Lunacharsky, 'Yunosheskie idealy Rikharda Vagnera', *Pravda*, 4 (1906), pp. 137–56.
20 See *Literaturnoe nasledie G. V. Plekhanova*, ed. A. V. Lunacharsky, 8 vols. (Moscow, 1934–40), III, pp. 199–200, 205–6.
21 A. Lunacharsky, 'Dlya chego my sokhranyaem Bolshoi teatr?', *O teatre* (Moscow, 1925), reprinted in A. V. Lunacharsky, *V mire muzyki*, ed. G. Bernandt and I. A. Sats (Moscow, 1958), p. 903.
22 Rikhard Vagner, *Iskusstvo i revolyutsiya*, tr. I. M. Katsenelenbogen (Petrograd, 1918).
23 See Lars Kleberg, '"People's Theater" and the Revolution' in *Art, Society and Revolution. Russia 1917–1921*, ed. N. A. Nilsson (Stockholm, 1979), p. 189.
24 R. Rollan, *Narodnyi teatr* (Petrograd-Moscow, 1919).
25 P. Kerzhentsev, *Tvorcheskii teatr* (Moscow, 1918).
26 See Kleberg, '"People's Theater"', pp. 189–91.
27 P. Kerzhentsev, *Tvorcheskii teatr*, 3rd edn (Moscow, 1919), p. 37.
28 Kerzhentsev, *Tvorcheskii teatr*, 3rd edn, p. 58.
29 Kerzhentsev, *Tvorcheskii teatr*, 3rd edn, p. 35.
30 See Lars Kleberg, 'Vyacheslav Ivanov and the Idea of Theater', *Theater and Literature in Russia, 1900–1930*, ed. N. A. Nilsson (Stockholm, 1984), pp. 57–70.
31 See V. I. Ivanov, 'K voprosu ob organizatsii tvorcheskikh sil narodnogo kollektiva v oblasti khudozhestvennogo deistva', *Vestnik teatra*, 26 (1919), p. 4.
32 Ivanov, 'K voprosu ob organizatsii tvorcheskikh sil', p. 4.
33 V. I. Ivanov, 'O Vagnere', *Vestnik teatra*, 31–2 (1919), pp. 2–3.
34 Ivanov, 'O Vagnere', p. 2.
35 Ivanov, 'O Vagnere', p. 3.
36 Ivanov, 'O Vagnere', p. 3.
37 Ivanov, 'O Vagnere', p. 2.
38 Ivanov, 'O Vagnere', p. 2.
39 Ivanov, 'O Vagnere', p. 3.
40 Ivanov, 'O Vagnere', p. 3.
41 See John Elsworth, *Andrey Bely: A Critical Study of the Novels* (Cambridge, 1983), p. 47.
42 Andrey Bely, *Revolyutsiya i kul'tura* (Moscow, 1917), p. 11.
43 Bely, *Revolyutsiya i kul'tura*, p. 11.

44 Bely, *Revolyutsiya i kul'tura*, p. 11.

45 Knipovich, *Ob Aleksandre Bloke*, p. 106.

46 See T. Khoprova and M. Dunaevsky, *Blok i muzyka* (Leningrad, 1980), p. 118. In the end they decided to publish the old version, however, and Blok's article finally appeared in *Zhizn' iskusstva* in August 1919. See Blok, *Sobranie sochinenii*, VI, pp. 24–5.

47 J. Forsyth argues that Blok's antithesis of 'culture' and 'civilisation' was inspired by Houston Stewart Chamberlain rather than Wagner (see his 'Prophets and Supermen: German Ideological Influences on Aleksandr Blok's Poetry', *Forum for Modern Language Studies*, 1 (1977), p. 41) but Blok's concept of 'culture' nevertheless clearly has much in common with Wagner's concept of 'nature', which, like Blok, he identifies with the common people, and the future 'free manhood of art'.

48 See Lukivskaya, *Biblioteka A. Bloka*, 1, p. 119.

49 L. L. Sabaneev, 'Rikhard Vagner. Ocherk', RGALI, *fond* 611, *op.* 1, *ed. khr.* 26, fols. 1–2.

50 See A. Gvozdev, A. Piotrovsky, 'Massovye prazdnestva' in V. Rafalovich, ed., *Istoriya sovetskogo teatra* (Leningrad, 1933), pp. 264–90.

51 See Huntly Carter, *The New Spirit in the Russian Theatre 1917–1928* (London, 1929), pp. 138–9.

52 Robert C. Williams, *Artists in Revolution: Portraits of the Russian Avant Garde, 1905–1925* (Indiana, 1977), p. 5.

53 See James von Geldern, *Bolshevik Festivals* (Berkeley, 1993).

54 Von Geldern, *Bolshevik Festivals*, p. 30.

55 See V. Shklovsky, 'Soglashateli', *Zhizn' iskusstva*, 430 (1920), cited in D. Zolotnitsky, *Zori teatral'nogo Oktyabrya* (Leningrad, 1976), p. 316.

56 See Von Geldern, *Bolshevik Festivals*, p. 80.

57 Gvozdev, Piotrovsky, 'Massovye prazdnestva', p. 270.

58 Von Geldern, *Bolshevik Festivals*, p. 189.

59 See *Petrogradskaya pravda*, 21 July 1920, cited in L. Polyakova, 'Vagner i Rossiya', *O Vagnere*, ed. L. Polyakova (Moscow, 1987), pp. 27–8.

60 See Yudin, *Emil Kuper*, p. 5.

61 S. Dreiden, *V zritel'nom zale – V. I. Lenin, novye stranitsy* (Moscow, 1970), p. 233.

62 Dreiden, *V zritel'nom zale*, p. 233.

63 See Dreiden, *V zritel'nom zale*, pp. 234–43.

64 E. Vakhtangov, 'S khudozhnika sprositsya' (March 1919), cited in N. M. Vakhtangova *et al.*, eds., *Vakhtangov: Zapiski, pis'ma, stat'i* (Moscow, 1939), p. 201.

65 See Polyakova, 'Vagner i Rossiya', p. 35.
66 For further information about Tairov's ideas about the theatre, see Nick Worrall, *From Modernism to Realism on the Soviet Stage: Tairov, Vakhtangov, Okhlopkov* (Cambridge, 1989), p. 35.
67 Robert Leach, *Vsevolod Meyerhold*, Cambridge, 1989, p. 17.
68 See *V. E. Meierkhold: stat'i, pis'ma, rechi, besedy*, ed. A. V. Fevralsky, 2 vols. (Moscow, 1968), II, p. 48.
69 See A. Z. Yufit, *Sovetskii teatr: dokumenty i materialy, 1917–1921* (Leningrad, 1968), p. 156.
70 See M. Mestechkin, *V teatre i v tsirke* (Moscow, 1976), p. 30.
71 See Marsily, '"Rientsi"', *Vestnik teatra*, 93–4 (1921), p. 18.
72 A. Lunacharsky, 'Teatr RSFSR', *Pechat' i revolutsiya*, 7 (1922), reprinted in A. V. Lunacharsky, *Sobranie sochinenii v 8 tomakh*, ed. I. I. Anisimov (Moscow, 1963–7) VIII, p. 508.
73 See A. Trabsky, ed., *Sovetskii teatr: Dokumenty i materialy. Russkii sovetskii teatr, 1921–1926* (Leningrad, 1975), pp. 287–8.
74 Trabsky, *Russkii sovetskii teatr, 1921–26*, p. 300.
75 See B. Asafiev, *Ob opere: izbrannye stat'i*, ed. L. A. Pavlova-Arbenina (Leningrad, 1976), p. 236.
76 See Asafiev, *Ob opere*, p. 236, and V. Karatygin, '"Rientsi"', *Zhizn' iskusstva*, 46 (1923), pp. 12–13.
77 See Trabsky, *Russkii sovetskii teatr 1921–26*, pp. 112–13.
78 See Trabsky, *Russkii sovetskii teatr, 1921–26*, p. 112.
79 See Gozenpud, *Russkii sovetskii opernyi teatr*, p. 60.
80 See N. Gilyarovskaya, *F. F. Fyodorovsky* (Moscow, 1946), pp. 64–7.
81 See Trabsky, *Russkii sovetskii teatr 1921–26*, p. 107.
82 Carter, *The New Spirit in the Russian Theatre*, pp. 170–1.
83 Carter, *The New Spirit in the Russian Theatre*, p. 171.
84 Nikolai Semashko 'Nado podderzhat'', *Izvestiya*, 11 May (1923), cited in Trabsky, *Russkii sovetskii teatr 1921–26*, p. 117.
85 See Y. Sakhnovsky, 'Itogy moskovskogo opernogo sezona', *Izvestiya*, 22 April (1923), cited in Trabsky, *Russkii sovetskii teatr 1921–26*, p. 117.
86 Boris Gusman, '"Loengrin" v Bol'shom teatre', *Pravda*, 1 April (1923), p. 6.
87 Khrisanf Khersonsky, '"Loengrin" v Bol'shom teatre', *Izvestiya*, 1 April (1923), p. 5.
88 See L. Sabaneev, 'Teatr i muzyka', *Pravda*, 17 April, 1923, p. 4.
89 See L. Sabaneev, '"Rientsi" v teatre Zimina', *Teatr i muzyka*, 8 (1923), p. 719.
90 S. Ch [Sergey Chemodanov], '"Rientsi" Vagnera', *Muzykal'naya nov'*, 1 (1923), pp. 33–4.

91 O. Litovsky, '"Rientsi" u Zimina', *Izvestiya*, 5 April 1923, p. 4.
92 See Nicoletta Misler, 'Designing Gestures in the Laboratory of Dance', in Baer, *Theatre in Revolution*, p. 161.
93 Carter, *The New Spirit in the Russian Theatre*, p. 144.
94 John Bowlt, 'The Construction of Caprice: The Russian Avant-Garde Onstage', in Baer, *Theatre in Revolution*, p. 66.
95 See R. Fülop-Miller and J. Gregor, *The Russian Theatre* (London, 1930), p. 118.
96 Bowlt, 'The Construction of Caprice', p. 80.
97 See Trabsky, *Russkii sovetskii teatr 1921–26*, p. 69
98 See Trabsky, *Russkii sovetskii teatr 1921–26*, pp. 73–4.
99 See Trabsky, *Russkii sovetskii teatr 1921–26*, pp. 93–5.
100 See Trabsky, *Russkii sovetskii teatr 1921–26*, p. 295.
101 Trabsky, *Russkii sovetskii teatr 1921–26*, p. 298.
102 Trabsky, *Russkii sovetskii teatr 1921–26*, p. 304.
103 See S. K. Khvorostin, 'Stranichka iz muzykal'noi zhizni Leningrada (Obshchestvo Vagnerovskogo iskusstva)', *Iz proshlogo sovetskoi muzykal'noi kul'tury* (Moscow, 1982), p. 231.
104 Khvorostin, 'Stranichka iz muzykal'noi zhizni Leningrada', p. 232.
105 Khvorostin, 'Stranichka iz muzykal'noi zhizni Leningrada', p. 233.
106 A model of the set was published in *Zrelishche*, 86 (1924), p. 7.
107 Lunacharsky, *V mire muzyki*, p. 305.
108 See Elizabeth Souritz, 'Constructivism and Dance', in Baer, *Theatre in Revolution*, p. 135.
109 E. Braudo, '"Val'kiriya" v Bol'shom teatre', *Pravda*, 9 December 1925, p. 8.
110 See V. Rudenko, *V. Suk* (Moscow, 1984), p. 212.
111 See Asafiev, *Ob opere*, pp. 242–5.
112 L. Sabaneev, '"Val'kiriya"', *Izvestiya*, 9 December (1925), p. 7.
113 See Trabsky, *Russkii sovetskii teatr 1921–26*, p. 304.
114 See V. Rappaport, '"Meisterzingery"', *Teatry i zrelishche*, supplement to *Zhizn' iskusstva*, 45 (1926), p. 1.
115 See, for example, N. Malkov, '"Nyurenbergskie mastera peniya"', *Zhizn' iskusstva*, 46 (1926), pp. 13–14.
116 See Trabsky, *Russkii sovetskii teatr 1921–26*, p. 300.
117 A. Ber, 'V oppozitsii protiv Vagnera', *Zhizn' iskusstva*, 50 (1924), p. 6.
118 Nikolay Malkov, 'Music and the Cultural Revolution', *Zhizn' iskusstva* 45, 6 November 1927, pp. 29–31, cited in William G. Rosenberg, ed., *Bolshevik Visions: First Phase of the Cultural Revolution in Soviet Russia*, (Ann Arbor, 1984), p. 466.

119 'Iz protokola no. 17. Zasedaniya organizatsionno-repertuarnoi kommissii khudozhestvennogo soveta Bol'shogo Teatra', in *Russkii sovetskii teatr 1926–1932*, ed. A. Trabsky (Leningrad, 1982) p. 112.

120 See E. Braudo, '"Meisterzingery"', *Sovremennyi teatr*, 4 (1929), p. 55.

121 See Grosheva, *Bol'shoi teatr*, p. 109.

122 [Anon], 'Tserkovniki i chastniki pod sovetskoi markoi', *Smena*, 5 March (1930), p. 5.

123 See Nancy Van Norman Baer, 'Design and Movement in the Theatre of the Russian Avant-Garde', in Baer, *Theatre in Revolution*, pp. 42–3.

124 See D. E. Gorbachev, *Oleksandr Khvostenko-Khvostov* (Kiev, 1987), pp. 50–3.

125 See Gorbachev, *Khvostenko-Khvostov*, pp. 68–9.

126 See Gozenpud, *Russkii sovetskii operny teatr*, pp. 245–6.

127 See *Leningradskii Gos. Ordena Lenina Akademicheskii Maly Operny Teatr*, ed I. V. Golubovsky (Leningrad, 1961), p. 28.

128 See R. Gruber, '"Zoloto Reina" v Leningrade', *Sovetskaya muzyka*, 3 (1933), p. 165.

129 See F. Syrkina *et al.*, eds., *Khudozhniki teatra o svoem tvorchestve* (Moscow, 1973), pp. 226–7 for further details.

130 See Gozenpud, *Russkii sovetskii opernyi teatr*, p. 246.

131 See Gruber, '"Zoloto Reina" v Leningrade', pp. 165–70.

132 R. Vagner, *Izbrannye stat'i* (Moscow, 1934).

133 R. Gruber, *Rikhard Vagner* (Moscow, 1934).

134 *Rabochii i teatr*, 4–5 (1933) contained articles by I. Sollertinsky, A. Piotrovsky, N. Malkov, B. Mazing, I. Ershov and G. Orlov. *Sovetskoe iskusstvo*, 7 (1933) featured articles by R. Gruber, M. Druskin, N. Volkov and S. Lapitsky.

135 Igor Glebow [Boris Asafiev], 'Wagner Heute', *Anbruch*, 1 (1933), pp. 26–7.

136 A. Lunacharsky, 'Put' Rikharda Vagnera', *Izvestiya*, 43 (1933), p. 2.

137 A. Lunacharsky, 'R. Vagner', *Sovetskaya muzyka*, 3 (1933), pp. 1–6.

138 Lunacharsky, 'R. Vagner', p. 4.

139 Lunacharsky, *Sobranie sochinenii*, VIII, p. 508.

140 Yury Elagin, *Ukroshchenie iskusstv*, 2nd edn (Tenafly, New Jersey, 1988), p 294.

141 See J. A. E. Curtis, *Manuscripts Don't Burn: Mikhail Bulgakov, A Life in Letters and Diaries* (London, 1991), p. 192. In 1926, Mikhail Bulgakov made some autobiographical notes for his friend Pavel Popov in which he declared a need to listen to music

as one of his 'characteristics': 'I could say that I worship good
music. It's very conducive to creative work. I am very fond of
Wagner. Best of all I like a symphony orchestra with trumpets'
(Curtis, *Manuscripts Don't Burn*, p. 79).

142 D. Gachev, 'Nasledstvo Vagnera', *Izvestiya*, 17 September
(1937), p. 3.
143 Gachev, 'Nasledstvo Vagnera', p. 3.
144 One concert took place in January 1938, and four in May 1938.
145 A. A. Alshvang, 'Rikhard Vagner: k 125-letiyu so dnya rozhdeniya', *Pravda*, 139 (1938), p. 6. Revised version printed in *A.
Alshvang: Izbrannye sochinenii v dvukh tomakh*, ed. G. B. Bernandt *et
al.*, 2 vols. (Moscow, 1964–5), I, pp. 78–9.
146 For a more detailed account of the production, see Rosamund
Bartlett, 'The Embodiment of Myth: Eizenshtein's Production
of *Die Walküre*', *Slavonic and East European Review*, I (1992),
pp. 53–76.
147 See Braun, *The Theatre of Meyerhold*, p. 179.
148 See Fevralsky, *Meierkhold: stat'i, pis'ma*, II, p. 370.
149 S. Eizenshtein, 'Voploshchenie mifa', *Teatr*, 10 (1940), p. 24.
150 See Eizenshtein, 'Voploshchenie mifa', p. 35.
151 See A. Gladkov, 'Meierkhold govorit', *Novy mir*, 8 (1961), p. 227.
152 See Konstantin Rudnitsky, 'Krushenie teatra', *Ogonek*, 22
(1988), pp. 10–14.
153 Y. Shaporin, '"Val'kiriya"', *Pravda*, 23 November (1940), p. 6.
154 See D. Rabinovich, 'Prem'era "Val'kiriya"', *Sovetskoe iskusstvo*,
24 November 1940 and A. Shavedryan, '"Val'kiriya"', *Izvestiya*,
23 November 1940, p. 4.
155 I. Sollertinsky, 'Postav'te Vagnera na tsene!', *Leningradskaya
pravda*, 51 (1940), p. 3.
156 See [Anon], 'Prosmotr opery "Loengrina"', *Za sovetskoe iskusstvo*,
14 June (1941), pp. 1–2.
157 See Ivan Sollertinsky, '"Loengrin"', *Leningradskaya pravda*,
21 June (1941), reprinted in I. Sollertinsky, *Kriticheskie stat'i*, ed.
M. Druskin (Moscow, 1963), pp. 43–6.
158 See John Elsworth, *Andrey Bely: A Critical Study of the Novels*
(Cambridge, 1983), p. 49.
159 Andrey Bely, *Glossaloliya [Glossolaliya]* (Berlin, 1922), p. 39.
160 Bely, *Glossolaliya*, p. 99.
161 Andrey Bely, *The First Encounter*, tr. and ed. Gerald Janecek,
preliminary remarks, notes and comments by Nina Berberova
(Princeton, 1979), p. 3.
162 See Bely, *The First Encounter*, p. 93.
163 Bely, *The First Encounter*, p. 59.

164 Bely, *The First Encounter*, p. 119.
165 'The Italian people, likewise standing nearer to the Welfs in their feud against the Kaisers, adopted these names from the German folk-mouth and turned them quite according to their dialect to 'Guelphi' and 'Ghibellini''.' See Ashton-Ellis, *Richard Wagner's Prose Works*, VII, p. 268.
166 See Bely, 'Nachalo veka. Berlinskaya redaktsiya', chapters 6–8, fol. 93.
167 See Andrey Bely, 'In Lieu of a Preface', *Maski* (Moscow, 1932), p. 9.
168 See Steinberg, *Word and Music*, p. 209.
169 Bely, *Maski*, p. 11.
170 This poem is in fact a variant of the second part of Bagritsky's 'Skazanie o more, matrosakh i letuchem gollandtse' (see E. Bagritsky, *Stikhotvoreniya* (Leningrad, 1940), pp. 66–76). For a comparison of the two versions, see Eduard Bagritsky, *Sobranie sochinenii*, 2 vols. (Moscow, 1938), I, p. 627.
171 Georgy Adamovich, 'Vagner. I' (1916), 'Vagner. II' (1918), 'Kogda, zabyv rodnoi ochag i goroda ...' (1920), *Chistilishche* (Petrograd, 1922), pp. 24–5, 40, 70–1.
172 Shmakov, 'Mikhail Kuzmin i Rikhard Vagner', pp. 31–2.
173 Shmakov, 'Mikhail Kuzmin i Rikhard Vagner', p. 33.
174 See Shmakov, 'Mikhail Kuzmin i Rikhard Vagner', pp. 33–42.
175 Shmakov, 'Mikhail Kuzmin i Rikhard Vagner', p. 34.
176 See Vladimir Nabokov, *Stikhi* (Ann Arbor, 1979), pp. 42–3.
177 See L. A. Ozerov, ed., *Boris Pasternak: Stikhotvoreniya i poemy* (Moscow-Leningrad, 1965), p. 128.
178 For further details of Pasternak's attitude to Wagner, see B. A. Kats, '*Raskat improvizatsii ...*': *Muzyka v tvorchestve, sud'be i v dome Borisa Pasternaka* (Leningrad, 1991).
179 Ozerov, *Pasternak: Stikhotvoreniya i poemy*, pp. 469–70.
180 See Y. Platek, *Ver'te muzyke* (Moscow, 1989), p. 233.
181 Letter from Pasternak to Tsvetaeva, 14 June 1926, in *Rainer Maria Rilke, Marina Zwetajewa, Boris Pasternak: Briefwechsel*, ed. Jewgenij Pasternak, Jelena Pasternak and Konstantin Asadowskij, tr. Heddy Pross-Weerth (Frankfurt, 1983), p. 185.
182 Pasternak *et al.*, *Rilke, Zwetajewa, Pasternak: Briefwechsel*, p. 201.
183 See 'Ne prislal li lebedya za mnoyu?' with its obvious associations with Lohengrin, and 'Putem vseya zemli' of 1940, which has an oblique reference to *Siegfried*, in Anna Akhmatova, *Stikhotvorenia i poemy*, ed. V. M. Zhirmunsky (Leningrad, 1976), p. 186. For further details, see B. Kats, R. Timenchik, *Anna Akhmatova i muzyka* (Leningrad, 1989), p. 145.

8 RECEPTION AND PERFORMANCE HISTORY, 1941–1991

1 Stark, *Peterburgskaya opera i ee mastera*, p. 256.

2 The concert held on 5 October in the Great Hall of the Moscow Conservatoire was conducted by Samosud; the concerts held on 13 and 18 October at the Hall of Columns were conducted by Golovanov.

3 For details, see Schwarz, *Music and Musical Life*, p. 206.

4 Samosud conducted a concert including extracts from *Die Meistersinger* at the Great Hall of the Conservatoire on 3 December 1952 (GTsMMK, *fond* 18, ed. *khr.* 810), but no other concerts included music by Wagner during this time, as far as can be established.

5 Schwarz, *Music and Musical Life*, p. 249.

6 See Schwarz, *Music and Musical Life*, p. 250.

7 Schwarz, *Music and Musical Life*, p. 257.

8 Card catalogues, GTsMMK.

9 See S. L. Uspenskaya, *Literatura o muzyke, 1948–1953: Bibliograficheskii ukazatel'* (Moscow, 1955), p. 96.

10 M. Druskin, 'Cherti realizma v tvorchestve Vagnera', *Sovetskaya muzyka*, 5 (1955), p. 61.

11 M. Druskin, 'Podlinnyi Vagner', *Sovetskaya muzyka*, 8 (1957), p. 96.

12 K. Ptitsa, 'S. A. Samosud i ego "epokha" na radio', *Sovetsksaya muzyka*, 7 (1978), pp. 87–8. Cited in Polyakova, 'Vagner i Rossiya', p. 30.

13 V. Aleksandrova, E. Bronfin, 'Vozrozhdenie "Loengrina"', *Sovetskaya muzyka*, 12 (1962), p. 44.

14 I. Nestiev, 'Moguchii talant', *Trud*, 22 May (1963), p. 7.

15 See Schwarz, *Music and Musical Life*, p. 485.

16 Schwarz, *Music and Musical Life*, p. 529.

17 See G. Ordzhonikidze, *Sovetskaya muzyka*, 2 (1983), p. 60.

18 See A. Ivashkin, '"Tangeizer"': Gastroli nemetskoi gosudarstvennoi opery', *Muzykal'naya zhizn'*, 24 (1986), p. 5.

19 See M. Rakhmanova, '"Tangeizer" v Moskve', *Sovetskaya muzyka*, 2 (1987), pp. 33–5.

20 A. F. Losev, 'Problema Rikharda Vagnera v proshlom i nastoyashchem', *Voprosy estetiki*, 8 (1968), pp. 66–197.

21 Polyakova, 'Vagner i Rossiya', p. 9.

22 N. Korzhavin, 'Na kontserte Vagnera', *Vremena* (Frankfurt, 1976), pp. 187–8. I am grateful to Oleg Chukhontsev for drawing this poem to my attention.

23 Korzhavin, *Vremena*, p. 188.
24 Natalya Kodryanskaya, *Remizov v svoikh pis'makh* (Paris, 1977), p. 313.
25 Aleksey Remizov, *Tristan i Isolda; Bova Korolevich* (Paris, 1957), pp. 5–6.
26 Olga Sedakova, 'Tristan i Isolda', *Vrata, Okna, Arki: Izbrannye stikhotvoreniya* (Paris, 1986), pp. 25–54.

Select bibliography

I WAGNER IN RUSSIA

(1) RUSSIAN TRANSLATIONS OF WAGNER'S LIBRETTOS (IN CHRONOLOGICAL ORDER OF PUBLICATION)

Tangeizer, tr. K. Zvantsov (St Petersburg, 1862)
Loengrin, tr. K. Zvantsov (St Petersburg, 1868)
Tangeizer, tr. G. A. Lishin (St Petersburg, 1875)
Tangeizer, tr. L. I. Palmin (Moscow, 1876)
Moryak-Skitalyets, tr. G. A. Lishin (St Petersburg, 1877)
Tristan i Izolda, tr. V. Cheshikhin (Leipzig/Riga, 1894)
Parsifal, tr. V. Cheshikhin (Moscow, 1898)
Nyurenbergskie mastera peniya, tr. I. Tyumenev (Moscow, 1899)
Val'kiriya, tr. I. Tyumenev (Moscow, 1900)
Zigfrid, tr. I. Tyumenev (Moscow, 1901)
Val'kiriya, tr. A. Abramova (Moscow, 1903)
Moryak-Skitalyets, tr. O. Lepko (Moscow, 1904)
Gibel' Bogov, tr. I. Tyumenev (Moscow, 1904)
Zoloto Reina, tr. I. Tyumenev (Moscow, 1906)
Tristan i Izolda, tr. V. Kolomiitsov (Leipzig, 1907)
Loengrin, tr. V. Kolomiitsov (Moscow, 1908)
Val'kiriya, tr. V. Kolomiitsov (Moscow, 1910)
Zoloto Reina, tr. V. Kolomiitsov (Moscow, 1910)
Zigfrid, tr. V. Kolomiitsov (Moscow, 1911)
Zakat Bogov, tr. V. Kolomiitsov (Moscow, 1912)
Nyurenbergskie mastera peniya, tr. V. Kolomiitsov (Moscow, 1912)
Parsifal, tr. V. Kolomiitsov (Moscow, 1913)
Tangeizer, tr. V. Kolomiitsov (Moscow, 1913)

(II) RUSSIAN TRANSLATIONS OF WAGNER'S WRITINGS
(IN CHRONOLOGICAL ORDER OF PUBLICATION)

Vagner, R, 'Ob uvertyure', tr. 'Sh', *Repertuar russkogo teatra*, 5 (1841), pp. 10–15

'Vstuplenie k ' "Loengrinu"', *Russkaya muzykal'naya gazeta*, 3 (1894), pp. 70–1

'Yvertyura k ' "Moryak-Skital'tsu"', *Russkaya muzykal'naya gazeta*, 12 (1894), pp. 270–1

'O simfonicheskikh poemakh Fr. Lista', *Russkaya muzykal'naya gazeta*, 8 (1896), pp. 899–914

'Avtobiograficheskii nabrosok', *Russkaya muzykal'naya gazeta*, 10 (1896), pp. 1255–72

' "Zapreshchenie lyubvi". Otchet o pervom predstavlenii opery Vagnera', *Russkaya muzykal'naya gazeta*, 10 (1896), pp. 1273–84

'Khudozhestvennoe proizvedenie budushchego', tr. A. Koptyaev, *Russkaya muzykal'naya gazeta*, 1 (1897), pp. 55–66; 2 (1897), pp. 291–9; 3 (1897), pp. 395–403; 5–6 (1897), pp. 715–24; 7–8 (1897), pp. 990–1000; 9 (1897), pp. 1141–58; 10 (1897), pp. 1307–13; 11 (1897), pp. 1533–41; 12 (1897), pp. 1679–87; 1 (1898), pp. 22–7; 3 (1898), pp. 253–7; 4 (1898), pp. 354–9; 5–6 (1898), pp. 449–55; 7 (1898), pp. 654–9; 8 (1898), pp. 727–31; 9 (1898), pp. 786–9; 10 (1898), pp. 856–9

'Ob uvertyure', *Russkaya muzykal'naya gazeta*, 12 (1898), pp. 1028–35

' "Geroicheskaya simfoniya" Betkhovena (iz programmnykh raz'yasnenii),' *Russkaya muzykal'naya gazeta*, 36 (1899), pp. 846–9

'O dirizhirovanii', *Russkaya muzykal'naya gazeta*, 38 (1899), pp. 900–5; 39 (1899), pp. 931–40; 41 (1899), pp. 1005–10; 42 (1899), pp. 1036–9; 43 (1899), pp. 1063–71; 44 (1899), pp. 1100–03; 45 (1899), pp. 1129–32; 46 (1899), pp. 1157–63; 47 (1899), pp. 1198–1201; 49 (1899), pp. 1264–6; 50–1 (1899), pp. 1335–8; 52 (1899), pp. 1351–5

O dirizhirovanii, tr. A. Koptyaev (St Petersburg, 1900)

'K dramaturgii "Loengrina"', *Russkaya muzykal'naya gazeta*, 25–6 (1900), pp. 632–5

'O "Tangeizere"', *Russkaya muzykal'naya gazeta*, 45 (1900), pp. 1077–80; 46 (1900), pp. 1108–15

'Vagner o proizkhozhdenii "Loengrina"', *Russkaya muzykal'naya gazeta*, 42 (1901), pp. 1045–52

Iskusstvo i revolyutsiya, tr. I. Ellena (St Petersburg, 1906)

'Opera i drama', *Russkaya muzykal'naya gazeta*, 2 (1906), pp. 43–5;

10 (1906), pp. 233–8; 12 (1906), pp. 303–7; 13 (1906), pp. 329–33

Opera i drama, tr. A. Shepelevsky and A. Vinter (Moscow, 1906)

Evreistvo v muzyke, tr. I. Yu-s (St Petersburg, 1908)

Iskusstvo i revolyutsiya, tr. I. Yu-s (St Petersburg, 1908)

Betkhoven, tr. V. Kolomiitsov (St Petersburg, 1911)

Moya zhizn'. Memuary, pis'ma, dnevniki, ed. A. Volynsky, 4 vols. (St Petersburg, 1911–12)

Moya zhizn', ed. A. Gretman (*Moscow, 1912*)

Vibelungi. Vsemirnaya istoriya na osnovanii skazanii, tr. S. Shenrok, introd. E. Metner [Medtner] and M. Tsenker [Zenker] (Moscow, 1913)

'Palomnichestvo k Betkhovenu', *Russkaya muzykal'naya gazeta*, 15–16 (1913), pp. 398–405; 18–19 (1913), pp. 468–73; 20–1; (1913), pp. 495–505

Iskusstvo i revolyutsiya, tr. I. M., Katsenelenbogen (Petrograd, 1918)

Palomnichestvo k Betkhovenu, tr. and ed. E. M. Braudo (Petrograd, 1923).

Izbrannye stat'i, ed. R. Gruber (Moscow, 1935)

Stat'i i materialy, ed. G. Krauklis and V. Gairat-Kurek (Moscow, 1974)

Izbrannye raboty, ed. I. A. Barsova and S. A. Osherova (Moscow, 1978)

Stat'i i materialy, ed. G. Krauklis (Moscow, 1988)

(III) CRITICAL LITERATURE IN RUSSIAN

Akimenko, F. 'O lire zlatostrunnoi Rikharda', *Russkaya muzykal'naya gazeta*, 15–16 (1913), pp. 385–8

Aleksandrova, V. *Lyudovik II, korol' Bavarskii. K istorii zhizni i tvorchestva R. Vagnera* (St Petersburg, 1911)

Alekseev, N. 'Neizvestnoe pis'mo Vagnera', *Sovetskaya muzyka*, 1 (1960), p. 78

Arkhivist [E. Braudo], 'Rikhard Vagner pod nadzorom III otdeleniya', *Vestnik teatra i iskusstva*, 2 (1922), p. 2

Asafiev, B. *et al.* eds., '*Zoloto reina' R. Vagnera. Sbornik statei* (Leningrad, 1933)

Ashkinazi, Zigfrid. 'Yunosheskie proizvedeniya R. Vagnera (k 100-letiyu so dnya rozhdeniya)', *Apollon'*, 7 (1913), pp. 38–46

Avraamov, Arseny. '"Parsifal"', *Zavety*, 4 (1914), pp. 1–6

Babaev, E. G. 'K voprosu o printsipe narodnosti v estetike L. N. Tolstogo', *Uchenie zapiski (Tashkentskii vechernyi pedagogicheskii institut)*, 4 (1957), pp. 103–40

Barsova, I. 'Sto let spustya', *Sovetskaya muzyka*, 11 (1983), pp. 112–20

Baskin, V. '"Kol'tso Nibelunga"'. Tetralogiya Vagnera', *Trud*, 9 (1889), pp. 288–307

Bazunov, S. A. *R. Vagner. Ego zhizn' i muzykal'naya deyatel'nost'. Biograficheskii ocherk* (St Petersburg, 1891)

Ber, A. 'V oppozitsii protiv Vagnera', *Zhizn' iskusstva*, 50 (1924), p. 6

Bernandt, G. B. 'Vagner i Odoevsky', *Sovetskaya muzyka*, 6 (1953), pp. 63–72

Bespristrastny, [V. Odoevsky], 'Rikhard Vagner i ego muzyka', *Sovremmenaya letopis'*, 11 (1863), pp. 11–16

Bogolyubov, N. N. '*Loengrin*'. *Romanticheskaya opera R. Vagnera. Opyt populyarnogo izlozheniya opery* (Perm, 1889)

'*Tangeizer*', *opera R. Vagnera. Opyt populyarnogo izlozheniya* (Kazan', 1901)

Braudo, E. M. '*Meisterzingery*'. *Razbor teksta i muzyki. Kratkoe libretto* (Moscow, 1929)

Rikhard Vagner. Opyt kharakteristiki (Petrograd, 1922)

'Richard Vagner v Peterburge', *Teatr i iskusstvo*, 19 (1913), pp. 418–20

'R. Vagner v Moskve', *Ogonek*, 6 (1929), p. 45

'Vagner i Bakunin (k 50-letiyu so dnya smerti Bakunina), *Novyi zritel'*, 27 (1926), pp. 6–7

'Vagner i Serov (dva neopublikovannykh pis'ma)', *Severnye zapiski*, 5–6 (1913), pp. 56–77

'Vagner v Bol'shom Teatre', *Moskovskii Bol'shoi Teatr (1825–1925). Yubileinyi sbornik* (Moscow, 1925), pp. 119–38

Vagner v Rossii (novye materialy k ego biografii) (Petrograd, 1923)

'Yunyi Zigfrid', *Ezhegodnik imperatorskikh teatrov*, 3 (1911), pp. 122–52

Burago, S. B. 'Blok i Vagner: kontseptsia cheloveka i esteticheskaya pozitsiya', *Izvestiya Akademii Nauk S.S.S.R. Seriya Literatury i Yazyka*, 43 (1984), pp. 522–36

Chechott, V. 'Baireit', *Artist*, 17 (1891), pp. 60–76

Chemberlen, G. S. 'Istoricheskoe znachenie R. Vagnera', tr. F. Lemberg, *Russkaya muzykal'naya gazeta*, 27–8 (1901), pp. 672–7; 29–30 (1901), pp. 703–8; 31–2 (1901), pp. 736–41

Cheshikhin, V. 'O zhelatel'nom tipe izdaniya sochinenii R. Vagnera', *Muzyka*, 130 (1913), pp. 364–5

'"Parsifal" (drama-misteriya R. Vagnera). Kriticheskii etyud', *Russkaya muzykal'naya gazeta*, 27–8 (1899), pp. 665–98

'Vagner kak dramaturg', *Russkaya muzykal'naya gazeta*, 11 (1895), pp. 647–66

'Vagner v Rige', *Muzyka*, 130 (1913), pp. 356–60

Cheshikhin, V., Dan, F. 'Pamyati Rikharda Vagnera', tr. S. Sviri-denko, *Russkaya muzykal'naya gazeta*, 15–16 (1913), p. 386
Denisyuk, N. 'Vagnerizm', *Teatral'nye izvestiya*, 442 (1896), p. 4
Dranishnikov, V. '"Nyurnbergskie mastera peniya"', *Rabochii i teatr*, 44 (1926), p. 7
Druskin, M. 'Cherty realizma v tvorchestve Vagnera', *Sovetskaya muzyka*, 5 (1955), pp. 61–70
'Gody izgnaniya', *Sovetskaya muzyka*, 2 (1958), pp. 47–60
'Podlinnyi Vagner ("Letuchii gollandets" v Malom Teatre)' *Sovetskaya muzyka*, 8 (1957), pp. 96–101
Rikhard Vagner (Moscow, 1958)
'Zakat Baireita', *Sovetskoe iskusstvo*, 7 (1933), p. 3
Durylin, S. *Vagner i Rossiya* (Moscow, 1913)
Eiges, K. 'R. Vagner i ego khudozhestvennoe reformatorstvo', *Russkaya mysl'*, 6 (1913), pp. 56–68
Eizenshtein, S. M. 'Voploshchenie mifa', *Teatr*, 10 (1940), pp. 13–38
Ellis, L. '"Parsifal" R. Vagnera', *Trudy i dni*, 1–2 (1913), pp. 24–53
Engel, Y. '"Gibel' Bogov Vagnera i Snegurochka Rimskogo-Korsakoga', *Ezhegodnik imperatorskikh teatrov*, 1 (1912), pp. 87–114
E. P. '"Loengrin"' (1850–1900)', *Russkaya muzykal'naya gazeta*, 35–6 (1900), pp. 727–86; 37 (1900), pp. 809–19; 38 (1900), pp. 851–4
Ess Iu [Yuferov], R. *Vagner i ego trilogiya 'Kol'tso Nibelunga'* (Moscow, 1889)
F. Nik. [Findeizen] 'Vagner v pis'makh venskogo kapel'meistera Essera', *Russkaya muzykal'naya gazeta* , 35 (1903), pp. 769–74
Famintsyn, A. *Rikhard Vagner i ego opera 'Loengrin'* (St Petersburg, 1868)
Ferman, V. E. *R. Vagner: opyt sotsiologicheskoi kharakteriski* (Moscow, 1929)
Findeizen, N. *'Nyurenbergskie meisterzingery'. 1. Tematicheskii razbor opery R. Vagnera. 2. Srednevekovye meisterzingery* (Moscow, 1914)
Rikhard Vagner: ego zhizn' i muzykal'noe tvorchestvo. Chasti I i II (1813–1859) (St Petersburg, 1911)
'Vagner i ego muzykal'naya drama', *Ezhegodnik imperatorskikh teatrov*, 2 (1913), pp. 1–33
'Vagner v Rossii', *Russkaya muzykal'naya gazeta*, 35 (1903), pp. 755–69
Gachev, D. 'Nasledstvo Vagnera', *Izvestiya*, 17 September 1937, p. 6
'Vagner i Feierbakh', *Sovetskaya muzyka*, 7 (1934), pp. 46–52
Gertsyk, E. 'R. Vagner kak poet i myslitel'', *Obrazovanie*, 7–8 (1900), pp. 48–59
Glebov, I. [B. Asafiev], '"Meisterzingery" v opernom tvorchestve Vagnera', *Maly opernyi teatr: Rikhard Vagner* (Leningrad, 1932), pp. 11–12
'"Tangeizer"', *Zhizn' iskusstva*, 15 (1923), p. 8

Gornfeld, A. 'Vagner i Dostoevsky', *Russkie vedomosti*, 114 (1913), p. 2

Gorodetsky, S. '"Meisterzingery"'. Kak ya rabotal nad perevodom "Nyurnbergskikh meisterzingerov"', *Sovremennyi teatr*, 5 (1929), p. 67

Gozenpud, A. A. 'Rikhard Vagner i russkaya kul'tura', *Sovetskaya muzyka*, 4 (1983), pp. 77–87; 5 (1983), pp. 84–90

Rikhard Vagner i russkaya kul'tura (Leningrad, 1990)

Russkii opernyi teatr mezhdu dvukh revolyutsii 1905–1917 (Leningrad, 1975) [See chapter 'R. Vagner na russkoi tsene', pp. 110–55]

Gruber, R. 'Rikhard Vagner i problema ego tvorcheskogo metoda', *Sovetskaya muzyka*, 2 (1933), pp. 32–49

R. Vagner (1883–1933) (Moscow, 1934)

'Skovannyi genii', *Sovetskoe iskusstvo*, 7 (1933), p. 2

'"Zoloto Reina" v Leningrade', *Sovetskaya muzyka*, 3 (1933), p. 165

Gunst, E. 'Rimsky-Korsakov o Vagnere', *Maski*, 5 (1912–13), pp. 39–46

Hochschüler, M. 'Pis'mo iz Baireita', *Vesy*, 9 (1904), pp. 39–46, 10 (1904), pp. 49–58

Ilinsky, A. *Rikhard Vagner, ego zhizn' i tvorchestvo* (Moscow, 1913)

Ivanov, V. I. 'O Vagnere', *Vestnik teatra*, 31–2 (1919), pp. 2–3

'Vagner i dionisovo deistvo', *Vesy*, 5 (1905), pp. 13–16

Ivanov, V. V. 'Sovremennaya nauka i teatr (k analizu postanovki "Val'kirii" Vagnera S. M. Eizenshteinom v Bol'shom teatre)', *Teatral'naya pravda: sbornik statei*, ed. Eteri Gugushvili and Boris Lyubimov (Tbilisi, 1981), pp. 388–40

Kapp, Y. *R. Vagner. Biografiya*, tr. G. Prokofiev (Moscow, 1913)

Karatygin, V. *'Parsifal'. Torzhestvennaya misteriya R. Vagnera. Tematicheskii razbor* (St Petersburg, 1914)

'R. Vagner', *Severnye zapiski*, 5–6 (1913), pp. 37–62

'Vagneriana', *Nash vek*, 65 (1918), p. 4

'Vagner i Dargomyzhsky', *Apollon*, 8 (1913), pp. 36–50

'"Val'kiriya"', *Nash vek*, 85 (1918), p. 4

Kashkin, N. F. 'Vagnerovskii teatr v Baireite', *Artist*, 41 (1894), pp. 153–7

'Vagner v Moskve (po lichnym vospominaniyam)', *Muzyka*, 131 (1913), pp. 372–78

Keilina, L. 'K pyatidesyatiletiyu Baireita', *Muzyka i revolyutsiya*, 11 (1926)

Kenigsberg, A. *'Kol'tso Nibelunga' Vagnera* (Moscow, 1959)

Opery Vagnera 'Letuchii gollandets', 'Tangeizer', 'Loengrin' (Moscow-Leningrad, 1967)

Rikhard Vagner. Kratkii ocherk zhizni i tvorchestva (Leningrad, 1972)

'Vokal'nyi stil' Rikharda Vagnera', *Sovetskaya muzyka*, 10 (1958), pp. 53–9

Khavsky, A. '"Tangeizer". Muzykal'naya drama R. Vagnera', *Russkaya muzykal'naya gazeta*, 9 (1901), pp. 263–71; 10 (1901), pp. 304–9; 11 (1901), pp. 327–34; 12 (1901), pp. 358–62

Khop, M. *'Parsifal'. Drama-misteriya v 3-x deistviyakh. Istor.-tsenicheskii i muzykal'nyi razbor*, tr. M. Goldberg (Moscow, 1913)

R. Vagner: *'Nyurnbergskie mastera peniya'. Muzykal'naya komediya i 3-x deistviyakh. Istoricheskii i muzykal'nyi razbor s mnogochislennymi notnymi primerami* (St Petersburg, 1914)

Tematicheskii razbor muzykal'nykh proizvedenii R. Vagnera (St Petersburg, 1908)

Khvorostov, S. K. ' Stranichka is muzykal'noi zhizni Leningrada (obshchestvo vagnerovskogo iskusstva, 1920-e gody)', in *Iz proshlogo sovetskoi muzykal'noi kul'tury*, vypusk 3, ed. T. N. Livanova (Moscow, 1982), pp. 231–7

Khvostenko, V. '"Vagneriana". Materialy k bibliograficheskomu ukazatelyu literatury na russkom yazyke', *Sovetskaya muzyka*, 11 (1934), pp. 85–95

Kitsner, F. 'Ars Wagneriana', *Maski*, 7–8 (1912–13), pp 53–7

K.N. *'Mastera peniya' R. Vagnera* (Moscow, 1909)

Knipovich, E. *Ob Aleksandre Bloke* (Moscow, 1987) [See chapter 'Moi Vagner', pp. 93–117]

Kolomiitsov, V. '"Kol'tso Nibelunga"', *Bayan*, 6 (1889), pp. 44–5; 8 (1889), pp. 63–4

'Kol'tso Nibelunga'. Tetralogiya R. Vagnera (Petrograd, 1922)

'"Meisterzingery" (k postanovku muzykal'noi komedii Vagnera v Bol'shom opernom teatre)', *Zhizn' iskusstva*, 293–4 (1919), pp. 2–3

'Rikhard Vagner i muzykal'naya drama v Rossii', *Muzykal'nyi kalendar na 1913 god A. Gabrilovicha*, (St Petersburg, 1913), pp. i–xxxii

'"Val'kiriya" (po povodu sotogo predstavlenii "pervogo dnya" trilogii Vagnera v Mariinskom teatre', *Vestnik teatra i iskusstva*, 6 (1922), pp. 3–4

Konen, V. 'O Rikharde Vagnere', *Sovetskaya muzyka*, 10 (1953), pp. 15–22

Konstant Smis, A. '"Val'kiriya" na radio', *Sovetskaya muzyka*, 7 (1934), pp. 66–8

Koptyaev, A. *Putevoditeli k operam i muzykal'nym dramam R. Vagnera* (St Petersburg, 1898)

'Vagner v epokhu "Tristana"' *Ezhegodnik imperatorskikh teatrov*, 5 (1909), pp. 36–56

'Zhenshchiny R. Vagnera (k stoletiyu so dnya rozhdeniya)', *Solntse Rossii*, 20 (1913), pp. 8–11

Korzukhin, I. *'Parsifal' R. Vagnera* (St Petersburg, 1914)

Rimsky-Korsakov i Vagner (Berlin, no date [?1914])

Krauklis, G. '*Loengrin*' *Rikharda Vagnera* (Moscow, 1963)
Opernye uvertyury R. Vagnera (Moscow, 1964)

Kutateladze, L. M. (ed.) *Pis'ma zarubezhnykh muzykantov iz russkikh arkhivov* (Leningrad, 1967) [see pp. 129–48 for Wagner's letters to Edith von Raden and A. N. Serov]

Kuznetsov, K. 'K istorii "Meisterzingerov"', *Sovetskaya muzyka*, 3 (1933)
'"Val'kiriya" Vagnera v Bol'shom Teatre SSSR', *Sovetskaya muzyka*, 2 (1941), pp. 76–8

K-verina, S. 'Vosem' dnei v Baireite', *Russkoe bogatstvo*, 8 (1889), pp. 103–20

Kyui, T. '*Kol'tso Nibelunga*' (St Petersburg, 1889)

Lapitsky, I. and Braudo, E. '*Nyurenbergskie mastera peniya*'. *Opera v 3-x d. R. Vagnera. Poyasnitel'nyi tekst* (Moscow, 1929)

Larosh, G. [H. Laroche], '"Loengrin" R. Vagnera', *Russkii vestnik*, 10 (1887), reprinted in *G. A. Larosh: Izbrannye stat'i*, iii, pp. 305–12
'"Nibelungov persten"', *Golos*, 235 (1876), reprinted in *G. A. Larosh: Izbrannye stat'i*, III, pp. 204–7
'O "Val'kirii"', Rikhard Vagner i vagnerizm', *Ezhegodnik imperatorskikh teatrov, prilozhenie 1-e* (St Petersburg, 1900), pp. 675–85

Levik, B. *Rikhard Vagner* (Moscow, 1978)

Levik, S. 'Opery Vagnera na Peterburgskoi tsene', *Sovetskaya muzyka*, 2 (1958), pp. 61–5

Lipaev, I. 'Baireit. Putevye zametki', *Russkaya muzykal'naya gazeta*, 28–9 (1902), pp. 675–85; 30–1 (1902), pp. 707–13; 32–3 (1902), pp. 737–44; 34–5 (1902), pp. 769–79; 36 (1902), pp. 801–11
Vagneriana: sputnik oper i muz. dram Rikh. Vagnera (Moscow, 1904)

Likhtanberger, A. *Rikhard Vagner kak poet i myslitel'*, tr. (from second French edition) S. Solovyov (Moscow, 1905)

Lishtanberzhe, A. 'Vzglyady Vagnera na iskusstvo', *Mir iskusstva*, 7 (1899), pp. 107–28, 11–12 (1899), pp. 195–206

Losev, A. F. 'Problema Rikharda Vagnera v proshlom i nastoyaschem', *Voprosy estetiki*, 8 (1968), pp. 67–197

Lovtsky, G. 'R. Vagner', *Sovremennik*, 13–15 (1914), pp. 262–9

Lunacharsky, A. 'R. Vagner', *Sovetskaya muzyka*, 3 (1933), pp. 1–6
'Yunosheskie idealy R. Vagnera', *Pravda*, 4 (1906), pp. 137–576

M. 'Svidetel'stvo pevtsa (E. van-Deik o Vagnere)', *Russkaya muzykal'-naya gazeta*, 18 (1900), pp. 500–4

Magomedova, D. M. 'Blok i Vagner', *Zbornik Radova Instituta za Strane Jezike i Knjizevnosti*, 6 (1984), pp. 194–220

Malkov, N. 'Vagner i russkaya muzyka', *Rabochii i teatr*, 4–5 (1933), pp. 7–9

Mazing, B. 'Ob ispolnitelyakh vagnerovskogo tsikla na nashei tsene', *Rabochii i teatr*, 4–5 (1933), p. 10

Melgunov, N. A. 'Kontserty gg. Rubinshteina i Vagnera', *Nashe vremya*, 64 (1863), reprinted in Popov, *Istoriya russkoi muzyki v issledovaniakh i materialakh*, pp. 80–1 and 72 (1863), p. 285–6

Mendes, K. R. *Vagner*, tr. S. D. Dukhovny, (Kiev, 1909)

Meyerhold, V. M. 'K postanovke "Tristana i Izoldy" v Mariinskom teatre', *Ezhegodnik Imperatorskikh teatrov*, 5 (1909), pp. 12–35

Mikhailovsky, V. G. 'Loengrin'. *Opyt analiza vagnerovskoi muzykal'noi dramy* (Moscow, 1923)

M. R. [Rappaport] 'Muzykal'naya letopis', *Syn otechestva*, 45 (1863), p. 345 and 59 (1863), pp. 458–9 [on Wagner's concerts in St Petersburg]

M. Yu. *Rikhard Vagner o muzyke. Mysli, aforizmy, fragmenty* (Moscow, 1913)

Nestiev, I. 'Rikhard Vagner: k 150 letiyu so dnya rozhdeniya', *Sovetskaya muzyka*, 10 (1963), pp. 11–12

N. S. O. 'Cherty iz literaturnoi deyatel'nosti Vagnera', *Muzyka i zhizn'*, 1 (1908), pp. 8–11

Odin iz publiki 'Kontserty Vagnera i ego muzyka', *Golos*, 59 (1863), p. 225

O. O. O. [V. Odoevsky] 'Pervyi kontsert Vagnera v Moskve', *Nashe vremya*, 57 (1863), reprinted in Braudo, *Rikhard Vagner i Rossiya*, p. 37

Orlov, G. 'Vagner v datakh. Po vystavke Leningradskoi filarmonii', *Rabochii i teatr*, 4–5 (1933), pp. 12–13

Pechersky, P. '"Tangeizer" v Rige', *Sovetskaya muzyka*, 5 (1957), pp. 104–7

Petrovsky, A. 'Teatral'noe delo Vagnera', *Rabochii i teatr*, 4–5 (1933), pp. 5–6

Piotrovsky, A. 'Vagner – teatral'nyi reformator i avtor "Meisterzingerov"', *Rikhard Vagner* (Leningrad, 1932), pp. 7–8

Polyakova, L. 'Rikhard Vagner i Rossiya', *Rikhard Vagner: sbornik statei*, ed. L. V. Polyakova (Moscow, 1987), pp. 9–41

Popov, S. 'Novoe o Vagnere v Rossii', *Sovetskaya muzyka*, 11 (1934)
  'Prebyvanie Rikharda Vagnera v Moskve i ego moskovskie kontserty v 1863 godu', *Istoriya russkoi muzyki v issledovaniakh i materialakh*, ed. K. Kuznetsov, vol. 1 (Moscow, 1926)
  'Rikhard Vagner v Rossii (Neizvestnye pis'ma Vagnera iz moskovskikh i leningradskikh arkhivov)', *Sovetskaya muzyka*, 11 (1934), pp. 51–2

Porfirieva, A. L. 'Meierkhold i Vagner', *Russkii teatr i dramaturgiya nachala XX veka. Sbornik nauchnykh trudov*, ed. A. A. Ninov (Leningrad, 1984), pp. 126–44

'Russkaya simvolistskaya tragediya i mifologicheskii teatr Vagnera (dramaturgiya Vyacheslava Ivanova)', *Problemy muzykal'nogo romantizma. Sbornik nauchnykh trudov*, ed. A. L. Porfirieva (Leningrad, 1987), pp. 31–58

Quod [V. Odoevsky] 'Vagner v Moskve', *Sovremennaya letopis'*, 8 (1863), pp. 13–14

Reingold, A. '*Kol'tso Nibelunga*'. *Sochinenie R. Vagnera. Izlozhenie teksta tetralogii s ob'yasneniyami i kriticheskami zametkami* (St Petersburg, 1889)

Rimsky-Korsakov, N. A. 'O Vagnere (iz pis'ma Rimskogo-Korskakogo k synu)', *Muzyka*, 133 (1913), pp. 419–20

'Vagner i Dargomyshky', *Sovetskaya muzyka*, 3 (1933), p. 137

Rogal-Levitsky, D. '"Rienzi" i "Parsifal" (orkestr i orkestrovka)', *Sovetskoe iskusstvo*, 7 (1933), p. 2

Rostislav, [Feofil Tolstoy] 'Pervyi kontsert Filarmonicheskogo obshchestva pod upravleniem Rikhard Vagnera', *Severnaya pchela*, 52 (1863), p. 1

'Vtoroi kontsert Filarmonicheskogo obshchestva', *Severnaya pchela*, 58 (1863), p. 1

Sabaneev, L. 'Rikhard Vagner i Rossiya', *Mosty*, 11 (1965), pp. 230–41

'Vagner i sinteticheskoe iskusstvo', *Muzyka*, 128 (1913), pp. 311–16

Saminsky, L. 'O nekotorykh obshchikh priemakh vagnerovskoi instrumentovki', *Muzyka*, 128 (1913), pp. 316–22

Savich, E. 'Vagner (k 40-letiyu so dnya smerti)', *Teatr i muzyka*, 6 (1923), pp. 637–9

Serov, A. N. 'Kontserty Filarmonicheskogo obshchestva pod upravleniem Rikharda Vagnera', *Sankt-Peterburgskie vedomosti*, 52 (1863), reprinted in *A. N. Serov: Izbrannye stat'i*, I, pp. 554–9

'"Loengrin" Rikharda Vagnera na russkoi opernoi tsene', *Novoe vremya*, 231, 233, 234 (1868), reprinted in *A. N. Serov: Izbrannye stat'i*, I, pp. 435–49

'"Nibelungov persten"'. Muzykal'naya dramaticheskaya poema R. Vagnera', *Yakor'*, 20 (1863), pp. 382–6; 21 (1863), pp. 405–9; 23 (1863), pp. 442–6; 24 (1863), pp. 465–8; 25 (1863), pp. 487–9; 29 (1863), pp. 584–6; 30 (1863), pp. 598–600; 32 (1863), pp. 637–9; 34 (1863), pp. 668–9; 36 (1863), pp. 700–1

'Rikhard Vagner i ego kontserty v Peterburge', *Yakor'*, 2 (1863), pp. 33–4

'Rikhard Vagner v Peterburge', *Sankt-Peterburgskie vedomosti*, 40 (1863), reprinted in *A. N. Serov: Izbrannye stat'i*, I, pp. 550–3

Serova, V. S. 'R. Vagner. Otryvok iz moikh vospominanii (pervaya poezdka zagranitsu v 1864 g.)', *Artist*, 12 (1891), pp. 64–72

'Vagner i Kozima (po lichnym vospominaniyam)', *Muzyka*, 132 (1913), pp. 386–98
Shaginyan, M. 'Chetyre pis'ma Aleksandra Bloka (otzyv o perevode M. Shaginyan tetralogii R. Vagnera "Kol'tso Nibelunga"', *Znamya*, 11 (1955), pp. 190–1
Shiller, F. 'Iskazhenniy oblik (fashistskaya legenda o Vagnere)', *Sovetskoe iskusstvo*, 7 (1933), p. 3
Shmakov, G. 'Kuzmin i Vagner', *Studies in the Life and Work of Mixail Kuzmin*, ed. J. Malmstad (Vienna, 1989)
Shpiller, N. 'Val'kiriya', *Sovetskaya muzyka*, 9 (1979), pp. 78–83
Shyure, E. *Drama R. Vagnera 'Tristan i Izolda'*, tr. V. Kolomiitsov (Moscow, 1909)
'M. Vezendonk i ee rol' v zhizni Vagnera', *Russkaya muzykal'naya gazeta*, 4 (1910), pp. 97–107; 5 (1910), pp. 129–36; 6 (1910), pp. 165–11; 8 (1910), pp. 209–15; 11 (1910), pp. 279–84; 12 (1910), pp. 309–14; 13 (1910), pp. 349–52; 14 (1910), pp. 377–81
Rikhard Vagner i ego muzykal'naya drama, tr. N. Rozen (Moscow, 1909)
Sidorov, A. A. *R. Vagner* (Moscow, 1934)
Sollertinsky, I. 'O puti Rikharda Vagnera', *Rabochii teatr*, 4–5 (1933), pp. 2–4
'Postav'te Vagnera na tsene', *Leningradskaya pravda*, 51 (1940), p. 3
'"Zoloto reina" i problema postanovki "Kol'tsa"', *Rabochii i teatr*, 8–9 (1933), pp. 46–52
Stanislavsky, M. *Vagner v Rossii* (St Petersburg, 1910)
Struve, A. 'Vagner (po povodu stoletiya so dnya rozhdeniya)', *Svirel' Pana*, 1 (1913), pp. 13–14
Sviridenko, S. 'List i Vagner', *Russkaya muzykal'naya gazeta*, 40–1 (1911), pp. 837–43
Nyurenbergskie meisterzingery' R. Vagnera (St Petersburg, 1914)
Parsifal'. Obshchedostupnoe posobie dlya oznakomleniya s vagnerovskoi misterii (St Petersburg, 1913)
Trilogiya 'Kol'tso Nibelunga' Rikharda Vagnera. Obshchedostupnyi ocherk (St Petersburg, 1907)
Tristan i Izolda'. Obshchedostupnyi ocherk dlya kratkogo oznakomleniya. V stikhotvornikh vyderzhkakh teksta, tr. S. Sviridenko and I. Ershov (St Petersburg, 1910)
'Vagner i drevnegermanskii narodnyi epos', *Russkaya muzykal'naya gazeta*, 15–16 (1913), pp. 388–407; 18–19 (1913), pp. 464–8; 20–21 (1913), pp. 490–4; 40–1 (1913), pp. 892–4; 43 (1913), pp. 947–53; 44 (1913), pp. 978–81; 45 (1913), pp. 1010–13
Vagnerovskie tipy trilogii 'Kol'tso Nibelunga' i artisty peterburgskoi opery (St Petersburg, 1908)

Taberio, N. '*Parsifal*'. *Istoricheskoe proiskhozhdenie skazanii o Parsifale. Soderzhanie i kratkii muzykal'nyi razbor dramy-misterii R. Vagnera* (St Petersburg, 1914)

Tchaikovsky, P. 'Baireitskoe muzykal'noe torzhestvo', *Russkie vedemosti*, (1876), reprinted in *P. I. Chaikovsky: Muzykal'no-kriticheskie stat'i*, ed. A. A. Shcherbakov, 4th edn (Moscow, 1986), pp. 261–84

Tigranov, F. '*Kol'tso Nibelunga': kriticheskii ocherk* (St Petersburg, 1910)

Tsvetaeva, P. '"Parsifal"', *Sovremennik*, 5 (1914), pp. 115–24

V-a, O. [A. V. Ossovsky] '20-letie Baireitskogo teatra', *Russkaya muzykal'naya gazeta*, 10 (1896), pp. 1247–54

'Pervyi russkii vagnerianets', *Russkaya muzykal'naya gazeta*, 15–16 (1913), pp. 408–12; 420–1 (1913), pp. 505–10

'Vagner i Berlioz (ocherk iz istorii frants. opery)', *Russkaya muzykal'naya gazeta*, 3 (1894), pp. 52–7

'Vagner v vospominaniyakh Kitsa', *Russkaya muzykal'naya gazeta*, 27–8 (1905), pp. 665–72

Valter, V. 'Baireit v 1906 g.', *Russkaya muzykal'naya gazeta*, 37 (1906), pp. 769–75; 38 (1906), pp. 801–9; 39 (1906), pp. 842–6; 40 (1906), pp. 870–4; 42 (1906), pp. 929–34

Obshchedostupnoe posobie dlya slushatelei muzykal'noi dramy R. Vagnera 'Kol'tso Nibelunga' (Moscow, 1908)

Obshchedostupnoe posobie dlya slushatelei opery R. Vagnera 'Nyurenbergskie meisterzingery' (Moscow, 1914)

Obshchedostupnoe posobie dlya slushatelei muzykal'noi dramy R. Vagnera 'Tristan i Izol'da' (Moscow, 1910)

'*Opera Vagnera 'Nyurnbergskie meisterzingery'. Muzykal'nye formy i dramaturgiya* (Moscow, 1912)

'R. Vagner (k 25-letiyu so dnya smerti)', *Russkaya mysl'* 1 (1908), pp. 1–19

'R. Vagner kak dirizher', *Russkaya muzykal'naya gazeta*, 4 (1908), pp. 900–12

Vagner, ego zhizn', tvorchestvo i deyatel'nost' (St Petersburg, 1911)

V. I. [V. Ignatovich], *Rikhard Vagner ('Kol'tso Nibelunga')* (St Petersburg, 1906)

Vieru, N. 'K 150-letiyu so dnya rozhdeniya Vagnera', *Sovetskaya muzyka*, 5 (1963), pp. 59–80

'"Meisterzingery" i opernaya reforma Vagnera', *Sovetskaya muzyka*, 2 (1958), pp. 55–70

Volkov, N. 'Na russkoi tsene (sud'ba vagnerovskogo repertuara)', *Sovetskoe iskusstvo*, 7 (1933), p. 3

Yastrebtsov, V. 'Po sluchayu "Nibelungov"', *Bayan*, 11 (1889), pp. 83–6

'Rimsky-Korsakov o Vagnere (po lichnym vospominaniyam)',
Russskie vedomosti, 130 (1911), pp. 122–5

(IV) CRITICAL LITERATURE IN LANGUAGES OTHER THAN
RUSSIAN

Altmann, Wilhelm. 'Briefe Wagners an Editha v. Rhaden', *Die
Musik*, 16 (1924), pp. 712–32
Andreevsky, A. 'Richard Wagner und die russische kultur', *Die
Lesestunde. Zeitschrift der Deutschen Buch-Gemeinschaft*, June 1936,
pp. xii–xv
Dilettanten und Genies: Geschichte der Russischen Musik, place and date
of publication unknown [See chapter 'Im Banne Richard
Wagners']
'Wagner und Russland', *Der Bayreuther Festspielbuch* (Bayreuth,
1951), pp. 64–6
Anon. *Richard Wagner im russischen Musikleben* (Berlin: Gesellschaft für
Deutsch-Sowjetische Freundschaft, ?1952)
Arro, Elmar. 'Richards Wagners Rigaer Wanderjahre: Über einige
baltische Züge im Schaffen Wagners', *Musik des Ostens*, 3 (1965),
pp. 123–68
Baedeker, Peer. 'Aller Schmerzen Ende', *Bayreuth Programmheft* (*Par-
sifal*), 1984 [On the relationship of Wagner and Josef Rub-
instein]
Bartlett, Rosamund. 'The Embodiment of Myth: Eizenshtein's Pro-
duction of *Die Walküre*', *Slavonic and East European Review*, 1
(1992), pp. 53–76
'Ivanov and Wagner', *Vjačeslav Ivanov: Russicher Dichter-europäischer
Kulturphilosoph*, hrsg. von Wilfried Potthoff (Heidelberg, 1993),
pp. 67–83
Boelza, Igor. 'Verkörperung der lichten Ideale des Deutschen
Volkes', *Der Bayreuther Festspielbuch* (Bayreuth, 1952), pp. 151–2
Burzawa, E. '*Die Walküre* von Sergej Eisenstein: Versuch der Rekon-
struktion', *Richard Wagner und sein Mittelalter*, ed. Ursula und
Ulrich Müller (Salzburg, 1989), pp. 299–313
Ejzenstein, S. M. *La Messinscena della Valchiria*, a cura di Pier Marco
di Santi, tr. Mass. Lenzi (Fiesole, 1984)
Fischer, K-D. 'Turgenev und Richard Wagner', *Zeitschrift für Slawis-
tik*, 31 (1986), pp. 228–32
Hetschko, Alfred. 'Zur Wagner-Pflege im ehemaligen Russland and
in der Sowjetunion', *Richard Wagner Festwochen* (Bayreuth, 1955),
pp. 18–21
Hughes, R. P. 'Nothung, the Cassia Flower and the Spirit of Music in

the Poetry of Aleksandr Blok', *California Slavic Studies* 6 (1971), pp. 49–60

Kobylinsky-Ellis, L. 'Der Tempel des Heiligen Grales asl Dichtung und Wahrheit', *Bayreuther Blätter*, 1 (1932), pp. 21–8; 2 (1932), pp. 94–108

Laux, Karl, *Die Musik in Russland und in der Sowjetunion* (Berlin, 1958) [see 'Richard Wagner', pp. 272–4]

Martynov, Sergey. 'Richard Wagner in Russland. Zum 100. Todestag des Musikdramatikers', *Sowjetunion Heute*, February 1983, pp. 60–1

Masing-Delic, Irene. 'The Metaphysics of Liberation: Insarov as Tristan', *Die Welt der Slaven*, 1 (1987), pp. 59–77

Mierau, F. 'Drei Anmerkungen zu Wagner im Russland', *Die Nibelungen: Bilder von Liebe, Verrat und Untergang*, ed. Wolfgang Storch (Munich, 1987), pp. 74–5

Reimers, Theresia. 'Wagner in Russland 'Ich wohne prachtvoll . . .', *Festspielnachrichten* (*Siegfried, Götterdämmerung*) (Bayreuth, 1990), pp. 2–7

Roesch, Friedrich. 'Richard Wagner, Franz Liszt und Hans von Bülow in ihren Beziehungen zur Philharmonischen Gesellschaft in St Petersburg', *Allgemeine Musik-Zeitung*, 22–3 (1896), pp. 292–8

Rosenthal, Bernice Glatzer. 'Wagner and the Russian Left', *Wagner in Retrospect*, ed. L. Shaw, N. Cirillo, M. Miller (Amsterdam, 1987), pp. 152–63

'Wagner and Wagnerian Ideas in Russia', *Wagnerism in European Culture and Politics*, ed. D. Large and W. Weber (Ithaca, 1984), pp. 198–245

II OTHER WORKS CONSULTED

(I) UNPUBLISHED (IN CHRONOLOGICAL ORDER)

Richard Wagner, four letters to Josef Standhartner (27 February, 8 March, 18 March, 7 April 1863), Nationalarchiv der Richard-Wagner-Stiftung, Bayreuth

Richard Wagner, letter to Marie Kalergis-Mukhanova (24 March 1863), Russian State Library, Manuscript Division (RGB), *fond* 175, *ed. khr.* 2, fol. 6

Richard Wagner, letter to Minna Wagner (20 April 1863), Nationalarchiv der Richard-Wagner-Stiftung, Bayreuth

Richard Wagner, two letters to Editha von Rhaden (8 September

1863, 16 January 1864), Nationalarchiv der Richard-Wagner-Stiftung, Bayreuth

Richard Wagner, letter to 'Graf Matthieu von Wielhorsky', Nationalarchiv der Richard-Wagner-Stiftung, Bayreuth

Karl Klindworth, letter to Richard Wagner, 24 December 1871, Nationalarchiv der Richard-Wagner-Stiftung, Bayreuth

Richard Wagner, letter to Karl Klindworth, 1 December 1873, Nationalarchiv der Richard-Wagner-Stiftung, Bayreuth

Marie von Wolkenstein, letter to Cosima Wagner, 19 March 1889, Nationalarchiv der Richard-Wagner-Stiftung, Bayreuth

Hans Richter, letter to Cosima Wagner, 19 April 1898, Nationalarchiv der Richard-Wagner-Stiftung, Bayreuth

Vsevelod Meyerhold, 'Zapisnye knizhki 1908', Central State Archive for Literature and Art (RGALI), *fond* 998, *op.* 1, *ed. khr.* 775

Vsevelod Meyerhold, 'O Vagnere i muzyka'noi drame. Chernovye nabroski i vypiski (1909)', RGALI, *fond* 998, *op.* 1, *ed. khr.* 414

Vsevelod Meyerhold, 'Zapisnye knizhki avgust 1909', RGALI, *fond* 998, *op.* 1, *ed. khr.* 838

Vsevelod Meyerhold, 'Zapisnye knizhki 1909–1910', RGALI, *fond* 998, *op.* 1, *ed. khr.* 839

Vsevelod Meyerhold, 'Zapisnye knizhki 1909' [Wagner bibliography], RGALI, *fond* 998, *op.* 1, *ed. khr.* 842

V. Kastorsky, 'Memuary', RGALI, *fond* 1922, *op.* 1, *ed. khr.* 10

Taneevy, S. I. and V. I., 'Pis'ma Katuara Egora L'vovicha', RGALI, *fond* 880, *op.* 1, *ed. khr.* 266

Andrey Bely, 'Material k biografii (intimnyi), prednaznachennyi dlya izucheniya tol'ko posle smerti avtora' (1923), RGALI, *fond* 53, *op.* 2, *ed. khr.* 3

Andrey Bely, 'Nachalo veka. Vospominaniya. Tom Tretii, Berlinskaya redaktsiya (1922–23)', RGALI, *fond* 53, *op.* 1, *ed. khr.* 26, 27

Andrey Bely, 'Istoriya stanovleniya samoznaniya dushi: chernovyi nabroski i oglyavleniya knigi', RGALI, *fond* 53, *op.* 1, *ed. khr.* 71

D. M. Pines, 'Literaturnoe nasledie A. Belogo: chernovyi avtograf (28/1/36)', RGALI, *fond* 391, *op.* 1, *ed. khr.* 71

D. M. Pines, 'Spisok proizvedenii Belogo unichtozhennye, propavshie, nenapechatennykh, sostavlennyi Belym (1927)', RGALI, *fond* 391, *op.*, 1, *ed. khr.* 67

Andrey Bely, 'Tablitsy i skhemy ideinoi preemstvennosti. Metafizicheskaya skhema (1912–1916)', RGB, *fond* 25, *k.* 37, *ed. khr.* 1

Andrey Bely, letters to Emil Medtner, RGB, *fond* 167, *k.* 2, *ed. khr.* 4, 6

Lev Ellis, letters to Emil Medtner, RGL RO, *fond* 167, *k.* 7, *ed. khr.* 24,

26, 34, 37, 39, 40, 42, 43, 51, 52, 54, 58, 59, 62, 63, 65, 68, 69, 74, 77, 78, 79,
Emil Medtner, letters to Andrey Bely, RGB, *fond* 167, *k.* 4, *ed. khr.*, 23, 42, 46, 54, 61
Sabaneev, L. L. 'Rikhard Vagner. Ocherk', RGALI, *fond* 611, *op.* 1, *ed. khr.* 26

(II) PUBLISHED

Abraham, G. *Slavonic and Romantic Music* (London, 1968)
Adamovich, G. *Oblaka. Stikhi* (Moscow-Petrograd, 1916)
   Chistilishche: Stikhi. Kniga vtoraya (Petrograd, 1922)
Adorno, T. *In Search of Wagner*, tr. Rodney Livingstone (London, 1981)
Albrekht, E. *Obshchii obzor deyatel'nosti vyshochaishe utverzhdennogo S.-Peterburgskogo Filarmonicheskogo Obshchestva s prilozheniyami i s pro-ektom izmeneniya ego ustava* (St Petersburg, 1884)
Altman, N. 'Iz besed s poetom Vyach. Iv. Ivanovym' (Baku, 1921)', *Uchenye zapiski Tartuskogo gos. universiteta. Vypusk 209. Trudy po russkoi i slavyanskoi filologii, XII. Literaturovedenie* (Tartu, 1968), pp. 304–25
Alexandrov, V. *Andrei Bely: The Major Symbolist Fiction* (Cambridge, Mass. 1985)
Apetyan, Z. A. ed. *N. K. Metner: stat'i, materialy, vospominaniya* (Moscow, 1981)
Apetyan, Z. A. ed. *N. K. Metner: pis'ma* (Moscow, 1973)
Arnshtam, L. 'Meierkhold i muzyka', *Sovetskaya muzyka*, 3 (1974), pp. 56–8
Asafiev, B. *Ob opere: izbrannye stat'i*, ed. L. A. Pavlova Arbenina (Leningrad, 1976)
Auer, L. *My Long Life in Music* (London, 1924)
Averintsev, S. 'Poeziya Vyacheslava Ivanova', *Voprosy literatury*, 8 (1975), pp. 145–92
Azbegauz, I. *Russkie muzykanty o muzyke zapada* (Moscow-Leningrad, 1950)
Baer, N. Van Norman, ed. *Theatre in Revolution: Russian Avant-Garde Stage Design 1913–1915* (London, 1991)
Bagritsky, E. *Sobranie sochinenii*, 2 vols. ed. I. Utkin (Moscow, 1938)
Balmont, K. *et al., My* (Moscow, 1920)
Barenboim, L. *A. G. Rubinshtein*, 2 vols. (Leningrad, 1957–62)
Barna, Y. *Eisenstein* (London, 1973)
Baskin, V. S. *A. N. Serov: Biograficheskii ocherk* (Moscow, 1890)

Beketova, M. A. *Pis'ma Aleksandra Bloka k rodnym*, 2 vols. (Leningrad, 1927–32)
Bely, A. 'Lettre autobiographique à Ivanov-Razumnik', *Cahiers du monde russe et soviétique*, 1–2 (1974), pp. 45–82
Arabeski (Moscow, 1911)
The First Encounter, tr. and ed. Gerald Janecek (Princeton, 1979)
Glossaloliya [*Glossolaliya*] (Berlin, 1922)
Kubok metelei. Chetvertaya simfoniya (Moscow, 1908)
Maski (Moscow, 1932)
Mezhdu dvukh revolyutsii (Leningrad, 1934)
Nachalo veka (Moscow-Leningrad, 1933)
Na perevale (Berlin-Petersburg-Moscow, 1923)
Na rubezhe dvukh stoletii (Moscow-Leningrad, 1931)
Peterburg [Literaturnye pamyatniki], ed. L. Dolgopolov (Moscow, 1981)
Petersburg, tr. Robert Maguire and John Malmstad (Harmsworth, 1983)
Pochemu ya stal simvolistom i pochemu ya ne perestal im byt' vo vsekh fazakh moego ideinogo i khudozhestvennogo razvitiya (Ann Arbor, 1982)
'Printsip formy v estetike', *Zolotoe runo*, 11–12 (1906), pp. 88–96, 115–18
'Protiv muzyki', *Vesy*, 3 (1907), pp. 57–60
Putevye zametki (Moscow-Berlin, 1922)
Revolyutsiya i kul'tura (Moscow, 1917)
Rudolf Shteiner i Gete v mirovozzrenii sovremennosti. Otvet Emiliyu Metneru na ego pervyi tom 'Razmyshleniya o Gete' (Moscow, 1917)
Simvolizm. Kniga statei (Moscow, 1910)
Stikhotvoreniya, 3 vols. ed. J. Malmstad (Munich, 1982–4)
Stikhotvoreniya i poemy (Moscow-Leningrad, 1966)
'Vospominaniya ob A. A. Bloke', *Epopeya*, 1 (1922), pp. 123–273; 2 (1922), pp. 105–299; 3 (1922), pp. 125–308; 4 (1923), pp. 61–309
Vospominaniya ob A. A. Bloke (Letchworth, 1964)
Benois, A. *Reminiscences of the Russian Ballet*, tr. Mary Britnieva (London, 1941)
Memoirs, tr. Moura Budberg, 2 vols. (London, 1960–4)
Benua, A. N. *Moi vospominaniya*, 2 vols. (Moscow, 1980)
Benua, A. N. Lunacharsky A. *et al*. *O teatre. Kniga o teatre* (St Petersburg, 1908)
Bernandt, G. *Aleksandr Benua i muzyka* (Moscow, 1969)
Bernandt, G. B. and Satta, I. A. eds. *A. V. Lunacharsky: v mire muzyki. Stat'i i rechi* (Moscow, 1958)
Bernandt, G. B. and Yampolsky, I. M. *Kto pisal o muzyke*, 4 vols. (Moscow, 1971–89)

Bialik, B. ed. *Literaturnyi protsess i russkaya zhurnalistika kontsa XIX–nachala XX veka. 1890–1904: Burzhuazno-liberal'nye i modernistskie izdaniya* (Moscow, 1982)

Blok, A. A. *Zapisnye knizhki*, ed. V. Orlov (Moscow, 1963)
Sobranie sochinenii, 8 vols. ed. V. N. Orlov *et al.* (Moscow-Leningrad, 1960–3)
Pis'ma k zhene, Literaturnoe nasledstvo, 89 (Moscow, 1978)

Boborykin, P. D. *Vospominaniya v dvukh tomakh*, 2 vols. (Moscow, 1953)

Bogolyubov, N. N. *Shest'desyat' let v opernom teatre* (Moscow, 1967)

Bondarenko, F. *Leningradskii gosudarstvennyi ordena Lenina akademicheskii teatr imeni S. A. Kirova* (Leningrad, 1960)

Borovsky, V. *Chaliapin* (London, 1988)
Moskovskaya opera S. I. Zimina (Moscow, 1977)

Bortnikova, E. *et al.* eds. *Vospominaniya o P. I. Chaikovskom* (2nd edn Moscow, 1973)

Braun, E. *Meyerhold on Theatre* (London, 1969)
The Theatre of Meyerhold (London, 1979)

Brown, D. *Tchaikovsky: A Biographical and Critical Study*, 4 vols. (London, 1978–91)

Bryantseva, V. *S. V. Rakhmaninov* (Moscow, 1976)

Buckle, R. *Diaghilev* (London, 1979)

Bugaev, B. (Andrey Bely), 'Amicus Plato, magis amica veritas', *Pereval*, 10 (1907), pp. 58–60

Burago, S. *Aleksandr Blok* (Kiev, 1981)

Burlyuk, D. *Rerikh: zhizn' i tvorchestvo 1917–1930* (New York, 1930)

Byaly, G. A. ed. *Poety 1880–1890kh godov* (Leningrad, 1972)

Calvocoressi, M. D. and Abraham, G. *Masters of Russian Music* (New York, 1936)

Carter, H. *The New Spirit in the Russian Theatre 1917–1921* (London, 1929)
The New Theatre and Cinema of Soviet Russia (London, 1925)

Chaikovsky, M. *Zhizn' P. I. Chaikovskogo*, 3 vols. (Moscow, 1900–3)

Chaikovsky, P. I. *Muzykal'no-kriticheskie stat'i*, ed. A. A. Shcherbakov, (4th edn Moscow, 1986)
Polnoe sobranie sochinenii: literaturnye proizvedeniya, vols. v–xvii (Moscow, 1959–80)

Chernyshevsky, N. G. *Polnoe sobranie sochinenii*, 16 vols. (Moscow, 1939–53)

Cheshikhin, V. *Istoriya russkoi opery s 1674 po 1903 g.* (St Petersburg, 1905)

Christa, B. *The Poetic World of Andrey Bely* (Amsterdam, 1977)

Chulkov, G. *'O misticheskom anarkhizme' so vstupitel'noi stat'ei Vyacheslava Ivanova 'O nepryatii mira'* (St Petersburg, 1906)
Pokryvalo Izidy (Moscow, 1909)

Cornwell, N. *The Life, Times and Milieu of V. F. Odoevsky, 1804–1869* (London, 1986)

Crookenden, J. 'The Chapter "Simvolizm" from Bely, "Istoriya stanovleniya samoznaiushchei dushi"', *Andrey Bely: Centenary Papers*, ed. Boris Christa (Amsterdam, 1980), pp. 39–51

Curtis, J. A. E. *Manuscripts Don't Burn: Mikhail Bulgakov, A Life in Letters and Diaries* (London, 1991)

Davidson, P. *The Poetic Imagination of Vyacheslav Ivanov: A Russian Symbolist's Perception of Dante* (Cambridge, 1989)

De la Grange, H. L. *Mahler*, (London, 1974–)

Deathridge, J. and Dahlhaus, C. *The New Grove Wagner* (London, 1984)

Deathridge, J., Geck, M. and Voss, E. *Wagner Werk-Verzeichnis* (Mainz, 1986)

Dianin, S. *Borodin: zhizneopisanie, materialy i dokumenty* (Moscow, 1960)

Dickinson, T. H. *The Theatre in a Changing Europe* (London, 1938)

DiGaetani, J. *Richard Wagner and the Modern British Novel* (London, 1978)

Dmitriev, N. [Kashkin], *Imperatorskaya opernaya tsena v Moskve* (Moscow, 1898)

Dombaev, G. *Tvorchestvo P. I. Chaikovskogo* (Moscow, 1958)

Donchin, G. *The Influence of French Symbolism on Russian Poetry* (The Hague, 1958)

Donington, R. *Wagner's 'Ring' and its Symbols* (London, 1963)

Dostoevsky, F. M. *Pis'ma*, ed. A. S. Dolinin, 4 vols. (Moscow, 1928–59)

Dreiden, S. D. *V zritel'nom zale: V. I. Lenin, Novye stranitsy* (Moscow, 1970)

Eisenstein, S. *The Film Sense*, ed. and tr. J. Leyda (London, 1953)

Izbrannye proizvedeniya, ed. S. Yutkevich, 5 vols. (Moscow, 1968–74)

Elagin, Y. *Ukroshchenie iskusstv* (Tenafly, New Jersey, 1988)

Elik, M. ed. *Blok i muzyka: sbornik statei* (Moscow-Leningrad, 1972)

Ellis (L. L. Kobylinsky). *Russkie simvolisty* (Moscow, 1910)

Ellis, W. A. *Richard Wagner's Prose Works*, 8 vols. (London, 1892–8)

Elsworth, J. *Andrey Bely: A Critical Study of the Novels* (Cambridge, 1983)

Engel, Y. *Glazami sovremennikami: Izbrannye stat'i* (Moscow, 1971)

V opere: Sbornik statei ob operakh i baletakh (Moscow, 1911)

Evans, E. *Tchaikovsky* (London, 1906)

Filosofov, D. *Slova i zhizn'. Literaturnye spory noveishogo vremeni (1901–1908 gg.)* (St Petersburg, 1909)

Findeizen, N. F. *Ocherk deyatel'nosti Sankt-peterburgskogo otdeleniya imperatorskogo russkogo muzykal'nogo obshchestva (1859–1909)* (St Petersburg, 1909)

Fitingof-Shel, B. A. *Mirovye znamenitosti: Iz vospominanii* (St Petersburg, 1889)

Forsyth, J. *Listening to the Wind: An Introduction to Alexander Blok* (Oxford, 1977)

'Prophets and Supermen: German Ideological Influences on Aleksandr Blok's Poetry', *Forum for Modern Language Studies*, 1 (1977), pp. 33–45

Frid, E. L. and Yankovsky, M. O. *Russkaya muzykal'naya literatura*, 2 vols. (Moscow, 1957–8)

Fülop-Miller R. and Gregor, J. *The Russian Theatre, Its Character and History* (London, 1973)

Furness, R. *Wagner and Literature* (Manchester, 1982)

Ganina, M. A. *A. K. Glazunov: pi'sma, stat'i, vospominaniya* (Moscow, 1958)

Garden, E. *Tchaikovsky* (London, 1973)

Geldern, J. von. *Bolshevik Festivals* (Berkeley, 1993)

Gertsen, A. I. *Polnoe sobranie sochinenii*, 30 vols. (Moscow, 1950–64)

Gladkov, A. 'Meierkhold govorit', *Novy mir*, 8 (1961), pp. 213–25

'Vospominaniya, zametki, zapisi o V. E. Meierkholde', *Tarusskie stranitsy*, ed. V. Koblikov *et al.* (Kaluga, 1961), pp. 292–307

Glebov, I. [B. Asafiev]. *Skryabin: opyt kharakteristiki* (Petrograd, 1921)

Glikman, I. *Meierkhold i muzykal'nyi teatr* (Leningrad, 1989)

Gojowy, D. *Neue Sojwetische Musik der 20 Jahre* (Regensburg, 1980)

Golubovsky, I. V. *Leningradskii Gos. Ordena Lenina Akademicheskii Maly Opernyi Teatr* (Leningrad, 1961)

Gomberg-Verzhbinskaya, E. P. and Podkopaev, Y. N. eds. *Vrubel: perepiska. Vospominaniya o khudozhnike* (Moscow-Leningrad, 1963)

Gorbachev, D. E. *Oleksander Khvostenko-Khvostov* (Kiev, 1987)

Gordeeva, E. *Iz istorii russkoi muzykal'noi kritiki XIX veka* (Moscow, 1950)

Gornfeld, A. *Boevye otkliki na mirnye temy* (Leningrad, 1924)

Gozenpud, A. A. *Dostoevsky i muzyka* (Leningrad, 1971)

Russkii opernyi teatr mezhdu dvukh revolyutsii 1905–1917 (Leningrad, 1975)

Ivan Ershov (Leningrad, 1986)

Russkii opernyi teatr 19 veka, 3 vols. (Leningrad, 1969–74)

Russii sovetskii opernyi teatr (1917–1941) (Leningrad, 1963)

Grechishkin, S. S. and Lavrov, A. V. 'Ellis – poet-simvolist, teoretik i kritik (1900–1910 gg.)', *XXV Gertsenovskie chteniya: 9. Literaturovedenie. Kratkoe soderzhanie dokladov* (Leningrad, 1972), pp. 59–62

Grigoriev, A. A. *Estetika i kritika* (Moscow, 1980)

Gronicka, A. von, *The Russian Image of Goethe*, 2 vols. (Philadelphia, 1965–85)

Grosheva, E. *Bol'shoi Teatr Soyuza SSSR* (Moscow, 1978)
Guichard, L. *La Musique et les Lettres au Temps de Wagnérisme* (Paris, 1963)
Gusin, I. ed. *Tz. Kyui: izbrannye stat'i* (Moscow, 1952)
Ivanov, E. 'Zapisi ob Aleksandre Bloke', ed. E. Gomberg and D. Maksimov, *Blokovskii sbornik* (Tartu, 1964), pp. 344–424
Ivanov, V. I. 'Ellinskaya religiya stradayushchego boga', *Novyi put'*, 1 (1904), pp. 110–34; 2 (1904), pp. 48–78; 3 (1904), pp. 38–61; 5 (1904), pp. 28–40; 9–10 (1904), pp. 47–70
'K voprosu ob organizatsii tvorcheskikh sil narodnogo kollektiva v oblasti khudozhestvennogo deistva', *Vestnik teatra*, 26 (1919), p. 4
Po zvezdam (St Petersburg, 1909)
'Religiya Dionisa', *Voprosy zhizni*, 6 (1905), pp. 185–220, 7 (1905), pp. 122–48
Sobranie sochinenii, vols. I–III ed. D. V. Ivanov and O. Deschartes, vol. IV, ed. D. V. Ivanov and O. Deschartes, A. B. Shishkin (Brussels, 1971–)
Ivanov, V. and Gershenzon, O. M. *Perepiska iz dvukh uglov* (Petrograd, 1921)
Ivanov, V. V. *Ocherki po istorii semiotiki v SSSR* (Moscow, 1976)
Ivanova, L. 'Vospominaniya o V. Ivanove', *Novy zhurnal*, 147 (1982), pp. 136–54; 148 (1982), pp. 136–60; 149 (1982), pp. 100–26; 150 (1983), pp. 130–59
Vospominaniya. Kniga ob otse, ed. John Malmstad (Paris, 1990)
Jackson, R. L. and Nelson, L. eds. *Vyacheslav Ivanov: Poet, Critic and Philosopher* (New Haven, 1986)
Janecek, G. 'Literature as Music: Symphonic Form in Andrey Bely's *Fourth Symphony*', *Canadian-American Slavic Studies*, 8 (1974), pp. 501–12
Jones, M. *Dostoyevsky: The Novel of Discord* (London, 1981)
Kandinsky, V. *Complete Writings on Art*, 2 vols. ed. K. Lindsay and P. Vergo (London, 1982)
Kashkin, N. D. *Stat'i o russkoi muzyke i muzykantakh* (Moscow, 1953)
Kashperov, A. V. *A. N. Skryabin: pis'ma* (Moscow, 1965)
Kats, B. *Muzyka v zerkale poezii*, 3 vols. (Leningrad, 1985–7)
'Raskat improvizatsii . . .': Muzyka v tvorchestve, sud'be i v dome Borisa Pasternaka (Leningrad, 1991)
Kats, B. and Timenchik, R. *Anna Akhmatova i muzyka* (Leningrad, 1989)
Keldysh, Y. et al. eds. *Russkaya khudozhestvennaya kul'tura kontsa XIX – nachala XX vekov*, 4 vols. ed. A. D. Alekseev et al. (Moscow, 1968–1981)
Kerzhentsev, P. *Tvorcheskii teatr* (Moscow, 1918)

Keys, R. and A. and Elsworth, J. tr. *Andrey Bely: The Dramatic Symphony and the Forms of Art* (Edinburgh, 1986)

Khessin, A. *Iz moikh vospominanii* (Moscow, 1959)

Khoprova, T. and Dunaevsky, M. eds. *Blok i muzyka* (Leningrad, 1980)

Kirilenko, K. N. ed. *Leonid Vitalievich Sobinov. Pis'ma, stat'i, rechi, vyskazyvaniya*, 2 vols. (Moscow, 1970)

Kleberg, L. and Nilsson, N. A. *Theatre and Literature in Russia, 1900–1930* (Stockholm, 1984)

Kleberg, L. 'Vyacheslav Ivanov and the Idea of Theater', *Theatre and Literature in Russia 1900–1930*, ed. N. A. Nilsson (Stockholm, 1984), pp. 57–70

Kloss, E. ed. *Richard Wagner an Freunde und Zeitgenossen* (Berlin, 1909)

Kluge, R-D. *Westeuropa und Russland im Weltbild A. Bloks* (Munich, 1967)

Knipovich, E. *Ob Aleksandre Bloke* (Moscow, 1987)

Kochik, O. Y. *Zhivopisnaya sistema V. E. Borisova-Musatova* (Moscow, 1980)

Kodryanskaya, N. *Remizov v svoikh pis'makh* (Paris, 1977)

Kommisarjevsky, T. *Myself and the Theatre* (London, 1929)

Konevskoy, I. *Stikhi i proza. Posmertnoe sobranie sochinenii* (Moscow, 1904)

Koptyaev, A. P. *A. N. Skryabin* (Moscow, 1916)

Korabelnikova, L. 'Muzyka' ('Iskusstvo i predmetnaya sreda v dukhovnoi zhizni Rossii vtoroi poloviny XIX veka') in Sternin, G. Y. ed. *Russkaya khudozhestvennaya kul'tura vtoroi poloviny XIX veka* (Moscow, 1988), pp. 98–138

Korotkina, L. V. *Rerikh v Peterburge-Petrograde* (Leningrad, 1985)

Korzhavin, N. *Vremena* (Frankfurt, 1976)

Kotrelyov, N. V. 'V. I. Ivanov: professor Bakinskogo universiteta', *Uchenye zapiski Tartuskogo gos. universiteta. Vypusk 209. Trudy po russkoi i slavyanskoi filologii, XII. Literaturovedenie* (Tartu, 1968), pp. 329–39

Kovač, A. *Andrei Belyj: The 'Symphonies' (1899–1908). A Re-Evaluation of the Aesthetic-Philosophical Heritage* (Frankfurt-Munich, 1976)

Krebs, S. *Soviet Composers and the Development of Soviet Music* (London, 1970)

Kremlyov, Y. A. ed. *A. V. Ossovsky: muzykal'no-kriticheskie stat'i (1894–1912)* (Leningrad, 1971)

Russkaya mysl' o muzyke, 3 vols. (Moscow, 1954–60)

Kremlyov, Y. A, *et al.* eds. *Mily Alekseevich Balakirev: issledovaniya i stat'i* (Leningrad, 1961)

Kryukov, A. *Turgenev i muzyka* (Leningrad, 1963)

Kuleshov, V. I. and Feierkherd, V. eds. *Iz istorii russko-nemetskikh literaturnikh vzaimosvyazei* (Moscow, 1987)

Kutateladze, L. M. *Artur Nikish i russkaya muzykal'naya kul'tura. Vospominaniya, pis'ma, stat'i* (Leningrad, 1974)

E. F. *Napravnik. Avtobiograficheskie, tvorcheskie materialy* (Leningrad, 1959)

Kutateladze, L. M. and Raaben, L. N. eds. *A. I. Ziloti: vospominaniya, pis'ma* (Leningrad, 1963)

Kyui, T. *Izbrannye pis'ma*, ed. I. L. Gusin (Leningrad, 1953)

Lakond, W. tr. *The Diaries of Tchaikovsky* (New York, 1945)

Lapshina, N. *Mir iskusstva* (Moscow, 1977)

Large, D. C. and Weber, W. *Wagnerism in European Culture and Politics* (Ithaca, 1984)

Larosh, G. A. *Izbrannye stat'i*, ed. A. A. Gozenpud, 5 vols. (Leningrad, 1974–8)

P. I. *Chaikovsky: muzykal'nye fel'etoni i zametki* (Moscow, 1898)

Lavrov, A. V. 'Yunosheskie dnevnikovye zametki Andreya Belogo', *Pamyatniki kul'tury. Novye otkrytiya na 1979* (Moscow, 1980), pp. 116–39

Lenrow, E. ed. and tr. *The Letters of Richard Wagner to Anton Pusinelli* (New York, 1932)

Lesnevsky, S. and Mikhailov, A. *Andrey Bely. Problemy tvorchestva: stat'i, vospominaniya, publikatsii* (Moscow, 1988)

Levik, S. Y. *Chertvert' veka v opere* (Moscow, 1970)

Zapiski opernogo pevtsa (Moscow, 1962)

Literaturnoe nasledstvo, vol. 85, *Valery Bryusov*, ed. V. R. Shcherbina et al. (Moscow, 1986)

Livanova, T. N. *Muzykal'naya bibliografiya russkoi periodicheskoi pechati XIX veka*, 6 vols. (Moscow, 1960–74)

Opernaya kritika v Rossii, 4 vols. (Moscow, 1966–73)

Lodder, Christina, *Russian Constructivism* (New Haven, 1983)

Loewenberg, A. *Annals of Opera*, 3rd edn (London, 1978)

Lukivskaya, K. P. ed. *Biblioteka A. A. Bloka: opisanie*, 3 vols. (Leningrad, 1984–6)

Lyapunova, A. S. and Yazovitskaya, E. B. eds. *Milii Alekseevich Balakirev: Letop. zhizni i tvorchestva* (Leningrad, 1967)

Magee, Bryan, *Aspects of Wagner* (London, 1968)

The Philosophy of Schopenhauer (Oxford, 1983)

Malcovati, F. ed. *Cultura e Memoria: Atti del terzo Simposio dedicato a Vjaceslav Ivanov*, 2 vols. (Florence, 1988)

Malmstad, J. 'Andrey Bely i Antroposofiya [Andrey Bely: 'Material k biografii (intimnyi)']', *Minuvshee*, 6 (1988), pp. 337–448; 8 (1990), pp. 409–71; 9 (1991), pp. 409–88

Malmstad, J. ed. *Andrey Bely: Spirit of Symbolism* (Ithaca, 1987)
Mandelshtam, O. *Sobranie sochinenii*, ed. G. P. Struve and B. A. Filippov (New York, 1955)
Mann, T. *Pro and Contra Wagner*, ed. and tr. A. Blunden (London, 1985)
Manykin-Nevstruev, N. *Imperatorskoe Russkoe Muzykal'noe Obshchestvo–Moskovskoe otdelenie. Simfonicheskie sobraniya 1–500. Staticheskii ukazatel'* (Moscow, 1899)
Matlaw, R. E. 'Scriabin and Russian Symbolism', *Comparative Literature* 1 (1979), pp. 1–23
Matskin, A. *Portrety i nablyudeniya* (Moscow, 1973)
Meck, G. von, *Tchaikovsky: Letters to His Family* (London, 1981)
Medtner, E. *Rasmyshleniya o Gete* (Moscow, 1914)
Mikhailov, M. *A. N. Skryabin* (Leningrad, 1971)
Modzalevsky, B. L. ed. *Perepiska L. N. Tolstogo s N. N. Strakhovym 1870–1894* (St Petersburg, 1914)
Müller, U. and Wapnewski, P. *Richard-Wagner-Handbuch* (Stuttgart, 1986)
Müller, U. ed. *Richard Wagner 1883–1983: Die Rezeption im 19 und 20 Jahrhundert* (Salzburg, 1984)
Murphy, A. B. *Melba: a Biography* (London, 1909)
Mylnikova, I. A. 'Stat'i Vyach. Ivanova o Skryabine', *Pamyatniki kul'tury. Novye otkrytiya. Ezhegodnik na 1983 god* (Leningrad, 1985), pp. 88–95
Nabokov, N. *Old Friends and New Music* (London, 1951)
Nabokov, V. *Stikhi* (Ann Arbor, 1979)
Neumann, A. *Erinnerungen an Richard Wagner* (Leipzig, 1907)
Newman, E. *The Life of Richard Wagner*, 4 vols. (London, 1933–47)
The Wagner Operas, 2 vols. (New York, 1949)
Newmarch, R. *The Life and Letters of Peter Ilich Tchaikovsky* (London, 1906)
Nietzsche, F. tr. F. Golffing, *The Birth of Tragedy Out of the Spirit of Music* (New York, 1956)
Nivat, G. 'Histoire d'une 'tératogénèse' Biélyenne: Les rapports entre Emilij Medtner et Andrej Belyj', *Cahiers du Monde Russe et Soviétique*, 11 (1974), pp. 93–131
Odoevtseva, I. *Na beregakh Nevy* (Moscow, 1988)
Orlov, G. *Muzykal'naya literatura: Bibliograf"icheskii ukazatel' knizhnoi i zhurnal'noi literatury o muzyke* (Leningrad, 1935)
Orlov, V. ed. *A. A. Blok-Bely: perepiska* (Moscow, 1940)
Orlova, A. tr. and ed. R. J. Guenther, *Musorgsky's Days and Works* (Ann Arbor, 1983)
Pachl, P. P. *Siegfried Wagner: Genie im Schatten* (Munich, 1988)

Palyukh, Z. L. and Prokhorova, A. V. eds. *Tolstoy i muzyka* (Moscow, 1977)

Pasternak, B. *Stikhotvoreniya i poemy*, ed. L. A. Ozerov (Moscow-Leningrad, 1965)

Pasternak, E. *et al. Rainer Maria Rilke, Marina Zwetajewa, Boris Pasternak: Briefwechsel*, tr. H. Pross-Werth (Frankfurt, 1983)

Pavlova Arbenina, L. A. ed. *Vospominaniya o B. V. Asafieve* (Leningrad, 1974)

Pekelis, M. A. S. *Dargomyzhsky i ego okruzhenie*, 3 vols. (Moscow, 1966–83)

Platek, Y. *Ver'te muzyke* (Moscow, 1989)

Pokrovsky, B. 'Dva slova o mastere' ['K 100-letiyu so dnya rozhdeniya Vs. E. Meierkholda'], *Sovetskaya muzyka*, 3 (1974), p. 59

Pokrovsky, N. *Muzykal'naya drama: Ee nedavnoe proshloe, sovremennoe polozhenie i nadezhdy na budushchee* (St Petersburg, 1904)

Porfirieva, A. L. ed. *Problemy muzykal'nogo romantizma. Sbornik nauchnykh trudov* (Leningrad, 1987)

Pozharskaya, M. N. *Russkoe teatral'no-dekoratsionnoe iskusstvo kontsa XIX–nachala XX veka* (Moscow, 1970)

Prokofiev, S. *Avtobiografiya*, ed. M. G. Kozlova (Moscow, 1973)

Pyast, V. *Vstrechi* (Moscow, 1929)

Pyman, A. *Alexander Blok: Selected Poems* (Oxford, 1972)
Aleksandr Blok: The Twelve (Durham, 1989)
The Life of Aleksandr Blok, 2 vols. (Oxford, 1979–82)

Rafalovich, V. ed. *Istoriya sovetskogo teatra* (Leningrad, 1933)

Remizov, A. *Tristan i Isolda; Bova Korolevich* (Paris, 1957)

Reutern, G. von, *Ein Freundshafts- und Familienkreis im 19. Jahrhundert: Biographisches* (Berlin, 1881)

Riasanovsky, N. 'Khomiakov on *Sobornost*'', *Continuity on Change in Russian and Soviet Thought*, ed. E. J. Simmons (Cambridge, Mass., 1955), pp. 183–96

Ricci, D. *La Rifrazione del Simbolo: Teorie del Teatro nel Simbolismo Russo* (Venice, 1989)

Ridenour, R. *Nationalism, Modernism and Personal Rivalry in 19th-Century Russian Music* (Ann Arbor, 1981)

Rimsky-Korsakov, A. N. *Letopis' moei muzykal'noi zhizni* (Moscow, 1955)

Rizeman, O. 'Rakhmaninov i Skryabin', *Studiya*, 12 (1911), p. 14

Rodina, T. A. *Blok i russkii teatr nachala XX veka* (Moscow, 1972)

Rolland, R. *Narodnyi teatr* (Moscow, 1918)

Rosenthal, B. G. ed. *Nietzsche in Russia* (Princeton, 1986)
'The Spirit of Music in Russian Symbolism', *Russian History*, 10 (1983), pp. 66–76

'The Transmutation of the Symbolist Ethos: Mystical Anarchism and the Revolution of 1905', *Slavic Review*, 4 (1977), pp. 608–27

Rossikhina, V. P. *Opernyi teatr Mamontova* (Moscow, 1985)

Rubinshtein, A. *Muzyka i ee predstaviteli* (St Petersburg, 1894, reprinted 1923)

Rudnitsky, K. *Russian And Soviet Theatre*, tr. R. Permar, ed. L. Milne (London, 1988)

Rusakov, A. V. E. *Borisov-Musatov* (Moscow, 1966)

Sabaneev, L. L. A. N. *Skryabin* (Moscow, 1922)
Vospominaniya o Skryabine (Moscow, 1925)

Salina, N. *Zhizn' i tsena. Vospominaniya artistki Bol'shogo teatra* (Moscow-Leningrad, 1941)

Schmidt, P. ed. *Meyerhold at Work* (Austin, 1980)

Scholz, H. ed. *Richard Wagner an Mathilde Maier (1862–1878)* (Leipzig, 1930)

Schopenhauer, A. *The World as Will and Representation*, tr. E. F. J. Payne (New York, 1969)

Schwarz, B. *Music and Musical Life in Soviet Russia* (Bloomington, 1983)

Sedakova, O. *Vrata, Okna, Arki: Izbrannye stikhotvoreniya* (Paris, 1986)

Serov A. N. *Izbrannye stat'i*, ed. G. N. Khubov, 2 vols. (Moscow-Leningrad, 1950–7)

Shaw, L. R., Cirillo, N. R. and Miller, M. S. eds. *Wagner in Retrospect: A Centennial Reappraisal* (Amsterdam, 1987)

Shcherbina, V. R. ed. *Aleksandr Blok: novye materialy i issledovaniya*, 4 vols., *Literaturnoe nasledstvo*, 92 (Moscow, 1980–7)

Shkafer, V. P. *Sorok let na tsene russkoi opery* (Leningrad, 1936)

Shostakovich, D. *The Memoirs of Dmitri Shostakovich as Related To and Edited by Solomon Volkov* (London, 1979)

Silk, M. S. and Stern, J. P. *Nietzsche on Tragedy* (Cambridge, 1981)

Sokhor, A. N. *Aleksandr Porfirievich Borodin: zhizn', deyatel'nost', muzykal'noe tvorchestvo* (Moscow, 1953)

Solovyov, B. *Poet i ego podvig* (Moscow, 1964)

Solovyov, V. S. *Stikhotvoreniya i shutochnye p'esy*, ed. Z. A. Mints (Moscow-Leningrad, 1974)

Stark, E. [Zigfrid] *Peterburgskaya opera i ee mastera 1890–1910* (Moscow-Leningrad, 1940)

Stasov, D. V. 'Muzykal'nye vospominaniya 1840–1860', *Russkaya muzykal'naya gazeta*, 11 (1909), pp. 289–95; 13–14 (1909), pp. 360–89

Stasov, V. tr. F. Jonas, *Pis'ma k rodnym*, 3 vols. (Moscow, 1953–62)
Selected Essays on Music (London, 1968)

Steinberg, A. *Word and Music in The Novels of Andrey Bely*, (Cambridge, 1982)

Steiner, R. 'Richard Wagner und die Mystik', *Die Drei*. *Monatschrift für Anthroposophie*, 10 (1929), pp. 713–31
Stephan, V. *Studien zum Drama des Russischen Symbolismus* (Frankfurt, 1980)
Stravinsky, I. *Poetics of Music* (New York, 1947)
Strunk, Oliver, *Source Readings in Music History*. v. *The Romantic Era* (London, 1981)
Stupel, A. *Russkaya mysl' o muzyke 1895–1917. Ocherk istorii russkoi muzykal'noi kritiki* (Moscow, 1980)
Syrkina, F. *Khudozhniki teatra o svoem tvorchestve* (Moscow, 1973)
Taneev, S. I. *Dnevniki*, ed. L. Z. Korabel'nikova, 3 vols. (Moscow, 1981–5)
Taruskin, R. *Opera and Drama in Russia as Preached and Practised in the 1860s* (Ann Arbor, 1981)
Tchaikovsky, M. *The Life and Letters of Peter Ilich Tchaikovsky*, ed. and abridged R. Newmarch (London, 1906)
Telyakovsky, V. A. *Vospominaniya* (Moscow-Leningrad, 1960)
Thode, D. ed. *Richard Wagners Briefe an Hans von Bülow* (Jena, 1916)
Thomson, R. D. B. *Lot's Wife and the Venus de Milo. Conflicting Attitudes to the Cultural Heritage in Modern Russia* (Cambridge, 1978)
'The Non-Literary Sources of "Roza i krest"', *Slavonic Review*, 45 (1967), pp. 292–300
Tomashevskaya, E. V. and Kremlyov, Y. A. *V. P. Kolomiitsov: stat'i i pis'ma* (Leningrad, 1971)
Trabsky, A. ed. *Sovetskii teatr: Dokumenty i materialy. Russkii sovetskii teatr, 1921–26* (Leningrad, 1975)
Russkii sovetskii teatr 1926–32 (Leningrad, 1982)
Uspenskaya, S. L. *Literatura o muzyke: 1948–53* (Moscow, 1955)
Literatura o muzyke: 1954–56 (Moscow, 1958)
Uspenskaya, S. L. and Yagolin, B. *Sovetskaya literatura o muzyke za 1957 god* (Moscow, 1959)
Uspenskaya, S. L. and Koltypina, G. *Sovetskaya literatura o muzyke: 1958–59* (Moscow, 1963)
Vakhtangova, N. M. ed. *Vakhtangov: zapiski, pis'ma, stat'i* (Moscow, 1939)
Valentinov, N. *Dva goda s simvolistami* (Stanford, 1969)
Vasilenko, S. I. *Stranitsy vospominanii* (Moscow, 1948)
Vospominaniya (Moscow, 1978)
Vengerov, S. A. *Russkaya literatura XX veka, 1890–1910* (Moscow, 1916)
Vickery, W. 'Blok's *Solov'inyj sad*: The Stuff of Tragedy', *Aleksandr Blok Centennial Conference*, ed. W. N. Vickery (Ohio, 1982), pp. 357–77

Vladykina-Bachinskaya, N. *Sobinov* (Moscow, 1958)

Vogel, L. ed and tr. *Blok: An Anthology of Essays and Memoirs* (Ann Arbor, 1982)

Volf, A. I. *Khronika peterburgskikh teatrov s kontsa 1855 do nachala 1881 goda* (St Petersburg, 1884)

Volfing [E. K. Medtner], 'Boris Bugaev protiv muzyki', *Zolotoe runo*, 5 (1907), pp. 56–62

Modernizm i muzyka (Moscow, 1912)

Volkoff, V. *Tchaikovsky* (London, 1974)

Volkonsky, S. *My Reminiscences*, tr. Mary Chamot, 2 vols. (London, 1924)

Volkov, N. *Meierkhold*, 2 vols. (Moscow-Leningrad, 1929)

Volman, V. *Russkie notnye izdaniya XIX–nachala XX veka* (Leningrad, 1970)

Voronin, S. D. 'Iz pisem Andreya Belogo k materi', *Pamyatniki kul'tury. Novye otkrytiya na 1986* (Leningrad, 1987), pp. 64–76

Vyazemsky, P. A. *Polnoe sobranie sochinenii*, 12 vols. (St Petersburg, 1878–96)

Wagner, R. *My Life*, tr. Andrew Gray (Cambridge, 1983)

West, J. *A Study of Vyacheslav Ivanov and the Russian Symbolist Aesthetic* (London, 1970)

White, E. W. *Stravinsky* (London, 1966)

Williams, R. C. *Artists in Revolution: Portraits of the Russian Avant-Garde, 1905–1925* (Indiana, 1977)

Wilson, C. *Rudolf Steiner: The Man and His Vision* (Wellingborough, 1985)

Wolzogen, H. von, ed. *Richard Wagner an Minna Wagner* (Berlin, 1908)

Woolley, G. *Richard Wagner et le symbolisme français* (Paris, 1931)

Worrall, N. *From Modernism to Realism on the Soviet Stage: Tairov, Vakhtangov, Okhlopkov* (Cambridge, 1989)

Yakovlev, V. *Izbrannye trudy o muzyke*, 3 vols. (Moscow, 1964–83)

N. D. Kashkin (Moscow-Leningrad, 1960)

Yankovsky, M. ed. *I. V. Ershov: Stat'i, vospominaniya, pis'ma* (Moscow, 1966)

Yaremich, S. *M. A. Vrubel: zhizn' i tvorchestvo* (Moscow, 1911)

Yudin, G. Y. *Emil Kuper: stat'i, vospominaniya, materialy* (Moscow, 1988)

Yufit, A. Z. ed. *Russkii sovetskii teatr. Dokumenty i materialy*, 2 vols. (Leningrad, 1968–78)

Zhadova, L. ed. *Tatlin* (London, 1988)

Zhdanov, V. A. and Zhegin, N. T. eds. *P. Chaikovsky: perepiska s N. F. fon Mekk*, 3 vols. (Moscow, 1934–6)

Zhdanov, V. A. ed. *Pis'ma P. I. Chaikovskogo i S. I. Taneeva* (Moscow, 1951)

Zhirmunsky, V. *Drama Aleksandra Bloka 'Roza i krest'* (Leningrad, 1964)

Zigmund [Andrey Bely], 'Chulkov. G. *Pokryvalo Izidy*. Kriticheskie ocherki (Moscow, 1909)', *Vesy*, 1 (1909), pp. 86–9

Zilbershtein, I. and Samkov, V. eds. *Sergey Dyagilev i russkoe iskusstvo*, 2 vols. (Moscow, 1982)

Valentin Serov v vospominaniyakh, dnevnikakh i perepiske sovremennikov, 2 vols. (Leningrad, 1971)

Zolotnitsky, D. *Zori teatral'nogo Oktyabrya* (Leningrad, 1976)

Zvantsov, K. 'A. N. Serov v 1857–71 gg. Vospominaniya o nem i ego pis'ma', *Russkaya starina*, 59 (1888), pp. 343–84

'O Rikharde Vagnere. Po sluchayu novogo sochineniya A. D. Ulybysheva', *Syn otechestva*, 25 (1857), p. 4

Index

CAMBRIDGE STUDIES IN RUSSIAN LITERATURE

General editor: MALCOLM JONES

Editorial board: ANTHONY CROSS, CARYL EMERSON,
HENRY GIFFORD, BARBARA HELDT, G. S. SMITH,
VICTOR TERRAS

Dostoyevsky and the process of literary creation
JACQUES CATTEAU
translated by Audrey Littlewood

The poetic imagination of Vyacheslav Ivanov
PAMELA DAVIDSON

Joseph Brodsky
VALENTINA POLUKHINA

Petrushka – the Russian carnival puppet theatre
CATRIONA KELLY

Turgenev
FRANK FRIEDEBERG SEELEY

From the idyll to the novel: Karamzin's sentimentalist prose
GITTA HAMMARBERG

The Brothers Karamazov *and the poetics of memory*
DIANE OENNING THOMPSON

Andrei Platonov
THOMAS SEIFRID

Nabokov's early fiction
JULIAN W. CONNOLLY

Iurii Trifonov
DAVID GILLESPIE

Mikhail Zoshchenko
LINDA HART SCATTON

Andrei Bitov
ELLEN CHANCES

Nikolai Zabolotsky
DARRA GOLDSTEIN

Nietzsche and Soviet culture
edited by BERNICE GLATZER ROSENTHAL

Russian literature and empire
SUSAN LAYTON